PIMLICO

826

# THE WORLD ON FIRE

Anthony Read is the author or co-author of ten previous non-fiction books, including *The Devil's Disciples* and *The Fall of Berlin*, and has written more than two hundred television scripts, winning awards in both areas. Before devoting himself full-time to writing, he had successful careers in advertising, journalism, publishing and as a BBC television drama producer. He has recently begun a new one with a well-received series of novels for children.

Also by Anthony Read

*The Devil's Disciples: Hitler's Inner Circle*

With David Fisher:

*Operation Lucy: Most Secret Spy Ring of the Second World War*
*Colonel Z: The Secret Life of a Master of Spies*
*The Deadly Embrace: Hitler, Stalin and the Nazi–Soviet Pact*
*Kristallnacht: Unleashing the Holocaust*
*The Fall of Berlin*
*Berlin: The Biography of a City* (published as *Berlin Rising* in the USA)
*The Proudest Day: India's Long Road to Independence*

With Ray Bearse:

*Conspirator: Churchill, Roosevelt and Tyler Kent, Spy*

For young people:

*The True Book about the Theatre*

The Baker Street Boys series:

*The Case of the Disappearing Detective*
*The Case of the Captive Clairvoyant*
*The Case of the Ranjipur Ruby*
*The Case of the Limehouse Laundry*
*The Case of the Stolen Sparklers*

# THE WORLD ON FIRE

## 1919 and the Battle with Bolshevism

---

# ANTHONY READ

PIMLICO

Published by Pimlico 2009

2 4 6 8 10 9 7 5 3 1

First published in Great Britain in 2008 by Jonathan Cape

Pimlico
Random House, 20 Vauxhall Bridge Road,
London SW1V 2SA

www.rbooks.co.uk

Addresses for companies within The Random House Group Limited can be fo
www.randomhouse.co.uk/offices.htm

The Random House Group Limited Reg. No. 954009

A CIP catalogue record for this book
is available from the British Library

ISBN 9781844138326

Typeset by Palimpsest Book Production Limited,
Grangemouth, Stirlingshire
Printed and bound in Great Britain by
Clays Ltd, St Ives plc

For Rosemary, Emma and Amelia,
my Three Graces

# CONTENTS

Murmansk

*Siberia*

GREAT
BRITAIN

FINLAND

Archangel

R U S S I A

Petrograd

Moscow  Cheliabinsk  Novonikolaevsk

London

Berlin  Warsaw  Kiev

TRANS-SIBERIAN RAILWAY

Paris  Milan

UKRAINE

Vladivostok

Madrid
Seville  Barcelona  Rome
Granada

Odessa

Caucasus

Baku

AFGHAN-
ISTAN

Lahore  Amritsar

C H I N A

Delhi

*A*

*F*

*R*

*I*

*C*

*A*

I N D I A

Bombay

*INDIAN OCEAN*

# THE WORLD ON FIRE, 1919

Boundaries shown are largely those constituted by
the post-war treaty settlements. Central European
borders were rather fluid at this time.

| 0 | 1000 | 2000 | 3000 miles |
|---|------|------|------------|
| 0 | 1000 | 2000 | 3000 | 4000 | 5000 km |

'We are running a race with Bolshevism, and the world is on fire.'

*President Woodrow Wilson, Paris, March 1919*

'They will say, "How can we leave them in peace when they set about setting the world on fire?" To that I would answer, "We are at war, messieurs!"'

*Lenin, on the founding of the Third International (the Comintern),*
*Moscow, March 1919*

# PROLOGUE: THE SPARK

IT is a common misconception that when the Armistice brought the Great War to a halt at the eleventh hour of the eleventh day of the eleventh month of 1918, the world was suddenly at peace. Certainly, the guns fell silent on the Western Front, and the millions of men dug into that lunatic two-way shooting gallery carved across Belgium and France from the North Sea to Switzerland were finally ordered to stop slaughtering each other. On all the other fronts – in Russia, Italy, Eastern Europe, the Middle East, Africa – the war between the Central Powers and the Allies had already fizzled out. But in vast stretches of Eastern Europe and Asia there was no peace, only a series of internecine struggles every bit as bloody as the world war itself. Winston Churchill, then Minister for Munitions in the British government, noted, as pithily as ever: 'The War of the Giants has ended. The wars of the pygmies begin.'

As the new year approached, revolution was everywhere, with civil wars and upheavals and the formation of new nation states all creating mayhem and uncertainty. On a line between the borders of France and the Sea of Japan, no old government remained in power. Three great empires, the Habsburg, the Ottoman and tsarist Russia, had imploded, leaving many of their subject peoples fighting among themselves over nationalism or ideology, or both. In a Germany bitter and bewildered by the sudden collapse of its army barely a month after their newspapers had proclaimed that the war was won, Berlin, Munich, Hamburg and other cities were torn by revolutionary violence. Everywhere, in the lands of both victors and vanquished and in the new states scrabbling for freedom, the relief of peace was overshadowed by a common fear, the dread of the Red Terror from the east: Bolshevism.

The general fear was only increased by the enthusiasm with which the prospect of revolution was greeted in some influential quarters. The British intellectual socialist, Beatrice Webb, co-founder with her husband of the London School of Economics, wrote in her diary on Armistice Day: 'Peace! Thrones are everywhere crashing and the men of property everywhere secretly trembling. How soon will the tide of revolution catch up with the tide of victory? That is the question which is exercising Whitehall and Buckingham Palace and causing anxiety even among the more thoughtful democrats.'[1]

In those days of slow and imperfect communications, the anxieties of the Western democracies sprang largely from the fear of the unknown. The very word 'Bolshevism' was new to most of their leaders: it had been in common circulation for barely a year – since 7 November 1917, to be exact, when Lenin's Bolshevik Party had seized power in Russia. In that short time, however, the name and the terror it represented had swept into the world's consciousness as quickly as the name 'al-Qaeda' would some eighty years later, to become as big a bogey in the Western world as militant Islam in the early years of the twenty-first century.

In many respects the early Bolsheviks in Russia were remarkably similar to the Taliban in Afghanistan: a fanatical sect determined to impose their puritanical vision first on their countrymen and then on the world. Internationally, it would not be entirely fanciful to compare the Bolsheviks to al-Qaeda, both regarding capitalism and Western democracy as corrupt and deadly enemies to be destroyed at all costs.

Lenin and Trotsky, the principal Bolshevik leaders, were convinced that what they were doing in Russia was the start of a world revolution, triggering a chain reaction through the developed and industrialised nations, which were 'ripe' for it. Although they despised nationalism, the Bolsheviks were happy to use the various nationalist movements to destabilise Central and Eastern Europe as a first step: as cold-blooded pragmatists, they believed the end justified whatever means they chose to employ, regardless of such Western bourgeois niceties as truth, humanity and honour, none of which they chose to embrace. As Trotsky himself put it later: 'We were never concerned with the Kantian-priestly and vegetarian-Quaker prattle about the sacredness of human life . . . To make the individual sacred, we must destroy the social order which crucifies him. And that problem can only be solved by blood and iron.'[2]

Bolshevik cynicism had been clearly demonstrated in the separate peace they had negotiated with Germany, ratting on Russia's allies and accepting a treaty, signed at Brest-Litovsk on 3 March 1918, which any normal power would have regarded as shameful. The Germans imposed such ferociously draconian terms that the later Treaty of Versailles, about which they complained so piteously, seems remarkably mild by comparison. Russia was stripped of 34 per cent of her population, 32 per cent of her agricultural land, 73 per cent of her iron ore output and a staggering 89 per cent of her coal, together with the major part of her industry. But Lenin and Trotsky did not care how much territory they gave away, since they believed frontiers would soon be irrelevant. The politicians and people of the West naturally found such Bolshevik attitudes as difficult to understand and as deeply disturbing as the phenomenon of the suicide bomber would be in later years.

The Bolsheviks came into being in 1903, at an angling club in London, of all places, where the fifty-seven delegates to the Second Congress of the minuscule Russian Social-Democratic Party had gathered after the Belgian police had hounded them out of Brussels. There was, of course, no possibility of holding such a meeting in tsarist Russia itself, an autocratic police state where all political parties were banned and where membership of any of the various Marxist parties brought automatic imprisonment or exile to the wilds of Siberia.

Like all such gatherings of the political left, the congress in London was extremely fractious, with interminable hair-splitting and violent argument dividing the party into two main factions, the more vociferous of which was led by the thirty-three-year-old Vladimir Ilyich Ulyanov, who had recently adopted the alias 'Lenin' – probably after the Siberian river Lena – in an attempt to confuse the tsarist police. Lenin initially called his group 'Hards' and his opponents 'Softs', names which accurately reflected their characters. However, after winning control of the editorial board for the party newspaper *Iskra* ('*The Spark*' – which was to 'start a big blaze'), he seized on a new name, referring to his group as the Bolsheviks (meaning 'those in the majority') and the others as the Mensheviks ('those in the minority'). In fact, within the overall SDP, the Bolsheviks were in a minority, but Lenin never missed a chance of furthering the illusion of power. From its very beginning, therefore, Bolshevism was founded on a lie, setting a precedent that was to be followed for the next ninety years.

Lenin had no time for democracy, no confidence in the masses and

no scruples about the use of violence. He wanted a small, tightly organised and strictly disciplined party of hard-line professional revolutionaries, who would do exactly as they were told. The young Leon Trotsky
(real name Lev Bronstein – he took his pseudonym from one of his
jailers, whose passport he stole to escape from Siberia in 1902), who
was then still a Menshevik, is reported to have protested to him, 'That's
dictatorship you're advocating.' To which Lenin replied, 'There is no
other way.'

Bolstered by a private income from his mother's country estate,
Lenin spent most of the next fourteen years in voluntary exile in
Western Europe, together with most of the main leaders of the other
Russian socialist parties. They were all abroad at the start of the
abortive revolution of 1905, which began in St Petersburg on 'Bloody
Sunday', 9 January, when a peaceful demonstration of workers led by
a priest, attempting to present a petition to the Tsar calling for basic
civil rights and a living wage, was turned into a massacre by armed
police and sabre-wielding Cossacks. In the upheavals of the following
weeks and months, few of the socialist leaders were eager to forsake
the safety and comfort of Paris or Geneva for the dangers of revolutionary Russia.

Trotsky was the first to return, living under a series of aliases and
editing *Izvestia*, the newspaper published by the Petersburg Soviet (the
word 'soviet' in Russian simply means 'council' – in this case a council
of workers formed to organise strikes and generally provide an alternative local government to that of the tsarist authorities). Lenin did
not return until November, by which time a highly reluctant Tsar
Nicholas II had been forced to grant some of the reforms demanded
by the people in order to avert a cataclysmic uprising. The Tsar promised a token amount of civil liberties, a constitutional order, Cabinet
government, and a legislative assembly – the Duma – Russia's first ever
parliament, to be elected on a broadly democratic franchise. For the
first time, political parties were permitted, and workers were allowed
to organise into rudimentary trades unions.

The euphoria over the concessions was short-lived. Traditionalists
and tsarists mounted a vicious backlash against the reforms, and the
empire was plunged into a sea of violent conflicts that foreshadowed
the later civil war. With the army and the police remaining almost
completely loyal, Nicholas ordered them to crush the reform movement, which they did with brutal enthusiasm. Repression returned with

mass arrests and thousands of summary executions; the soviets were eliminated and political prisoners soon filled the jails once more. In the countryside, and especially in the Baltic lands, the Tsar sent in army and Cossack units to unleash a war of terror, shooting, flogging, burning down whole villages, raping women in front of their men and hanging the men from trees in front of their women. All told, between mid-October 1905 and the opening of the first state Duma in April 1906, the Tsar's men are believed to have executed some 15,000 people, shot or wounded at least 20,000 and deported or exiled another 45,000.[3]

Lenin, who had naturally opposed all the moves towards democracy, had tried to seize the opportunity to foment violent revolution, but with only a few hundred Bolshevik supporters he had failed to ignite the necessary spark. He left Russia again to return to his books and his theorising in Switzerland, from where he issued a stream of exhortations and pontifications. Trotsky was arrested and exiled to Siberia, escaping once more in 1907 and fleeing first to London, then to Vienna and Paris. Expelled from Paris in 1916, he spent a year in New York before slipping away via Canada to return to Moscow to join in the revolution of October/November 1917.

The outbreak of the Great War in 1914 appeared to mark the end of international socialism, as patriotism on both sides took precedence over proletarian brotherhood. Lenin, however, welcomed the war as the great opportunity for which he had been waiting. He looked forward to the defeat of Russia – which would bring down the tsarist regime and all it stood for. But even more than that, he expected the imperialist powers to exhaust themselves, leaving the way open for him to turn the war into a great European civil war that would result in the masses of peoples, regardless of nationalities, uniting to overthrow their rulers and establish the international 'dictatorship of the proletariat'. Not surprisingly, he found little support for his ideas, even among left-wing socialists, most of whom were pacifists simply wanting an end to war. But there were a few hard-core believers who agreed with him, including Trotsky, who had by then converted to Bolshevism and was if anything even more extreme than Lenin in his views, seeking to create a state of 'permanent revolution'. And these few souls kept the faith through the hard years, biding their time until their moment should come.

*

For all their hopes and plans, the Bolsheviks were taken completely by surprise and played virtually no part in the Russian Revolution of February/March 1917 – which was in any case less a revolution than simply the collapse of the rotten tsarist regime, albeit accompanied by considerable bloodshed. Lenin, of course, was still living in exile in Switzerland, and few people in Russia took either him or his party seriously, even after he returned in April by courtesy of the Germans, who gave him safe passage across their country in a sealed train. Indeed, when he began trying to bring down the Provisional Government by seeking to turn anti-war demonstrations in Petrograd (as St Petersburg had been patriotically renamed) into armed insurrection, he was branded a German agent and forced to flee to Finland. Trotsky, who had already returned from New York, took a more canny approach, going underground while creating a power base in the Petrograd Soviet of Soldiers, Sailors and Workers, the de facto governing body in the capital.

By the autumn, Alexander Kerensky, leader of the Provisional Government, was planning to hold elections for a constituent assembly, which would bring genuine democracy to Russia. Aware that this would scupper his chances of seizing power, Lenin slipped back into Petrograd in disguise, covering his bald head with a dark wig and baring his chin in a reversal of the more usual false beard cover-up, to begin preparing his plans for a coup. He was aided by a hard core of Bolsheviks, headed by Trotsky, who had by then gained control of the key Military-Revolutionary Committee of the Petrograd Soviet and won the support of vital elements of the army and navy. On the night of 25 October (7 November in the Western Gregorian calendar, which was not adopted by Russia until early 1918) Bolshevik pickets quietly surrounded all government buildings. Next morning at 10 a.m. Lenin issued a proclamation:

To the citizens of Russia

The Provisional Government has been deposed. Government has passed into the hands of the organ of the Petrograd Soviet . . . the Military-Revolutionary Committee, which stands at the head of the Petrograd proletariat and garrison. The task for which the people have been struggling has been assured – the immediate offer of a democratic peace, the abolition of the landed property of the landlords, worker control over production, and the creation of a Soviet Government. Long live the Revolution of Workers, Soldiers and Peasants![4]

It was all a gigantic bluff, a blatant and misleading untruth. But it worked, simply because there was no one with the will or the organisation to oppose it.

Unlike the savagery of February and March, the 'October Revolution' was virtually bloodless – later tales of the storming of the Winter Palace, where the Provisional Government was in session, were yet more lies, deliberately created to glorify the Bolshevik achievement, and perhaps to underline their belief in violence. At the time, few residents of Petrograd were aware that anything unusual was happening in their city. The organisational genius of Trotsky was equally mythical at this stage – the coup on 7 November was a complete shambles, and only succeeded because the other side was even more disorganised. Rival left-wing parties felt they could not attack a fellow revolutionary party, and so held back. The army was disaffected, confused and at odds with the government. The government ministers simply did not know what to do, and so did nothing, apart from huddling together in the Winter Palace waiting to be rescued.

At 9.40 p.m., Bolshevik sailors on the cruiser *Aurora* moored on the River Neva fired a few noisy blank rounds at the Winter Palace by way of a warning – fresh from the dockyard for repairs, the ship had no live ammunition on board. Military cadets in the palace replied with machine guns, until they realised that no shells were actually being fired at them. An hour later, Red troops in the Peter and Paul Fortress finally managed to fire about thirty shells from hastily assembled field guns – a feat that had taken them all day to organise after discovering that the fortress's own guns were rusty and useless museum pieces. Even then, most of the shots landed harmlessly in the river. Nevertheless, at 2.30 a.m., the ministers surrendered.

Petrograd, the capital, was in Bolshevik hands. Moscow, where they faced slightly more organised opposition, fell to them eight days later, and within a few more days they had control of most provincial centres. On 3 December a Bolshevik detachment occupied the army's supreme headquarters at Mogilev, and within two days they had concluded a preliminary armistice with the Central Powers, which was formally concluded on 15 December. A week later they started negotiations at Brest-Litovsk for a peace treaty.

The Bolsheviks were in power, but their grasp on it was still tenuous. Lenin himself believed that the revolution in Russia could only survive as part of the worldwide revolution, for which his own was providing the vital spark. First, however, he had to consolidate his power in Russia, which in itself was no easy task, especially considering that the core membership of the Bolshevik Party itself was probably no more than 10–15,000, though the number of supporters was growing exponentially. He bought time by allowing the promised election to take place, but when his Bolsheviks secured only 24 per cent of the votes, he promptly shut down the new assembly. When some 50,000 unarmed citizens staged a peaceful march in support of the assembly, Bolshevik troops stationed on rooftops opened fire on them with machine guns, killing at least ten people and wounding several dozen more in an uncomfortable echo of 1905's Bloody Sunday.

The whole machinery of government was dismantled and private enterprise abolished along with property rights. Factories were handed over to the workers, banks closed and land appropriated, resulting very quickly in starvation and famine. To help secure his position amid the continuing unrest, Lenin set up the 'All-Russian Extraordinary Commission for Struggle against Counter-Revolution and Sabotage', better known by its acronym as the Cheka, the successor to the tsarist Okhrana and forerunner of the KGB, to imprison, torture and murder his political opponents – and anyone else who could be labelled an 'enemy of the people'. 'The people', meanwhile, were taking matters into their own hands in a nationwide orgy of violence, murder and looting. Peasants and the urban poor left their hovels and slums and simply moved into the houses and apartments of the middle and upper classes, helping themselves to whatever they found there, with the blessing of the new regime. Law and order gave way to anarchy; lynch mobs ruled everywhere.

As word of atrocities and indignities reached the outside world, culminating in the brutal murder of the Tsar and his family in a cellar in Ekaterinburg, the Western democracies were filled with a growing sense of horror. During that first year of the revolution, however, they were naturally preoccupied with the Great War: Lenin's withdrawal of Russia from the war was of more concern to them than the turmoil he and his followers were inflicting on their own country. Trotsky, who initially led the peace negotiations with the Central Powers, played for time in the belief that the German Army was about to succumb to Bolshevik propaganda and stage its own revolution. But Lenin overruled him, cynically accepting the Germans' unbelievably harsh terms, to the dismay and disgust not only of his own people but also of the Western Allies. Britain, France and America were aghast at what they saw as a treacherous betrayal releasing vast numbers of German troops to the Western Front and giving the Central Powers access to vital sources of food and raw materials, including oil from the rich fields around Baku and coal from the Don Basin.

The *New York Times* ran headlines like 'RUSSIANS SELL OUT TO GERMANS' and 'BOLSHEVIKI YIELD RUSSIA'S RICHES TO BERLIN'. In London, *The Times* published a leading article declaring that 'The remedy for Bolshevism is bullets' – an attitude that did not change with the coming of peace. 'Every British and French soldier killed last year,' Winston Churchill proclaimed in a speech in April 1919, 'was really done to death by Lenin and Trotsky, not in fair war, but by the treacherous desertion of an ally without parallel in the history of the world.'[5]

Lenin was impervious to the Allies' anger. Coldly pragmatic as always, he saw the treaty signed at Brest-Litovsk as an essential move to save the Bolshevik Revolution, his first and only priority. By removing the German threat and taking Russia out of the war, he could concentrate on dealing with his many internal enemies, who posed a much greater danger. He could then keep the spark alive until the war between the Western nations turned into a great European civil war, leading to the universal victory of the proletariat. The civil war, however, when it came shortly afterwards, was not in the West, but in Russia itself. It would last three years, cost at least ten million lives – considerably more than losses on all sides in the Great War – and confirm the world's worst apprehensions about the nature of Bolshevism, sending alarm signals right around the globe.

The civil war has usually been seen as a fight between Whites and Reds for the soul of Russia or, to put it more prosaically, for control of the central Russian government. In fact, it was not a single war but a series of civil wars and a series of international wars, all happening at more or less the same time in an inglorious free-for-all. And there were not two but three principal antagonists, the Reds, the Whites and the Greens, who mainly represented Russia's vast peasant population and were led by the Socialist Revolutionaries (SRs), less extreme socialists whom Lenin and the Bolsheviks hated even more than they did the Conservatives and tsarists. All three of these main elements were fighting each other, as well as other revolutionary groups: the

Whites inadvertently gave enormous help to the Bolsheviks by defeating their principal rivals, the Greens, in a series of battles during 1918.

It had all begun immediately after the October Revolution with brief but savage struggles, first in Petrograd itself, then in Moscow and other major towns and cities in northern Russia. Lenin and his followers saw civil war as simply an extension of the class war and a vital phase in their revolution. They welcomed it, and even incited it, as the most effective way of strengthening and enlarging their power base. In the spring and early summer of 1918 they deliberately extended it to the countryside in a 'bread war', provoking the peasants by requisitioning their grain to feed the army and the starving cities – and thus creating rural starvation as well. To obtain the grain and other foodstuffs, the government created a 76,000-strong 'Food Army', empowered to occupy villages and extract their 'surplus' grain. Their authority was generally interpreted as a licence to plunder, which naturally led to vicious struggles in which men were burnt alive, chopped up with scythes, tortured and beaten to death. As a direct result, there were over two hundred peasant uprisings in July and August which the Bolsheviks tried to portray as 'SR-Kulak revolts' – the kulaks, better-off farmers and peasants, were seen as the rural equivalent of the urban 'burzhoois'. It is estimated that some 250,000 people were killed in the bread wars.[6]

Sporadic and uncoordinated fighting spread throughout the rest of the old tsarist empire as resistance gradually coalesced, then merged with the ongoing conflicts with and within the breakaway republics along the borderlands. In stripping Russia of a huge swathe of territory, the Treaty of Brest-Litovsk liberated the subject nations of Finland, Estonia, Latvia, Lithuania, Poland, Belorussia, the Ukraine and the Transcaucasus from Russian imperialism. Granted, they would have become economic and political satellites of a victorious Germany, but Germany's defeat gave them the chance of independence, free at last from Russian domination. They seized it gleefully, though not always unanimously; for much of the time their citizens were fighting each other as well as the Russian Reds.

By mid 1918, the whole of the old Russian Empire was ablaze with a myriad small fires, which together became a massive conflagration, involving not only Russians and their former subjects, but also American, British, French, Czech, Canadian, Japanese, Serb, Italian, Romanian and German troops. Surrounded on all sides by hostile armies, the Bolsheviks had been forced back into a central region barely six hundred miles in diameter, much the same size as the old Grand Duchy of Muscovy ruled by Ivan the Terrible in the sixteenth century. However, this region still contained some 60 million people, mostly Great Russians, and covered an area of nearly a million square miles, bigger than all the warring countries of Europe put together.[7] Significantly, it also contained most of Russia's war industry, most of the stores and establishments of the old army and navy, and the national communications network based on Moscow. 'The ancient capital,' as Churchill wrote, 'lay at the centre of a web of railroads . . . and in the midst a spider! Vain hope to crush the spider by the advance of lines of encircling flies!'[8]

Lenin had moved his government to Moscow in March 1918, since Petrograd was uncomfortably close to Russia's western borders and vulnerable to German attack. He and Trotsky took over the Tsar's former quarters in the Kremlin and had the tune played by the bells in the musical clock on the Spassky Tower changed from 'God Save the Tsar' to the 'Internationale'. He also changed the official name of the party to the Communist Party – but everyone, both at home and abroad, continued to call its members Bolsheviks.

Allied troops – for convenience I include Americans, though strictly speaking the United States was not a member of the wartime Alliance but an 'associated power' – had been sent to various Russian ports during the year, initially to support the Bolshevik regime and bolster the Eastern Front against the Central Powers. But with Russia's withdrawal and then the end of the war, their purpose became less clear. Hampered by the lack of an agreed overall objective, Allied intervention into the Russian civil war was piecemeal, indecisive and for much of the time accidental.

On 6 March 1918, immediately after the signing of the Brest-Litovsk Treaty, British ships had landed an advance party of 170 Royal Marines in Murmansk, a small settlement at the head of a long fjord in the Barents Sea 150 miles north of the Arctic Circle. Murmansk, which was later to become the main base of the Soviet Union's Northern Fleet, had been built in 1915–16 at British insistence and with British money and technicians, to provide the Allies with an ice-free port to handle war supplies to the Russian Army. Archangel, on the White Sea – 350 miles south-east of Murmansk on the map but 600 miles away by sea or land – the only port in north-west Russia that was not blockaded by the German Navy, was ice-bound for up to seven months of the year. The great danger for the Allies was that Murmansk might fall to the Germans and provide them not only with the war materiel held there but also with a secure base from which their U-boats could push out into the Atlantic, bypassing the barrage of 70,000 mines laid across the North Sea by the British and Americans, to attack the troopships crossing the Atlantic loaded with eager young doughboys heading for the Western Front.

Murmansk and Archangel had been the two points of entry for British supplies during the Great War, and as such were protected by a British naval squadron, which provided the marines for the landings at Murmansk. These were made at the express invitation of the local soviet, which had been ordered by Trotsky to accept Allied help to defend the port against possible attack by Germans and White Finns from across the nearby border, and to stop them getting their hands on the huge quantities of weapons and munitions stored there, which they could then use against the Bolsheviks. A few hundred Serb troops and a detachment of French artillery were already in the general area. They were joined in late June by six hundred British reinforcements and a month later by a battalion of French colonial infantry. With little resistance, they quickly pushed out their perimeters to establish a sizeable enclave.

By late spring, there was a new reason for landing Allied troops in north Russia – and this time it was not one that enjoyed Trotsky's support. With Ludendorff's armies inflicting terrible casualties on the Allies in France, it was vital to find ways of relieving the pressure there. Winston Churchill had one answer, pressing the War Cabinet: 'Above all, reconstitute the fighting front in the east.' Otherwise, he said, there might be no end to the war.[9] Thus, from June to September, American, British, Canadian and French troops were also poured into Archangel, with the aim of linking up with White Russian forces to reconstitute the Eastern Front against the Germans. Trotsky, however, had no intention of being dragged back into the war, and determined to throw the invaders out, regarding this incursion in a very different light from the token force in Murmansk. 'We cannot regard interference by the Allied imperialists in any other light than as a hostile attempt on the freedom and independence of Soviet Russia,' he declared. 'If they try to effect a landing, we shall resist with all the means at our disposal. We see no difference between encroachment by the Germans and "friendly" encroachment by the Allied armies.'[10]

The Americans had by far the largest contingent in Archangel: at 4,800 men – mostly Polish-Americans from Michigan and Wisconsin who had no idea why they were there – nearly twice as many as the British and more than five times as many as the French. Although President Wilson had agreed to their going only on condition that they would be used solely to guard stores and 'to give such aid as may be acceptable to the Russians in the organisation of their self-defense', they soon found themselves in action against Bolshevik forces sent by Trotsky to resist the invasion. Inevitably, in defending themselves as well as their White Russian allies, they found themselves sucked into a conflict from which there could be no quick and easy exit.

Some of their operations bore a striking resemblance to episodes in other wars many years later. In January 1919, for instance, a combined British, American and Canadian force had to abandon the small town of Shenkursk on the White Sea shore south of Murmansk, which they had originally occupied to guard the rail link to Archangel and as a recruiting centre for White Russians. With a thousand Bolshevik troops about to outflank them, the Americans set about destroying the town. 'We started burning the houses,' one US veteran recalled many years later, 'so we would take and throw straw and feed, scattering it through the houses, set up a fire, beat the old man over the head with your musket or rifle, chase them out, screaming and a'hollering and yelling at you. But we did it. Anyway, we had to do it.' They then withdrew to the edge of the town, and opened fire on the people left inside, who they presumed were Bolsheviks. 'We killed so many that day it was unbelievable. I sat there with a machine gun, and poured bullets into that town just continuously. It was not over a quarter of a mile away, so with a good machine gun you can do good work in there. They were scattered in between those houses, you could see them, they could not get in or out of a house, there was no cover for them.'[11]

The fighting was by no means all one-sided, however. By the time they sailed for home on 14 June 1919, the Americans in north Russia had suffered 2,845 casualties, including 244 dead. The British, who finally left Archangel on the night of 26–27 September and Murmansk two weeks later, had casualty figures of 106 officers and 877 other ranks – typically, the British made a distinction between the two – of whom respectively 41 and 286 were killed.[12]

*

In the far east, Allied intervention in the Russian civil war centred on the Siberian port of Vladivostok on the Sea of Japan, ostensibly to protect the 40,000 men of the Czechoslovak Legion, who had been part of the Russian Army. Originally formed from Czech nationalists working inside Russia at the outbreak of war, the Legion had been enlarged by Czech and Slovak prisoners of war and deserters from the Austro-Hungarian Army, until it constituted a self-contained corps of two divisions. After Russia pulled out of the war, they resolved to join the Czechoslovak Army in France, but obviously could not pass through enemy lines to get there. Their only viable route appeared to be to travel east rather than west, right around the world, via Vladivostok, across the Pacific, the United States and the Atlantic. The Soviet government had agreed in March to let them leave the country by the Trans-Siberian Railway, as 'free citizens' with a 'specified number of weapons for self-defence' against freed Magyar and German prisoners.

All should have been simple from then on – but in Russia in 1918 nothing was ever simple, and certainly not the movement of an army corps across 4,900 miles of a country seething with mistrust and unrest. The writ of the central government barely extended through Siberia, where local soviets ruled, usually by force. At every stop, they held up the trains, subjecting the Czechs to a barrage of Bolshevik propaganda, trying to recruit them for the new 'Internationalist' Red Army or to disarm them. This served only to strengthen the determination of the Czechs, who suspected that the Bolsheviks were preparing to hand them over to the Germans and Austrians, a fear that seemed justified when they tried to split the Legion into two, directing one half to go north to Murmansk. The aggrieved Czechs did not know, or believe, that this change was made at the request of the Allies, and refused to go. Czech–Bolshevik relations nosedived.

Things came to a head in May 1918, at Cheliabinsk in the Urals, when a trainload of Czechs heading east clashed with former Hungarian prisoners travelling west for repatriation. There was little love lost between the Czechs and Hungarians, who regarded each other as renegade traitors and imperialist oppressors respectively. Insults led to blows, and the whole thing exploded when a Hungarian threw part of a broken cast-iron cooking stove (or a crowbar – accounts vary) out of the train window, hitting and killing (or seriously injuring) a Czech soldier. The result was instant mayhem: the well-armed Czechs lynched the

Hungarian and beat up as many others as they could lay their hands on until the local Red Guards arrived to restore order. When the Red Guards arrested those responsible for the lynching, two Czech battalions marched into town, disarmed the small Red Guard unit, freed their comrades and took over the town.

The Czechs quickly reached an amicable agreement with the local soviet, but the Bolshevik leaders in Moscow overreacted. One of Trotsky's lieutenants sent a telegram to every soviet along the line of the railway, ordering that all Czechs were to be taken from their trains and drafted into the Red Army as labour battalions. The Czechs at Cheliabinsk, who controlled the telegraph office along with the railway station, intercepted this telegram, and a further message two days later from Trotsky himself, stating: 'All soviets are hereby ordered to disarm Czechoslovaks immediately. Every armed Czechoslovak found on the railway is to be shot on the spot. Every troop train in which even one armed man is found shall be unloaded and its soldiers interned.'[13]

Trotsky's ill-considered directive, and particularly the order to shoot any Czech who refused to surrender his arms, was described by the Petrograd correspondent of the Associated Press as having 'lost the Bolsheviks practically all their friends among the Entente officials in Russia' – including the British diplomatic representative in Moscow, Robert Bruce Lockhart, and Raymond Robins, the United States Red Cross commissioner. It was, according to the correspondent's report, 'the greatest error the Soviet Government has made'.[14] To the Czechs, it amounted to a declaration of war. Within twenty-four hours, they were fighting the Bolsheviks at several points along the railway.

The Czechs' main problem was that they were split into four main groups: one in the Volga region, one near Vladivostok, one at Cheliabinsk in the Urals, and one in central Siberia around Novonikolaevsk (now Novosibirsk). The distances separating them were immense: relating them to American geography, Evan Mawdsley in his history of the Russian civil war puts the Volga group three hundred miles *east* of New York, the Vladivostok group a thousand miles *west* of San Francisco, the Cheliabinsk unit in Pittsburgh and the Novonikolaevsk group in Salt Lake City.[15] That they were able to join up at all was a considerable achievement, made possible only by the weakness of their opponents. The Red Army was still not properly organised; ill-equipped and undisciplined units of Red Guards, generally made up of local factory workers, were no match for the experienced and well-trained Czechs, who within days were capturing one town after another almost at will. Soon, they were threatening Moscow itself.

The Czechs' successes created focal points for anti-Bolshevik opposition groups, whose resistance until then had been confined to sporadic local skirmishes. Now they rose and swept away Soviet control in vast areas of Siberia and European Russia. The Czechs, inevitably, found themselves supporting the new anti-Bolshevik governments that were springing up like weeds in all directions, and were soon hopelessly entangled in the turmoil. By the end of June, they had taken Vladivostok, throwing out the local soviet. On 6 August, in company with a White Russian force, they took the town of Kazan and with it the huge tsarist gold reserves, which had been sent there from Petrograd for safety from the Germans. By the end of August, their forces in the different parts of the railway joined hands, giving them control of its entire eastern section from the Volga to the Pacific, the only east–west line of communication across the vast and largely trackless spaces of Siberia.

By any standard, the Czechs were a force to be reckoned with, but their 'plight' provided Britain and France with an added excuse to send troops into Siberia, and to bring pressure on their Allies to join them. 'We must not take "No" for an answer, either from America or from Japan,' Churchill wrote in a memorandum to the British Cabinet on 22 June 1918. '. . . Surely now when Czech divisions are in possession of large sections of the Siberian Railway and in danger of being done to death by the treacherous Bolsheviks, some effort to rescue them can be made? Every man should ask himself each day whether he is not too readily accepting negative solutions.'[16] Both David Lloyd George, the British Prime Minister, and Georges Clemenceau, the French Premier, agreed. On 2 July they appealed jointly to President Wilson – who had rejected their previous pleas for US involvement in Russia no fewer than six times during the last four months – to give US military support to the Czechs. Three days later, he finally agreed, albeit with considerable reservations.

The Japanese began landing troops at Vladivostok later that month, alongside a British battalion of the Middlesex Regiment known as the 'Hernia Battalion', since it was made up entirely of men declared unfit to fight. They were joined in mid August by 9,000 American troops under the command of Major General William S. Graves, who had been given the unnerving warning by the Secretary of War, Newton

D. Baker: 'Watch your step. You'll be walking on eggs loaded with dynamite.'[17]

Graves's sealed orders, originally typed by the President himself on his portable machine, told him that he must at all costs refrain from doing anything that might lead to further US involvement in Russia. 'Military intervention there,' the orders stated, 'would add to the present sad confusion in Russia rather than cure it, injure her rather than help her, and it would be of no advantage in the prosecution of our main design, to win the war against Germany. [The government of the United States] cannot, therefore, take part in such intervention or sanction it in principle . . . Military action is admissible in Russia . . . only to help the Czecho-Slovaks consolidate their forces and get into successful co-operation with their Slavic kinsmen and to steady any efforts at self-government or self-defense in which the Russians themselves may be willing to accept assistance . . . The only legitimate object for which American or allied troops can be employed, it submits, is to guard military stores which may subsequently be needed by Russian forces and to render such aid as may be acceptable to the Russians in the organisation of their own self-defense.'

The US, Wilson said, was in any case not 'in a position, and has no expectation of being in a position, to take part in organised intervention in adequate force from either Vladivostok or Murmansk and Archangel'. The President's ultimate aim, he said, was 'to send to Siberia a commission of merchants, agricultural experts, labor advisers, Red Cross representatives, and agents of the Young Men's Christian Association accustomed to organizing the best methods of spreading useful information and rendering educational help of a modest sort'.[18]

Odd as Wilson's plans may have seemed, they were not unhelpful by comparison with the declared – and undeclared – intentions of Britain, France and Japan. Indeed, one major factor underlying his decision to send US troops was distrust of the Japanese and a desire to prevent their establishing a permanent foothold in the area. There was a strong suspicion that the Japanese had ambitions to annex the territory, a suspicion that was soon shown to be justified: invited to send 7,000 men into Siberia, the Japanese poured in some 72,000, and kept them there until October 1922, three and a half years after the last Americans had been withdrawn. They could not be prised out of Sakhalin Island until 1925, by which time they had invaded Manchuria. Their soldiers, incidentally, were issued with pocket Russian dictionaries, in

which the word 'Bolshevik' was equated with 'barsuk', meaning badger
or wild beast, followed by the instruction: 'to be exterminated'.[19]

In marked contrast to the Japanese attitude, General Graves, a typical
desk soldier who did everything absolutely by the book, followed his
instructions to avoid involvement punctiliously. When a US officer
arrested a Russian because he had confessed to being a Bolshevik,
Graves ordered the man's immediate release. 'You have no orders to
arrest Bolsheviks or anybody else unless they disturb the peace of the
community,' he said. 'The United States Army is not here to fight Russia
or any group or faction in Russia. Because a man is a Bolshevik is no
reason for his arrest.'

When the British commander, Major General Alfred Knox, and the
British consul, Sir Charles Elliott, complained to Graves that Russia
would become Bolshevik unless he did something to prevent it, the
American pointed out that his orders were quite explicit: his job was
neither to assist nor to prevent the Bolsheviks taking power, but merely
to keep the peace. For twenty months he did his best to carry out that
thankless task, though for much of the time the peace that needed to
be kept was between the various partners in the intervention – Poles,
Italians, Canadians, French, Romanians, Serbs, Czechs and, above all,
Japanese, as well as the British. Jealousies and misunderstandings flourished on all sides, just as they did among the many factions of White
Russians with whom the intervention forces were supposed to be co-
operating. Alongside Graves's non-fighting troops, Wilson's Red Cross
and YMCA workers struggled to carry out the President's high purpose,
their numbers reaching some 2,500 within a short time.

The Allies also intervened in southern Russia, but these incursions were
shorter and less significant. At the end of 1917, on the assumption that
the revolution would fail, the British and French, as was their custom,
had carved up the Russian Empire into 'spheres of influence' corre-
sponding with the two powers' economic interests. The British zone,
reflecting heavy investments in Russian oilfields, included the Caucasus,
Armenia, Georgia and Kurdistan; the French, who had invested mainly
in the coal and iron mines of the Ukraine, earmarked Bessarabia, the
Ukraine and the Crimea.

The British already had a relatively small Anglo-Indian force in the
Transcaucasus to counter the German and Turkish threat to Afghanistan
and northern India. In mid August they sent a detachment from Persia

across the Caspian Sea to occupy the port of Baku, centre of the Russian oil industry, from which the Bolsheviks had been driven by Whites. Their intention was to keep the Bolsheviks out, and deny the oil both to them and the Germans and Turks. A month later, however, the British were themselves driven out by a force of Turks who outnumbered them by ten to one. The brief occupation had little effect, but became notable for the abduction from Baku of twenty-six Bolshevik commissars and their murder by local White tribesmen, which became a Soviet cause célèbre. The Bolsheviks blamed the British, and used the incident to damn them to Central Asians until the fall of the Communist regime seventy years later allowed the truth to be revealed.

The French landed forces including Greek and Polish contingents in the Black Sea ports of Odessa and Sevastopol in December 1918. They linked up uneasily with the White armies in the region, tried to raise local units of Russians under French officers, and actually engaged in fighting the Reds until the alliance with the Whites finally broke down and they pulled out, ignominiously, in April 1919, with their soldiers and sailors on the brink of mutiny.

Leaving aside the activities of the Czechoslovak Legion, which were in any case quite separate, and the Japanese, who had their own agenda in eastern Siberia, Allied intervention made virtually no military impact on the civil war as a whole. With only a few thousand raggle-taggle troops in a handful of tiny enclaves in the furthest corners of the vast Russian land mass, under conflicting orders from unenthusiastic governments, there was never any real chance that they could alter the course of the revolution. What the intervention did achieve, however, was to convince Lenin and the Bolsheviks that they were the victims of an international conspiracy, a belief that came naturally to any good Marxist. In a clear demonstration of his blinkered paranoia, Lenin told his Central Executive Committee in July: 'What we are involved in is a systematic, methodical, and evidently long-planned military and financial counter-revolutionary campaign against the Soviet Republic, which all the representatives of Anglo-French imperialism have been preparing for months.' As an analysis of the shambles of intervention, it could hardly have been more wrong. But, as the world was to find to its cost for most of the twentieth century, few committed Marxists are capable of accepting that cock-ups are more common than conspiracies.

The paranoia was by no means confined to the Bolsheviks. As the

civil war became ever more bloody, reports of Red atrocities created a
growing sense of alarm in the West. After the murder of the Romanov
family, there was further outrage at news that Cheka agents had flouted
diplomatic convention by breaking into the British Embassy in Petrograd
and killing its acting head, the naval attaché Captain Francis Cromie,
in a gunfight. Nothing was said, of course, of the fact that the embassy
had itself blatantly flouted diplomatic convention by operating as a
base for espionage and sabotage against the Soviet government. However,
the diplomatic community in the city was appalled that Cromie's killers
mutilated his body and hung it from the window of the embassy. It
was not removed until all the neutral diplomats, including those broadly
sympathetic to the regime, threatened to leave the country.[20]

Assassinations soon became almost as common as executions in
Russia: the new German Ambassador was another prominent victim,
and Lenin himself was shot and very nearly killed in August 1918 by
a young woman who turned out to be a member of the rival Socialist
Revolutionaries, though the Bolsheviks tried unsuccessfully to prove
that the British had been involved. At the same time as the attempt on
Lenin, a young SR officer shot and killed the head of the Petrograd
Cheka, Mikhail Uritsky. The Bolsheviks' reaction was instant and savage.
Three days later, on 2 September, the government declared an official
state of Red Terror.

The use of terror as a weapon in Russia was nothing new – its history
went back to Ivan the Terrible and beyond. It had been an essential
part of the October Revolution, as Trotsky confirmed: 'Intimidation is
a powerful weapon of policy . . . The Revolution . . . kills individuals
and intimidates thousands. The Red Terror cannot be distinguished
from armed insurrection, of which it is the direct continuation.'[21] *Pravda*,
the party organ, had already been urging workers and the poor to take
up arms against those 'who agitate against the Soviet Power, ten bullets
for every man who raises his hand against it . . . The rule of Capital
will never be extinguished until the last capitalist, nobleman, Christian
and officer draws his last breath.'[22] Throughout the country, Bolshevik
supporters had seized the chance to settle old scores with a wave of
arbitrary murders of civil servants, engineers, factory managers and
priests – in short, anyone who had previously held a position of responsibility or authority.

With the assassination attempt on Lenin, coupled with a left-wing
revolt within the party, a botched attempt at an uprising by the SRs,

the growing success of the various White armies and the landings of Allied troops in Russia, the regime was under serious threat. The Red Terror was its immediate response. The front page of *Pravda* announced:

Workers, the time has come when either you must destroy the bourgeoisie or it will destroy you. Prepare for a merciless mass onslaught upon the enemies of the Revolution. The towns must be cleared of this bourgeois putrefaction. All the bourgeois gentlemen must be registered, as has happened with the officer gentlemen, and all who are dangerous to the cause of revolution must be exterminated . . . Henceforth, the hymn of the working class will be a hymn of hatred and revenge.[23]

On a more popular level, the tone was set by newspapers such as the mass circulation *Krasnaia Gazeta* which screamed:

Without mercy, we will kill our enemies in scores of hundreds. Let them be thousands, let them drown themselves in their own blood. For the blood of Lenin and Uritsky let there be floods of bourgeois blood – more blood, as much as possible.[24]

The Chekists were ordered to 'arrest all SRs at once' and to take hostages from the 'bourgeoisie and officers', who were to be executed 'on the least opposition'.[25] They needed no second bidding. One of their chief lieutenants, the Latvian M. Ia. Latsis, issued clear directions on what was expected:

We are out to destroy the bourgeoisie as a class. Hence, whenever a bourgeois is under examination the first step should be not to endeavour to discover material proof that the accused has opposed the Soviet Government, in deed or word, but to put to the witness the three questions: 'To what class does he belong?' 'What is his origin?' 'What is his upbringing, education and profession?' And it is solely in accordance with the answers to these three questions that his fate should be determined.[26]

Under the leadership of the Pole Felix E. Dzerzhinsky, the Cheka had grown at a remarkable rate since its formation less than a year before, and was rapidly becoming a state within a state, completely outside the law. From its headquarters in the Lubianka building, the former Moscow home of Lloyd's Insurance, its tentacles spread across the whole of Russia through a network of local offices, all vying with each other for the depth of their depravity. Dzerzhinsky, like many of his agents, had spent more than half his life in prisons and labour camps under the care of the Okhrana, the tsarist secret police, where he and they had been brutalised and stripped of all emotions apart from hatred. With total indifference to human suffering, the Chekists set about emulating their former captors and exacting a terrible vengeance for their own ill treatment.

Many Chekists were sadists, who took pleasure in inflicting the most unspeakable tortures on their victims. 'Hostages' were shot by the hundred for supposed provocations by their class or families. The number of executions soared into tens of thousands, often for the most trivial reasons. On one infamous occasion, during a session of the Council of People's Commissars, Lenin passed a note to Dzerzhinsky asking how many dangerous revolutionaries they had in prison. Dzerzhinsky wrote 'About 1,500' on the note and returned it. Lenin pencilled a cross beside the figure, and passed the note back to the Cheka leader, who that night ordered the shooting of 1,500 prisoners. Lenin, however, had not ordered their execution – Dzerzhinsky was not aware that he always marked anything he had read with a cross, to show that he had seen it.[27] There is no record of Dzerzhinsky's being disciplined or even reprimanded for his action. It was simply accepted as part of the Terror.

Reports of the Red Terror were received with revulsion in the West. Many of the stories came, of course, from Russian émigrés, mostly aristocrats and dispossessed businessmen or *burzhooi*, who had lost everything and were naturally both bitter and biased. They found a receptive audience, especially among the many investors in France, Belgium and Britain who had lost heavily when the Soviets cancelled all foreign debts, including government bonds, and nationalised property and industrial and commercial enterprises without compensation. The émigrés linked their anti-Bolshevism with anti-Semitism, a combination that chimed with the views of many influential figures and most of the press, who held that the Bolshevik Revolution was essentially a Jewish plot financed from Germany. It was a belief that was to retain its grip for many years, with tragic results for the world. In fact, not many Jews were Bolsheviks, but many of the leading Bolsheviks were Jews, which made it easy to blame their race for the whole thing.

Although the truth was so terrible that it needed no embellishment, fantastical rumours about the Red regime flourished and were accepted without question: women were being 'nationalised' and regarded as communal property; several American newspapers reported that the Bolsheviks had set up an electrically operated guillotine in Petrograd, capable of chopping off five hundred heads an hour, and so on. The *New York Times* referred to the Bolsheviks as 'human scum', while in London the Conservative *Morning Post* described the regime as a farce in which 'unpractical visionaries, emancipated criminals, wild idealists, Jewish Internationalists, all the cranks and most of the crooks, have joined hands in an orgy of passion and unreason'.

Less was heard in the West of the atrocities committed by the Whites and the Cossack hosts on workers and peasants in general and the Jews in particular. These were generally the work of individual White generals and warlords and were not systematic or matters of official policy, but they often matched and sometimes even outdid the Red Terror. No Bolshevik, for instance, could equal the White General Baron Roman von Ungern-Sternberg, a German Balt born in Estonia, who was sent by the Provisional Government to the Russian far east, where he claimed to be a reincarnation of Genghis Khan and did his best to outdo the Mongol conqueror in brutality. A fanatical anti-Semite, in 1918 he declared his intention of exterminating all the Jews and commissars in Russia, a task he set about with great enthusiasm, having his men slaughter any Jews they came across in a variety of barbarous ways, including skinning them alive. He was also noted for leading his men in nocturnal terror rides dragging human torches across the steppe at full gallop, and for promising to 'make an avenue of gallows that will stretch from Asia across Europe'.[28]

Ungern-Sternberg was by no means unique in his views: savage anti-Jewish pogroms were a common feature of many areas in the war zone, in which Jews were slaughtered in their thousands and even tens of thousands. Recently uncovered archives from 1920 speak of 'more than 150,000 reported deaths' and up to 300,000 victims, including the wounded and the dead.[29]

While the outside world reacted in horror to events in Russia, the Soviet leaders were far more sanguine. Even as the Red Terror approached its peak, they found the time and money to mark the first anniversary of their revolution in grand style. It was reported that they had voted 25 million roubles for the celebrations, and that the centres of Moscow and Petrograd had been festooned with red flags and banners. Immense crowds, including 'twenty thousand children of the proletariat', marched in procession through the main streets, singing the 'Internationale'. According to a Reuter report, '1,100,000 free dinners are being distributed. Extraordinary "autos da fé" are being held by the Bolsheviks, who are burning dummies representing "Imperialists", officers, bankers, and priests, wrapped in old Russian flags.'[30] Motor vehicles were decorated with flowers, and 'many artistes were carried through the town on lorries, reciting revolutionary poems and singing revolutionary songs'.[31] It was a pattern of self-delusion that would be followed for the next seventy years, displaying an unshakeable confidence that sent waves of trepidation surging through the West.

As 1918 drew to a close, Winston Churchill, with his usual hyperbole, defined the new spectre that was looming over the free world. 'Russia,' he told his constituents in an election speech in Dundee on 26 November, 'is being rapidly reduced by the Bolsheviks to an animal form of barbarism . . . Civilisation is being completely extinguished over gigantic areas, while Bolsheviks hop and caper like troops of ferocious baboons amid the ruins of cities and the corpses of their victims.' The leaders of the Western democracies were filled with dread that such a situation might be repeated in their own countries in 1919.

# I

## 'THE RED FLAG FLIES OVER BERLIN'

UNTIL November 1917, revolutions had always been domestic affairs, mainly confined to one country and only indirectly affecting the rest of the world. But Lenin, Trotsky and the other Bolsheviks made no secret of the fact that they were intent on starting a universal revolution, to be exported through a defeated Germany; they boasted that they had already sent agents out to prepare the ground and organise revolt. So, as the end of the Great War and the defeat of German militarism finally came into sight, Germany was seen as posing a new threat to the world order.

On 18 October 1918, French Foreign Minister Stephen Pichon told Lord Derby, the British Ambassador in Paris, that

he and the Government here were very much disturbed by certain information that they had got from Germany as to that Country being on the eve of a revolution. He says that they are as full of Bolshevism as Russia itself was before the Revolution, and it may break out at any time. They have got a Provisional Committee which he says is practically a Provisional Government actually established with its Headquarters in the Russian Embassy at Berlin. In fact he says the position is exactly the same there as it was before Kerensky brought off the Russian Revolution. What frightens him is the fact, as he says, that Bolshevism is very contagious and he is evidently considerably alarmed as to what may happen in this country [France].[1]

What was happening in Germany soon became all too clear, and all too ominous. Over the previous few months, as the tide of war had turned inexorably against it, the country had become a vast tinderbox of revolution waiting for a spark. On Sunday 3 November, that spark was struck in Kiel, base of the Imperial Navy's High Seas Fleet. Thoroughly demoralised by poor and inadequate food, harsh conditions and brutal repression, and with defeat staring them in the eyes, German sailors refused orders to raise steam for what they dubbed a 'Death Cruise', a suicidal last battle in the North Sea. When their officers tried to discipline them, the revolt escalated into full-scale mutiny.

The men stormed the armouries, seized weapons, attacked the military prisons and liberated the prisoners. Dockyard and arsenal workers downed tools and joined them. Next day, after a brief but bloody fight with soldiers still loyal to the Kaiser, they marched through the town, calling for revolution. The workers' unions declared a general strike. By evening, the whole city was in rebel hands, including the harbour and all the warships in it – when the battleship *König* raised the imperial war flag the mutineers opened fired on the ship with rifles, until the ensign was hauled down and replaced with the red flag. And when the naval commander of the town, Captain Heine, resisted arrest by a revolutionary patrol that had forced its way into his home, he was shot dead by a soldier.[2] The port admiral, the Kaiser's brother Prince Heinrich, was forced to flee for his life, hiding behind a set of false whiskers and the red flag flying on his car. Even so, the car was shot at several times, the driver was seriously wounded, and the Prince was forced to take the wheel himself in a mad dash for the Danish frontier at Flensburg.

The Cabinet in Berlin, under Prince Max of Baden, who had been appointed Chancellor at the beginning of October, was preoccupied with the problems of ending the war without surrendering. Most histories have depicted Prince Max as a liberal, simply because he was described as such by General Erich Ludendorff, the legendary Quartermaster General of the German Army, and virtual military dictator, with Field Marshal Paul von Hindenburg, of Germany from 1916 to 1918. But Ludendorff's idea of a liberal was anyone whose views were less extreme than the Kaiser's, or his own. In fact, Max, a cousin and brother-in-law of the Kaiser, was a dyed-in-the-wool monarchist with little sympathy for revolutionaries of any shade. But he was also a realist: his main concern at that moment was trying to persuade the Kaiser to abdicate, a prerequisite for any armistice negotiations. He saw the events in Kiel as an unwelcome diversion, a localised mutiny that had to be put down without delay. Since communications with the port were virtually non-existent, he and the Cabinet dispatched his friend Conrad Haussmann, a progressive Reichstag deputy, and Gustav

Noske, a tough former master butcher and leading Social Democrat deputy, to find out what was going on and to calm the situation.

Arriving in Kiel, the two deputies quickly realised that this was no simple mutiny. They were met at the station by a great crowd of demonstrators, and when Noske made a speech, promising that an armistice would be signed in a few days, and 'the just wishes of the soldiers and sailors would be speedily fulfilled', he was frequently interrupted by cheers for a republic, and by shots that scattered his audience.[3] When he managed to telephone the Cabinet that evening, he reported that all naval discipline had broken down, that the mutineers were demanding amnesty, an armistice, and the abdication of the Kaiser – and that they had elected him, Noske, governor of the region.

Any hopes that the mutiny at Kiel was an isolated incident were soon squashed. Extreme left-wing socialists, led by Karl Liebknecht, Rosa Luxemburg, Wilhelm Dittmann and Hugo Haase, seized the chance they had been waiting for and immediately began orchestrating events. Dittmann, who had only recently been released from a prison sentence for inciting a previous naval mutiny at the beginning of the year, rushed from Berlin to Hamburg, where he addressed a huge gathering of soldiers, sailors and workers. Condemning the existing German government, he demanded a Socialist republic, and urged the workers to 'go the whole hog' to bring it about. In typical Socialist style, he proposed a series of resolutions – which were, of course, all passed by acclamation – sending fraternal greetings to their comrades in Kiel, calling for a general strike in sympathy with them, and demanding the release of all 'victims of the existing civil and military justice'. This last was quickly achieved with a mass march on the law courts, where they freed a number of military prisoners who were awaiting trial. What the London *Daily Telegraph* described as 'sanguinary battles' took place in several parts of the city. Meanwhile, 15,000 dockers left work and marched on the military barracks. After a brief firefight, the officer in charge surrendered the barracks and the troops joined the rebels, who had by then disarmed all the police in the city.

At the railway station, trains carrying soldiers back to the front were stopped, and the men joined the mutineers. When the military set up machine guns around the harbour to prevent marines leaving their posts, the crowd charged the guns and forced their withdrawal. Soon, all the German flags in Hamburg harbour had been replaced with the red flag, which was also flying on a torpedo boat that returned to the port from

the open sea under the command of its own soviet and with its officers under arrest. Clearly, the mutiny was no sudden whim but an
organised revolt that had been planned in some detail, with leaders in
place and red flags provided for all flagstaffs.

Word of the revolt spread quickly throughout the navy, and soon
there were similar scenes in all the other northern ports – Bremen,
Wilhelmshaven, Altona, Lübeck, Cuxhaven, Tilsit – mutiny and insurrection were everywhere and were soon moving inland. A convoy of
thirty cars carried revolutionary soldiers into Hanover, headquarters of
the Seventh Army Corps, where they occupied the military barracks,
disarmed the officers, arrested the commanding general and frogmarched
him off in handcuffs. In Dresden, the capital of Saxony, soldiers
demanding immediate peace led huge street demonstrations and took
control of the city. 'Reds are streaming with every train from Hamburg
to Berlin,' Count Harry Kessler, socialite, diplomat and Social Democrat
supporter, recorded in his diary on 6 November. 'An uprising is expected
here tonight. This morning the Russian Embassy was raided like a
disreputable pot-house and Joffe [the ambassador] with his staff,
deported. That puts paid to the Bolshevik centre in Berlin. But perhaps
we shall yet call these people back.'[4]

By 7 November, as the Bolsheviks in Russia were celebrating the first
anniversary of their revolution, the conflagration had spread far beyond
north Germany. Modelling themselves on the Russian soviets, soldiers',
sailors' and workers' councils seized control in towns and cities and
barracks. Gangs of sailors roamed the country, spreading the message
of revolution. Kessler, who always had an eye for a good-looking sailor,
noted that those he saw occupying the Reichstag building in Berlin
looked 'healthy, fresh, neat and, most noticeable of all, very young', in
contrast with the soldiers, who were 'old and war-worn, in faded
uniforms and down-at-heel footwear, unshaven and unkempt, remnants
of an army, a tragic picture of defeat'.[5]

An uneasy calm hung over most of Berlin, and indeed over much of
Germany. There was very little fighting. 'Events at Kiel, Lübeck, Altona,
Hamburg and Hanover have as yet passed off fairly bloodlessly,' Kessler
recorded. But he then added: 'That is the way all revolutions start. The
thirst for blood grows gradually with the strains involved in setting up
the new order . . . The shape of the revolution is becoming clear: progressive encroachment, as by a patch of oil, by the mutinous sailors from
the coast to the interior. Berlin is being isolated and will soon be only

an island . . . The sea sweeps down on the land, Viking strategy. Perhaps we shall become the spearhead, against our own wish, of the slaves' revolt against Britain and American capitalism. Liebknecht as war-lord in the decisive battle and the Navy in the van.'[6]

Karl Liebknecht, rightly singled out by Kessler as the potential leader of the threatened battle, was the most prominent left-wing Socialist in Berlin, and indeed the whole of Germany. Born in Leipzig in 1871, he was the son of Wilhelm Liebknecht, a close friend of Karl Marx and one of the founders of the Social Democratic Party and of the foremost Socialist newspaper, *Vorwärts* (*Forward*). Karl was more radical than his father, embracing the full Marxist doctrine while studying law and political economy at the universities of Leipzig and Berlin. He opened a law office in Berlin in 1899, specialising in defending his fellow Socialists against charges such as smuggling subversive literature, some of which he had written himself, into tsarist Russia.

Liebknecht's anti-militarist writings brought him an eighteen-month jail sentence in 1907, the year he became president of the Socialist Youth International. He was elected to the Reichstag as a Social Democrat in 1912, and in December 1914 was the only member to vote against the war. At the end of that year, he joined a group of other extreme left-wingers in forming the Spartacus League, named after the slave who led a revolt against ancient Rome, using its newspaper *Spartakusbriefe* (*Spartacus Letters*) to call for a workers' revolution and an end to the war. The paper was soon banned, and Liebknecht was arrested and sent to the Eastern Front, where, refusing to fight, he was assigned to collecting and burying the dead. Discharged from the army when his health collapsed, he was arrested again on May Day 1916 for leading an anti-war demonstration, and sentenced to four years' imprisonment for high treason. He was released in October 1918, under Prince Max's amnesty for political prisoners, and immediately resumed his leadership of the Spartacists, in partnership with the Polish activist, Rosa Luxemburg.

Luxemburg, born in Lublin, Poland, in the same year as Liebknecht, was the daughter of a Jewish timber merchant and had become involved in revolutionary anti-tsarist activities as a schoolgirl. She had fled from Poland to Switzerland, where her lover, Leo Jogiches, a wealthy Lithuanian socialist, financed her studies in philosophy, history, economics, politics and mathematics at Zurich University, and also backed her in founding the Social Democratic Party of Poland and

Lithuania, whose members included Felix Dzerzhinsky and several others who became leading Communists in Russia. Suffering from a growth defect that left her very short and with a slight hunchback, she made up for her physical deformity with an intense intellectualism, and was if anything even more extreme in her views than Liebknecht, demanding world government under a single international Socialist party.

Migrating to Germany, Luxemburg obtained German citizenship through marriage, joined the SPD and set about radicalising the party, teaching Marxism and economics at its training centre. She was imprisoned three times between 1904 and 1906, and again during the war, when she still managed to write a series of violently anti-war pamphlets that were smuggled out of jail and printed and distributed among workers and soldiers by Jogiches. On her release in October 1918, she plunged back into Spartacist politics, feverishly drawing up the blueprints for her revolution while leaving Liebknecht to present its public face on the streets. 'The future belongs to Bolshevism everywhere,' she declared.

This poisonous pair, like Lenin and Trotsky in Russia, saw the moderate Socialists of the SPD as their principal enemies. 'The party must be recaptured from below,' Luxemburg wrote, 'by mass rebellion.' Their allies were the anti-war left-wingers who had split from the main SPD in 1917 and formed their own Independent Social Democratic Party (USPD), and who were only slightly less extreme than the Spartacists. The moderate Socialists responded by sneering at them in *Vorwärts*, contrasting the 'pathological instability' of Spartacus with their own 'clear-headed and sensible calm'.[7] But while the moderate Socialists were maintaining their sensible calm, the Spartacists were meeting returning troop trains at the rail termini to beg or buy rifles, pistols and machine guns.

The calm in Berlin was finally broken on Saturday 9 November, while Prince Max was still trying to persuade the Kaiser to step down. But even then there was virtually no violence. On that beautiful autumn day the city, the greatest industrial centre in the Reich and possibly the whole of Continental Europe, was paralysed by a general strike of all its major factories. The S-Bahn, the elevated train system, was brought to a halt when radical workers seized the power stations and cut off the electricity supply. Most Berliners stayed quietly at home, but a few tens of thousands began marching towards the centre, peacefully and in good order. They were joined by soldiers from various barracks, including the Maybug barracks, where one of the few incidents occurred: when an officer drew his revolver and ordered his men to shoot a group of mutineers, they shot him instead, seriously wounding him. The entire barracks then joined the demonstrators.

By 11 a.m., sailors and troops were pouring into Berlin from Hamburg and the north. Among the earliest arrivals was a group of sailors who had commandeered a Zeppelin airship from Kiel, and who landed at the Johannisthal airfield in eastern Berlin with red flags flying, cheered by striking ground staff. Those travelling by train were delayed by the removal of rails on the orders of the military governor of the city – he had originally wanted to bomb the trains, but thankfully his order had been blocked by the War Ministry on the grounds that many of the passengers were civilians. The delays were only temporary, however: among the mutineers on the trains were units of engineers who made short work of restoring the track. That evening there were twenty-six mass meetings in Berlin, in all the major public halls. In the meantime, workers' and soldiers' councils were being formed on the streets, rapidly coalescing into an organised network with a central council or soviet of twenty-eight members, half soldiers and sailors and half civilian workers, ready to take over the government.

The old order in Germany collapsed. Beginning with the ageing King Ludwig III, whose House of Wittelsbach had ruled Bavaria without interruption for more than a thousand years, Germany's twenty-two lesser kings, princes and dukes were all deposed without resistance. By midday on 9 November, only the king of Prussia and emperor of Germany, Kaiser Wilhelm II, remained.

The Kaiser was not in Berlin, having left for military headquarters in Spa on 30 October in the mistaken belief that 'his' soldiers would always honour their oath to protect him. His Chancellor knew better. With thousands of armed and rebellious troops and workers threatening the capital, Prince Max sought to forestall the violence of the revolution by issuing a press statement announcing that the Kaiser had renounced the throne – though in fact Wilhelm had bluntly refused to do any such thing. Prince Max then bowed out, handing over the government to the moderate leader of the Social Democrats, Friedrich Ebert, a forty-seven-year-old former saddler and trade union leader, who had been one of Rosa Luxemburg's students at the party's training school.

Like many other Social Democrats, Ebert favoured the establishment of a constitutional monarchy on the British pattern, but his hopes were scuppered by his deputy, Philipp Scheidemann, who proclaimed a republic almost by accident. Scheidemann had rushed to the Reichstag to tell his colleagues of Ebert's appointment. Having done so, he was eating lunch in the restaurant when he was told that Karl Liebknecht and his Spartacus League were setting up camp in the Royal Palace, from where they intended to announce a soviet-style republic modelled on Lenin's Russia. 'I saw the Russian madness before me,' Scheidemann wrote later, 'the replacement of the Tsarist terror by the Bolshevist one. No! Not in Germany.'⁸ Leaving his meal, he strode out to the small balcony outside the Reichstag library. The crowd gathered below cheered his appearance, then quietened as he began an off-the-cuff speech. He told them of the new government, and spoke briefly about the horrors of war and the misery of defeat. Then, needing a rousing finish, he cried: 'The rotten old monarchy has collapsed. Long live the new! Long live the German Republic!' And so it was done, almost as an afterthought.

Liebknecht had spent that morning touring the city centre in a lorry loaded with armed guards and festooned with red carnations, calling on the workers to rise and take over the revolution. Responding to his bidding, armed workers, soldiers and sailors had stormed the Admiralty, locking up over a hundred officers, including several admirals, and had broken open the Moabit prison. He had led a huge crowd through the gates of the palace, and stood on the balcony from which the Kaiser had addressed cheering crowds on the declaration of war in 1914. A red carpet was torn from the floor and draped over the parapet. 'Comrades!' he cried. 'The red flag flies over Berlin! The proletariat is marching. The reign of capitalism which has turned Europe into a graveyard is over. We must summon our strength to build a new government of workers and peasants, to create a new order of peace and happiness and freedom not merely for our brothers in Germany but for the whole world. Whoever is resolved not to cease from the fight until the Free Socialist Republic and the world revolution shall be realised, let him raise his hand and swear!' The crowd roared back 'We swear!'

But Liebknecht was two hours too late. Ebert had already persuaded Liebknecht's left-wing allies, the Independent Socialists, to join him in forming a government by agreeing that workers' and soldiers' councils should exercise 'all power' until the election of a new national assembly.

Next day, the councils elected the first official government of the German Republic. With the revolutionary title of the Council of People's Commissars, it consisted of six members: three Majority Social Democrats (Ebert, Scheidemann and Otto Landsberg) and three Independent Socialists (Haase, Dittmann and Emil Barth). But Ebert would be in charge.

For the rest of Saturday and through Sunday there were scattered skirmishes in the city centre, with some sporadic shooting. Officers who dared to venture on to the streets had their epaulettes and badges of rank torn off, as was happening throughout Germany. The most serious fighting was around the palace, where Liebknecht and the Spartacists had established their headquarters, and the adjoining imperial stables, a baroque four-storey building which was occupied by a group of loyalist officers and cadets of the Youth Defence Force. In the Alexanderplatz to the east of the palace, there was a twenty-minute gun battle for control of police headquarters, at the end of which some 650 prisoners were freed and an Independent Socialist, Emil Eichhorn, proclaimed himself Berlin's new police president.

By Monday 11 November, when the rest of Europe was celebrating the Armistice, things were generally quiet, and by the next day Harry Kessler could write in his diary:

In the city everything is peaceful today and the factories are working again. Nothing has been heard of shootings. Noteworthy is that during the days of revolution the trams, irrespective of street fighting, ran regularly. Nor did the electricity, water, or telephone services break down for a moment. The revolution never created more than an eddy in the ordinary life of the city which flowed calmly along on its customary course. Moreover, though there was so much shooting, there were remarkably few dead or wounded. The colossal, world-shaking upheaval has scurried across Berlin's day-to-day life much like an incident in a crime film.[9]

A soviet revolution in Berlin had been averted, at least for the moment. But it was a different story in Munich, Germany's second city and the capital of Bavaria, Germany's second largest state. There, Socialist street demonstrations and upheavals forced the King to flee, and a Council of Workers, Soldiers and Peasants meeting, inevitably in a beer hall, proclaimed an independent Bavarian Republic, under the unlikely leadership of Kurt Eisner, head of the Independent Socialist Democratic Party.

Eisner, the drama critic of the *Münchener Post* newspaper, had never held elected office in his life. He was a wild-haired, shaggy-bearded Berlin Jew, the very epitome of the bohemian café intellectual with his spindly frame and pince-nez spectacles perched on a prominent hooked nose. He had been a protégé of Karl Liebknecht's father, Wilhelm, who had made him his successor as editor of *Vorwärts* in 1899. He was dismissed in 1905, after falling out with his colleagues on the paper, and emigrated to Bavaria, where he worked as a political journalist, first in Nuremberg and then in Munich. But his views moved steadily further to the left, and in 1915, after he had begun openly criticising Germany's 'aggressive spirit' and regularly falling foul of the military censors, he was sacked again. He was, however, allowed to go on writing dramatic and literary criticism, more or less on a freelance basis.

With plenty of time on his hands, Eisner took to holding court in the Golden Anchor coffee house on Monday evenings, leading a regular group of about thirty young people in interminable philosophical discussions on subjects such as 'Socialism as the religion of the proletariat'. Such political talking shops were a regular feature of the Munich scene: some six years later, Adolf Hitler was to preside over one, also every Monday evening, in the Café Neumaier on the edge of the Viktualenmarkt.

By the spring of 1917, in common with other left-wing Socialists in Berlin and elsewhere, Eisner had parted company with the Majority Social Democrats; he formed the Bavarian USPD, with an increasingly radical programme. Linking up with other Independent Socialist parties in the rest of Germany, he led calls for a general strike in January 1918, with the declared intention 'to overturn the monarchy, and not only the Prussian, but to bring down militarism entirely'.[10] He succeeded in bringing out some 8,000 workers from the Krupp armaments factory, the Rapp Motor Works and the Bavarian Aircraft Plant, before he was arrested. He was never tried or convicted, but spent the next eight and a half months in Stadelheim jail, until on 14 October he was suddenly released to stand in a Reichstag by-election.

The Bavarian authorities refused to take Eisner seriously. Allowing him to stand was meant as a sop to the radical left; it was a foregone conclusion, they believed, that his moderate Social Democrat opponent, the hearty, popular and typically Bavarian Erhard Auer, would waltz home. But they had failed to recognise the sea change that was taking place in popular feeling. On the verge of defeat and starvation, the people were weary of war. They were also bitter and angry at discovering that they had been lied to and kept in ignorance of Germany's true situation. After years of rejection, Eisner's anti-militarist message was suddenly acceptable, even desirable, and his incarceration had turned him into a martyr figure attracting sympathy rather than derision.

For all his other-worldly attitudes and appearance, Eisner proved himself to be a highly effective political operator, and he made the most of the situation with a brilliant campaign. Looking like an Old Testament prophet with his long white hair and beard, he proclaimed, 'You see me just as Stadelheim gave me back to freedom,' and compared his ordeal with the well-fed comfort of his opponent. He insisted that a vote for Auer would be a vote for continuing the war and more mass murder. He called openly for revolution and the overthrow of established authority. His audiences increased daily as his bandwagon started to roll, aided by the news on 27 October that Austria-Hungary had surrendered, raising the awful possibility of the war arriving on Bavarian soil with an Italian invasion from the south. And then, at the start of November, Eisner's calls for a republic were given a fillip by news that the Austrians had thrown out the Habsburg dynasty. 'Across the border,' he declared, 'we greet the new Austrian Republic, and we demand that a Bavarian regime instituted by the people proclaim peace together with the German republicans of Austria in the name of Germany, since neither the will nor the power exists in Berlin to reach an immediate peace.'[11]

When Eisner called for a mass demonstration on 7 November to demand an immediate end to the war, Auer was forced to give his party's support in order to avoid being outflanked. The result was staggering: in warm autumn weather more than 80,000 people crowded on to the Theresienwiese, the great meadow close to the centre of Munich on which the annual Oktoberfest is held. Eisner stood on a soapbox and orated for more than an hour, without interruption. When he was done, one of his aides shouted: 'Comrades, our leader Kurt Eisner has spoken. There is no reason to waste any more words. Follow us!' And follow him they did, first to a temporary barracks and munitions depot at the nearby Guldein School, where they helped themselves to arms with the active help of the guards, who promptly joined them. They then moved on into the city centre, gathering more weapons and more men from various military posts on the way, until they reached the massive Türkenstrasse barracks, where they met their first opposition. After a few bullets and a little tear gas, resistance in the barracks ceased. The last bastion of royal authority had fallen, leaving the city open to Eisner and his men and women.

Not content with invading barracks, one group of demonstrators invaded the Mathäserbräu, Munich's biggest beer hall in the heart of the city, alongside the municipal and state administrative buildings, and in an impromptu but well-lubricated political meeting on the second floor set up a council of soldiers and sailors. On the ground floor, meanwhile, Eisner presided over a separate meeting of workers which established a council of workers with him as its chairman – the first elected office he had ever held. It was then a simple step to combine the two into a unified council of workers, soldiers and peasants. The revolution was in business. The council sent out trucks loaded with armed soldiers to patrol the city and enforce order. They occupied key buildings and took over transportation and communications centres, then finally seized the major newspaper and publishing houses, printing and posting up hundreds of yellow placards announcing the new regime.

At about 10 p.m., Eisner and the members of his new council marched to the Landtag, the Bavarian state parliament, escorted by some sixty armed men. Opening up the closed building, the council members took seats at the deputies' desks in the lower house, while Eisner climbed on to the presidential podium, rang for order, then proclaimed the end of the Wittelsbach dynasty and the foundation of the Bavarian Republic. 'The Bavarian revolution is victorious,' he announced. 'It has put an end to the old plunder of the Wittelsbach kings. Now we must proceed to build a new regime . . . The one who speaks to you at this moment assumes that he is to function as the provisional prime minister.'[12] No one disagreed.

Next morning, the city awoke to find red flags flying over public buildings and the main churches, and Eisner's yellow posters everywhere proclaiming the new republic. The old King had fled, first to one of his country estates near the Austrian frontier, and then into Austria, where he remained briefly before moving on to permanent exile in Hungary. There had been no battles, no street fighting and virtually no resistance. And so things were to remain for some weeks, with the vast majority of Bavarians passively accepting the new regime, at least for the moment.

To the relief of all but the extreme left, Eisner promised to maintain public order, security of individuals and of private property, and to hold free and universal elections for a constituent assembly. His proclamation of the revolution and its aims ended on a remarkably positive – one might say almost naive – note: 'In this time of wild murder we abhor all bloodshed. Every human life should be holy. Long live the Bavarian Republic! Long live the peace! Long live the creative work of all labour activity!'[13]

The new regimes in both Berlin and Munich, and the almost bloodless revolutions that had brought them into being, seemed to offer hope that the worst excesses seen in Russia might be avoided in Germany. The revolutions were so new, however, and accurate information on what was really happening so hard to come by that it was impossible to be sure about anything. None of the Western leaders could forget that the civilised Kerensky had been the forerunner for the brutality of the Bolsheviks. They dared not lower their guard even, or especially, when the Germans sought an armistice. Ironically, while they had suspected in 1917 that the Bolshevik revolution in Russia was aided if not engineered by the Germans, they now feared that the German revolution was inspired and orchestrated by the Russian Bolsheviks.

It would have been satisfying for the Allies to ignore pleas for an armistice and to press on with the war, driving the German armies back into their homeland and delivering a knockout blow that would lead to an unconditional surrender. Marshal Foch, the Allied Commander-in-Chief, told Clemenceau and Lord Derby on 11 November that 'within another fortnight the German Army would have been completely surrounded and would have been obliged to lay down their arms'.[14] It would have been satisfying, certainly, but highly dangerous, as Britain's Chief of the Imperial General Staff, Field Marshal Sir Henry Wilson, noted in his diary on 9 November:

Cabinet meeting tonight . . . Lloyd George read two telegrams from the Tiger [Clemenceau] in which he described Foch's interview with the Germans. The Tiger is afraid that Germany may collapse and Bolshevism gain control. Lloyd George asked me if I wanted that to happen or if I did not prefer an armistice. Without hesitation I replied 'Armistice'. The whole cabinet agreed with me.

And so, at 5.12 a.m. two days later, in a railway carriage parked in a clearing of the forest of Compiègne, the Armistice was signed after brief but frantic negotiations. Significantly, one clause required German Army units in south Russia and the Baltic States to stay where they were, fully armed, to hold back the Red Army. At a Cabinet meeting in London the day before, Churchill had stressed the Allies' new priority: 'We might have to build up the German Army, as it was important to get Germany on her legs again for fear of the spread of Bolshevism.'[15] In Paris, Foch even began drawing up plans for German troops to be joined with Americans and French to mount an attack on the Bolsheviks – an idea that found an echo a quarter of a century later at the end of another world war, when Heinrich Himmler, Hermann Göring and other leading Nazis entertained the naive hope that the Allied armies could be persuaded to join the Germans in pushing back Stalin's Red Army and crushing the Soviet Union.

While the two sides were still at war, Western governments' nervousness at events in Germany was compounded by lack of reliable information. The only reports they saw came from news agencies and correspondents of neutral countries, picked up in Amsterdam, Copenhagen, Stockholm and so on. And those neutral countries themselves were not immune to the dangers. As a *New York Times* report from London warned:

The most serious question of the hour . . . is how far Europe is infested with Bolshevism. Dispatches show that the revolution in Germany has made an impression in Sweden, where organs of the Independent Socialists publish a manifesto urging the establishment of Soldiers' and Workmen's Councils everywhere in order to establish a Socialist Government and republic. General demobilization of the army and an eight-hour working day are also demanded of them.

In Holland also, say dispatches from Amsterdam, popular joy over the end of the war is overshadowed by fear of Bolshevist troubles and doubts whether a partial demobilization of the army, with an increase in the bread ration, will stave off subversive infection.

The revolutionary Socialist Party has already issued a manifesto advocating Russian methods. Moreover, a new republican party has arisen in Holland aiming at the abolition of the court, army, navy and diplomacy.

Newspapers in Spain, Holland and even Norway also express apprehension over the spread of the Red Flag movement. The troubles in Switzerland also cause uneasiness. A general strike began there today.[16]

Once the Armistice was signed, journalists rushed to cross the lines to report on the true situation in Germany. From the east, Morgan

Philips Price, a British journalist who had been the *Manchester Guardian*'s special correspondent in Russia since December 1914, contacted the Provisional Government in Berlin at the end of November and obtained permission to enter Germany. Price, born into a family which had made a fortune from cotton, timber and land and had a long involvement in Liberal politics, was a committed Marxist. Regarded as an apologist or even a propagandist for the Bolshevik cause, he was encouraged to go to Berlin by the Soviet Foreign Commissar, G.V. Chicherin, and the head of the ministry's Central European Department, Karl Radek. His aim was not only to report on the situation in Germany but also to counteract the horror stories spread by anti-Bolshevik refugees and project a more sympathetic image of what was going on in Russia. Unfortunately, by the time he arrived he had been sacked by his editor for biased reporting, though since the letter never found him he did not discover this until he had sent half a dozen cables, all but two of which were stopped: although the war was over, the British military censors were still hard at work monitoring and blocking information on Germany.

It took Price six days to reach Berlin from Moscow, passing train-loads of returning Russian prisoners going in the opposite direction. The first frontier post, forty miles east of Minsk, marked the start of territory still occupied by the Germans. There, he was passed from the Russian Revolutionary Frontier Commission to the German Soldiers' Soviet, which he said was composed mainly of 'backward Bavarian peasants'. Price noted caustically that they 'allowed the officers still much power and even elected them to the Soviets'. He seemed happier to report that the soldiers' soviets got more revolutionary the nearer he got to the German frontier, where the customs was run entirely by 'common soldiers'. And that during the journey through East Prussia, soldiers boarding the train turned the officers out of the compartments and made them stand in the corridors. 'The trains were packed with troops returning home,' he wrote, 'and the atmosphere became more revolutionary as I approached Berlin . . .'[17]

In Berlin, Price interviewed Hugo Haase, leader of the Independent Socialists in Ebert's Cabinet, whom he found sitting at Bismarck's old copper-topped desk in the Chancellery. Haase told him that the German government intended to publish all its documents relating to the start of the war in 1914, from the ultimatum to Serbia to the invasion of Belgium, so that the world could 'judge better as to the responsibility for the war' – though it is not clear whether he believed this would vindicate or condemn Germany. Dismissing what he described as 'local disorders that have broken out in some districts', he said they were due to 'old reactionary officials who have not yet been got under control'.

Haase admitted that the great masses of returning soldiers knew nothing of politics and might not immediately 'rise to the occasion', aiding the bourgeois parties by their apathy. In the long run, however, he believed the organised urban workers would achieve a Socialist republic. But the only way the Spartacus group could gain control, he said, was if social and industrial conditions got so bad that the working masses saw a more radical government as their only hope. The Allies could help to avoid this by concluding an immediate preliminary peace, and relieving the food situation by raising the blockade.[18]

The Allied naval blockade had been one of the most potent weapons in the later stages of the war, and one of the most successful, preventing supplies, especially of food, reaching Germany: in the end, hunger had proved as effective as millions of tons of artillery shells in bringing Germany to her knees. Starving munitions workers had lost the will to keep slaving for a victory that was becoming more and more illusory. Soldiers at the front, although marginally better fed than civilians, were demoralised by news of the suffering of their families back home. And one of the factors that weakened Ludendorff's final offensives in 1918 had been the fact that German troops advancing through British positions had been unable to resist the temptation to stop and plunder what to them were luxurious stocks of food and drink left behind in the rear areas. 'Entire divisions totally gorged themselves on food and liquor,' one of Ludendorff's staff officers complained, and so had failed 'to press the vital attack forward'.[19]

With the signing of the Armistice, the Germans had hoped that the blockade would be lifted, allowing desperately needed food to be shipped in to relieve the suffering of the civilian population. But an armistice is not the same as a peace treaty. Technically, the two sides were still at war, and while they were at war, many wartime restrictions remained in force – including the blockade, even though its results encouraged the spread of Bolshevism. As an American journalist who reached Berlin from the west at about the same time as Price reported: 'Karl Liebknecht and famine are the two black beasts of Berlin. The German capital presents a compact picture of conditions throughout the shattered empire, with the difference that Berlin suffers most from a lack of food and most from the daily fear that Liebknecht's Spartacus group will plunge the city and country into bloody Bolshevism.'[20]

The situation was aggravated by the terms of the Armistice, which demanded that Germany hand over to the Allies not only great quantities of armaments but also 5,000 rail locomotives, 150,000 freight wagons and 5,000 lorries, effectively removing the principal means of distributing food. Frederick A. Smith, writing for the *New York Times* and *Chicago Tribune*, was the first American journalist to reach Berlin, having been flown there in an airplane provided by the Workers' and Soldiers' Council in Frankfurt, specifically so that he could report on the food shortage. He duly obliged in his first dispatch, saying: 'All Germans are united in a plea to President Wilson and America to relieve quickly the food situation, thus saving them from the peril of the Bolsheviki, who from the first have been receiving money and counsel from the leaders of the Russian terrorists.'[21]

Smith had crossed the border from Alsace-Lorraine near Metz on 21 November, together with four other American reporters. They had driven past the returning German Army that had fought battles in the Argonne and on the Meuse, whose troops were greeted in villages with cries of 'Welcome home, heroes!' and garlanded with paper flowers. At Trier they met their first revolutionary – a young lieutenant wearing a white armband who, when he had recovered from the shock of finding American civilians alongside German troops, directed them to the mayor, a sailor called Fritz Harris. Harris was one of the seamen who had swarmed south from Kiel. Together with a mere fifty other revolutionaries recruited in Trier, he had disarmed the 70,000 soldiers garrisoned there, and was now running the entire administration of the city. His orders were being 'readily and apparently willingly obeyed by the former civilian rulers, including the burgomaster, the railroad, telegraph and Post Office officials, and even the military leaders'.

Harris had the American journalists put on a train to Coblenz, where they found a bombastic army sergeant, Fritz Donath, in charge. After listening to their plans, Sergeant Donath sent for a major general. 'Formerly,' Smith wrote, 'when a general of the German Army entered any room the clicking of heels of subordinates could be heard as they came to the salute, but it was not so with this band of rebels against Prussianism. The only salute for the General was an informal nod from Donath, who bluntly ordered him to get two military cars to take us on to Frankfurt.' The General complied without complaint.

While the cars were being prepared, Donath pointed to the red flag flying over the town hall. That, he said, was their answer to President Wilson's urging them to throw out their militaristic leaders. The people, Donath said, had waited a long time for the right moment to strike, but their decision had been brought on by the food crisis. 'The soldiers,' he said, 'had two hearts, one heart at the front and another at home with their wives and children. When they returned to their homes occasionally and found their families undernourished, they lost their spirit for further battling.' The revolution, Donath told Smith, was the most peaceful in the history of the world's upheavals. He stated proudly that 'not a drop of blood was spilled in Coblenz on Nov. 9, 10 or 11 while the revolution was taking place'.[22]

The real testing ground for the revolution, however, would not be in traditionally conservative towns like Coblenz or Trier. Nor would it be in the great provincial cities like Hamburg and Frankfurt, though since 1848 Frankfurt had always been touted as the capital of an alternative federation of German states. The city that counted, particularly to the outside world, was Berlin, the Reich capital, Germany's only true metropolis. Like most metropolises, Berlin was not typical of Germany, or even of Prussia. Labelled 'Red Berlin', it was regarded with suspicion and distrust by the rest of the country. Outside the elegant and affluent centre and west end, two-thirds of its population were immigrants, or the children of immigrants. Though nobody had counted, the largest ethnic group was almost certainly Silesian, more Polish than German, mainly labourers who had flocked to the city as factory fodder during the industrial explosion of the previous fifty or sixty years. Alongside them were thousands of Poles, Russians, Ukrainians, Moravians, Bohemians and, of course, Jews, all adding their own contribution to the mix, and all cooped up together in vast tenement blocks that were labelled, sardonically, *Mietskasernen* (rental barracks), where multiple families were often crammed together in one room and a single toilet had to serve up to a dozen families. Berlin was clearly a fertile breeding ground for violent revolt, and yet it stayed calm and relatively trouble-free for some weeks after the almost bloodless revolution of 9 November.

To a large extent, all was relatively quiet because the forces of the right, and indeed the centre, were keeping their heads down. While thousands of soldiers and sailors were forming councils and tearing badges of rank from officers, the high command and the bulk of the regular officer corps appeared to do nothing, simply holding their ground and waiting for things to settle down. And tens of thousands of their troops, mostly hard-bitten regular soldiers with nationalist and right-wing views, also stayed quiet in their barracks, keeping out of harm's way and waiting for orders. It was essential that they made no moves to smash the councils before the time was right, for this would have provoked a civil war.

Although Field Marshal Hindenburg was nominally in command of the army, the man responsible for holding it together was General Wilhelm Groener, who had taken over from Ludendorff as First Quartermaster General on 26 October. Groener was an unusual general in several ways: for a start, he was not a Prussian but a southerner from Württemberg; he was also the son of a sergeant, was an expert on railways and was politically savvy. After spending two years in the War Ministry organising logistics and supplies, he had good connections with industrialists and the trade unions, knew how things worked, and knew how to negotiate and bargain. He also knew Ebert, and on 10 November, while the new Chancellor was still in the process of moving into the Chancellery, Groener called him on the secret direct line from General Headquarters, to offer him a deal. As Groener himself put it, he 'informed him that the Army would put itself at the disposal of his regime in return for the regime's support for the Field Marshal and the officer corps through the maintenance of order and discipline in the Army'. In other words, he promised to support Ebert and his government, provided they left him alone to run the army as the self-governing state-within-the-state that it had always been. He made one other condition: 'The officer corps demands of the regime a battle against Bolshevism, and is ready for such an engagement.'[23] Ebert accepted his offer – and in doing so handed the lever of real power back to the generals.

Recognising that he could not hope to stop the councils movement as it gained momentum, and needing to get between four and five million soldiers back across the Rhine from France in good order, Groener chose cooperation over confrontation. Following the old dictum 'if you can't beat 'em, join 'em', he ordered the election of a soldiers' council for every battalion, company and squadron, then set about getting reliable officers placed on each council. It was a bold move, and it worked – for about three weeks, when the supposedly tame councils asserted their independence and refused to agree to a programme that would have resurrected the old order in the army. The brief era of collaboration with the councils was over. Groener had nine divisions of returned front-line troops stationed around Berlin, quartered outside the city both to avoid straining its resources and to keep them away from contamination by the radical left. He now showed his true colours by proposing to send them into the city 'to disarm the citizens', a move that Ebert wisely vetoed.

Ebert's first priority was to keep the lid on the revolutionary pot by restoring and then maintaining order. He and his Majority Socialists believed that the best and safest way of doing this was by holding early elections for a national assembly, which would dissolve the councils, draw up a new constitution and work out the best way of establishing a representative and legitimate government. This, of course, was anathema to Liebknecht, Luxemburg and the Spartacists. Like Lenin and Trotsky, they abhorred democracy, knowing they could never hope to win a majority. Such elections would inevitably expose the narrowness of their support, and wipe them out as a political force. If this was to be avoided, the elections must be stopped and Ebert's government brought down, fast. Liebknecht's revolutionary shop stewards went to work in the factories and public services, which were plagued by an ever increasing number of strikes. The plan was that these should lead to a massive general strike, which would bring down the government.

Alarmed at the prospect of further disorder, a group of senior civil servants, who had been quietly keeping the administrative wheels turning, persuaded several hundred soldiers and sailors to demonstrate outside the Chancellery and proclaim Ebert President of the Republic. This they duly did, after declaring that Germany faced a 'total catastrophe' if the rule of the councils was not ended and free elections for a national constituent assembly were not held before 20 December. In response to their cheering acclamation, Ebert came out on to the balcony, but declined the honour they were trying to bestow on him. Extolling the rule of law, he advised them to concentrate on helping to restore the economy instead of taking 'unauthorised measures' and making 'individual experiments', then returned to his desk.

Word of the attempt to make Ebert President reached Liebknecht very swiftly, and he reacted just as swiftly to what the Spartacist newspaper *Die Rote Fahne* (*The Red Flag*) described somewhat melodramatically as 'the Putsch of 6 December'. As it happened, two Spartacist meetings were taking place in halls to the north of the city centre, and those attending were called out to take part in a counter-demonstration. They set out in good order, but as they reached the corner of Invalidenstrasse found their way blocked by a line of machine guns manned by troops from the nearby Maybug barracks. Without warning, the machine guns opened up. They continued for a full five minutes, mercilessly cutting down everyone and everything in their field of fire – including passengers and crew on a number 31 tramcar, which had the misfortune to turn the corner at the wrong moment.

Leaving their dead, dying and wounded victims lying on the ground, the machine-gunners then calmly withdrew into the barracks, and anonymity. No one has ever established who they were, or who they represented, or who gave the order to open fire. No one can be sure what the political situation was at that time in the Maybug barracks, though it was certainly very different from what it had been less than a month before, when the troops shot their officers and joined the revolutionaries. The soldiers were most probably part of a new phenomenon that was to play a vital role in German political life over the next decade and more: the Freikorps, an abbreviation of *Freiwilligenkorps*, a name that properly translates as 'volunteer corps', and dates back to the struggle for liberation and a national German identity during the Napoleonic occupations of Berlin in 1806 and 1813.

The Freikorps of 1918 and 1919 were not bands of freedom fighters but freebooting private armies of embittered ex-servicemen, mainly composed of former officers and NCOs who refused to disband, determined to maintain military discipline and organisation in the face of what they saw as the disorder of the soldiers' councils. Steeped in the harsh traditions of the Prussian Army, they were fiercely nationalist and violently anti-Bolshevik. Their formation was encouraged if not actually initiated by Groener, both as a means of keeping alive the ethos of the officer corps during those uncertain times and of providing tough, trained units of loyal troops who could be relied on to fight the revolutionary forces of the extreme left. Their relationship with the army was kept deliberately vague, but they were equipped by it with machine guns, mortars and even field guns as well as rifles and pistols, and there is little doubt that their pay came from army funds. Many of their commanders were serving regular officers.

The Freikorps' first function was to police Germany's eastern frontiers with the new Baltic States and the newly independent and deeply hostile Poland, which after centuries of German, Russian and Austrian oppression could be expected to try and grab as much territory as it could get away with. Protection against Bolshevism spreading from the east was a secondary consideration in this area, but nonetheless it was a real consideration, especially when Russia went to war with Poland in 1919. In Berlin and the rest of Germany, however, the battle with Bolshevism in all its forms was the Freikorps' very *raison d'être*.

On 10 December, five days after the last German forces had been evac-uated from France and Belgium in accordance with the terms of the Armistice, the first army units marched back into Berlin. It could hardly be described as a victory parade, but the Brandenburg Gate and Pariser Platz were garlanded and decorated with fir fronds and palm leaves. The newspapers stressed that the soldiers had never been defeated, that they had returned 'in good order ... their shield of honour unstained' and that they were 'welcomed back to the Reich capital with warm hearts and warm thanks as true conquerors'.[24] They were allowed to carry their arms, but without ammunition, and many had flowers stuck in the barrels of their rifles, just like the troops who marched out of the city in August 1914. An estimated 100,000 spectators had turned out to greet them, but according to the *Berliner Morgen-Zeitung* there were only eight to ten policemen on duty. Ebert made a long speech from a podium in front of the Adlon Hotel, welcoming the troops back to their Socialist Republic and assuring them, in a phrase that would echo around an incredulous world next day, that 'No enemy has vanquished you'. After four years of horrific warfare and 9,450,000 deaths – more than two million of them Germans – it seemed that Germany had learned nothing.

Few of the returning soldiers were properly demobilised, either in Berlin or elsewhere in the country. Mostly, they just melted back into the general population – and exacerbated the government's problems with up to six million men suddenly needing work, housing and food in an economy where some 95 per cent of industry was still geared to war production. It was a situation that was ripe for Bolshevik exploit-ation, particularly as the Allied blockade had been extended for another month, and with it the threat of starvation. The Spartacists were quick to seize on the opportunity. 'Bolshevism,' Frederick Smith reported, 'impersonated by Liebknecht and supported by the Spartacus group, trades on famine conditions in an effort to enlist civilians and returning soldiers in a program of terror and destruction.'[25]

Berlin remained in a state of confusion for the rest of December, with various groups all claiming authority: Ebert's Council of People's Commissars in the Chancellery, the Congress of Workers' and Soldiers' Councils in the Reichstag, the Workers' and Soldiers' Councils of Berlin in the Prussian Landtag building, Eichhorn's 3,000-strong 'Security Service' in police headquarters on Alexanderplatz, the Revolutionary Shop Stewards and, of course, Liebknecht's and Luxemburg's alternative Spartacist government in the Royal Palace, supported by a volunteer force of about 2,000 Red sailors based in the Royal Stables and calling themselves the People's Naval Division. There were daily street demonstrations, mass meetings and spasmodic gunfights, and virtually every day until Christmas another returning division from the regular army marched back through the Brandenburg Gate and up the Unter den Linden before dissolving into the crowds.

The first national Congress of Workers' and Soldiers' Councils met in the Reichstag on Monday 16 December, with representatives from all over Germany, though the delegates from the Independent Socialist Republic of Bavaria saw themselves as fraternal observers rather than participants. Outside the Reichstag, from the top of a truck, Liebknecht harangued what he claimed were a quarter of a million demonstrators. And on Thursday the 19th, a force of armed Spartacist sailors charged the entrance, but were repelled by truncheon-wielding guards. To the dismay of the Spartacists and the Independent Socialists, whose constant cry was 'All power to the soviets', it was clear that for many delegates, the excitement of government was wearing thin. Most of them wanted nothing more than to get back to some sort of normality as quickly as possible. Morgan Philips Price noted a marked 'absence of the revolutionary enthusiasm so noticeable at recent Russian Congresses . . . and a general desire to throw responsibility for the future on the National Assembly', which would be elected to draw up a new constitution.[26] The congress voted overwhelmingly to dismantle the council system and hold early elections, setting the date at 19 January, just one month ahead. It would be a short campaign but a bloody one as the Spartacists and Independent Socialists ratcheted up their efforts to disrupt it and prevent the elections taking place.

Violence erupted again on 23 December, when the sailors of the People's Naval Division, having already been given 125,000 marks as back pay, demanded another 80,000 marks as a Christmas bonus. When they were refused, they stormed the office of the City Commandant,

General Otto Wels, in the splendour of the eighteenth-century Arsenal at the top of the Unter den Linden. Having taken Wels and two other officers hostage, they marched off to the Chancellery, where they interrupted a Cabinet meeting and occupied the building while they squabbled with the ministers over how the money was to be paid. The major condition demanded by the ministers was for the sailors and their Spartacist allies to evacuate the Royal Palace and hand over the keys.

As the dispute escalated, Ebert decided that the time had come to call in Groener's promise. Using the secret direct line to Supreme Headquarters at Kassel, he asked for military help. Groener's assistant, Major Kurt von Schleicher – later to become Adolf Hitler's immediate predecessor as Chancellor – took the call and was more than happy to oblige by sending a force of trustworthy troops. Within the hour, the Third Battalion of the Uhlan Guards made the short train journey from Potsdam, determined to put an end to the People's Naval Division.

The 'Battle of Christmas Eve' started at dawn next day, in and around the Royal Palace and the stables. Both sides were armed with machine guns, but the troops also had 75mm field guns, with which they bombarded the palace, smashing down the gates and windows, including the famous balcony from which both the Kaiser and Karl Liebknecht had made their historic speeches. It was a bizarre battle, with regular breaks for talks and speeches. The fighting was hampered by huge crowds milling around in front of the palace, gawping at the damage before moving on to the Christmas Fair, which carried on as normal in the nearby Lustgarten, or the brightly lit shops and stores, which continued to do good business in the Linden, Friedrichstrasse and Leipziger Strasse. By one o'clock in the afternoon, the battle had fizzled out, inconclusively. Most of the 'trustworthy troops' had simply melted into the crowd. Groener blamed the failure of the operation on Christmas – but clearly made a mental note to make use of troops who could be truly relied on when the next emergency (or opportunity) arose: the Freikorps, whose numbers were growing fast.

On Christmas Day, while Ebert rested in the Chancellery and Groener celebrated quietly with his staff in Supreme Headquarters at Wilhelmshöhe Castle, there was no let-up in the Spartacus campaign. Liebknecht staged yet another demonstration, marching from the Victory Column in front of the Reichstag, up the Linden to join the sailors at the Royal Palace, where curious sightseers inspected the damage from the previous day. They then moved on to the newspaper quarter in Belle-

Allianz-Platz (named for the famous Russian victory over Napoleon, which the British insisted on calling 'Waterloo'), and occupied the offices of *Vorwärts*, taking over the presses to run off leaflets on red paper claiming: 'Today, 25 December 1918, *Vorwärts* has passed into our, the revolutionary workers', possession, in accordance with the new justice born with the Revolution of 9 November,' and filled with slogans calling for 'the international Socialist world revolution' and 'all power to the Soldiers' and Workers' Councils' and the overthrow of the Ebert–Scheidemann government.[27]

This was too much for Eichhorn at Police Headquarters: he sent in soldiers from his 'Security Section' to reinstate the usual management. *Vorwärts* instantly became the most virulent anti-Spartacist paper in the city, declaring war on the 'bloody dictatorship of the Spartacus League'. 'The despicable actions of Liebknecht and Rosa Luxemburg soil the Revolution and endanger all of its achievements,' it raged. 'These brutal beasts . . . want to demolish and destroy everything that dares to oppose them, with lies, slander and violence.'[28]

Undeterred, Liebknecht ended the year by inviting about a hundred Spartacists to a conference starting on 29 December in the banqueting hall of the Prussian Landtag. After two days of typically fractious argument, they voted to make a complete break with Social Democracy and align themselves unequivocally with Soviet Russia, renaming themselves the Communist Party of Germany (KPD). Among the guests was Karl Radek, who had been smuggled into Germany to help foment the civil war that was an essential part of a Bolshevik revolution. In a long speech, he denied that the regime in Russia was a reign of terror, and asserted that civil war was not as awful as was sometimes thought: a whole year of civil war in Russia, he claimed, had killed fewer people and destroyed less property than a single day of international war. 'What we are now carrying out in Russia,' he declared, 'is nothing but the great unperverted teaching of German Communism. The Council of Peoples' Commissars of Europe will yet meet in Berlin. Spartacus will conquer. It is destined to seize power in Germany.'[29] Liebknecht responded enthusiastically with a call to arms: 'We do not want a lemonade revolution. We have to hasten the internationalisation of civil war.'

Rosa Luxemburg, always the supreme intellectual with a distaste for violence, was deeply suspicious of Radek, whom she had known, disliked and distrusted since they had clashed during the formation of the Polish

Social Democratic Party. She did her best to cool the passions of the meeting by stressing that they needed to build up their strength before rushing into precipitate action. But her efforts were in vain. For the young Spartacists, the lure of action was more attractive than her lectures on Marxist theory. And so the new German Communist Party entered the new year of 1919 looking for trouble and thirsting for blood.

They would not have to look very far. After the debacle of the Battle of Christmas Eve, the three Independent Socialists in the government had resigned, angry that Ebert had not consulted them, or indeed the rest of the Cabinet, before calling for help from Groener. Ebert had promptly replaced them with three of his own men, one of whom was Gustav Noske, the tough ex-butcher who had been sent to Kiel to calm down the mutineers. Ebert appointed him Defence Minister. Noske had a good reputation – Kessler said he was regarded as 'energetic and intelligent'[30] – and it was also a popular appointment with the troops, who carried him shoulder-high into the Chancellery. Fully aware of the importance of the task that faced him, Noske growled: 'Someone's got to be the bloodhound,' and wasted no time in establishing contact with Groener. While Liebknecht was turning Spartacus into the Communist Party and calling for a new revolution, Noske took Ebert to the military base at Zossen, on the outskirts of Berlin, where 4,000 men paraded before them, fully equipped, fully trained and fully motivated: General Georg von Maercker's Volunteer Rifles, the best of the early Freikorps.

'You can relax now,' Noske told Ebert. 'Everything will be all right!'[31]

# II

## 'COULD IT HAPPEN HERE?'

THE people of the United States approached 1919 in high spirits: the war to end all wars was over, and they were convinced that they had won it, for democracy. But the threat of 'Radicalism' was already casting its shadow across the sunny prospects of peace. Less than two weeks after the last shot had been fired in France, the *New York Times* was asking:

Is Bolshevism a menace to the peace and security of America? What is the significance of the movement? These are enticing questions just now, when every cable brings further news of the spread of the Red Terror through Europe. Every day the situation grows worse, until many people are ready to declare that the United States will be the next victim of this dangerous malady.[1]

America was already involved, albeit mainly indirectly, in the battle against Bolshevism in Russia, but in early 1919 it found itself fighting it on the home front as well. Unfortunately, Woodrow Wilson was an absentee president, physically and/or mentally, for most of the year, too obsessed with the Paris Peace Conference and his dream of a League of Nations to provide the steady leadership in domestic affairs that was needed to control a dangerous and volatile situation.

By insisting on going to France, the first US president to leave the country to conduct business with foreign powers, Wilson had demonstrated his obstinacy and egotism. The other leaders of what would be thought of as the 'Big Four' at the conference – Georges Clemenceau of France, David Lloyd George of Great Britain and Vittorio Orlando of Italy – were politicians and prime ministers, not heads of state, and there were many Americans who thought their President had no place

in such a gathering, even though he was also his country's chief executive. But to Wilson, the fact that the other leaders were politicians,
and therefore venal, meant that he had to be there, to provide dis-
interested moral guidance and ensure the triumph of democracy and
freedom.

Wilson believed not only that American arms had won the war, but
also that he had been largely responsible for persuading Germany to
sue for peace on the basis of a set of principles that he had outlined
to Congress in January 1918. Labelled the 'Fourteen Points', these
encompassed his vision for a future in which the nations would coexist
in brotherly harmony, and where disputes would be settled peacefully
through an international forum, the League of Nations. He could not
trust the Europeans to bring his utopian dreams to fulfilment, and still
less could he trust his American colleagues and opponents. And so,
ignoring their criticisms and concerns, he set sail from New York on
4 December 1918 on a former German passenger liner, renamed the
*George Washington*, at the head of a delegation of five commissioners
or plenipotentiaries to the Peace Conference in Paris. Apart from his
closest confidant, 'Colonel' Edward House, who was already preparing
the way in Europe, the commissioners were an unimpressive lot,
described by former Republican President William Taft as 'a bunch of
cheapskates'.[2] It seemed that Wilson had chosen them for their quali-
ties as yes-men, who could be relied on to agree with whatever he
decided.

The *George Washington* docked at the French port of Brest on Friday
the 13th, a date that did not worry the strictly Presbyterian President
– he claimed not to be superstitious, but said that in any case thirteen
was his lucky number. He enjoyed a tremendously enthusiastic reception in Paris, and remained there until 26 December, when he and his
wife crossed the Channel to England, to stay in Buckingham Palace as
the guests of King George V and Queen Mary. Despite his English
ancestry, and the warm welcome he received, Wilson struck up no
rapport with Britain and the British, and indeed went out of his way
to deny any special relationship. 'You must not speak of us who come
over here as cousins, still less as brothers,' he admonished a British
diplomat and an American Embassy official at the state banquet in the
palace. 'We are neither.'[3] Following a similar line in his public speeches,
he caused no little offence by pointedly avoiding any mention of Britain's
enormous sacrifices or her massive effort during four long years of war

against German militarism. Lloyd George, though, was not abashed. Buoyed up, perhaps, by a landslide victory in a general election, the results of which were announced during Wilson's stay, he determined to use all his famed Welsh wizardry to win the President over. In Paris, he was to succeed brilliantly, but for the moment relations remained somewhat prickly.

After brief visits to his mother's church in Carlisle and then to Manchester, at both of which he spoke piously of his great crusade to ensure a moral peace for the world, Wilson returned to Paris on New Year's Eve. He originally intended to stay in Paris for just a few weeks, to see the Peace Conference started along the right lines, but soon found himself embroiled in the detailed work and could not bear to hand over his precious baby to anyone else. So there he remained for the next six months, apart from a brief and disastrous visit to Italy early in the new year – when he received the usual tumultuous welcome from crowds in the streets but still managed to offend the government, the Church and parliament – and a quick trip home in mid February. Officially this was for the closing sessions of Congress; unofficially it was to try to deal with the growing band of opponents to his League of Nations ideas. Wilson may have been regarded in Europe, at least in the popular view, as a knight in shining armour, but in America he was a lame-duck president, with hostile Republican majorities in both the House and the Senate. Even so, he stayed in Washington for only a few days before hurrying back to the Peace Conference, obsessed with saving the world even at the expense of neglecting a serious domestic crisis in his own nation.

While Wilson was in London lecturing King George and the British on the high moral stance needed to reshape the Old World, America had suddenly found itself facing a new challenge, partly real but mostly imagined, that would last throughout the whole of 1919. At 10.45 p.m. on 30 December a bomb exploded at the home of Ernest T. Trigg, President of the Philadelphia Chamber of Commerce, followed ten minutes later by another at the apartment of Acting Superintendent of Police William B. Mills, blowing him out of his bed and into a corridor ten feet away; minutes after that, a third bomb blew the front off the house of Supreme Court Justice Robert von Moschzisker. By some miracle no one was killed or seriously injured in any of the blasts. In crudely printed circulars found at the scenes of the explosions, addressed 'To the exploiters, the judges, policemen, the priests, the soldiers', unnamed anarchists claimed responsibility. 'Science triumphed over Torquemada's century,' they declared in a reference to the Spanish monk who revived the Inquisition in 1483 and tortured and burnt some 2,000 'heretics'. 'Anarchy will triumph over the present Torquemadas of our century. We have demanded the freedom of all political prisoners, freedom of press and speech. You have refused. We war against you.'[4]

Ignoring the anarchist connection, Captain Mills announced that the bombings 'were part of the plot which the Bolsheviki are starting on a nationwide scale. I think that they started in Philadelphia, and that outbreaks may be expected any day and in any part of the country.'[5] In a massive security operation, Mills sent out scores of detectives to question every known radical sympathiser in the city and called in agents of army and navy intelligence, the Department of Justice, the Post Office and the Shipping Board. Home Defense Reservists were posted to guard churches and the homes of city officials and wealthy citizens.

Almost immediately, Mills's officers picked up a fifty-six-year-old former hat-maker, Edward Moore, whom the *Philadelphia Inquirer* labelled 'one of the city's most intractable revolutionists', on the grounds that he had associated with such well-known troublemakers as the Socialist presidential candidate Eugene V. Debs, who had been sentenced in September 1918 to a ten-year prison term for speaking out against the war, and 'Big Bill' Haywood, leader of the syndicalist union, the Industrial Workers of the World (IWW), who had been convicted of a similar offence.

'We are holding him [Moore] right here in City Hall, incommunicado,' Mills told reporters. 'I don't give a damn if he is being held without the advice of an attorney. I will even refuse him the rights of Habeas Corpus. This is not the time for legal technicalities. They used brute force, and the Police Department, in hunting these criminals down, will resort to the same methods.' The Chief Postal Inspector, whose agents were involved in the search, added his own gloss: 'There is a lamp post for every Bolshevist who has taken part in these murderous and insane outrages.'

Moore was released four days later on the orders of a judge, who found that there was no evidence of any kind against him. The real perpetrators were never identified, but the press and the general public had little doubt who was responsible. William H. Wilson, Director of the Department of Public Safety, announced that he would not tolerate any further meetings of radical organisations in Philadelphia, declaring that 'this is America – not Russia'.[6] The Great Red Scare had begun.

In Britain, Lloyd George started the new year of 1919 still jubilant from his election victory on 28 December, which had given his coalition the greatest parliamentary majority in history, with 529 seats in the Commons as against 177 for all other parties. The euphoria, however, was as short-lived as that felt by the exhausted men of the British Army at their victory over the Germans. All the servicemen wanted now was to shed their uniforms and go home. When they learned that this was not to be, and that Churchill and others were demanding a slow-down in demobilisation and more conscription for a fresh war, against the Bolsheviks in Russia, they rebelled. Suddenly, the spectre of revolution loomed menacingly over Britain. Mindful of events in Russia and Germany, both government and people began asking, 'Could it happen here?'

At the time of the Armistice, the British Army numbered 625,000 officers and nearly six million other ranks.[7] For two months, in France and Flanders, in Italy and Greece, in Palestine and Mesopotamia, officers and men demanded to be brought home. In camps throughout England they clamoured to return to civilian life. But by the new year a mere 261,000 had been released, an average of 37,000 a week:[8] by contrast, the United States had by then demobilised some 600,000, and the sight of American ships steaming out of French and British ports crammed with doughboys bound for home was particularly galling to war-weary Tommies still trapped in khaki, many of whom had jobs as well as families waiting for them.

There were in fact some genuine difficulties over demobilisation, not least of which was the urgent need to organise several armies of occupation. The western and Rhineland provinces of Germany had been divided into three zones of occupation, and the British were responsible for the area around Cologne; British troops also had to be found for Palestine, Mesopotamia and German East Africa. Field Marshal Sir Douglas Haig, the Commander-in-Chief in France, estimated that the armies of occupation would need over a million men – a large number for a country that traditionally maintained only a token standing army. Meanwhile, still more were needed for India, where the independence movement was burgeoning rapidly. But while these may have been cogent reasons for commanders and Cabinet ministers to hang on to the men they had, they counted for little to the men themselves, who saw only muddle and inefficiency and decided to take direct action.

The first mutiny began at the Channel port of Folkestone early on Friday 3 January 1919, when orders were posted in No. 1 Rest Camp that 1,000 men were to parade at 0815 hours for embarkation and a return to France, followed by another 1,000 at 0825. Someone scrawled across the orders 'No men to parade'.[9] And none did. Word spread swiftly through the town's three camps that 3,000 men from No. 1 camp had decided not to march to the boat but to head instead for the town hall, where they would hold a general meeting. Men from the other camps rushed to join them: some 10,000 assembled outside Folkestone town hall, where several of them climbed on to the portico to deliver speeches voicing their complaints, which were received with loud cheers. The town mayor appeared and assured the men that if they went back to camp they would hear good news – an announcement that was greeted with a loud chorus of the popular song, 'Tell me the Old, Old Story'.[10]

Only when the town commandant, Lieutenant Commander H.E.J. Mill, promised that 'any complaints would be listened to' did the men march back to their camps in a long column headed by a big bass drum. Once there, they were told that henceforth there would be only voluntary embarkation for France; those who had work to go to in Britain could be demobilised at once, from Folkestone, and those who had complaints could have seven days' leave in which to pursue them. It seemed that the revolt had ended quietly – *The Times* correspondent reported that there had been 'no rowdyism'.[11] The mailboat sailed for France with no soldiers on board. Next day, however, new orders for the embarkation of 'a certain number' were posted. This provoked another demonstration, this time to picket the harbour and troop trains carrying men returning from leave, who joined the strike en masse. An armed guard posted at the harbour entrance was hurriedly withdrawn when the striking troops threatened to collect their own weapons from their camps and remove it forcibly.[12]

There were similar scenes at Dover that same morning, when about 2,000 men turned back from the Admiralty Pier where they were about to board ship for France:

They streamed off along the railway, in spite of official protests, and on their way to the town met a train loaded with returning troops bound for the pier. The soldiers called on the newcomers to join them, and the carriages were soon emptied. Continuing their march, and all in full field kit and carrying their rifles, the troops mustered at Cresswell, and from the railway bridge some of their number addressed the others on demobilisation grievances. They decided to send a deputation to the military and civil authorities, and the men then fell in and marched to the Town Hall, which was reached just before 10 o'clock ... The troops represented scores of different units, and a number of Canadian and Australian men.[13]

The Mayor let them into the town hall and the adjoining Connaught Hall, where they passed the time in community singing while waiting for a reply from the military authorities. Later, he commandeered the local cinema and had a free picture show put on for their entertainment. Although the men were all armed, there was never any threat that they might have used their weapons – and in any case it is very unlikely that they had any ammunition for them. It was a very British rebellion, carried out with typically British restraint and even good humour. Nevertheless, alarm bells started ringing when the men tore down a 'For Officers Only' sign above the door of a comfortable station waiting room, formed a 'Soldiers' Union' and elected a committee composed entirely of rank and file. Recognising the awful smell of the soviets, the government acted fast, sending staff from London that same night to rush through demobilisation procedures in all the camps affected.

Word of the events in Folkestone and Dover reached the newspapers, but the war censorship, which was still in operation, soon clamped down on any reports of further unrest. Many newspapers protested, and some even defied the ban, apparently without incurring any penalties, but *The Times*, as ever the voice of the Establishment, toed the official line with a self-righteous editorial:

We are asked to publish, but have no intention of publishing, a great many letters on the subject of demobilisation which show a deplorable lack of responsibility on the part of the writers ... fanning an agitation which is already mischievous and may become dangerous ... These demonstrations by soldiers have gone far enough.[14]

So, the British public was kept largely in the dark about fifty other mutinies, at home and abroad, during the month of January. In several cases, particularly in camps in and around London, mutineers tried to cram as many men as they could into lorries and drive to Whitehall to deliver their protests at the centre. Mostly they were dissuaded by their officers, but some got through, and in every case their reception was conciliatory.

On 8 January, 1,500 soldiers based at Park Royal in west London marched on Downing Street to confront Lloyd George and the Cabinet. The Prime Minister was willing to meet the soldiers, but Lord Milner warned that if he did so, 'similar processions would march on London from all over the country'. General Sir Henry Wilson declared somewhat pompously, 'The Prime Minister should not confer with soldiers who had disregarded their officers. The soldiers' delegation,' he said, 'bore a dangerous resemblance to a *Soviet*. If such a practice were to spread, the consequences would be disastrous.' General Sir William Robertson, GOC Home Forces, was sent out to meet a delegation of one corporal, one lance corporal and one private, talked to them for half an hour and agreed to their demands for better conditions and the end of drafts for Russia, whereupon the troops marched back to their barracks in good order.

Unrest continued to bubble and simmer throughout the army, however, both in the UK and in France, Greece and Russia, leading a nervous General Wilson to write a warning note to Winston Churchill shortly after Churchill had taken office as Secretary of State for War and Air: 'We are sitting on top of a mine which may go up at any moment.'[15] Churchill did not disagree: he feared that the unrest would spread to other camps throughout Britain, and that 'widespread disobedience would encourage Bolshevism in Britain'. To counter this, according to Wilson's diary, he wanted to bring back from France 'all reliable regiments, ie Household and Cavalry, Yeomanry, Home County regiments, etc'.[16]

One of the most worrying developments at this time was the formation of the Soldiers', Sailors' and Airmen's Union (SSAU), which began trying to organise the men of the armed forces, despite servicemen being specifically forbidden by King's Regulations from belonging to a trade union. The founders of the SSAU got around this by enlisting men as honorary members. The union continued to grow for nearly five months, claiming forty-nine branches, including Calais and Boulogne, by the beginning of April, when military intelligence estimated its strength at 10,000 members. In truth, the SSAU never amounted to very much, but in the climate of the times it caused considerable unease among civil and military authorities, who feared that it was part of the great Bolshevik plot. They felt, understandably, that unionised and indoctrinated troops could not be relied on to suppress civil disorder, and would be inclined to fraternise with strikers rather than shoot at them. The whole thing petered out in early May, as more and more temporary soldiers were demobilised, leaving the army with an ever greater proportion of regular soldiers for whom unionism held little attraction.[17]

In spite of all the efforts of Churchill and at least some of the generals to sort out the mess of demobilisation, the mutinies continued throughout January. There is no evidence that the SSAU played a significant part in any of them, though it undoubtedly made use of the men's dissatisfactions as a recruiting tool. The troops were often protesting against bad food and living conditions, but most of the trouble was caused by the slow pace of demobilisation, coupled with the suspicion that this had a sinister purpose. 'The excitement . . . is attributed in many quarters,' reported the *Pall Mall Gazette*, 'to oft-repeated rumours that plans are being prepared for the sending of a considerable force to Russia.'[18]

The most serious mutiny was in Calais, on 27 January, among detachments of the Army Ordnance Corps and the Mechanical Transport Corps. The mutineers persuaded many soldiers returning on leave-boats to join them, so that by the second day of the revolt there were between 3,000 and 4,000 armed men occupying the whole town and port. Women nurses joined in, with their own demands. Soon there were 20,000 mutineers out in the Calais area, with strike committees in every camp, coordinated by an elected council of twenty to thirty soldiers and sailors which met in cafés and issued daily orders and even permits. This was looking dangerously like a soviet-style insurrection, and to counter it Sir Douglas Haig had two divisions of fighting troops recalled from deployment in Germany and placed under the orders of General Julian Byng, commander of the Third Army. On the night of 30 January, Byng surrounded Calais with troops equipped with armoured cars and machine guns. There could have been a bloodletting as serious as those in Berlin, but fraternisation between the mutineers and Byng's forces quickly frustrated any action, and the authorities were once again forced to give way.

Under the wartime Defence of the Realm Act, which was still in force, mutiny was punishable with the death penalty. With all the sensitivity that had allowed him to send hundreds of thousands of infantrymen 'over the top' to be mown down by enemy machine guns during the war, Haig wanted to shoot the leaders of the Calais strike. Fortunately, Churchill, who had actually served in the trenches for a brief period while out of office during the war, had more sense and quashed the idea. The government's fear of provoking an explosion and even a revolution was demonstrated by the fact that the only revolt that resulted in punishment was not in the army but the navy, where one sailor was sentenced to two years' hard labour, three to one year and three to ninety days' detention, for refusing to go to sea, taking over their ship, the patrol vessel HMS *Kilbride* at Milford Haven in Wales, hauling down the white ensign and hoisting the red flag in its place.

At first sight, the events at Milford Haven might have sounded like an uncomfortable echo of those at Kiel two months earlier. But any resemblance started and ended right there. Royal Navy ships were already deployed off Murmansk, Archangel and Vladivostok and there was little sympathy among their crews for the Bolsheviks, even though the men who had signed up for the duration were eager to get home for demobilisation. With the Armistice, however, the new presidents of Finland and two of the nascent Baltic States – Estonia and Latvia – begged Britain to help them maintain their newly found independence in the face of any Bolshevik invasion. The third Baltic State, Lithuania, had more complex relationships with Russia, Germany and Poland, and had not yet asserted its independence.

The danger of attack by the Red Army when the Germans withdrew from Latvia and Estonia was very real. 'The end of German occupation places before Soviet Russia the task of liberating the Baltic territories,' Lenin had announced in *Pravda* and *Izvestia*. 'Soviet Russia must gain access to the Baltic coast and replant the Red Flag of the Proletarian Revolution there. Soviet troops must occupy Lithuania, Latvia and Estonia. The Baltic must become a Soviet sea.' In the face of such blatant threats, the Estonians and Finns begged for protection by British warships and troops. Estonia was particularly vulnerable, since the German Army there simply disintegrated with the Armistice, its troops throwing down their weapons and demanding to go home.

And although a provisional government had been established in Reval (Tallinn) on 11 November, within days the Bolsheviks had set up a rival government at Narva, near the frontier, and the Red Army began moving into Estonian territory. By 10 December, Soviet troops had occupied more than half the country. In Latvia, the German Army had not mutinied, but many units were on the side of the Bolsheviks, as was a large proportion of the population.

The British Foreign Office told the Estonians that there was no chance of sending troops, but that Britain might send warships, and supply arms and equipment to help them to defend themselves. The Admiralty, though, was not so sanguine about warships, pointing out that during the war the Germans, Russians and even the Swedes had liberally sown the Baltic with mines, many of which had had the safety devices required by The Hague Convention removed, and few of which were charted. Warships could not be safely sent in until minesweepers had first cleared the way – and minesweepers were in short supply, being needed urgently to clear mines around Britain's own shores. Among the other problems were ice – the Estonian capital Reval was ice-bound for most of the winter – and the Soviet Navy, whose main base at Kronstadt was less than 180 miles away. Vice Admiral Sydney Fremantle, the Deputy Chief of Naval Staff, warned that although it was 'scarcely credible that the Russian ships could be in good order after having been for a year in Bolshevik possession, we have had some surprises from the Bolshevik Army and must be on our guard against unexpected efficiency in some, at any rate, of the Russian ships'.[19]

Despite the Admiralty's reservations, political considerations outweighed naval caution, and on 20 November Lloyd George's Imperial War Cabinet decided that a show of force was needed in the Baltic, 'to help strengthen the populations of that part of the world against Bolshevism and to assist British interests there'.[20] Two days later, a squadron of five light cruisers and nine destroyers, plus minesweepers and support vessels, under the command of Rear Admiral Edwyn Alexander-Sinclair, set sail for the Baltic, led by the light cruiser HMS *Cardiff*. *Cardiff*'s last mission, completed only the day before, had been to escort the German High Seas Fleet into the Firth of Forth for internment. Her crew had been looking forward to ten days' shore leave with their families or, in the case of 'duration of hostilities' men, to speedy demobilisation. They were not best pleased to find themselves sailing off to an icy sea they didn't know, where they might well be shot at or blown up by mines, to protect countries they had mostly never heard of.

The mission started badly. The collier carrying coal to refuel the minesweepers at Copenhagen ran aground, and since there were no stocks of coal available in the Danish capital, Sinclair was forced to carry on without them: Bolshevik forces were reported to be advancing on Reval, where the situation was desperate, and there was no time to wait for another collier. The other ships, being oil-fired, were quickly refuelled from their accompanying tankers, but would have to rely on their own paravanes, torpedo-shaped devices towed by the ship to cut the mooring cables of submerged mines. It was not enough. The cruiser *Cassandra* struck a mine in an uncharted German field which broke her back in two places and killed ten seamen. She sank within twenty minutes. All but one of the remaining 440 crew were saved by two accompanying destroyers, and were taken back to Britain on a second cruiser, the *Calypso*, which hit an unmarked submerged wreck and had to limp home for repairs. The tale of woe was still not finished: two destroyers also had to return to Britain after damaging themselves in a collision.

Sinclair's orders were to show the flag at Reval and the Latvian port of Libau (Liepaja), and cover the landing of rifles, ammunition and field guns that were on their way to the Baltic in two minelayers. But when he arrived at Reval, he discovered that the 7th Red Army was only forty miles from the city, and that if he did nothing it was doomed to fall within days. Ignoring the Admiralty's orders restricting him to patrol duties, he sailed up the coast to Narva with two cruisers and five destroyers and shelled the rear of the advancing army for several hours, knocking out the only bridge across the river on the frontier, and halting the Reds' advance. Sailing on to Libau with half his force, Sinclair encountered two Soviet destroyers, which he pursued, captured and handed over to the Estonians for their navy, which until then consisted of little more than one gunboat. A week later, two of the British cruisers and a destroyer supported an Estonian counter-attack near Narva with a devastating display of close-range shellfire which broke and scattered the Russian forces.

By the end of the first week in January, with the help of the Royal Navy, the Russians were in full retreat. For the moment, Estonia was safe. The same could not be said, however, for Latvia, where Sinclair's ships could do little to support the Latvian forces from the sea. The

Latvian President, Karlis Ulmanis, who had been a high-school teacher in Nebraska, USA, had organised a force of sharpshooters, the Latvian Rifles, but they were too weak to stop Trotsky's Red Army, or to put down an uprising by Latvia's own Bolsheviks.

Sinclair invited Ulmanis on board his flagship, and explained that his orders prevented him from putting his Royal Marines ashore to fight alongside the Latvians, and that in any case they were too few to make any significant effect. He did agree to send Marine officers to organise local volunteers, and then stopped a mutiny of Latvian troops by shelling their barracks, but could only advise Ulmanis to do a deal with the Germans, who still had some 40,000 troops in the country and were committed under the terms of the Armistice to protect the Baltic States against attack. The German Army in Latvia, however, was disintegrating fast into ill-disciplined gangs run by soldiers' councils or local German warlords, and most of the soldiers wanted only to get out as fast as possible, leaving behind their arms, equipment and stores for the Bolsheviks to pick up. With the ice closing in and the Latvian Army in full retreat and facing full-scale mutiny, Sinclair evacuated British citizens from Riga, then withdrew. On 2 January the British ships sailed for Copenhagen and home. Ulmanis and his ministers fled to Libau, to continue their struggle from there.

Following Sinclair's advice, Ulmanis approached Germany for help – and the Germans were delighted to oblige. For hundreds of years there had been large numbers of ethnic Germans in the region as settlers, merchants or landowning 'Baltic barons', known collectively as 'Balts', and for generations it had been a German, or more precisely a Prussian, dream to turn it into a grand duchy, extending German territory northwards from East Prussia. Seeing the chance of furthering the dream, the Germans were happy to sign a treaty with Latvia. Like most treaties imposed on weaker nations by Germany from the end of the Franco-Prussian war to Brest-Litovsk, its terms were swingeing and designed to give Germany the greatest possible long-term advantage. German troops would serve only under German officers; any increase in the size of the Latvian Army would be matched by an increase in German troops; Germans who served for a month would be automatically entitled to Latvian citizenship and therefore the right to settle, and even to a grant of land on the vast estates of the 'Baltic barons'.[21] It was an attractive proposition and before long, queues were forming outside the recruiting offices in Berlin for new Freikorps units – it would not have been practicable or safe to try to use the army proper. It would take some time before the new units were ready for action, of course. Until then, the Latvians would simply have to suffer, as indeed they did.

The Red Army had marched into Riga on 3 January, and the new regime had wasted no time before making its aims clear, posting proclamations in Russian, Latvian and German at every street corner:

We shall begin without delay to construct in Latvia a new Socialist Proletarian State. We shall exterminate the social traitors of this as of other countries. Behind us stands the Russian Soviet State, with which we shall henceforth remain intimately united. Behind us, too, stands the Communist Revolution, which will soon change not only Germany but the rest of Europe into a Federation of Soviet Socialist Republics, of which we shall be a constituent part. From the Rhine to Vladivostok, from the Black Sea to Archangel, the great civil war rages. Soon it will smash down the ramparts raised by victory-drunk Imperialism. In France, in England, in Italy, the first mutterings of the Proletarian Revolution are already heard ... To Arms! Long Live the Soviet Government of Latvia! Long Live the World Revolution![22]

The new government was headed by Peter Stutchka, son of a prosperous Latvian family, who had been a lawyer in St Petersburg. With long white hair and saintly face, he bore an obvious resemblance to Kurt Eisner in Munich: like Eisner, he was a utopian intellectual with no experience of government in any form. However, with the help of a band of tough, professional Bolshevik revolutionaries, he was determined to go much further than Eisner in imposing his idealistic vision on his countrymen.

Stutchka's first act – surprisingly perhaps for a lawyer – was to abolish the legal profession, swiftly followed by an announcement that money, too, was to be done away with. As soon as money was out of circulation, he argued, swindling and thieving would vanish and murder would dwindle. 'Money has not always existed,' he declared. 'In the earliest days of humanity, in the age of primitive communism, money was unknown. We are beginning again in the present age of transition with the original barter of goods. Later each person who works will simply receive from the state the quantity of food and manufactured goods necessary for the maintenance of his capacity to work. Money is now living in the last days of its domination! Be this our slogan – AWAY WITH MONEY!'[23] As a first step, all bank accounts were limited to a maximum of 10,000 roubles, and any surplus confiscated. Naturally, people avoided banks and hid their money under their mattresses or anywhere they could, but this was risky – it was likely to be found when their homes were raided for clothing, boots and bedlinen to be seized for the Red Army.

Efforts to root out the 'parasitical bourgeoisie, bring them into closer relations with proletarian circles, and accustom them to useful work' began at once. All bourgeois were ordered to register themselves within five days, on pain of death, and the inevitable firing squads were soon at work executing landowners, farmers, lawyers, bankers, businessmen, clergy, students – anyone who could be classed as a 'counter-revolutionary'. It was the start of a long winter of discontent.

The revolutionary events in the Baltic States may have been taking place in a remote corner of Northern Europe but they were linked with other upheavals elsewhere as well as those in Russia. Bolshevik agitation as much as a military collapse had forced Bulgaria to desert the Central Powers and pull out of the war at the end of September. King Ferdinand had abdicated and his successor, the young King Boris III, lasted only a month before being ousted by a new revolutionary government. The news was received with glee in Moscow, with huge headlines in *Izvestia* proclaiming the death throes of imperialism and the imminence of social revolution everywhere. Lenin optimistically offered the German Communist Party a million Russian soldiers and unlimited aid, including grain shipments, to support their coming revolution.

Hungary and Austria, too, were in a state of upheaval. The old Emperor, Franz Josef, had died in 1916 at the age of eighty-six and his successor, his twenty-nine-year-old great-nephew Karl, had spent the next two years trying to save the Habsburg dynasty by intriguing with the Allies for a separate peace and promising his subject nationalities – Poles, Czechs, Slovaks, Slovenes, Bosnians, Croats, Romanians – greater autonomy if not independence. It was a vain bid, completely trumped by President Wilson's Fourteen Points and the promise of self-determination for all. Already tottering, the Habsburg dual monarchy was finally finished by defeat in the war. After violent demonstrations in Vienna and Budapest, Karl abandoned the throne and fled, and revolutionaries took control in both cities.

Greatly encouraged by the news of turmoil in Berlin, Vienna and Budapest, Lenin and Trotsky launched an offensive to reconquer the

Ukraine, to create a physical link with the European revolution. On another tack, they were reported to have sent back to Germany and Austria 2,000 prisoners of war who had been specially trained for Bolshevik propaganda work, while 5,000 prisoners were said to have enlisted in the Red Army.[24]

Ordinary Berliners started the new year desperately trying to normalise their lives in the midst of all the political chaos swirling around them. Most of the violence and danger was concentrated in the central area of the city, between the Alexanderplatz and the Brandenburg Gate and the Reichstag, but even here, in the fashionable Leipziger Strasse and bustling Friedrichstrasse, the shops and stores and cafés were still doing good business, in spite of the nightly curfew. For most people, what caused the greatest disruption was not the shooting but the wave of strikes that plagued the city. The Revolutionary Shop Stewards had brought out the workers at factories like the giant AEG plant in Moabit and had closed down the gasworks and some power stations, so that thousands of Berliners suffered in cold and darkness.

For the middle and upper classes there was the added inconvenience of a waiters' strike affecting many cafés and restaurants – surprisingly, most were still open, despite the chronic food shortage. Harry Kessler records how he was just sitting down to dinner in a restaurant on New Year's Day when a deputation of strikers marched in and presented the manager with an ultimatum: agree to their demands within ten minutes, or be closed down. The manager capitulated, and according to Kessler: 'The strikers, with red tabs stuck in their hats and carrying a red flag, left. Blackmail completed, we could return to the matter of food. Many places have already been shut, others attacked and wrecked . . . We are returning to the days of strong-arm law. The Executive is wholly powerless.'[25]

The Executive, in fact, was more concerned with the coming National Assembly elections on 19 January. Ebert announced his manifesto on New Year's Day, and he and Noske began preparing for the showdown with the Spartacists and Independent Socialists who were determined to wreck the elections. One of the first things Ebert needed was a reliable police force, something he could never have while Emil Eichhorn ruled as Police President. Several newspapers were already running a campaign against Eichhorn, the former telegraphist at the Russian Embassy who had seized control of the Berlin police and renamed it the Security Service during the first days of the revolution in November. The campaign was largely inspired by a news agency with close ties to the government, which circulated stories such as that he was being paid 1,700 marks a month by Rosta, a Russian news service spreading Bolshevik propaganda, that he had been interfering with the city's telephone and telegraph lines, was in cahoots with the Red sailors in the Royal Palace, and had turned his headquarters on Alexanderplatz into a personal fortress packed with weaponry, including machine guns and artillery.

Since the Battle of Christmas Eve and the breaking of General Wels by the Red sailors, Eichhorn had been acting more and more as the military governor of the city. This posed an intolerable threat to Ebert's authority, and clearly had to be stopped. Protected by the strongest military force in the city, Eichhorn had seemed invulnerable. But everything changed on 2 January, when Noske took Ebert out to Zossen, to review General von Maercker's Freikorps. Two days later, on Saturday 4 January, Ebert persuaded the Prussian state government to dismiss Eichhorn and reinstate his predecessor, Eugen Ernst.

Eichhorn, of course, had no intention of going quietly. His first reaction was to appeal for support from his own Independent Socialist Party, which was immediately joined by the Revolutionary Shop Stewards and the Communists, issuing a joint proclamation condemning the Ebert–Scheidemann government's 'new contemptible conspiracy to strike down the whole German proletariat and the entire German Revolution'. It called for a mass demonstration the next afternoon, to defend 'the fate of the Revolution', a challenge that Ebert and his associates were only too ready to accept.

The demonstrators assembled on the Sunday afternoon in the Siegesallee (Victory Avenue), a broad walk in the Tiergarten lined with incredibly kitsch white marble statues of past Hohenzollern rulers. At an estimated 150,000, it was reputed to be the biggest crowd ever seen in Berlin, moving slowly past the Reichstag, through the Brandenburg Gate and up the Linden, past the palace and on to the Alexanderplatz, to the thump and blare of military bands. Red flags flying, the marchers swirled like a vast tide around army lorries packed with heavily armed soldiers. In their midst, Karl Liebknecht rode in an open car, revelling in the belief that his moment of glory was approaching.

At the Alexanderplatz, Liebknecht joined a meeting of seventy-one shop stewards and Independent Socialists in the red-brick Police

Presidium. He and Wilhelm Pieck were the only Communists present, but it was Liebknecht who appeared on the balcony to address the multitude. According to Kessler, who was present as always, he spoke 'with unctuous solemnity, like a parson, intoning his words slowly and expressively', his sing-song inflexion carrying over the heads of the silent crowd, though only part of what he said was intelligible. When he finished 'there was a roar of approval, red flags were flourished, and thousands of hands and hats rose in the air'.

To Kessler, Liebknecht seemed like 'an invisible priest of the revolution' and he continued the religious simile by saying that the demonstration seemed 'half-way between a Roman mass and a Puritan prayer meeting' before drawing another, more ominous comparison: 'The wave of Bolshevism surging in from the East resembles somewhat the invasion by Islam in the seventh century. Fanaticism and power in the service of a nebulous fresh hope are faced, far and wide, by nothing more than the fragments of old ideologies. The banner of the prophet waves at the head of Lenin's armies, too.'[26]

Buoyed up by the size and apparent fervour of the crowd outside the windows, the meeting in Police Headquarters called for another mass demonstration next day, and elected a fifty-three-member Revolutionary Committee with three presidents – Liebknecht, George Ledebour of the Independent Socialists, and Paul Scholze representing the Shop Stewards – who declared in yet another proclamation to be issued the following morning:

Comrades! Workers!
The Ebert–Scheidemann Government has rendered itself impossible. It is hereby declared deposed by the undersigned Revolutionary Committee, the representative of the revolutionary socialist workers and soldiers (Independent Social Democratic Party and Communist Party).

The undersigned Revolutionary Committee has provisionally assumed the conduct of the business of government.
Comrades! Workers!
Support the measures of the Revolutionary Committee, 6 January 1919.
The Revolutionary Committee
LEDEBOUR, LIEBKNECHT, SCHOLZE[27]

In fact, Liebknecht and Ledebour had both jumped the gun, carried away by their enthusiasm. Neither of their own central committees had agreed to such a decisive step – indeed, Rosa Luxemburg, always more thoughtful and less impulsive than Liebknecht, strongly disapproved, believing the Spartacists were not yet ready for power. But it was too late to go back. The battle lines had been drawn. Overnight, armed groups of Spartacists seized several important public buildings, including the Reich Printing Office where the nation's banknotes were produced, the central telegraph agency, all the main railway stations and most of the major newspaper offices on and around Belle-Allianz-Platz. The *Vorwärts* offices were a particular target for the Spartacus fighters, who occupied the building and dumped the day's entire edition into the River Spree, then set about using the presses to publish their own version of the paper.

Next morning, even larger crowds assembled on the streets. But this time they were more or less equally divided between supporters of the Revolutionary Committee and those of the Ebert government – and it was hard to tell which was which. 'They are made up of the same sort of people,' noted Kessler, 'artisans and factory girls, dressed in the same sort of clothes, waving the same red flags, and moving in the same sort of shambling step. But they carry slogans, jeer at each other as they pass, and perhaps will be shooting one another down before the day is out.'[28]

The shooting started at around 5 p.m., outside Wertheim's, the fashionable department store on Leipziger Platz, and quickly spread to Wilhelmplatz, Potsdamer Platz and the Linden. Soon, the whole of central Berlin was engulfed in the rattle of rifle and machine-gun fire, the booming of trench mortars and the crash of grenades. Liebknecht toured the city in his open car, surrounded by a ring of trucks with mounted machine guns, all flying red flags, constantly orating: 'The time for action has come! Make the dream of a Socialist Republic reality! Today is the start of the Socialist revolution that will spread throughout the whole world!' The new, Spartacist *Vorwärts* announced that the Russian government hoped that Bolshevism would be supreme throughout Germany by March at the latest, and that 'the entire national property in Russia will be unreservedly placed at the disposal of the German Communists for the achievement of this end'.[29]

That evening it poured with rain, but the shooting continued, and the confusion multiplied. A general strike was called, twice – once by the government, as a protest against the Spartacus takeover of *Vorwärts*, and once by the Independent Socialists and Revolutionary Shop Stewards against the government. The rebel unity began to break up, as the Independent Socialists approached Ebert and Scheidemann with an offer of .negotiation. The sailors in the palace, to which the Revolutionary Committee had moved on Sunday evening, decided to take no further part in the battle and threw Liebknecht and his partners out, declaring themselves neutral. They were now interested only in getting their pay. Whole sections of Eichhorn's Security Service began defecting, reporting to the Charlottenburg police headquarters for service against the rebels.

Meanwhile, regular army commanders of the city's barracks formed a 'garrison council' and sent out two small but well-equipped units of highly professional troops. One was posted to protect the Chancellery and Interior Ministry, the other the Reichstag and the area around the Brandenburg Gate, on top of which they set up a machine-gun post under the giant copper horses of the Quadriga with a field of fire that included the whole of Pariser Platz, the entrance to Wilhelmstrasse, Unter den Linden and the approaches to the Reichstag. The soldiers did not have things all their own way, however: the indefatigable Kessler, hurrying from one trouble spot to another to satisfy his curiosity, was passing through the square at about 4 p.m. on Tuesday 7 January, when he suddenly found himself having to dodge bullets and grenades. A group of Spartacists had somehow managed to climb to the top of the gate, overpower the troops and take over their gun. They were now shooting up the crowds in the Tiergarten.[30]

Even before the shooting started on the Monday afternoon, Noske had moved from the Wilhelmstrasse to the prosperous western district of Dahlem, where he took over an empty girls' school and turned it into what he described as a 'war camp', a military headquarters complete with motor pool, map room, telephone switchboard and radio transmitters. Volunteers began pouring in, demobilised soldiers, students, professional men and, most significantly, hordes of workers, all eager to fight for the government. They were swiftly armed and organised. At Noske's call, the Freikorps units at Zossen, plus others at the military garrison town of Potsdam, on Berlin's south-western border, began preparing for action, under the overall military command of Lieutenant General Freiherr von Lüttwitz.

By Wednesday 8 January, with his government's strength growing rapidly, Ebert could confidently proclaim 'The hour of reckoning is near!' and announce that the elections would take place as planned in ten days' time. Next day, Noske gave the order for the Freikorps and government forces to move into the city. Over the next two days, they recaptured the railway stations, riddled the *Rote Fahne* offices on Wilhelmstrasse with heavy machine-gun fire, and shelled the Spartacus/KPD offices on Friedrichstrasse until the building collapsed. Twelve hundred Freikorps troops from Potsdam moved on to Belle-Allianz-Platz, shooting anyone who came within ten steps of them, and began attacking the *Vorwärts* offices. Three hundred and fifty Spartacists with rifles lay in wait behind barricades of baled papers and huge rolls of newsprint, but they stood little chance against troops armed with machine guns, flame-throwers, mortars, field artillery and captured British tanks, with which they proceeded to bombard the rambling building even after a white flag had been raised. Some three hundred Spartacist men and women surrendered. They were marched off to the nearby dragoon barracks, where several of them were beaten to death. The rest were lined up and shot.

The only notable centre of resistance now remaining was the Police Presidium. It fell overnight on Saturday/Sunday, after a vicious and bloody battle, to a force composed mainly of men who had defected from Eichhorn's Security Service, led by officers and regular soldiers from the formerly mutinous Maybug barracks, again using artillery to smash holes in the walls. Eichhorn himself had escaped earlier in an armoured car and taken refuge in the giant Bötzow Brewery on Friedrichstrasse, from where he fled to Brunswick, never to return to Berlin.

The army and Freikorps began to clean up the city, moving methodically block by block, street by street, flushing out suspected radicals and Spartacist gunmen sniping from rooftops. They recaptured the Brandenburg Gate and established control over central Berlin. The Revolutionary Shop Stewards called off their ineffective general strike, but when the workers refused to disperse after a peaceful demonstration in front of the Reichstag, Lüttwitz's troops opened fire on them with machine guns, killing forty-two and wounding 105. Noske claimed that the demonstration had been 'an insurrection', and declared martial law throughout northern Germany, killing dozens of suspected radicals and cracking down on subversive organisations.

The January revolution, 'Spartacus Week' as it is often called, was over. But its effects were not confined to Berlin and were still being felt in various parts of Germany. In Bremen, Communists took over the workers' council from the Majority Socialists and declared the city state to be a Socialist republic. There was disorder in Hamburg when the workers' and soldiers' council banned the local Socialist newspaper for supporting the Ebert government. A general strike was declared in Brunswick 'in sympathy for Liebknecht', and 10,000 people marched through the town 'pillaging shops and public buildings, and occupying the printing and newspaper offices'. In Stuttgart, Spartacists demonstrated outside the local infantry barracks, where shots were fired, occupied the town hall and dismissed the chief burgomaster and councillors. In Leipzig, there was fighting between police and troops heading for Berlin on military trains, resulting in eight dead and thirteen wounded, after the workers' and soldiers' council had decreed that it would not allow armed counter-revolutionary troops to pass through the station on their way to the capital; the soldiers were eventually disarmed and sent on their way. There was fighting in Dresden, when soldiers and Spartacists tried to take over the parliament building and the local newspaper offices. In Halle, the Spartacists had more success, occupying the offices of the Democratic *Hallesche Zeitung*, arresting the editor and forcing the local magistrate to recognise the workers' and soldiers' council as the sole executive authority. In Schwerin, sailors from Berlin joined the Spartacists and Independent Socialists in trying to overthrow the Mecklenburg-Schwerin state government: they occupied the railway station, post office and arsenal, but were driven out by troops from the Schwerin garrison with artillery and machine guns.

Some of the most serious trouble was in Düsseldorf, a major industrial city with a population of 470,000 and a long tradition of Socialism. The end of the war had brought sudden, large-scale unemployment – the Rheinische Metallieren, for instance, one of the largest munitions works in Germany, had reduced its 30,000 workforce by half – and the Spartacists had taken full advantage of the situation. They organised a mass demonstration which, according to the Press Association's special correspondent with the British forces in Germany, 'was swollen by all the rougher elements and unemployed in the town'. They were also joined by the volunteer police, ex-soldiers who were paid fifteen marks a day and who were disgruntled at rumours that they were about to be disbanded by the Allies. They disarmed the regular police, surrounded the burgomaster's house and helped themselves to arms handed in by the returning troops in November. They closed the banks and big businesses, opened the prisons, took several leading citizens hostage and seized control of the telegraph, telephone and, of course, the local newspapers, renaming the *Düsseldorfer Nachrichten* the *Rote Fahne von Niederrhein* (the *Lower Rhine Red Flag*).[31] Order was finally restored by British and Belgian troops, who were already established in the residential quarter of the city on the west bank of the river as part of the Allied occupation of the Rhineland.

From Munich, Bavarian Prime Minister Kurt Eisner sent a telegram to the Berlin government on 10 January, expressing his horror at the 'murderous civil war', and warning that 'all Germany would perish' if it were not stopped. 'Berlin's example,' he admonished, 'is having a disturbing effect everywhere, and is producing an epidemic of insanity.' Anger against Berlin was growing everywhere in south Germany, he said, while at the same time 'various evil-disposed persons here are calling for fratricidal war'.[32]

Eisner's nervousness was understandable. Munich had remained generally calm throughout November and December, though there was no shortage of political arguments or demonstrations. At one point, a group of about four hundred anarchists and radicals had invaded the offices of several conservative newspapers and used the presses of one of them to publish a special edition urging a new revolution. They had then broken into the house of Eisner's Majority Social Democrat partner, Erhard Auer, and forced him at gunpoint to write a letter of resignation as Minister of the Interior. Eisner, forever reasonable, had talked them into backing down and another crisis had been averted. Auer continued in government, and forced Eisner to call a general election, which was set for 12 January. Surprisingly, the election campaigns were comparatively trouble-free, though nine people were killed in street brawls on New Year's Eve and two more a couple of days later.

Receiving nothing worse than a scolding from Eisner for their attack on Auer, the radicals formed themselves into a Bavarian branch of Spartacus, and prepared to emulate their Berlin brothers and sisters in trying to overthrow the government. By the new year they were calling for a boycott of the elections and rejection of parliamentary democracy, demanding that the councils should be given total power. Their calls went unanswered: some 86 per cent of voters turned out on the day, including newly enfranchised women, who made up 53.4 per cent of the electorate. They voted overwhelmingly against Eisner and his

Independent Socialists, who received less than 3 per cent of the total
and won only three of the 180 Landtag seats. But Eisner, who was
still chairman of the Congress of Workers', Soldiers' and Peasants'
Councils as well as head of the Provisional Government and Foreign
Minister, was in no hurry to quit, or to convene the new parliament.
He hung on for over a month, while the political chaos continued to
mount.

It is not possible to say precisely how many casualties there were in
Berlin during the Spartacus uprising. Official estimates were that one
hundred rebels were killed and about four hundred wounded, with
thirteen Freikorps dead and about twenty wounded, but the
Communists claimed the overall deaths numbered well over a thousand, which sounds a more likely figure. Even at a thousand-plus, the
toll was overshadowed by the worldwide influenza pandemic, which
had killed 4,732 Berliners during December and was still raging through
the city, adding to the nightmare. But at least the flu was something
that could not have been avoided, whereas the revolutionary violence
was entirely man-made. *Vorwärts*, publishing again in an improvised
format on 13 January, pointed the finger of blame in a bitter poem
on its front page:

> Many hundred dead are lying in a row –
>     Proletarians!
> Iron, powder, and lead do not ask if a person belongs to the Right, to
> the Left or to Spartacus,
>     Proletarians!
> Who has brought violence into the streets?
>     Proletarians!
> Who first took up arms and relied on their results?
>     Spartacus!
> Many hundred dead are lying in a row –
>     Proletarians!
> Karl, Radek, Rosa and companions –
> None of them is there, none of them is there!
>     Proletarians![33]

Liebknecht, Luxemburg and Radek were not there because they and
the other Spartacus leaders had all gone into hiding. Liebknecht and
Luxemburg were in safe houses in the central working-class district of

Neukölln, where they continued writing inflammatory articles for *Die Rote Fahne*, which somehow was still being published and distributed. 'Order Rules in Berlin' was the heavily ironic title of a Luxemburg editorial, which admitted that the revolution had failed, but claimed a moral victory. 'The masses were up to the mark,' she wrote. 'They have forged this defeat into the chain of those historic battles which are the strength and pride of international Socialism ... "Order Rules in Berlin?" You stupid lackeys! Your order is built on sand. Tomorrow the revolution will rise again, in a blare of trumpets, to announce "I was, I am, I always will be!"'[34]

Liebknecht was equally defiant. In an article headed 'In Spite of All', he wrote: 'Hold hard. We have not fled. We are not beaten. For Spartacus – that means fire and spirit, heart and soul, will and deed of the workers' revolution. For Spartacus – that stands for all the longing for achievement, all the embattled resolution of the class-conscious proletariat. Whether or not we survive, our programme will live. It will dominate the world of liberated peoples. In spite of all.'[35]

On 14 January, Liebknecht and Luxemburg, together with Wilhelm Pieck, moved to a new safe house, an apartment at 53 Mannheimer Strasse, in the middle-class district of Wilmersdorf. It proved to be not so safe: next day, prompted perhaps by a 10,000-mark reward posted by a Russian émigré organisation calling itself the 'Association for Combating Bolshevism', someone reported their whereabouts to the Guards Cavalry Division, a Freikorps unit based at the Eden Hotel. When troops burst into the apartment and arrested them, Luxemburg calmly packed a small suitcase, putting in some books, expecting a stay in prison. Instead, she and her two companions were pushed into cars and driven to the Eden for interrogation.

The interrogation was harsh but not violent, though the three Spartacists were abused, spat at and struck as they were hustled through the hotel lobby, and Luxemburg enraged her captors by her heavily sarcastic answers to their questions and her insufferable air of intellectual superiority. But when they were marched out of the hotel's side entrance, individually, everything suddenly changed. As Liebknecht emerged, he was hit over the head with a rifle butt by a burly soldier called Runge. Semi-conscious from the blow, he was bundled into a waiting car and driven off at speed into the nearby Tiergarten. Near the park's New Lake he was pushed out of the car and shot several times in the back 'while attempting to escape'. His body was found in the early hours of the morning, and delivered to an aid station near the Kaiser Wilhelm Memorial Church as that of an unknown man.

Luxemburg was also struck down by Runge's rifle butt, which crushed her skull. She was then shoved, half dead and bleeding profusely, into a car, where a Freikorps officer, a Lieutenant Vogel, shot her several times in the head, blowing her brains out while the car sped from the hotel into the Tiergarten. It stopped on the Lichtenstein Bridge over the broad Landwehr Canal, which at that point separates the Tiergarten from the Zoological Gardens. Luxemburg's body was heaved uncere-moniously over the parapet, crashing through the thin sheet of ice into the dark water, where it stayed, trapped under the winter ice until the thaw in May.

The third Spartacist leader, Wilhelm Pieck, somehow managed to get away from the Eden Hotel unharmed. The official story was that he escaped while being transported to Moabit jail, but another account says he was allowed to leave the hotel with a letter from a military intelligence officer guaranteeing his safety. Either way, he survived to become President of the East German Democratic Republic from 1949 until his death in 1960, while Liebknecht and Luxemburg were cele-brated as martyrs in the Communist annals.

Liebknecht was buried on Sunday 25 January, along with thirty-three Spartacist dead. Taking no chances, the government sealed off the entire central area of the city and only those with passes were allowed through the barricades. Troops with machine guns and artillery were posted along the route to the cemetery in east Berlin but the event passed off without any serious incident.

A government inquiry into the deaths of the Spartacus leaders found Private Runge guilty of 'leaving his post without being properly relieved' and of 'improper use of his weapons'. He spent several months in jail before being released. Lieutenant Vogel, diagnosed as 'psychopathic', probably as the result of his fine war record, was sentenced to two years in jail – which he never served. He was allowed to escape to Holland, to return a few months later when everything had blown over.

The Bolsheviks in Russia responded to the murders of Liebknecht and Luxemburg in typically savage fashion. Two days after Liebknecht's funeral they took four grand dukes – Georgi and Nikolai Mikhailovich, Dmitri Konstantinovich and Pavel Aleksandrovich – lined them up against a wall in Petrograd's Peter and Paul Fortress, and shot them.

Lenin then had the complete works of Liebknecht and Luxemburg published by his printers in Moscow.

As polling day for the German elections approached, Noske and the Freikorps imposed order of a sort on Berlin. Morgan Philips Price noted in his diary for 17 January:

A deathly quiet prevails in the city. The quiet of the grave. Military patrols streets, artillery posted everywhere. Armed White Guards being organised by a certain Reinhardt go about arresting and terrorising at pleasure. Several of my friends disappeared. A fine condition for eve of election for National Assembly. Attended sitting of Berlin Soldiers' Soviet. Most of the delegates from garrison seemed frightened at having called in spirits they cannot lay.[36]

The elections went ahead as planned on 19 January, with a massive 83 per cent turnout. In a complex system of proportional representation, the voters gave no single party an overall majority, but Ebert's Majority Social Democrats were confirmed as the biggest party with 37.9 per cent of the votes, while the Independent Socialists could manage only 7.6 per cent. The Communists, of course, were not represented since they had boycotted the elections, but it was clear that they would have received only minimal support. That same day, Noske issued a decree reducing the soldiers' and workers' councils to a purely consultative role.

Its leaders might have been dead, but Spartacus was by no means finished, and nor was the violence in Berlin and the rest of Germany. Because of the continuing danger, Noske persuaded Ebert to convene the Constituent Assembly not in Berlin but in the quiet, small town of Weimar, 160 miles south-west of the capital, where he believed it would be easier to defend the delegates against insurgents. On 30 January, he sent in an advance guard of 120 men from Maercker's Volunteer Rifles to establish security, but before they even reached the centre of the town they were surrounded by Spartacist fighters, who disarmed and imprisoned them. It took Maerker's entire force of 7,000 men three days to free them and drive out the rebels, after which they dug trenches right around the town as a first line of defence against a concerted attack.

On 15 January, the Liberal *Manchester Guardian* had reported: 'The formidable military machine, which seemed to be crushed for ever, has risen again with astonishing rapidity. Prussian officers are stalking the streets of Berlin, soldiers are marching, shouting and shooting at their command. Indeed, Ebert and Scheidemann very likely got more than they bargained for.'[37] The reaction to the Bolshevik threat became increasingly ruthless as Noske applied the same tactics that he had used to quell insurrection in Berlin to the other trouble spots in the rest of the country. The Freikorps became the government's fire brigade, dealing with riots, strikes and demonstrations. But although the flames of revolution were damped down, they continued to smoulder, ready to flare up again at the first opportunity.

# III

## 'EVERY STRIKE IS A
## SMALL REVOLUTION'

IT would be an oversimplification to say that the Western leaders at
the Paris Peace Conference were moved solely or even primarily by
their fear of Bolshevism, but its spectre inevitably cast its shadow
over their deliberations: while it may not have been always at the front
of their minds, it was constantly at the back of them, a lurking dread
of revolution, anarchy and economic collapse. It had even affected the
choice of location for the conference. Neither Wilson nor Lloyd George
had wanted to meet in Paris, since France had been both a belligerent
and a victim of the war and so would be emotionally involved in the
outcome. For similar reasons, Wilson had refused to visit the trenches
of the Western Front, in case the sight of so much devastation should
affect his own high-minded impartiality. He had wanted the venue to
be on neutral ground, in a quiet Swiss town such as Lausanne or Geneva,
forgetting that for years such towns had sheltered exiled revolutionaries, including Lenin himself. He was given a sharp reminder when
Swiss Social Democrats staged mass rallies to celebrate the first anniversary of the Bolshevik Revolution and brought the country to a standstill with a general strike 'against military and bourgeois dictatorship'.
Suddenly, Wilson accused Switzerland of 'harbouring the most poisonous
elements in Europe' – and agreed that the Peace Conference should be
held in Paris after all.

And so, at precisely the same moment as the Freikorps were crushing
the Spartacus rising in Berlin, Clemenceau, Wilson, Lloyd George and
Italian Prime Minister Orlando gathered in the French Foreign Ministry
at the Quai d'Orsay in Paris to decide on the procedures for the Peace

Conference. Since the start of the year, the press, particularly in Britain, had been clamouring for an early start to the conference, 'to stem the tide of chaos threatening Germany because of the introduction of Bolshevism'.[1] The Liberal *Observer* Sunday newspaper warned that 'A tidal wave of Russo-German Bolshevism sweeping over Europe might give more embarrassment at Paris than the escape of Napoleon did at Vienna.'[2]

By early 1919, only the defeated nations had been infected to any serious degree by the plague bacillus of Bolshevism, but it had not yet been proven that the victors had automatic immunity. One of the most recognisable early symptoms was industrial unrest – and this seemed to be growing rapidly in the Western nations. On the other hand, there were those, particularly among employers, who saw such unrest not as a symptom but as a cause of Bolshevism, which had to be stamped out quickly and ruthlessly with no regard for underlying reasons. Either way, it was a matter of grave concern.

During the final months of the war, there had been a growing number of strikes on both sides. In Germany they had led on to revolution, just as they had in Russia in 1917, and Britain, France and even America were fearful that the same thing might happen in their countries. In Britain and America, governments had always done their best not to get involved in industrial relations, but this had changed with the war, when strikes could have seriously damaged the vital supply of armaments. In addition, both governments had taken control of the mines and railways for the duration, and were therefore directly responsible for them. In Britain, legislation such as the War Munitions Act of July 1915 had banned strikes and imposed compulsory and binding arbitration of disputes, while the Defence of the Realm Act gave the government almost unlimited powers akin to martial law. In fact, these measures failed to stop strikes altogether, but those that did occur were settled quickly, either by the government's conceding to the strikers' demands or by the use of force.

The most worrying disputes had not involved miners, railwaymen or munitions workers, but London's Metropolitan Police, who came out on strike on 30 August 1918, calling for better pay and conditions but most of all for recognition of their National Union of Police and Prison Officers. At a mass meeting on Tower Hill, speakers declared that they were fighting on a matter of principle and threatened to call for a general strike if their demands were not met that day. Lloyd George intervened at once, conceding practically everything apart from union recognition, which the newspapers warned would have 'transferred the control of the force from the Home Secretary and the Chief Commissioner to the officials of the Union'.[3] To underline his kid-gloves approach, Lloyd George sacked the Chief Commissioner at Scotland Yard and replaced him with a new man, Sir Nevil Macready, who had a reputation for 'great tact', which it was hoped would 'enable him to placate the discontent without weakening essential discipline'. The policemen may have been placated, but a few days later the prison officers also struck, as did London firefighters and postal workers.

Because union officials had given an undertaking not to call strikes during the war, many workers considered that the unions had sold out to government, and turned instead to the more radical shop stewards for leadership. The most notable example of this was in Scotland, where militant shop stewards formed themselves into the Clyde Workers' Committee, initially to fight the Ministry of Munitions' policy of directing unskilled labour into factories to do skilled men's work. But when they started a series of strikes in 1916, and began distributing pamphlets with titles such as 'Should the Workers Arm?', the government used its powers to break the committee and arrest its leaders.

The CWC reappeared in September 1918 with a slight but significant change of name – the Clyde Workers' Soviet Committee – publishing a manifesto that was unashamedly Bolshevik:

(a)  Removal of Parliament and Municipal Councils, to be taken over by the Revolutionary Council.

(b)  Immediate seizure of all means of subsistence to secure the success of the revolution.

(c)  Disarming of all non-proletarian soldiers.

(d)  Seizure of arms and ammunition by the Workers' and Soldiers' Councils.

(e)  Arming of the entire labour population as a Red Army.

(f)  All superiors to be nominated by the rank and file.

(g)  Abolition of Courts martial.

(h)  Creation of a revolutionary tribunal to try men chiefly responsible for all the harsh treatment accorded to our comrades now in prison and to political prisoners.

(i)  Abolition of all class distinctions, titles and orders.

(j)  Six hours day and £7 per working week.

(k)  Confiscation of all Crown estates, which will become public property.

(l)  Annulment of State debts and other debts.

(m)   Expropriation of all land and properties, funds, and other securities now in possession of the ruling classes.

(n)   Expropriation of all banks, mines, industrial and commercial establishments by the Revolutionary Committee.

(o)   Republican Committee to take over all means of communication, traffic and means of transport.

The police seemed remarkably relaxed about this Bolshevik plot. The public need not be alarmed, they said – they had seen similar literature before and were fully aware of 'the seditious propaganda that was being carried on surreptitiously in various parts of the country and more particularly in the Clyde area, by revolutionaries', whose following, 'as far as could be ascertained', was insignificant. If the leaders of the movement were wanted, they continued, the police would have no difficulty in laying hold of them, 'as they are well known'. As to stores of arms and explosives, the police were incredulous: 'There have been attempts now and again to smuggle in arms and ammunition in small quantities, but the ports are too strictly watched for anything of that sort to take place on any scale.'[4]

The police's confidence – or complacency – was largely based on reports from a special intelligence service that had been set up during the war by Basil Thomson, head of the CID and Special Branch at Scotland Yard, who made weekly reports to the Cabinet on the labour situation throughout the country. The service was too useful to be disbanded when the war ended, and went on monitoring union activities for potential revolutionary threats.[5] One of its greatest fears was that workers and mutinous soldiers would join forces, as they had done in Russia and Germany, with similar results. A report of 10 January to Lloyd George's Deputy Prime Minister, Bonar Law, said that

a certain section of the workers (whose names and activities are well known to Scotland Yard and the Home Office) are only too ready and eager to fan and foment a passing grievance to inveigle the soldiers into an alliance with themselves, on the lines of the Soviet Committees. The ultimate end of this manoeuvre would be Revolution and a Soviet form of Government.

The dangers consequent upon even the slightest success of such a scheme must be patent to anyone who has studied the course of events in Russia. The spread of this spirit is alarming, and evidence can be obtained of a determined effort to emulate the Russian Bolshevik movement in this country.[6]

As well as keeping an eye on subversives in industry, the security services were also watching the ports for Bolshevik agents and couriers carrying money and revolutionary literature from the Continent, supposedly under the direction of a Russian woman named in the report as Angelica Balabaroff (in actual fact Balabanova, daughter of a wealthy Ukrainian businessman), who was said to work chiefly between Berne, Berlin, Stockholm and Moscow. The Bolshevik agents, the security service reported, were usually smuggled into the country on foreign ships by crew members who were paid handsomely for every stowaway who succeeded in landing in Britain. Late in 1918, according to a Central News report, eleven foreign Jews who arrived as stowaways on a Dutch steamer were caught in the East End, and deported.[7] They may well have been economic refugees, but the fact that they were Jewish would undoubtedly have labelled them as dangerous Bolsheviks.

With or without Bolshevik support from overseas, industrial tensions in Britain escalated rapidly in January 1919: unemployment rocketed when munitions production was cut and increasing numbers of men were demobilised and returned to the jobs market. At the heart of the discontent were coal miners, railwaymen and transport workers, who made up the powerful 'Triple Alliance' of unions formed during the war. Although unions in the three sectors acted independently, they were pledged to support each other in any dispute and could bring the entire country to its knees in a very few days.

The miners, more than a million strong, were in the most powerful position, for Britain ran on coal. Coal was needed for heating homes and factories, for cooking, for power generation. Without coal there could be no electricity from power stations and no gas – every town had its own gasworks, where coal was heated to make gas, with coke as a by-product; the tall chimneys of virtually every mill and factory belched out smoke from coal-fired boilers powering their machinery; iron and steel furnaces were fired by coal and coke; all trains ran on it, including those carrying coal to depots and power stations, and so did most ships – including those carrying coal from ports in Scotland, South Wales and the north-east. During the war, the miners had used their muscle to back claims for higher wages, shorter hours and better conditions. As early in the war as July 1915, 200,000 Welsh miners struck; as late in the war as August 1918, 60,000 went on strike.

In their wartime disputes the miners had been generally successful –

though their pay was still shamefully inadequate for an industry where an average of three men were killed every working day and those who survived to retirement were often crippled by injury or lung disease. With the end of the restraints imposed by the war, the struggle began again in earnest. In the week ending 14 January there were eighteen new miners' strikes, and twenty more in the following week.[8] The miners still won consistently: a week later several large disputes were settled, involving 150,000 men in Yorkshire who had been out for thirteen days, 50,000 in the Nottingham and Derbyshire field, 12,000 in Fife, and so on. One of the things that worried the government most was that the majority of these strikes were 'unofficial', without the support of the unions, and the men's demands were not only economic but also political. They included a 30 per cent wage increase, a reduction of working hours from eight to six a day, and – most worrying – nationalisation of the industry with joint control by government and miners.

It was not miners, however, or other members of the Triple Alliance, who caused the greatest upsets at that time, but workers in Belfast and Glasgow, two great centres of shipbuilding and engineering that had been most affected by the end of the war. Their principal union, the Amalgamated Society of Engineers (ASE), had negotiated a forty-seven-hour week, but the men were having none of it. They struck in Belfast for a forty-four-hour week and in Glasgow for forty hours, with no loss of pay. Their justification was that this would reduce unemployment and make way for demobilised soldiers.

Belfast, home to the giant Harland & Wolff shipyard, builders of the *Titanic* among thousands of other vessels, was the scene of the first eruption, on Saturday 25 January, when the shipyard workers walked out. On the Monday, they were joined by municipal electricity and gas workers, seeking the same hours, with the immediate result that electrical power in the city was reduced by 90 per cent. Trams stopped running and other workers were forced to trudge on foot through a heavy snowfall to their unheated and unlit factories and offices, where they were turned round and sent home again – only factories which generated their own power were working. In abattoirs, butchers had to dispatch animals with poleaxes, since their stun guns would not operate. Theatres and cinemas could not open. Only hospitals were spared, given special dispensation by the strikers to receive power. 'Belfast is like a dead city,' reported the *New York Times*, 'a city of candles.'[9]

But the candles lighting homes had to be used sparingly. Any residents using more than one in their homes at night risked having their houses stoned in punishment.

The strikes quickly escalated as other workers came out in sympathy, and a General Strike Committee was formed with representatives of no fewer than twenty-six unions. It was soon running the city from its base in Artisans' Hall.

'The workmen have formed a "Soviet" committee,' a telegram to the Cabinet in London reported, 'and this Committee had received 47 applications from small traders for permission to use light.'[10] On a bigger scale, no ships could move into or out of the harbour or dry docks without its permission, increasing the strikers' stranglehold on the economic life of the city. 'It is syndicalism pure and simple,' the right-wing *Belfast News-Letter* fulminated. 'The strike leaders are not relying on the strength or justice of their demand. Their weapon is the paralysis of the city's daily life.'[11]

The strike in Belfast proceeded with remarkable calm – the only recorded violence, apart from stones thrown at houses burning more than a single candle, was when a delegate from Dublin attempted to make a mildly revolutionary speech at a mass meeting in Donegall Square North. He was knocked off the platform to yells of 'We want no Papist Bolsheviks here!' Sectarian tensions were already evident in Ireland between the loyalist Protestant north and the secessionist Catholic south, where the Sinn Fein MPs elected in December had refused to take their seats at Westminster and had set up their own rebel parliament in Dublin, the Dáil Éireann, declaring an independent Irish republic on 21 January. Before the year was out, those tensions would erupt into the start of a civil war that was almost unique for the time in not having a significant Bolshevik component, but for the moment the men of Ulster were more concerned with work and wages.

The chairman of the Belfast Strike Committee, Charles McKay, had a much more enthusiastic reception than the Dublin delegate when he told the crowd: 'The city has been ours since Saturday. The workers simply go down and show themselves and the municipal staff come out either on principle or for safety.' This sally was greeted with a roar of laughter, and he went on, more seriously: 'The employers know that the workers' cause is just. The government intervened quickly enough during the war in the so-called national interest when there were any disputes. Why don't they intervene now? We can't rely on

the government. We can't rely on our unions. We have to rely on
ourselves. The little tin gods over there,' he pointed at the City Hall,
'know we are right, though there is not a man among them who has
the courage to say so.'[12]

The Belfast stoppage remained civilised: emergency services were kept
running and when the managing director of Harland & Wolff died
during the strike, a contingent of workers joined the funeral procession as a mark of respect for their employer. The same could not be
said of Glasgow, where there was a much greater tradition of militant
Marxism, and where the reconstituted Clyde Workers' Committee had
been agitating for some time. The Forty-Hours Strike, as it became
known, was the culmination of more than a decade of confrontation
with capitalism on Clydeside. Union strength had been building steadily:
membership had almost quadrupled since 1910, with four out of every
five workers in a union, mainly in the Amalgamated Society of Engineers.
Now, with unemployment suddenly soaring to 11 per cent, it was time
for that strength to be tested.

From the beginning of January, all the various unions in the region
came together in a joint committee to prepare for the battle. The average
working week in Glasgow at the time was fifty-four hours: sinking their
sectional differences – the CWC, for instance was all for demanding a
thirty-hour week, while the ASE executive favoured its already agreed
forty-seven hours – the committee finally settled on a target of forty.
This was the figure promoted by Emmanuel Shinwell, a future Cabinet
minister in the 1945 Labour government, an adroit political operator
who chaired the joint committee and was also president of the Glasgow
Trades Council, and Willie Gallacher, a future Communist MP (one of
the very few ever to sit in the House of Commons), who was elected
strike organiser.

Gallacher made no bones about his political ambitions for the coming
strike. 'Into it then, comrades, as never before,' he exhorted. 'Let this
be the class war started at last. Too long have we been groping about
in the dark. Now at last we begin to see the light, and come what may
we must sustain the fight until we emerge into the full, bright day of
the Socialist Republic!'[13] Shinwell, more canny, drew up a manifesto
stating that 'This movement . . . is not revolutionary in character, nor
is it inspired by the legitimate demand for more leisure. It is attribut-
able solely and entirely to the fear of possible unemployment in the

near future and the desire of the workers generally to make room for demobilised servicemen.'[14] To underline his determination to keep out political agitators, Shinwell and his committee decreed that only strikers would be allowed to speak at mass meetings. Writing several years later, Gallacher lamented what he regarded as a lost opportunity: 'We had forgotten we were revolutionary leaders of the working class . . . we were carrying on a strike when we ought to have been making a revolution.'[15]

The Glasgow strike began on Monday 27 January, when 40,000 workers stayed away from work. By the third day, the number had reached 70,000, and mass pickets five to ten thousand strong, some of them composed of strikers' wives and women workers, were marching through the city from factory to factory, until every one was closed down, together with all the privately owned power stations and one of the city's two corporation-owned stations. The other, supplying electricity to the tram system, managed to stay in operation by providing its men with board and lodgings under the protection of a company of armed troops.

Shinwell and Gallacher led a deputation to the Lord Provost, Glasgow's mayor, persuading him to ask the government to intervene. At noon on Friday 31 January, they returned to hear the government's decision: after telephoning Lloyd George in Paris, Bonar Law had refused to get involved. Outside the City Chambers, an estimated 35,000 strikers had assembled in George Square, many of them marching in behind pipe bands and drummers. The atmosphere was explosive. Already antagonised by being kept waiting while the Lord Provost attended a meeting of the Magistrates' Committee, the crowd turned nasty. A giant red flag was raised on the city flagpole, windows were smashed, a tram was overturned, the police drew their batons and charged, beating and knocking down anyone who got in their way. Mounted police joined in, clubbing and trampling people indiscriminately. Forty people were severely injured. As the melee mounted, Sheriff Alastair Oswald Morison Mackenzie emerged from the City Chambers together with Chief Constable J.V. Stevenson and began to read the Riot Act, ordering the demonstrators to disperse. He never finished – a broken bottle sailed from the crowd, struck the Chief Constable on the head, then cut Mackenzie's hand. Someone snatched the Riot Act document from him and made off with it. David Kirkwood, one of the deputation, ran down the steps from the building to see what was happening, and was

bludgeoned to the ground, unconscious. Gallacher punched the Chief
Constable on the jaw, and was also beaten. He, Kirkwood and Shinwell
were arrested. The crowd, fleeing from the mounted police, retreated
along nearby streets, looting shops and grabbing beer bottles as ammunition to hurl at their pursuers and overturning a further thirty trams.

'This was not a strike but a Bolshevist rising,' the jittery Secretary
of State for Scotland, Robert Munro, told the Cabinet in London.
General Sir William Robertson, C-in-C Home Forces, reported that
one hundred motor lorries and six tanks were already on their way
north by rail and that Scottish troops from Highland regiments were
available to quell the disturbances and restore order.[16] Over the next
few days some 10,000 troops were deployed at strategic points in and
around Glasgow in full battle order and with fixed bayonets; the City
Chambers were surrounded with barbed wire and machine guns.
Glasgow was a city under siege. Soldiers in the local barracks at
Maryhill, meanwhile, were kept inside and inactive – their loyalty to
the government could not be relied on. To Gallacher's regret, the strikers
failed to emulate their counterparts in Germany by approaching the
soldiers, fraternising with them and trying to win them over to their
cause, and the faint hope of revolution faded. Troops broke up the
pickets at power stations and workers began to drift back to the shipyards and factories.

As the focus shifted further south on 3 February, with a walkout of
train drivers on the London Underground, the Glasgow Joint
Committee's *Strike Bulletin* remained bullish: 'London is now in the
turmoil of a new strike movement, the profiteers of Belfast are still
helpless before the united forces of the workers . . . the surrender of
the employers and the government is only hours away. No one knows
better than they do that they are beaten to a frazzle by the greatest
strike movement this country has ever seen.'[17]

The London Underground stoppage was only one of 105 continuing
strikes throughout Britain at that time, but it had the most immediate
impact as it disrupted the affairs of the nation's capital. The seemingly
trivial cause was over meal and comfort breaks in the newly negotiated eight-hour working day, but it was enough to plunge the city into
chaos, aggravated by snowy weather, as the rest of the workforce struggled to reach their offices and factories. The situation was made worse
when drivers of surface trains on the Southern Railway's suburban

services also struck. Once again, the government refused to intervene, but once again made use of troops, this time as volunteer drivers of over a thousand motor lorries mobilised from Army Service Corps depots to supplement the overstretched bus services and carry passengers through the streets. Members of the Royal Automobile Club also rallied to the cause, turning out with their cars to provide 'free transport for tired workers'.

As the tube strike was beginning to bite, the government was faced with an even greater threat when members of the Electrical Trades Union decided they would stop work at 6 p.m. on 6 February, in sympathy with the Glasgow strikers, and 'plunge London into darkness' unless the government acted to resolve the Forty-Hours Strike. This was finally too much. The government acted at last, but not as the electricians wanted: using the draconian Defence of the Realm Act it declared that any electrical worker who stopped work without notice, or anyone who incited others to do so, faced six months' imprisonment and/or a fine of £100. At the same time, it ordered army engineers to stand by to man the power stations. The electricians backed down, but the general unrest continued: among many smaller disputes, 8,000 London waiters and hotel workers stopped work, forcing restaurants to close or offer only the most basic menus and service.

Lloyd George hurried back from Paris on 8 February to impose his authority and try to sort things out – but as he arrived some 3,000 soldiers in transit to France from camps in northern England were marching from Victoria Station to Whitehall in protest at having been forced to spend the night on the station platforms with poor food and no sleeping arrangements. They were stopped at Horse Guards Parade by a battalion of Grenadier Guards with fixed bayonets, who shepherded them to the nearby Wellington barracks, where they were given breakfast and sent on their way to France. The soldiers' protest had passed off peacefully, with no violence, but Lloyd George was sufficiently concerned by the situation to warn his daughter not to bring her baby to London.[18]

The Glasgow strike petered out on 11 February, when the joint committee admitted defeat and postponed the fight for the forty-hour week. In Belfast, the strikers held out until the 20th, before reaching a compromise settlement granting them slightly shorter hours. But the threat of action by the Triple Alliance still loomed: at a special conference on 12 February, miners' leaders rejected a government wage offer and decided to ballot their members on a national strike, and the railwaymen began putting together their demands for shorter hours and higher pay. Meanwhile, the Alliance leaders decided to canvass their members on making 'Hands off Russia!' one of the aims of direct action. *The Times*, which together with the *Daily Telegraph* and the *Morning Post* had been appealing for middle- and upper-class solidarity 'in the defence of the nation', condemned what it saw as 'a planned campaign drawn up by intellectuals in the background who wish to emulate Lenin and Trotsky and the Spartacus leaders in Germany'.

The result of the miners' ballot, announced on 25 February, was an overwhelming endorsement of the strike call, by a majority of almost six to one. It was what Lloyd George and his ministers had been expecting, and they had already planned their response: instead of confrontation, they offered conciliation, in the form of a Royal Commission under a High Court judge of the King's Bench, Mr Justice Sankey, who as Sir John Sankey had been an advocate for the South Wales miners during his years as a barrister. The commission was to inquire into wages, hours and conditions in the pits and to consider 'any scheme . . . for the future organisation of the coal industry, whether on the present basis, or on the basis of joint control, nationalisation, or any other basis'. The miners were to nominate or approve half the members of the commission. It was a classic case of jam tomorrow, an offer so reasonable that the miners could not possibly refuse. Nor did they.

Lloyd George had defused the situation and bought time: the miners' leaders spent the next four months having their teeth drawn in the august setting of the Robing Room of the House of Lords. Without the miners, there was no Triple Alliance, and the threat of joint action with the railwaymen and transport workers was lifted, at least temporarily. In another master stroke, the Prime Minister spiked the guns of the unions outside the Triple Alliance by setting up the National Industrial Conference, another talking shop where representatives of management and labour could sit down together to discuss their problems and consider reforms that would be referred to the government for decisions in due course.

In the United States, just as in Britain, the early part of 1919 was a time of considerable uncertainty as the country struggled to cope with a sudden return to a peacetime economy. Nine million people had been engaged in war industries, and four million men were in the armed forces, 600,000 of whom were released almost immediately, creating enormous stresses, both socially and economically. Because Germany had collapsed so suddenly, there had been no time to make plans for the best ways of demobilising and redeploying them all; nor had there been time for a softening of wartime attitudes, particularly over the need for unquestioning loyalty and patriotism. Conformity, however blinkered, was everything; dissent, in any shape, was highly suspect.

Since there had as yet been no peace treaty to bring the war to an official end, the wartime Espionage and Sedition Acts, which prohibited any deed, word or even thought that could be interpreted as anti-war or anti-government, were still very much in operation. Indeed, a number of prosecutions were still proceeding against people who had been foolish or determined enough to criticise either the government or the war. In addition to Eugene Debs and Bill Haywood, the most prominent of these was the veteran leader of the American Socialist Party, Victor Berger, who had served as Congressman for the Fifth Wisconsin District since 1910. The first Socialist to serve in Congress, Berger was regarded as an honourable, if slightly eccentric, member of the House of Representatives. He had been against the war from the start, but in June 1917 declared that since America was in it, he wanted to win it, 'for democracy'. Later, however, he said that in his opinion America's war could not be justified, and that 'the blood of American boys [was] being coined into swollen profits for American plutocrats'.[19] These typically Socialist sentiments had been enough to get him indicted for violating the Espionage Act in February 1918, but it was not until January 1919 that he was brought to trial; in the meantime he had stood for the US Senate in the spring elections, when he was only narrowly defeated, and been re-elected to the House of Representatives in November on a peace platform. His popular support, however, was not enough to save him from being sentenced to twenty years' imprisonment in Fort Leavenworth.

Since the war was over, it seems likely that the savagery of Berger's sentence was the result of a growing neurosis about Socialism in any form, energetically fanned by a press that was largely owned by the 'plutocrats' whom he had castigated. Alongside the plutocrats, but not necessarily separated from them, were the patriotic organisations such as the National Security League and the American Defense Society, which were still active and eager to continue with the chauvinist agendas that were their reason for existing. The Evil Hun had been defeated, but they soon found a new target for their alarmist propaganda: radicalism in general, and Bolshevism in particular.

Within a week of the Armistice, the Mayor of New York, John Hylan, banned the red flag from the city's streets, and ordered the police to 'disperse all unlawful assemblages'. A few nights later, a Socialist mass meeting in Madison Square Garden was invaded by an estimated five hundred soldiers and sailors, who stormed the doors. It took twenty-two mounted policemen to restore order. Next night, there was another riot, again involving soldiers and sailors, outside the Palm Garden on 58th Street, where the Women's International League was holding a meeting of sympathy for Revolutionary Russia. Six people were badly beaten up, including a respectable stockbroker who happened to be walking up Lexington Avenue with a lady. When he stopped to ask what all the excitement was about, a sailor yelled, 'Hey, fellers, here's another of the Bolsheviks!' and a gang of men leapt on him and beat him nearly unconscious.[20]

In such a climate, the Philadelphia bombs, like other bomb plots later in the year, naturally provided wonderful ammunition for the super-patriots. So, too, did the labour unrest that would dominate the American industrial scene throughout 1919. For the most part, this was caused by simple economics – inflation had reduced the value of the 1913 dollar to forty-five cents, and while the cost of living for the average family was 99 per cent higher than it had been five years before, wages had barely increased at all.

What had increased was union membership and the organisation of labour. Building on the gains made during the pre-war Progressive era and Wilson's New Freedom programme, American Federation of Labor membership had climbed to 4,169,000 by 1919. During the war, there had been an uneasy truce between organised labour and industrial employers, but when the war ended, so did the truce. Most employers were not averse to granting modest wage increases; but they were solidly opposed to the idea of collective bargaining by organised labour, and they were ready to fight against that with every weapon at their disposal. The battle lines were drawn for a year of industrial mayhem – altogether during 1919 there would be 3,600 strikes in the United States, involving more than four million workers – for which it was all too easy, and convenient, to blame Bolshevik agitators.

It was particularly easy to blame the Reds for the general strike that hit Seattle in February, since Industrial Workers of the World (IWW) agitators had long been active in the Pacific Northwest. Although they were in fact very few, the Wobblies, as they were generally known, were extremely noisy and troublesome, with wildcat strikes, red-flag parades, rabid speeches and violent propaganda, all of which convinced West Coast newspapers that labour in the region was dangerously radical. Seattle, with its huge harbour and shipbuilding and lumber industries, was the queen city of the north-west. It had long been the strongest centre of labour unions in the whole of America, and by the end of the war more than 50 per cent of its entire labour force was organised, with over 110 craft unions affiliated to the American Federation of Labor, all offering each other mutual support through a Central Labor Council. The Seattle unions were among the most radical in the country, regularly casting the one dissenting vote in national AFL conventions against the re-election of the conservative president, Samuel Gompers. But they were models of conformity compared with the IWW.

The IWW had been founded in Chicago in 1905 with the support of the Socialist Party, largely through to the efforts of William D. 'Big Bill' Haywood, a tough but gentle one-eyed giant, born near Salt Lake City, Utah, in 1869. Haywood had worked as a miner, a cowboy, a homesteader and a general roustabout before becoming the national secretary-treasurer of the Western Federation of Miners, leading it in some of the most bitter strikes ever seen in the West. He had then helped form the IWW to represent the millions of unskilled and itinerant workers in industries such as lumber, mining and agriculture, who were at the mercy of ruthless employers. It was never more than a few tens of thousands strong, and its membership fluctuated from month to month, mostly drawn from the migrant hoboes who 'rode the rails', walking along the railroad tracks or jumping freight cars to travel the enormous distances between Californian fruit farms and canning factories, the harvest belt of the Midwest and the lumber camps of the far north-west to find work. These homeless and rootless men formed a brotherhood of the road with its own myths and legends, celebrating their shared hardships in anthems such as 'Hallelujah, I'm a bum' and 'Paint 'Er Red!', collected in their *Little Red Songbook*. Regularly abused, beaten, jailed, thrown off moving trains by brakemen – in four years 4,000 of them were killed and 25,000 injured on the railroads – they were well schooled in violence and had little to lose by using it.

Haywood and the IWW had consistently opposed the war. Slogans such as 'Don't be a soldier, be a man', and appeals not to fight the battles of Rockefeller, J.P. Morgan and other monopoly capitalists, had enraged a population conditioned by powerful government propaganda to support the fighting and hate the Germans. Newspapers, particularly those owned by the capitalists vilified by the IWW, openly encouraged their readers to exterminate Wobblies: 'Kill them,' screamed the *Tulsa Daily World*, 'as you would any other kind of snake.' Members were beaten, whipped, tarred and feathered and, during a miners' strike at Butte, Montana, lynched. It was against this background of anger and suspicion that Haywood was arrested under the Espionage Act in 1918, along with 165 other leading Wobblies, ninety-nine of whom were found guilty after a five-month criminal trial, the longest in American history.

Red journalist John Reed, just back from an assignment in Soviet Russia, was struck by the sight of the accused men in the courtroom, lounging at their ease in shirtsleeves, reading, talking, smoking, making liberal use of the thoughtfully provided spittoons. 'I doubt if ever in history there has been a sight like them,' he wrote in the *Liberator*. 'A hundred men better fitted to stand up for the social revolution could not have been collected from all America. Lumberjacks, harvest hands, miners, editors . . . who believe that the wealth of the world belongs to those who create it . . . the outdoor men, hardrock blasters, tree fellers, wheat binders, longshoremen, the boys who do the strong work of the world . . . The scene was strangely familiar – it looked like a meeting of the Central Executive Committee of the All-Russian Soviets in Petrograd!'[21] Reed was a sympathetic supporter of the IWW men, as well as the Soviet Russians, but he could hardly have chosen words that would condemn them more in the eyes of loyal Americans.

In spite of Haywood's pronouncement that the Russian Revolution was 'the IWW all feathered out',[22] the union's main philosophy was not Bolshevik but syndicalist, with a strong dash of anarchism thrown in. It aimed to smash capitalism but did not believe in the Communist ideal of state ownership, instead seeking workers' control of their own industries. Its opponents, not unnaturally, found such distinctions hard to make, lumping anarchists, syndicalists, Communists and Socialists together under the single heading of dangerous radicals. The IWW's other principal tenet and ambition was its clarion call for 'One Big Union', to replace all the individual craft and industry unions which it believed the employers played off against each other in a strategy of divide and rule. They may have been right, but such a policy did not endear the Wobblies to the traditional unions, who understandably saw it as a threat to their own existence.

As its name implied, the IWW did not confine its message or its activities to the United States. Immigrant workers from countries such as Poland, the Ukraine, Germany and Hungary spread the word to families and friends back home, while seamen Wobblies carried it around the world. IWW influence was seen in 1918 in strikes and direct action as far afield as Australia, South Africa, Spain and Norway. It was felt especially strongly in South and Central America, feeding on an existing tradition of individualist anarchism, with growing militancy in Mexico, Uruguay, Bolivia, Peru, Chile and Argentina, where a general strike throughout the republic was called on 10 January.

There were bloody street battles in Buenos Aires, as the strikers attempted to take over the Central Police Prefecture and the Post and Telegraph Offices, with heavy casualties. The police chief's car was torched, as were many tramcars, and the strikers demonstrated their anti-religious views by pillaging churches and attacking a monastery. By the end of the night, known casualties included twenty-seven dead, fifty-one seriously wounded and 105 slightly wounded. Next day, there were some 10,000 heavily armed troops on the streets, aided by strong naval forces.

Although the strike was officially called off after the second day, following the intervention of President Irigoyen, the shooting and general disorder continued for some time. Strikers who attacked the Post Office and the Nasena Ironworks were dispersed with machine-gun fire, leaving another twenty dead and sixty wounded. Significantly, the worst of the fighting was reported to be in the Russian quarter of the city, and General Dellepiane, who had been put in charge of the police, ordered all Russian agitators to be rounded up and interned on warships in the harbour.[23]

After a few days, the troubles in Argentina and Peru, where another general strike had led to bloody clashes with the military, finally died down and things in South America returned to a semblance of normality. But news of what appeared to be Bolshevik- or IWW-inspired disturbances in the western hemisphere added to the unease in the United States. American nervousness was increased by growing unrest nearer home, in western Canada, where there had been a brief general strike in the spring of 1918 in Winnipeg, barely fifty miles across the border from Minnesota. In December of that year, following a Socialist rally in the city, the *Western Labour News,* the organ of the city's Trade and Labour Council, had talked of a Dominion-wide strike in defiance of the government. And in January 1919, a prominent member of the council had warned in an inflammatory public speech: 'In Germany the workers are shooting. In Winnipeg we are still fighting with ideas – but we shall soon be fighting with rifles.'[24]

The IWW was not directly responsible for the strike in Seattle, but its influence, especially in the pressure it exerted on the conventional unions for more radical action, could not be denied. It had organised lightning strikes in the city during the war, and had created an atmosphere of militancy that increased with the coming of peace. Alongside the IWW, but separated by a vital difference in philosophy, was the Socialist Party of America, led by the anti-war 'traitors' Eugene Debs and Victor Berger. This was a bigger and more important organisation than the IWW, but one which sought revolution through political means rather than the direct action espoused by the Wobblies.

Seattle's Central Labor Council, made up of all the regular craft unions, had already expressed sympathy with the Bolshevik regime in Russia, and was spoiling for a fight with the employers to prove its own revolutionary credentials. The employers meanwhile, well organised under the umbrella of the Employers' Businessmen's Association, were equally determined to celebrate peace by crushing the unions and clawing back the gains they had made during the war. The showdown came on 21 January, when 35,000 members of the Metal Workers Union at the shipyards struck for higher pay and shorter hours. The Emergency Fleet Corporation, a wartime agency of the US government, had granted the union permission to renegotiate its contract with management, but the agency's head had then sent a telegram to the employers' Metal Trades Association, threatening to withdraw its steel allotment if it did not resist all union demands. By a farcical mischance, the telegraph boy, perhaps flustered because his bicycle had just been stolen, delivered the telegram to the unions' Metal Trades *Council.* Furious at the double-dealing revealed by the telegram, and faced with a flat refusal by the employers to negotiate, the union members voted to strike.

The Metal Workers immediately called on the Central Labor Council for support. Led by their aggressive secretary, James A. Duncan, a Wobbly in all but name, all 110 of the council's unions agreed to poll their members, who voted by overwhelming majorities in favour of a general strike, the first in American history. The press immediately went into a frenzy. The Seattle *Star* warned strikers: 'This is America – not Russia.' Not to be outdone, the Seattle *Post-Intelligencer* displayed a massive cartoon on its front page showing the red flag flying above the Stars and Stripes, over the caption 'Not in a Thousand Years'. Every newspaper printed the IWW's proud boast that 'every strike is a small revolution and a dress rehearsal for the big one'[25] – and whole-page advertisements demanding that labour leaders be 'hanged on the nearest telephone pole' lest they turn Seattle into 'the most labor-tyrannized city in America'. Ignoring the warnings, 60,000 workmen downed tools at 10 a.m. on 6 February, paralysing the economic life of the city. The stoppage was not confined to the shipyards and industry, but spread out into every area of activity. Schools closed, streetcar services stopped, theatres did not open as four out of every five theatrical employees walked out; truck drivers, barbers, janitors, elevator operators, newspaper typesetters, waiters, men and women from every type of job, came out in sympathy with the shipyard workers. Within two days, the number of strikers had risen to 75,000.

The council's own newspaper, the *Union-Record*, reassured the public that the Strike Committee would feed the people, care for babies and the sick, preserve law and order, and run all industries necessary to the public health and welfare. The committee was as good as its word, exempting garbage and laundry trucks, milk wagons, ambulances and the like, and making sure that the city was at no time without food, water, coal, heat or light. Several thousand union men of the War Veterans Guard wearing white armbands patrolled the streets to maintain order. Although there were some 3,500 Wobblies involved, and a certain amount of revolutionary literature was distributed, the strikers' behaviour was exemplary: there was no violence and not a single arrest had to be made – which did not prevent stories being published elsewhere of the city's being in the hands of lawless mobs, and, of course, whipping up anti-revolutionary fervour. 'REDS DIRECTING SEATTLE STRIKE – TO TEST CHANCE FOR REVOLUTION' was a typical headline. Other inflammatory comments included 'The Seattle strike is Marxian', 'a revolutionary movement aimed at existing government', 'the stepping stone to a Bolshevised America', 'the Bolshevik beast comes into the open', 'it is only a middling step from Petrograd to Seattle', and so on.

In the absence of the employers, who had gone to ground and so were unavailable for negotiations, opposition to the strike was led by Seattle's mayor, the forty-four-year-old Ole Hanson. Hanson, born in Racine, Wisconsin, the son of Norwegian immigrants, had started work in the law, but had soon tired of both the job and his home town and had headed west on a buckboard in search of something more adventurous. After dabbling in grocery-store ownership, selling real estate, advertising copywriting and investment broking, he had decided to try politics, winning a seat in the Washington State Legislature. A man with mixed political affiliations, he had started as a Republican, then became a Progressive, and in 1916 supported Wilson; he had named three of his sons Theodore Roosevelt Hanson, William Taft Hanson and Bob La Follette Hanson, and two daughters gloried in the names Lloyd George Hanson and Eugene Field Hanson. In 1918, after failing to win a seat in the US Senate, he had run for mayor with no definite party tag, and had been elected, presumably because the people of Seattle liked his independent spirit and his opponent was an even more unlikely candidate. Clearly a man with an eye for the main chance, Hanson was quick to realise that the general strike was his passport to immortality. Ignoring the Central Labor Council's promise to maintain law and order, he deputised a thousand extra police and called for support from the army, and Secretary of War Newton Baker swiftly obliged.

Eight hundred federal troops from Camp Lewis marched into the city on the morning of 6 February, led by Mayor Hanson in a car draped with a huge American flag. At the same time, a train left the city carrying fifty-four so-called 'IWW leaders and troublemakers' in two heavily guarded tourist sleeping cars, bound for New York, Ellis Island, and deportation. They had been rounded up two hours before the strike was due to start, to be sent back to their native lands – a few to Britain, half a dozen to Russia, most to Scandinavia. Twenty-four of them were charged with belonging to 'an organisation which advocates the destruction of property', in other words, the IWW; nine were described as anarchists; four were 'ex-convicts'; two were 'diseased'; three were alleged to have violated the white slavery laws; the rest were deemed likely to become public charges. The US Commissioner General of Immigration, Anthony Caminetti, announced that a further 6,000 aliens would be deported. In the event, wiser counsel prevailed, and after further investigation only three of the original fifty-four were actually removed from the country.

Next day, a further contingent of troops arrived, and Hanson notified the Strike Committee that unless they called off the strike by 8 a.m. next morning he would use the troops to crush it and operate all essential enterprises. 'Any man who attempts to take over control of municipal functions here,' he announced, 'will be shot on sight.' To back up his brave words, he then proclaimed: 'We have 1,500 police officers, 1,500 regulars from Camp Lewis, and will get the services of every soldier in the Pacific Northwest to protect life, business and property. The time has come for the people in Seattle to show their Americanism ... the anarchists in this community shall not rule its affairs.'[26]

In the face of savage criticism from the press, increasing hostility from the general public and considerable pressure from a hostile AFL, which feared irreparable damage to the labour movement as a whole, the local craft unions decided to pull out of the general strike. It was officially called off by the Strike Committee at midday on 11 February. Hanson trumpeted his triumph: 'The rebellion is quelled, the test came and was met by Seattle unflinchingly.' The Seattle *Star*'s headline read 'FULL STEAM AHEAD ... Today this Bolshevik-sired nightmare is at an end.' The *Post-Intelligencer* reprised its earlier cartoon, but this time the red flag was in tatters while the Stars and Stripes still flew proudly. Hanson found himself promoted as a national hero – though to liberals he remained 'the Seattle Clown' – and shortly afterwards he resigned as mayor to tour the country giving lectures on the dangers of Bolshevism, and earning $38,000 in the first seven months. His salary as mayor had been $7,500 a year. The 35,000 shipyard workers who had started the whole thing stayed out on strike, having gained nothing.

The Seattle general strike had been an industrial dispute based on the usual industrial factors: wages, hours and the right of workers to collective bargaining. But in the climate of the times it had become a symbol of political revolt and impending revolution. On the day the strike ended, two special agents of the Justice Department's Bureau of Investigation, forerunner of the FBI, raided the IWW's Propaganda

Committee, confiscated two large boxes of literature, together with the records, minute books and correspondence, and took the acting secretary, James J. Exstel, in for questioning. The following day, they raided the IWW Defense Committee and arrested twenty-six members, turning the aliens over to the immigration authorities for possible deportation and the US citizens to the local police for prosecution under the Washington Criminal Anarchy Law.[27]

The Bureau had waited until the strike was over, knowing that any federal action was bound to make the workers dig in their heels, and that the strike was about to fail anyway. But the agents had been watching the Wobblies on the West Coast since 1915, as indeed had various local authorities and other federal agencies. During the war, the Justice Department had been forced to send a special assistant, Clarence L. Reames, to stop a wave of illegal arrests of radicals by local authorities and patriotic groups, but he had then joined the Bureau of Immigration and local businessmen in planning the detention of some 3–5,000 suspected alien IWW members in internment camps for future deportation. One hundred and fifty had already been arrested when the Secretary of Labor vetoed the scheme and ordered their release.[28]

Immigration officials stepped up their active investigation of IWW and other radical elements in Seattle in November 1918, when the first rumblings of the discontent that led to the general strike were felt. Reames reported that shipyard workers were dissatisfied with the basic national wage of $6.40 a day, and drew attention to what he described as the growing Bolshevik or revolutionary propaganda being distributed in the city. He asked for a force of special agents to be dispatched to check out whether the situation was developing into a seditious conspiracy. The Bureau chief, A. Bruce Bielaski, ordered the Seattle office to keep him informed, since he had also received disquieting reports from the Office of Naval Intelligence on IWW and Bolshevik activities.

From then on, Bielaski received a steady stream of information on the Red menace from the Bureau's Seattle office. Unfortunately, most of it came from members of patriotic societies like the American Protection League and the Minutemen, financed by local business interests, and agents of the Pinkerton Detective Agency, employed by those same interests. The Pinkerton men, who were regularly used as strikebreakers by the employers, had infiltrated the IWW, the shipyards and the Central Labor Council. Since they were never averse to acting as agents provocateurs, their reports were at best highly suspect. The wildly exaggerated reports from both sources, taking radical dreams at face value, fed the growing hysteria in official circles, helping to spark a great rash of apocalyptic predictions by politicians and the press.

In Washington DC, Vice President Thomas R. Marshall denounced foreign radicals as 'anarchists and wild-eyed theorists', and went on: 'If I had my way all such who have naturalisation papers would be deprived of them and all others would be driven from the country.'[29] Senator Knute Nelson of Minnesota stated that 'the strike posed greater danger to the nation than the war against Germany', Senator William King of Utah declared that its instigators were all confirmed Bolsheviki, and Washington's own Representative Albert Johnson climbed on the bandwagon with the cry: 'From Russia they came and to Russia they should be made to go.'

As the general strike call went out in Seattle, the senators were given fresh cause for anxiety by a radical meeting held in the Poli Theatre, almost in the shadow of the Capitol itself in Washington DC, on the afternoon of Sunday 2 February, followed by another meeting in the old Masonic Temple the next evening. The chief speaker at these meetings was Albert Rhys Williams, a writer and former Congregationalist minister recently returned from Russia, who told his audience: 'America sooner or later is going to accept the Soviet Government, and when America discards some of the ideas current in the papers it will find it not so hard to swallow.'

The press, naturally, reacted furiously to the implied slur, and so did the senators. According to the *Washington Post*, 'indignation in the Senate reached the boiling point over the "red" meetings . . . resulting in the unanimous adoption of a resolution, introduced by Senator Walsh of Montana, extending the scope of the Overman subcommittee of the Senate Judiciary Committee investigating German propaganda, and ordering a sweeping investigation into the Bolshevik propaganda'.[30]

Wasting no time, the committee, headed by Senator Lee Overman of North Carolina, began its hearings on 11 February, the day the strike collapsed, and continued them for a month until 10 March. Its first, subpoenaed witness was Rhys Williams. It then took testimony from some twenty-four other witnesses, two-thirds of whom were violently anti-Bolshevik, providing an eager press with a wealth of lurid and often entirely unsubstantiated horror stories about life in Soviet Russia during and after the Bolshevik Revolution. It also took evidence from US Army Intelligence officers detailing a vast network of subversive intellectuals including many distinguished professors in American universities and colleges. When its final 1,200-page report was published, the press really went to town with sensational headlines: 'RED PERIL HERE', 'PLAN BLOODY REVOLUTION' and 'WANT WASHINGTON GOVERNMENT OVERTURNED'.[31] For the American public, the Red Scare had been given the official approval of the US Congress. It was set to run and run.

In line with the Overman Committee's inquiries, Representative John L. Burnett of Alabama introduced a bill to ban virtually all immigration for four years. 'The time has come,' he said, 'when we should begin cleaning house in the United States. The people are in the right temper for it, and it can be done more easily and thoroughly now than ever before.' Although the AFL unions endorsed the bill, the *Los Angeles Times* demurred, posing the question that has echoed down the years: who else but the aliens, it asked, would do the 'hard grueling, rough, dirty, back-breaking work that is especially repugnant to the American notion of living'?[32]

# IV

## 'I HAVE SEEN THE FUTURE, AND IT WORKS'

IN mid February, having scored a personal triumph in Paris by persuading delegates from twenty-seven countries to endorse his proposal for a League of Nations as an integral part of the Peace Treaty, President Wilson was preparing to sail home for a brief visit. In the meantime, however, he was waiting for a reply from the Soviet government and the White Russians to an invitation to peace talks, acceptance of which would be an equally noteworthy achievement. While his country was convulsed with fear of the Red menace, Wilson, with the support of Lloyd George, had made several attempts to come to terms with the Russian Bolsheviks, offering them food and other much-needed relief supplies in return for promises of good behaviour. When, at the insistence of the French and Italian Foreign Ministers, the Council of Four heard lurid eyewitness reports of the Red Terror from the French and Danish ambassadors who had just returned from Russia, he and Lloyd George dismissed them out of hand as exaggerations.

Wilson had sent an American diplomat from the London Embassy, William Buckler, to Stockholm in January, to talk to the Soviet Deputy Foreign Commissar, Maxim Litvinov. Buckler had returned with an encouraging report saying, among other things, that the Soviet government was ready to drop its calls for worldwide revolution and the use of terror. Litvinov had claimed that all his government wanted was peace in which to build a better society, but that the blockade and Allied intervention in the civil war were preventing this.

Clemenceau had refused to contemplate inviting the Bolsheviks to Paris for talks – in fact, he would not even allow the invitation to be sent over French telegraph lines.[1] So Lloyd George, ever the wily politi-cian, had suggested holding them in a distant location equally conven-ient for the Russians and the Allies: the Turkish islands of Prinkipo, 'Princes' Islands', just off Constantinople. This would allow the Allies to talk to the various Russian factions, including the Bolsheviks, without compromising the French premier's principles. Clemenceau was not alone in his attitude to the Soviets: Orlando and the Italians were equally adamant, and Churchill spoke for many in Britain when he told Lloyd George, 'One might as well legalise sodomy as recognise the Bolsheviks.'[2] Churchill and Clemenceau need not have worried – the Soviets demanded conditions and concessions that both Wilson and Lloyd George described as insulting, and any lingering hopes that the Prinkipo proposal could be salvaged in some form were swept away on 16 February, when the White Russians, who had been quietly incited by the French and by Churchill and his associates, finally sent their refusal.

With the Prinkipo talks abandoned, the whole Russian question remained in the air: were the Allies at war with the Soviets or not? Should they step up their half-hearted intervention in the civil war, or withdraw and leave the Russians to it? To Churchill, both as Secretary of State for War and as an individual, the answer was important and urgent. As the grandson of one of England's premier dukes, there was no doubting where he stood as an individual; but as a minister he was responsible for the army and needed a clear decision one way or the other, something that Lloyd George avoided making, knowing that whichever way he chose would cause him trouble. He told Churchill that any decision could only be made in Paris, with the personal involve-ment of President Wilson.

Realising that the President was leaving for America the next day, Churchill and General Sir Henry Wilson made a madcap dash to Paris on 14 February to catch him before he left. They crossed the Channel at full steam on the destroyer HMS *Plucky*, then drove from Dieppe to Paris non-stop – apart from an accident that left Wilson's car with a shattered windscreen and a broken steering wheel – arriving cold, wet and weary at 3 p.m. Three and a half hours later Churchill faced an emergency meeting of the Supreme Council, to try to persuade it to make a firm decision. 'Great Britain,' he said, 'had soldiers in Russia who were being killed in action. Their families wished to know what purpose these men were serving. Were they just marking time until the Allies had decided on a policy, or were they fighting in a campaign representing some common aim?' He went on to stress the problems the uncertainty was causing among the White Russian troops, who were 'weakening and quavering' and infecting the Allied troops who were 'intermingled with them'.

President Wilson agreed that the Allied troops 'were doing no sort of good in Russia. They did not know for whom or for what they were fighting.' He believed, therefore, that 'the Allied and Associated Powers ought to withdraw their troops from all parts of Russian territory'. But these, he hedged, were purely his personal thoughts. Churchill conceded that withdrawal was at least 'a logical and clear policy', but said that he feared that the consequences would be like 'pulling out the linch-pin from the whole machine. There would be no further armed resistance to the Bolsheviks in Russia, and an interminable vista of violence and misery was all that remained for the whole of Russia.'

Churchill's florid phraseology failed to move Wilson. The existing Allied forces, the President pointed out, were not capable of stopping the Bolsheviks, but none of the Allies were prepared to send reinforcements. And when Churchill, backed by Italian Foreign Minister Baron Sonnino, suggested they might send 'volunteers, technical experts, arms, munitions, tanks, aeroplanes, etc', Wilson hedged again, warning that 'in some areas they would certainly be assisting reactionaries'. The best Churchill could get out of him was that he would go along with whatever the rest of the council decided. And with that, Wilson left to board his train for Cherbourg, where the USS *George Washington* was waiting to carry him back across the Atlantic to face a hostile Congress.[3]

During the voyage, Wilson was briefed by Ambassador David Francis, returning home after his tour of duty as envoy to Russia, who gave him full details of the chaotic situation there, and of the 'reign of terror instigated by the Bolsheviki'. Like so many Americans, Francis still related the Bolshevik threat to Germany. 'I think it is impossible to restore peace in Europe with chaos prevailing in Russia,' he told the President. 'In fact, with Germany practically uninjured industrially, I am persuaded that if peace is negotiated with Bolshevik rule continuing in Russia, Germany in twenty years will be stronger than she was at the beginning of the war.'

Wilson chose to land at Boston, partly because he had never made an official visit to the city since taking office, and partly because it was the home base of Senator Henry Cabot Lodge, the most obdurate opponent of his League of Nations, who was to chair the Senate Foreign Relations Committee when the new Congress convened. When he finally landed on 24 February, he was greeted with wild enthusiasm by half a million people who had been given a public holiday for the event. But the packed streets were lined shoulder to shoulder by rows of federal and state troops, supported by nine hundred police, while sharpshooters with high-powered rifles were in position on the roofs of high buildings and other vantage points, in a security operation that was at that time unprecedented in American history.

A short while earlier, an undercover agent of the Justice Department had claimed to have uncovered a conspiracy whereby two radicals from each major city in America were to meet in New York for a murder conference, at which they would draw lots to decide which of them would assassinate the President in Boston.[4] The day before Wilson's arrival, a force of Secret Service agents, with the help of New York City detectives and police bomb squad operatives, raided premises at 1722 Lexington Avenue in New York, arrested fourteen Spanish Wobblies and seized quantities of seditious literature – or so they supposed, since it was in Spanish, which they couldn't understand. They also discovered the parts of a complicated machine, which they suspected was for making bombs.[5] At the same time, ten more Spaniards and Cubans were arrested in another raid in Philadelphia, where memories of the new year bomb outrages were still fresh. The men, most of whom turned out to be cigar-makers, were held without bail during a long investigation. No bombs were ever discovered, but the fear of Bolshevism continued to grow.

Churchill stayed on in Paris when Wilson left, trying to get the rest of the council to give him a straight answer, but in the absence of Wilson and Lloyd George, and the Italian premier, Orlando, who had hurried back to Rome to deal with another of his country's recurrent Cabinet crises, it was a hopeless task. It was made even more impossible by the machinations of Lloyd George, operating through his secretary Philip Kerr, the future Lord Lothian, British Ambassador to the United States in 1939–40. Kerr remained in Paris, telegraphing daily reports to the Prime Minister in London and circulating his responses to other members of the British Empire delegation and, to Churchill's fury, to Colonel House, who reported them by wire to Wilson.

Preoccupied with the industrial turmoil in Britain, Lloyd George was playing a cautious game. 'Winston is in Paris,' he told the newspaper magnate Lord Riddell, with whom he was spending the weekend. 'He wants to conduct a war against the Bolsheviks. That *would* cause a revolution. Our people would not permit it.'[6] To Churchill, he telegraphed that the War Office – Churchill's own department – felt that the presence of British soldiers in Russia was a mistake, and that he agreed with this assessment. 'If Russia is pro-Bolshevik,' he wrote, 'not merely is it none of our business to interfere with its internal affairs, it would positively be mischievous; it would strengthen and consolidate Bolshevik opinion. An expensive war of aggression against Russia is a way to strengthen Bolshevism in Russia and create it at home . . . [it] is the road to bankruptcy and Bolshevism in these islands . . . Were it known that you had gone over to Paris to prepare a plan of war against the Bolsheviks it would do more to incense organised labour than anything I could think of; and what is still worse, it would throw into the ranks of the extremists a very large number of people who now abhor their methods.'[7] Wilson concurred from mid-Atlantic: 'Greatly surprised by Churchill's Russian suggestion,' he radioed. 'It would be fatal to be led further into the Russian chaos.'

Despite mounting personal friction with Lloyd George, who wanted to go on sitting on the fence as long as possible, Churchill persisted in trying to get a straight answer to his question: what were they to do, 'fight or quit; get on or get out'? The next meeting of the council on 19 February was due to discuss the problem, and hopefully even resolve it. But that morning, shortly after leaving his home to drive to the meeting, Clemenceau was shot by a young man named Emile Cottin, who leapt out from behind a cast-iron *pissoir* and fired nine shots at the Tiger's car from a Browning automatic pistol. All but one of the bullets either missed or were absorbed by the thick upholstery, but one found its mark in Clemenceau's back, penetrating his left shoulder blade and lodging near vital organs. The old man – he was seventy-seven – tried to pass it off as not serious, and indeed it had caused little real damage. But the doctors decided that because of his age and the location of the bullet it would be safer to leave it where it was, and ordered him to rest for ten days.

Everyone automatically assumed that Cottin was a Bolshevik (though in fact he was an anarchist, acting alone). On hearing the news in London, Lloyd George immediately wired Kerr that it meant Prinkipo was definitely off, as it was now 'quite impossible' to deal with the

Bolsheviks. They would have to consider alternatives. He said he now agreed with Churchill, who had just spoken at a Mansion House luncheon saying that 'If Russia is to be saved, as I pray she may be saved, she must be saved by Russians'. Recognising that it was time to abandon his hopes of sending an army, Churchill fell back on the next best thing. Britain, he said, could help smash the 'foul baboonery of Bolshevism' by sending munitions and volunteers.[8]

Any decision about Russia by the Supreme Council was postponed indefinitely, but the American government had already announced that it would withdraw its troops from north Russia. Two weeks later the British Cabinet followed suit, deciding to pull out of north Russia, the Caucasus and Siberia, but to increase its missions to the White Russian forces under General Anton Denikin in south Russia and Admiral Alexander Kolchak on the Urals front, both of whom were scoring notable victories against the Red Army. There was news from the Baltic, too, that was both heartening and disturbing: a force of 12,000 German troops and Freikorps volunteers under Count Rüdiger von der Goltz, a Prussian major general who had aided the Finns in defeating the Bolsheviks a year earlier, had begun driving the Bolsheviks out of western Latvia. The good news was that this was a significant setback for Lenin's plans to dominate the region. The bad news was that Goltz had his own agenda, and it did not include complete independence for the Baltic States.

The day after the Prinkipo plan was finally abandoned, Colonel House briefed a young Russian expert in the American delegation, the twenty-eight-year-old William C. Bullitt, to visit Moscow on a fact-finding mission. Bullitt, a brilliant young Philadelphia socialite who has been compared by some to the Great Gatsby, had been fascinated by Russia for some time, and despite his patrician background was sympathetic to the Bolsheviks. 'Trotsky,' he had written to House in February 1918, 'is the kind of man we need to have in power in Russia.' He urged the recognition of the Soviet government and suggested that the United States should send an envoy to Moscow, 'to see what the Bolsheviki are about'. Now, it seemed, he was to be that envoy.

Because of his patrician background, Bullitt had inflated ideas of his own worth, and tried to imbue his mission with greater significance, claiming that House, on behalf of Wilson, and Lloyd George's secretary Philip Kerr, on behalf of the British Premier, had charged him with negotiating armistice terms with the Bolsheviks. It is worth noting that neither Wilson nor Lloyd George were in Paris at the time. In Wilson's absence, his Secretary of State, Robert Lansing, was in charge of the American delegation. He noted in his diary on 16 February that on that day he had 'talked with House about sending Bullitt to Russia to cure him of Bolshevism';[9] he then wrote to Bullitt: 'You are hereby instructed to proceed to Russia for the purpose of studying conditions political and economic, therein, for the benefit of American commissioners plenipotentiary to the peace.'[10]

Bullitt set off on 22 February, taking with him three other Americans: the radical journalist Lincoln Steffens; a naval secretary, R.E. Lynch; and a military intelligence officer and Russian expert, Captain W.W. Pettit. Lynch only travelled as far as Helsinki, Pettit got no further than Petrograd. So Bullitt was finally accompanied to Moscow only by Steffens, whose starry-eyed attitude to the Soviet regime was summed up in his memorable statement: 'I have seen the future, and it works.' The only problem with this was that he wrote it on the journey out, before he had seen anything of the present, let alone the future.

The two men had a wonderful week in Moscow, staying in a former palace, eating caviar and watching the opera from the Tsar's box. They talked to the Foreign Commissar, Chicherin, and to Lenin himself, with whom they were mightily impressed, and by the end of the week Bullitt thought he had a deal. The Russian proposals, which added little to those made by Chicherin in response to the Prinkipo invitation, called for an immediate armistice between the various regimes fighting on Russian territory, the withdrawal of all Allied forces and the ending of the blockade. Bullitt bore them proudly back to Paris, proclaiming optimistically: 'The Red Terror is over!' He was shattered to find that nobody wanted to know. Wilson, newly returned from America and suffering from debilitating headaches, said he was simply too busy to see him. Lloyd George did agree to have breakfast with him, but explained that he was under too much pressure at home to consider the report: the press had got wind of Bullitt's mission, and had presented it as proof that the British and American governments were about to recognise the terrorist Bolshevik regime. The climate of fear was not eased by news of a Bolshevik *coup d'état* in Hungary the previous weekend. And to cap it all, the latest news from the civil war seemed to indicate that the Whites were about to secure a final victory, making any deal with the Reds totally unnecessary.

Bullitt smarted at this slight for six weeks before resigning when the published terms of the German treaty completed his disillusionment with Wilson. After a stay on the French Riviera, 'to lie on the sand and watch the world go to hell', he returned to the United States and testified to the Senate, bitterly attacking the Treaty of Versailles, and managing to get his Moscow report into the record. Ironically, when the United States did finally recognise the USSR, as it had then become, in 1934, Bullitt was chosen as the first US Ambassador. By the time he left Moscow again at the end of his term, he had become a fervid opponent of Communism in all its forms: Lansing's idea of sending him to Russia to cure him of Bolshevism had finally worked.

At the beginning of 1919, Marshal Foch, the Allied Commander-in-Chief in France, had begun seriously exploring the possibility of sending large numbers of American troops to Poland, to ward off Russian advances into the eastern frontier area, known as the 'Ober-Ost' (short for the German Oberkommando-Ostfront, High Command Eastern Front), a 1,500-mile-long strip of heavily fortified territory snaking down from the Gulf of Bothnia in the north to the Sea of Azov in the south, which had been formerly occupied by the Germans. On 25 February, Foch produced a vast scheme stretching from the Rhine to Vladivostok, in which preliminary peace terms would be imposed on Germany without more ado, to be followed by an immediate crusade in which Finns, Poles, Czechs, Romanians and Greeks would be sent to fight against the Bolsheviks alongside the Allies and the White Russians. 'If this were done,' he proclaimed, '1919 would see the end of Bolshevism, just as 1918 had seen the end of Prussianism.'[11]

The Bolsheviks saw Poland as the 'Red Bridge', across which they would carry the revolution to Germany and the West, believing the revolution in Russia could not survive unless it was joined by revolutions in Lithuania, Poland and, essentially, Germany. In 1919, as far as the Soviet Russians were concerned, the question was not whether the Polish bridge should be crossed but how and when. In the event, 'how' became the overriding question, a problem that could only be solved by force.

For more than 120 years, Poland had been partitioned between Russia, Prussia and Austria. During the world war the Germans had pushed the Russians back, and occupied the tsarist Kingdom of Poland. They were still there on 11 November 1918, when the Poles disarmed German troops on the streets of Warsaw, and declared themselves an independent republic. As their new head of state and commander-in-chief, they chose Marshal Josef Piłsudski, newly released from German imprisonment in Magdeburg Castle and escorted back to Warsaw by none other than Count Harry Kessler, who had been appointed Germany's first diplomatic representative to the new nation. Sadly, Kessler's mission was short-lived: the antagonism of the Poles to Germany was so great he was forced to close the legation and return to Berlin in less than a month.

Having seen the Germans defeated and about to be expelled from his country, Piłsudski had no intention of allowing them to be replaced by Russians of any colour. As the Germans withdrew from the Ober-Ost, which was now the border region between Russia and Poland, both countries rushed to fill the vacuum with their own troops. The inevitable clash came in Belorussia at 6 a.m. on 14 February 1919, when a Polish cavalry patrol disturbed a Bolshevik encampment at breakfast. An hour later, a Polish detachment of fifty-seven men and five officers rode into the nearby small town of Bereza Kartuska and found it occupied by the Bolsheviks. There was a short, sharp engagement in which eighty Red Army soldiers were taken prisoner. The Polish–Soviet War had begun.[12] It was to smoulder and flare intermittently for the rest of the year, involving Lithuanians, Latvians, Ukrainians and Belorussians as well as Russians and Poles, until it burst into full flame in April 1920.

In the meantime, however, Poland was still faced with internal problems. At the beginning of March, the city council in Cracow was forced to appeal to Warsaw for aid in fighting Bolshevism. Workers' and soldiers' councils were established in Cracow, there were demonstrations in Lublin, and Bolshevik troops were advancing through Galicia.[13]

In Germany, Friedrich Ebert convened his National Assembly in Weimar on 6 February, in the Court Theatre where the plays of Goethe and Schiller had first been performed and where Franz Liszt had conducted the premiere of Wagner's *Lohengrin*. The auditorium had been transformed into a passable legislative chamber, with writing desks for the deputies – thirty-four of whom were women – and the old presidential chair from the Reichstag, complete with the imperial eagle emblem, set on a raised dais on the stage. The dress circle was reserved for local dignitaries, with the press and public accommodated in the upper circle and gallery. The stage was heaped with a mass of red, pink and white carnations and rows of lilies of the valley. According to *The Times,* the general effect was 'frankly rather like that of an English harvest thanksgiving service'.[14] To Harry Kessler, it looked 'quite cosily provincial and respectable' with its pale green silk and white decoration, but not very impressive. 'Danton or Bismarck,' he thought, 'would seem monstrous apparitions in these dainty surroundings.'[15]

The town itself was hermetically sealed by several divisions of infantry, backed by units of artillery and cavalry, and the streets were constantly patrolled by mounted troops. No one could enter without an official pass, or obtain a room or food or do virtually anything without one of a bewildering array of colour-coded cards. Morgan Philips Price, who had obtained a press permit to attend the opening session, found the atmosphere of the town 'more fitting for a literary and scientific congress than a political assembly at the greatest crisis in its history'.[16]

Ebert, dressed in a plain black frock coat, opened the proceedings with a claim for a 'Wilson peace' in response to Germany's having laid down her arms in reliance upon his Fourteen Points. 'We warn our opponents,' he said, 'not to drive us to the uttermost. Hunger is preferable to disgrace and deprivation is to be preferred to dishonour.'[17] He was duly elected President, and nominated Scheidemann as Chancellor and 'the Bloodhound' Noske as Defence Minister. It was all very low-key. Scheidemann's first speech as Chancellor gave Price 'the very worst impression. The whole spirit of his party and of the democrats supporting him is Prussian militarism dressed up with another sauce.'[18]

After interviewing various party leaders, Price soon wearied of Weimar, and headed off to the Ruhr, where things were very much more lively. The miners had been more or less permanently on strike since Christmas, when they had stopped work demanding better pay, shorter shifts and more food. The mine owners had offered some concessions, but then called in troops to break the strikes. Workers' and soldiers' councils had been set up throughout the Ruhr, and were dominated by left-wing Independent Socialists. In Essen, they occupied the Mine Owners' Association headquarters and announced the socialisation of the coal industry. This was denounced as illegal by the government in Berlin, at which the miners elected more councils and took over the mines. They elected a Commission of Nine to negotiate on their behalf with the government, which refused to recognise it and threatened to send in more troops. The miners promptly formed their own Red Army, and in February began fighting government troops and Freikorps units who were occupying the smaller mining towns.

At the same time, a delegate conference at Mülheim proclaimed a general strike with the support of more than half the Ruhr miners and many workers in other industries. The strike soon collapsed, but fighting continued. When the government troops ignored an agreement by both sides to withdraw to specified points, the miners' leaders called a new general strike, with support increased to 25 per cent. Martial law was declared in most Ruhr cities, and the miners' leaders were either arrested or forced into hiding. Nevertheless, the strike continued until the last week in April before it finally collapsed, after vicious attacks by the Freikorps which left a legacy of great bitterness in the Ruhr for decades.

While the miners in the Ruhr were striking and fighting, there were more upheavals further south in Bavaria, sending fresh shivers through the West, and the rest of Germany. Despite receiving only a humiliating 3 per cent of the vote in the elections of 12 January and losing his own seat into the bargain, Kurt Eisner had clung to power, refusing to resign as Prime Minister on the grounds that he was still chairman of the Council of Soldiers, Workers and Peasants, which saw itself as the true government. His intransigence increased his unpopularity on all sides. Everyone had a reason to hate him – they said he was a Galician Jew, a Berliner, a café intellectual, a left-wing Socialist, a betrayer of true Socialism, too radical, not radical enough, he was ineffectual and incompetent, the list seemed endless. Above all, he was blamed for the collapse of the economy – Bavaria was virtually bankrupt, suffering like so many other places from a huge loss of jobs as munitions production ceased and soldiers were demobilised, and yet he had vastly increased spending on unemployment benefits.

Eisner finally managed to infuriate just about everybody in Bavaria when he attended the first post-war conference of the Second Socialist International in Berne. As the only head of government there, he was held in great respect and listened to with some reverence, particularly when he publicly acknowledged German responsibility for the Great War and named Wilhelm Hohenzollern, the former Kaiser, as the one man most to blame for four and a half years of carnage. Speaking calmly and quietly, he lambasted all aspects of Prussianism, condemned Germany's harsh treatment of French civilians and Allied prisoners of war, and appealed to German prisoners to help rebuild the devastated regions of France and Belgium. All this was well received by the comrades in Berne, but in Munich it was regarded as treason, and he was branded a traitor. 'Eisner is the most cursed man in Germany,' his close friend the radical poet Gustav Landauer admitted,[19] and there were few Bavarians who disagreed with him. In Eisner's absence, his great rival Erhard Auer seized the initiative and announced that the Landtag would reconvene on 21 February. Eisner would have to resign then, if he had not already done so. As he left Berne the day after his speech, to face his critics at home, a friend congratulated him on his courage in speaking out. 'In nine days' time, I shall be finished,' he replied with great sadness.[20]

Back in Munich, Eisner immediately caused more confusion by joining a mass demonstration on the Theresienwiese, followed by a march through the streets of the old city, which was ostensibly against the policies of his own regime. Estimates of the number of people involved were as confused as the purpose of the demonstration, which included supporters and opponents of both parliamentary government and the councils system: according to the *Neue Zeitung* there were 150,000 marchers, while the *Münchener Post* put the figure at a modest 9,000. Some demonstrators carried placards saying 'Against Bolshevism' and 'For the Landtag', others waved banners reading 'Long Live the Council System'. Prime Minister Eisner and his wife posed for a photograph in the middle of a group holding up a large sign reading 'Reaction is on the march! Up with the Council System!'[21]

The confusion was only increased on 19 February, when a force of six hundred sailors arrived from Wilhelmshaven, apparently at the request of the Social Democrat Minister for Military Affairs, Albert Rosshaupter. They arrested the Security Service chief and the Chief of Police, and occupied the main railway station and the central telegraph office, then forced their way into the Landtag building, where two separate and contradictory meetings were taking place: in one wing, the Congress of Councils was passing a resolution demanding its integration in the constitution; in another, a conference of Social Democrats was deciding that the councils should be deprived of all power. The natural assumption was that the sailors were there to support the councils, as they had done throughout Germany in November. But in the topsy-turvy world of 1919 Munich, it turned out that they were calling themselves 'the Committee for the Protection of the Landtag' – against the councils. When the Social Democrat ministers denied all knowledge of any such committee and insisted that they leave, the sailors meekly complied, announced that their action had been 'an error', and promptly disappeared.[22]

In a final speech to the last session of the Congress of Councils, Eisner said that what he called 'the sailors' putsch' showed once again that the revolution was constantly threatened by militarism and by compromises with the bourgeoisie, in the form of the Landtag. So, he said, the councils must continue to press for the goals of Socialism and the aims of the revolution. But, he went on, propounding his romantic vision:

The second revolution will not be plundering and street fighting. The new revolution is the assembling of the masses in city and countryside to carry out what the first revolution has started . . . The bourgeois majority is now to implement bourgeois policies. We shall see whether they are capable of ruling. In the meantime, the Councils should do their job: to build the new democracy. Then perhaps the new spirit will also arrive in Bavaria . . .

Tomorrow the Landtag begins – tomorrow the activities of the Councils should also begin anew. Then we shall see where are to be found the force and vitality of a society consecrated by death.[23]

With only hours to go before the new Landtag, Eisner finally accepted the Cabinet's ultimatum that he must go. On the morning of 21 February he wrote his resignation speech in his office at the Foreign Ministry, then dismissed his secretarial staff and set off on foot for the opening session, accompanied by two aides and two armed guards. Typically, he refused to take a different route from his regular one, dismissing his aides' concerns for his safety with a blithe: 'They can only shoot me dead once.' As he turned the corner into the Promenadestrasse, a young man in a trench coat ran up behind him, pulled out a pistol and shot him at point-blank range in the head and back. The first shot smashed his skull, the second pierced a lung. He fell to the ground dead, amid a spreading pool of blood.

Eisner's assassin was Count Anton Arco-Valley, an aristocrat who had served as a lieutenant in the Bavarian cavalry during the war, and who had, like most returning officers in Munich, suffered the indignity of having his badges of rank torn from his uniform by revolutionaries in the street. His exact reason for killing Eisner was never made clear: he was filled with bitterness at being rejected for membership of the ultra-right Thule Society because his mother was Jewish, his girlfriend had taunted him as a weakling, and he hated the revolution. But why he should have chosen to kill Eisner, at the precise moment when he was stepping down, remains a mystery. Having fired his shots, he turned to run, but was belatedly shot down by one of Eisner's bodyguards, who then pumped four more bullets into him as he lay on the pavement. He was not dead, however, when soldiers carried him to hospital, where Germany's most eminent surgeon, Professor Ernst Sauerbruch, operated on him and saved his life.

Eisner, of course, was beyond help. His aides carried his body back to the Foreign Ministry, while one of his guards rushed to the Landtag to tell the delegates what had happened, holding up Eisner's bloodied spectacles as proof. In the shocked silence after his announcement, someone in the public gallery shouted: 'Revenge for Eisner! Down with Auer!' The session was adjourned for an hour, after which Auer delivered a short eulogy in praise of his dead opponent. Eisner, he said, choosing his words carefully, had been 'a man of the most unsullied idealism'. He was in the middle of condemning Eisner's murder when a member of the Revolutionary Workers' Council, a butcher named Alois Lindner, burst into the chamber, pulled a Browning rifle from under his coat and shot him at close range. Lindner then walked calmly back towards the door, shooting at the benches of the bourgeois BVP, the Bavarian People's Party, as he went. When a guard tried to disarm him he shot him dead, and escaped. Meanwhile, an unidentified man in the public gallery also pulled out a gun and began firing at the deputies, killing one BVP member and wounding others, while deputies dived for cover under their seats, or tried to escape from the building on their hands and knees. Auer's wounds were serious, but his life was saved by the same Professor Sauerbruch who had just operated on Count Arco-Valley. He survived, but was unable to return to public life for several years.

From being reviled and derided on all sides, Eisner suddenly became a martyr. Sobbing proletarian women knelt on the pavement where he had fallen, soaking their handkerchiefs in his blood. Shortly afterwards his followers erected a bizarre shrine there, consisting of a dozen rifles stacked like a tepee over a pile of flowers and with a picture of the dead man hanging on a wire in the middle. A sign was erected saying: 'Proletarians! Hats off before the blood of Kurt Eisner.' But not everyone approved: a member of the Thule Society sprinkled the shrine with the

1. Setting the world on fire: Vladimir Lenin preaches the doctrine of Bolshevism, while Leon Trotsky (*right*) gauges the reaction of the crowd in Sverdlov Square, Moscow.

2.–3. Germany's Bolshevik martyrs, Karl Liebknecht and Rosa Luxemburg, founders of the Spartacus League, brutally murdered for trying to import Lenin's revolution.

4. Luxemburg and Liebknecht's killers were photographed next day, showing no shame. Runge, who clubbed them with his rifle butt, sits centre, with moustache.

5. Friedrich Ebert, a former saddler who became the first president of the German Republic, struggled to impose order on a turbulent nation.

6. Philipp Scheidemann, former minister of finance, proclaimed the republic almost by accident, and became its first chancellor.

7. Demonstrators, here seen marching on the Reich Chancellery in the New Year, regularly packed the streets of Berlin during 1919.

8. Other scenes in the city were less peaceful, as street battles raged between government troops and Spartacist revolutionaries.

9. Steel helmets, Homburg hats and sailors' caps signified the broad range of Spartacist supporters, seen here manning a machine gun behind a makeshift barricade in the newspaper district.

10. The Royal Palace, including the famous balcony from which the Kaiser announced the outbreak of the world war and Liebknecht tried to proclaim a Red republic, suffered severe damage in the January uprising.

11. Mutinous British soldiers, refusing to go to Russia or back to France, descended on the government in Whitehall, demanding immediate demobilisation.

12. Bavaria's unworldly left-wing minister-president, Kurt Eisner (*left*), with his SPD rival, Erhard Auer. Shortly afterwards, Eisner was assassinated on the street and Auer narrowly escaped with his life after being shot in the Bavarian Landesrat.

3. (*Above right*) Revolutionary troops guard their improvised shrine at the spot where Eisner was gunned down in Munich.

14. Hungarian Communist leader Béla Kun (*right*), seen here strolling happily in Budapest with two fellow members of the ruling council, Joseph Pogany and Sigismund Kanh, achieved power peacefully. But he needed Red Terror to hold on to it, and was soon ousted by reactionary White forces.

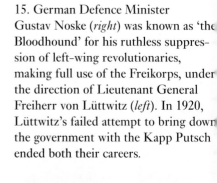

15. German Defence Minister Gustav Noske (*right*) was known as 'the Bloodhound' for his ruthless suppression of left-wing revolutionaries, making full use of the Freikorps, under the direction of Lieutenant General Freiherr von Lüttwitz (*left*). In 1920, Lüttwitz's failed attempt to bring down the government with the Kapp Putsch ended both their careers.

16. The staunch traditionalists of the Bavarian Freikorps, seen here marching into Munich with flowers in their hats, were mainly responsible for driving out the Communists of the *Räterepublik* in bitter fighting.

17. The 'Big Three', British Prime Minster David Lloyd George, French Prime Minister Georges Clemenceau and US President Woodrow Wilson, were in jubilant mood as they approached the Palace of Versailles for the signing of the Peace Treaty with Germany.

18. Herbert Hoover, seen here supervising the shipping of relief supplies from the Bush Docks in Brooklyn, New York, organised a massive operation to deliver American food to the starving millions in post-war Europe. He later became the 31st president of the United States.

19. Posing here for a presidential campaign that never happened, US Attorney General A. Mitchell Palmer presented himself as America's saviour – but only succeeded in fuelling the Great Red Scare and ultimately losing all credibility.

20. Although essentially a desk-bound filing clerk, Palmer's special assistant, J. Edgar Hoover, liked to picture himself as the nation's chief protector against 'Commonists'. Setting up the General Intelligence Department, he swiftly compiled a card index of 200,000 suspected radicals, before going on to head the FBI.

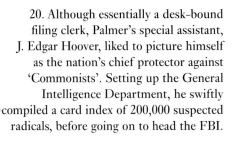

21. Britain's constant worries about Communi[st] incursion into India led [to] the Third Anglo–Afgha[n] War, and the closure of the Khyber Pass frontie[r]

22. German troops, see[n] here guarding a pile of frozen Bolshevik bodies in north-west Russia, were heavily involved in the fighting around the Baltic states.

23. One of the high-speed forty-foot coastal motor boats of the Royal Navy, which sank a battleshi[p], a heavy cruiser and a submarine depot ship in the heavily fortified Soviet naval base at Kronstad[t]

urine of a bitch on heat, attracting all the male dogs for miles around to lift their legs on the spot.

As news of the killing spread, the city stopped. With the Cabinet and the Landtag deputies scattered in panic, the councils reigned unopposed, moving immediately to take on the task of trying to restore order from the chaos into which Eisner's death had plunged Munich. At an emergency general meeting, they declared martial law, ordered revolutionary troops to patrol the streets and set up machine-gun posts at strategic points, and issued warnings that anyone caught stealing or robbing would be shot immediately. They called a three-day general strike – which fell conveniently over the weekend – and imposed a 7 p.m. curfew. And they distributed placards announcing a council assembly for next morning, ending with the cry: 'Long live Eisner's legacy! Long live the second revolution! Long live the Soviet Republic!'

At the assembly, they formed a new body, the Zentralrat (Central Council), with eleven members drawn from all the various Socialist and council factions, both in the city and the countryside, which was intended to govern not only Munich but the whole of Bavaria. As chairman, and therefore the de facto Prime Minister of Bavaria, the Zentralrat elected Ernst Niekisch, a burly twenty-eight-year-old schoolteacher from Augsburg, capital of the province of Swabia and centre of Bavaria's depressed textile industry. On the face of it, Niekisch was a good choice, well suited to reconciling the various competing interests. He was a member of Auer's Social Democratic Party, albeit on its left wing, but was also chairman of the executive committee of the combined Bavarian Workers' Councils; as a Swabian from Augsburg he was not closely identified with either the capital or the countryside.

The first thing Niekisch did was to sit down with representatives of the councils, the free trade unions and the Socialist parties, and thrash out a programme of Socialist unity designed 'to preserve the successes of the revolution and to avoid fraternal and civil war'.[24] 'Preserving the successes of the revolution', like 'Eisner's legacy', was a suitably ambiguous phrase that was used a great deal in those hectic days to sanctify any possibly controversial decision. And virtually all the decisions made by Niekisch and his colleagues were controversial. The Landtag was to be recalled 'as soon as conditions permit'; at the same time the councils were to be incorporated into the constitution, with 'advisers' in every government ministry and their members enjoying the same legal immunity as parliamentary deputies. The standing army was to be disbanded and replaced by a Republican Security Force. Registered members of all the Socialist parties aged over twenty were to be supplied with arms from army stockpiles, so that they could serve in the 'Arbeiterwehr', the Workers' Defence Force, while bourgeois citizens were ordered to hand in any weapons they possessed. Munich University, which had strongly opposed Eisner, was closed down; so, too, were the leading bourgeois newspapers.

Perhaps the most controversial of the Zentralrat's immediate actions was the taking of fifty hostages from prominent bourgeois organisations, with a warning that three of them would be shot for every revolutionary that was harmed. Under a storm of protest from the BVP, and considerable pressure from the SPD, Niekisch managed to persuade his colleagues to back down and release the hostages, on condition that they remained in Munich. The Zentralrat also allowed the banned newspapers to resume publication, under a fairly indulgent censorship, but forced the Catholic *Bayerische Kurier* to publish atheistic articles, and the National Liberal *Münchener Neueste Nachrichten* to print Socialistic ones.

The Zentralrat also back-pedalled on the central issue of whether Bavaria should be ruled by a parliamentary government elected by general franchise or by a soviet-style council system. Instead of simply proclaiming a soviet republic, as voted for by a packed open meeting of the Munich Councils in the Deutsches Theater, the Zentralrat decided to convene a Congress of Bavarian Councils to debate the matter. When it opened on Tuesday 25 February, mobs of radical soldiers and unemployed workers gathered in two of Munich's biggest beer halls, then marched to the Landtag building to demand a soviet regime and a Red Army. Inside, Niekisch called the congress to order under a huge portrait of Eisner draped in red and black. He asked the delegates to rise as he paid tribute to 'this man, our Eisner', in typically vacuous words. 'I do not believe it necessary,' he intoned, 'to state explicitly what Comrade Eisner has meant for the proletariat . . . Now it is our duty to realise our responsibilities . . . and to help our people through these difficult hours. We can best do that when we set as our task the fulfilment of the legacy of the precious deceased.'[25]

The congress broke off the next day to honour Eisner with a funeral as grand as that of any Bavarian king. The casket was borne on a carriage from the royal collection, driven by a coachman wearing

Wittelsbach livery and followed on foot by the civic and state officials. Cannon salutes, muffled drums and clanging church bells, some tolled by priests at gunpoint, sounded as the procession moved through the old city past the town hall draped in black and churches flying red flags. Aircraft flew low overhead in salute, military bands played solemn dirges. In the cemetery chapel there were no prayers and no religious rites, but Eisner's friend Gustav Landauer gave a eulogy in which he compared him to Goethe, Jesus, Jan Hus and the Old Testament prophets. Like Jesus and Hus, he said, Eisner had been killed by stupidity and greed, and like the prophets he had 'wrestled with weak, wretched human beings because he loved humanity'.[26] The writer Heinrich Mann, no doubt to the fury of his conservative younger brother, Thomas, added his own encomium: 'The hundred days of Eisner's government brought more ideas, more joys of rationality, more intellectual stimulation, than the fifty years that went before.'

The congress resumed after the funeral, and worked on through the rest of the week against a background of shooting and demonstrations in the streets and interruptions and demands for a 'second revolution' in the chamber. When it decisively rejected a motion calling for a soviet republic, and voted equally decisively to recall the Landtag, with instructions to elect a new Cabinet and draw up a new constitution based on parliamentary principles, the Communists stormed out of the congress and withdrew from the Zentralrat – to the relief of the moderate members. Several thousand radicals staged an angry demonstration on the Theresienwiese, which was broken up by the new SPD militia, the Republican Security Force, killing three men. The congress was wound up and its members dispersed to their own towns and cities across Bavaria to consult their parties, almost all of which endorsed their decisions. For the moment everything was relatively calm.

While the revolutionary fires in Munich seemed to be damped down, the volatile situation in Germany as a whole was still worrying foreign observers. A British secret agent, code-named V.77, reported that the Spartacist organisation had much improved since the beginning of the year, and that funds were getting through to it from Russia. He said squads of unemployed workers were being trained as agitators and sent from one trouble centre to another to foment strikes; the Berlin garrison was honeycombed with disaffection, and the loyalty of some of the Freikorps was questionable. He claimed to have spoken to workers in cheap cafés and beer halls: 'In nine cases out of ten they say "We are not Spartacists, but if we don't get food very soon we'll smash everything up, plunder the rich, plunder the farmers, join the Russians and plunder Europe."' He went on to warn that 'Their temper is becoming more and more dangerous. If some light does not very soon pierce the gloom, it is absolutely certain that in the shortest possible time complete and universal anarchy will break out, every industrial centre will be destroyed, the rich will be robbed of everything they possess, and the state of Germany will be at least as bad as that of Russia.'[27]

The British Officers' Commission added to the doom and gloom with its report that although in their opinion the workers' and soldiers' councils offered the best hope for democracy, the Weimar Assembly seemed determined to smash them. 'Berlin,' they reported, 'was a fair representation of the mood of the people . . . Dirt, disorder, dancing and death. Once the cleanest city in the world, it is now filthy . . . Every dancing-hall in the city is filled to overflowing, and almost within sound of the orchestras Spartacists and government troops shoot each other down.'[28]

British apprehensions over Berlin were borne out when a second Spartacist revolt erupted at the beginning of March, the day after the last returning troops, 'the heroes from East Africa', paraded through the Brandenburg Gate in front of cheering crowds. The first draft of the new national constitution had been presented to the Weimar Assembly by its author, the Interior Minister Professor Hugo Preuss, on 24 February. It proposed a two-chamber parliamentary legislature under a strong president, but made no provision for the councils, or the socialisation of industry. To Spartacus and the Independent Socialists, this promised the dictatorship not of the proletariat but of the bourgeoisie. In protest, they joined Richard Müller, chairman of the Congress of Workers' and Soldiers' Councils, in calling a general strike aimed at bringing down the Ebert–Scheidemann government and replacing it with one controlled by the Independent Socialists, operating with the council system.

The strike began quietly on Monday 3 March, at first involving only the newspapers. The *Rote Fahne*, one of the few papers published that day, called on workers and party comrades to occupy their factories peacefully, and not to let themselves be 'drawn into pointless shooting'. The government tried to assert its democratic credentials by plastering walls all over the city with posters proclaiming 'Socialism is Here!' – but few workers agreed with this. According to Kessler, not only the extreme left but also 'a large part of the Majority Socialist workers' were rumoured to be against it. 'This could be the start of the second revolution,' he wrote in his diary[29] – but this may have been wishful thinking: at the time he was actively plotting a *coup d'état* with Foreign Minister Count Ulrich Brockdorff-Rantzau, the only government minister then in Berlin, to unseat Scheidemann and bring in the Independent Socialists. In Kessler's opinion, the council system was the only way to bring about Germany's economic reconstruction. Brockdorff-Rantzau, however, could not make up his mind whether it would be better for him to line up with the Independents at once, or wait for a month or six weeks and join the Spartacists and Russians. Both of these well-placed aristocrats seemed certain that the Reds would ultimately triumph.

During the morning, armed gangs took to the streets, plundering and looting stores around Alexanderplatz and exclusive apartment buildings at the Tiergarten, smashing nightclubs, gambling halls and expensive restaurants in the city centre. They were joined by sailors from the remnants of the People's Naval Division in the Royal Stables and over a thousand renegade soldiers from the Republican Security Guard – all of whom were seeking their pay – and very soon their numbers had grown to an estimated 15,000.

Anticipating trouble, the Prussian state government had already called in 'the Bloodhound', Gustav Noske, and put him in command of its armed forces, which meant mostly Freikorps units stationed around the outskirts of the city. His first move was to declare martial law, but this failed to deter the rebels. That night they stopped all the trams, occupied the main railway termini, and seized some thirty police stations, all without any significant violence. Next day, at a meeting at trade union headquarters, they spelled out their demands: recognition of the councils; the freeing of all political prisoners; the creation of a Red Army, in which, among other things, officers would be elected by the men; the disbanding of the Freikorps; and recognition of Soviet Russia.

The fighting finally broke out early on the Wednesday morning, when a detachment of Lieutenant General Freiherr von Lüttwitz's Freikorps, the men who had destroyed the *Vorwärts* building during the earlier uprising, clashed with troops from the Maybug barracks at the Halle Market. The battle quickly spread to Alexanderplatz, where it centred once again on the Police Presidium. Wilhelm Reinhardt's pro-government Freikorps unit housed in the battered building was besieged by a combination of

Republican Guards, sailors of the People's Naval Division, Maybug troops and various other armed groups. Both sides were equipped with artillery and mortars as well as small arms, but that did not stop sight-seers gathering behind a barrier erected by the Republican Guards to listen to the shooting – 'There is nothing to be seen,' wrote Kessler, who was, naturally, among them. But, he added, 'Bullets are whizzing across the Alexanderplatz and from time to time the dull thud of a mortar can be heard.' The 'fairly phlegmatic crowd', he noted, did not seem very enthusiastic. He was told that two officers from the Naval Division, one of them its commander, who had gone to the Presidium to negotiate, were shot dead by Reinhardt men as they were leaving.

The bizarre nature of the day's events was underlined when a force of Republican Guards marched down the nearby Unter den Linden with its band playing, past a unit of Reinhardt troops grouped around an armoured car with mounted machine guns. They passed each other without challenge. Even more bizarre were the posters that appeared on walls that day asking 'Who has the Prettiest Legs in Berlin? Caviar-Mousey-Ball. Evening 6 March.' The question was never answered, because at 6.30 p.m. all the lights went out – the power station workers had joined the strike. The Reinhardt troops extended the siege condi-tions to other parts of central Berlin, saying Spartacus forces were preparing to seize Potsdamer Platz. This, Kessler thought, indicated a much more serious civil war situation, 'a major operation instead of a guerrilla one'.[30] He was right. By next morning, there were 30,000 Freikorps troops in the city. They relieved the men in the Police Presidium, and ejected the sailors from the Royal Stables with the help of aircraft and heavy machine guns.

'The last two days have seen more bloodshed in Berlin than any since the start of the revolution,' Kessler noted. '. . . All the abomina-tions of a merciless civil war are being perpetrated on both sides. The hatred and bitterness being sown now will bear harvest. The innocent will expiate these horrors. It is the beginning of Bolshevism.'[31] Posters appeared on the city's Litfass columns showing a woman dancing with a skeleton, over the message: 'Berlin, can't you see? Your dancing partner is Death.' The strike was called off, the electricity was back on and it was business as usual in the cabarets, bars, theatres and dance halls, but the fighting continued. Noske issued an unequivocal order: 'Any person who bears arms against government troops will be shot on sight.' The rebel militias were driven back into the eastern working-class district of Lichtenberg, where they were attacked with tanks, flame-throwers and heavy artillery. 'They must all be killed,' General Lüttwitz told an American reporter. 'I am glad they are still fighting for it gives us a chance to kill more of them.'[32]

The main fighting was over by the end of Monday 10 March, but there was still more killing to come as old scores were settled. Next morning, twenty-four of the surviving sailors of the Naval Division reported to their paymaster's office in Französische Strasse to draw the money owing to them and receive their demobilisation papers. When they arrived, they discovered that the building had been occupied by Reinhardt men under the command of a Lieutenant Marloh. The sailors were lined up against a wall in the courtyard, and shot down in cold blood. 'Sheer gruesome murder,' Kessler commented. But worse was happening elsewhere in central Berlin, especially in Moabit prison. One American correspondent saw Freikorps troops herd ten white-faced Spartacist prisoners into the jail – six were boys hardly more than seventeen years old, one was a woman covered in mud and bleeding from the corners of her mouth.[33]

Another American journalist, Ben Hecht, stood outside the walls and watched Reinhardt troops march 220 prisoners inside while an organ grinder played a merry tune nearby. Hecht heard the prisoners pleading for mercy on the other side of the wall, then heard the sound of machine guns. 'Above the sound of the guns,' he wrote, 'came the cries of men. I could not distinguish the words. The cries changed to howling. The machine guns continued. I waited till the howling and the sputtering were both over. It had grown dark in the street. The sun was setting.' One of the executioners later told Hecht what had been happening, claiming that he had helped kill 2,000 in one morning: 'Units of twenty-five men, women and boys chained to one another were marched across the prison yard. Three machine guns opened fire on them and kept up the firing until all the bodies had stopped moving.' Next day, the German government expelled Hecht 'for reporting lies'.[34]

By 16 March, it was all over. As always, there are no reliably accurate figures for those killed and injured. Noske estimated that about 1,200 died during the 'week of bloodshed', about a hundred of whom were Freikorps men; left-wing sympathisers put the deaths at about twice that number. Berlin was left battered and severely bruised from all the fighting. Buildings were holed and shattered, barbed wire still littered the streets, and machine guns still guarded strategic points and the entrances to the major hotels. But order had been restored, albeit at great human cost, and the city was firmly in the hands of the non-radicals.

While the Spartacists in Berlin were being slaughtered by Noske's Freikorps, Trotsky's Red Army was suffering significant reverses in the Russian civil war. Although the Allies were about to end their intervention, the White armies of Admiral Kolchak and General Denikin mounted a powerful spring offensive with spectacular successes in the south and in the Urals, while in Latvia, Goltz's German troops were continuing to drive the Bolsheviks back. Lenin, meanwhile, was sitting safely in a room in Moscow, presiding over a meaningless talk-shop that called itself the first Congress of the Third Communist International. Soon abbreviated in the Russian fashion to the 'Comintern', this new organisation embodied his plan for one universal Communist Party that was to rule first Europe and then the rest of the world. The First International, originally known as the International Working Men's Association, had been formed in London in 1864 by Karl Marx himself, but had foundered amid squabbles over dogma, mainly between Marx and the Russian anarchist Michael Bakunin. The Second International, set up in 1889, soon became embroiled in its own sectarian infighting, and fell apart in 1914 as Socialist parties took sides in the war. The congress held in Berne in February 1919, which was attended by most of the 'soft' Socialists whom Lenin so despised, from Britain's Ramsay MacDonald to Bavaria's Kurt Eisner, was an effort to re-establish it. It proved, however, to be its last gasp.

The Berne congress aimed to re-establish traditional social democracy as the predominant force in the international workers' movement. Lenin's response to this threat was to call for a radical alternative committed to revolution rather than reform. In late December 1918 he had suggested to Chicherin that a Third International might meet 'in Berlin (openly) or in Holland (secretly), let's say by 1.ii.1919'.[35] Holland or Berlin would have offered the Bolsheviks another high-profile stepping stone to the West, but Noske's brutal suppression of the Spartacists had ruled out Berlin, and the Dutch authorities had clamped down on revolutionary activities. So, Moscow it was: the congress opened on 2 March 1919, in the Courts of Justice built by Catherine the Great in the eighteenth century.

The Third International was planned in great secrecy, with invitations sent out in the name of the Central Committee of the Russian Communist Party and the exiled or barely existent Communist Parties in Poland, Hungary, Austria, Latvia and Finland, the Socialist Labour Party in America, and a mysterious 'Balkan Revolutionary Social Democratic Federation', which seems to have been specially invented for the occasion. The purpose of the Moscow congress was stated as being to establish 'a fighting organisation for permanent co-ordination and systematic leadership . . . subordinating the interests of the movement in each particular country to the interests of the revolution on an international scale',[36] a pointed reference to the failure of the Second International. Thirty-nine organisations from various countries were summoned, as diverse as the IWW in America, Sinn Fein in Ireland and the Shop Stewards Movement in Britain.

In the event, few of those invited managed to get to Moscow: only one delegate each from Germany, France, Norway and Switzerland made the journey to Russia. Everyone else who attended was rounded up from foreigners who happened to be living in Moscow at the time. Henri Guilbeaux, for example, was there because he had just been expelled by the Swiss government and knew nothing of the Third International until Lenin personally knocked on the door of his hotel room and invited him to attend and make a speech; the party he was supposed to represent had barely a dozen members. America was represented by the émigré Boris Reinstein, who also just happened to be in Moscow at the time. There was no one from Italy or Britain: the Ukrainian Angelica Balabanova, who spoke six languages fluently and was acting as official interpreter, was instructed to speak for Italy and to announce the affiliation of the Italian Socialist Party; a former Russian political exile called Fineberg, now working in the Foreign Affairs Commissariat, was appointed 'consultant for the British Communist group'. And a Dutch engineer named Rutgers represented Holland, the Socialist Propaganda League of America and Japan, which he had once visited. And so it went on.

Because the Russians had only been able to scrape together thirty-five full delegates and sixteen 'consultative' delegates, the congress was held in a relatively small room, decorated entirely in red, including the floor, and festooned with banners proclaiming 'Long Live the Third International' in various languages. Lenin presided from the centre of a long, red-covered table set on a raised dais, quietly listening and speaking when necessary in almost every European language with astonishing ease. Clearly, he had whipped his followers into line for this significant occasion: 'Everybody of importance was there,' wrote Arthur Ransome, who was himself present as an observer. 'Trotzky [sic], Zinoviev, Kamenev, Chicherin, Bucharin, Karakhan, Litvinov, Vorovsky, Steklov, Rakovsky, representing here the Balkan Socialist Party, Skripnik, representing the Ukraine.'[37] Trotsky, wearing a long, black leather coat, breeches and gaiters and a fur hat with Red Army insignia, kept disappearing into another room, to work on the draft of a New Communist Manifesto, and to dash off newspaper articles extolling the contrived congress, to be printed once it had been decided to go public.

One traveller, Hugo Eberlein, actually had an official mandate from the German Communist Party, but proved to be the most difficult delegate present when he stubbornly insisted on questioning the legitimacy of the Comintern, and the timing of its creation. Before her murder, Rosa Luxemburg had been opposed to the idea, and her successors in Germany did not believe the movement was strong enough internationally to support such an organisation. 'Real Communist parties,' Eberlein pointed out, 'exist in only a few countries. In most they have only come into being in the last few weeks. In many countries where there are Communists, there is no organisation. The whole of Western Europe – and America – is missing.' This was not the time, he argued, to turn a 'consultative' assembly into a 'full congress'.

Patiently, Lenin and the other Russians tried to convince Eberlein that one of the aims of the congress was to provide the organisation that nascent national parties urgently needed. The dictatorship of the proletariat, Lenin told him, was already taking hold in different parts of Europe, 'thanks to Soviet power in Russia, thanks to the Spartacists in Germany and analogous organisations in other countries such as, for example, the Shop Stewards Committees in England'. To Arthur Ransome's bemusement, Lenin was convinced that a revolution was about to break out in Britain, where, he told the delegates, the government had recognised workers' councils as 'economic organisations'. 'The temporary defeat in Germany,' he said, 'was less important than this durable triumph.'

There was, Ransome thought, 'a make-believe side to the whole affair'. He noted with affectionate amusement that Balabanova 'seemed happy at last, even in Soviet Russia, to be in a "secret meeting"', and that 'in spite of some childishness, I could not help realising that I was present at something that will go down in the histories of Socialism, much like that other strange meeting in London in 1848.'[38]

For five days, the delegates wallowed in endless talk, expressing their total hostility to parliamentary government and the orthodox traditions of social democracy, which benefited only the bourgeoisie, and rejecting the so-called 'civic freedoms' of a capitalist society. They demanded the establishment of soviets as the only appropriate form of proletarian power everywhere. 'Through the soviets,' Trotsky's manifesto declared, 'the working class, having conquered power, will manage all spheres of economic and cultural life, as is currently the case at present in Russia.' The main target of the manifesto, after the conventional Socialist parties, was Great Britain, which was charged with 'unleashing the Great War through direct and deliberate provocation'. Britain was the bête noire of the Comintern, and would remain so for many years: the Communists saw Britain and her empire as the main props of the world capitalist order; British diplomacy was seen as especially wily and perfidious, intent on playing off states against each other. But the United States was in turn moving into the British position, 'weakening one camp by helping the other, intervening in military operations only so far as to secure for itself all the advantages of the situation'.[39] In one long-winded thesis, Nikolai Osinsky, an ardent supporter of party centralisation, condemned the 'imperialist' Paris Peace Conference for trampling underfoot the principles of national self-determination, and declared the League of Nations to be a scheme whereby the United States could challenge British and French colonial interests. The imperialist capitalism that lay behind the entire conference, he said, would make further arms races and wars certain.

Finally, on the sixth day, the secrecy that had surrounded the proceedings was dropped and the formation of the Communist International was trumpeted in the morning papers. An executive committee was elected, with Zinoviev as president and Karl Radek as secretary. Since Radek was then in prison in Berlin, Balabanova, to her astonishment, was deputed to act in his place. That evening, a celebratory meeting was held in the Bolshoi Theatre, attended by members of the Moscow Soviet and every conceivable trade union and factory committee. The huge theatre was packed, and great queues formed outside all the doors. When Kamenev opened the meeting by announcing the founding of the Third International, Ransome recorded, 'there was a roar of applause from the audience, which rose and sang the *Internationale* in a way that I have never heard it sung since the All-Russian Assembly when the news came of the strikes in Germany during the Brest negotiations [in January 1918]'.⁴⁰

When Lenin stood up, his efforts to speak were drowned by roar after roar of applause. 'It was an extraordinary, overwhelming scene,' wrote Ransome, who seemed prepared to believe that it was all spontaneous, 'tier after tier crammed with workmen, the parterre filled, the whole platform and the wings. A knot of workwomen were close to me, and they almost fought to see him, and shouted as if each one were determined that he should hear her in particular.' Lenin finally managed to make himself heard, and when he did he left no one in any doubt about his ambitions for the new organisation. The Soviet movement was spreading through countries 'such as England', he claimed. 'The victory of the proletarian revolution around the world is guaranteed. The foundation of an international Soviet republic is at hand.' These were words intended to send shivers of apprehension down every Western spine. Next day was declared a public holiday in honour of the Third International, and regiments of Trotsky's Red Army paraded through Red Square to mark the occasion.

The day after the parade, Ransome, who was about to leave for home, went to see Lenin, who told him: 'I am afraid that the Jingoes in England and France will make use of yesterday's doings as an excuse for further action against us. They will say "How can we leave them in peace when they set about setting the world on fire?" To that I would answer, "We are at war, Messieurs! And just as during your war you tried to make revolution in Germany, and Germany did her best to make trouble in Ireland and India, so we, while we are at war with you, adopt the measures that are open to us." . . . Balfour had said somewhere, "Let the fire burn itself out." That it would not do.' Lenin said he was sure England and America would come to terms if their hands were not tied by France. But intervention was no longer an option. 'They must have learnt,' he said, that Russia could never be governed as India is governed, and that sending troops here is the same thing as sending them to a Communist university.'

When Ransome spoke about the general hostility to Bolshevik propaganda in other countries, Lenin amazingly played down its importance. 'If the conditions of revolution are not there,' he said, 'no sort of propaganda will either hasten it or impede it. The war has brought about those conditions in all countries, and I am convinced that if

Russia today were to be swallowed up by the sea, were to cease to exist altogether, the revolution in the rest of Europe would go on. Put Russia under water for twenty years, and you would not affect by a shilling or an hour a week the demands of the shop stewards in England.'

Ransome once again tried to convince Lenin that there would not be a revolution in England. But the Soviet leader was not about to be diverted from his obsession that easily. 'We have a saying,' he replied, 'that a man may have typhoid while still on his legs. Twenty, maybe thirty years ago I had abortive typhoid, and was going about with it, had had it some days before it knocked me over. Well, England and France and Italy have caught the disease already. England may seem to be untouched, but the microbe is already there.'[41]

Trotsky's New Communist Manifesto, although couched in the usual impenetrable political jargon, left no doubts about the purpose of the Comintern. It was 'to generalise the revolutionary experience of the working class, to cleanse the movement of opportunism and social-patriotism, to mobilise all genuinely revolutionary forces, and hasten the victory of the Communist revolution throughout the world'. For all its grand words, however, the Comintern organisation was based on very shaky foundations: its secretary was in jail in Germany and the acting secretary, Balabanova, resigned after a short while, disgusted by Lenin's utter ruthlessness in destroying his Socialist opponents abroad, especially those in her beloved Italy, by any means including deliberate lies and slander. Its president, Grigori Zinoviev, an earnest thirty-four-year-old with a puffy face and pallid skin, was Lenin's chief aide, a long-standing member of the Central Committee, and the party boss of Petrograd, but he was also a fantasist, with little practical knowledge of the outside world. He was ambitious and unscrupulous, and clearly hoped to use his position as a stepping stone to succeeding Lenin in due course, to the disgust of rivals such as Trotsky and Bukharin, who had distrusted him since he had opposed the November uprising.

The executive of the Comintern consisted for some time of two men, Victor Serge and Vladimir Mazin, both experienced political operators. Serge, born in Brussels in 1890 to Russian parents who had fled their homeland after being implicated in terrorist plots, had grown up in an atmosphere of radical idealism and had become an anarchist living in Paris until moving to Petrograd in early 1919. Mazin, whom he met there, had been a Social Revolutionary terrorist and was imprisoned for ten years after an attack on a Treasury van. Both men were highly literate – Mazin had studied Marx and written a book called *Goethe and the Philosophy of Nature*, Serge had taught adult education classes and gave lectures to militiamen – and highly resourceful. They had been responsible for buying weapons for the Petrograd Soviet from dealers in Finland, which they had paid for by printing tsarist notes bearing the image of Catherine the Great and the signature of a non-existent bank director. Now, they were given a bare, unheated room in the Smolny Institute, furnished with a wooden table and two hard chairs, and were left to get on with organising the world revolution under the uncertain direction of Zinoviev.

# V

## 'CAN BOLSHEVISM BE ANY WORSE?'

THE Allies' principal weapon in the ongoing battle against Bolshevism was food. It was a weapon wielded with total determination by a man who had more managerial skill, intelligence and, ultimately, power than most of the army generals combined: the American engineer Herbert Hoover. Hoover was a sober, industrious Quaker from the Midwest, the son of a blacksmith in the small town of West Branch, Iowa, on the banks of the Wapsipinicon River. His father's family, originally the Hubers, had left their native Switzerland in the late seventeenth century to escape religious persecution, arriving in America via the German Palatinate. True frontiersmen, they had moved steadily westwards in covered wagons, through Lancaster County in Pennsylvania, the mountains of North Carolina, and Ohio, crossing the Mississippi River in the 1850s. His mother's family, the Minthorns, were originally from England, sailing for America in 1725 and trekking west from Boston through Ontario and Detroit before winding up in Iowa. Both families had been involved in anti-slavery campaigns and good works among the Indians, a legacy of moral responsibility that Herbert embraced wholeheartedly but with a total lack of sentimentality. His benevolence was a stern duty, not a soft touch.

Hoover's father died of 'rheumatism of the heart' when he was ten, and he was moved to another Quaker settlement in the frontier village of Newburg, Oregon, under the care of an uncle, a doctor who had made a fortune from fruit farming. Four years later, his devout mother died of typhoid fever. Put to work as an office boy in the Oregon Land Company, he was soon earning a good wage and discovering a head for business. In 1892 he enrolled at the brand-new Stanford University to study mechanical engineering and geology, with the aim of becoming a mining engineer, filling his spare time as treasurer of the college's *Daily Palo Alto* newspaper.

After graduating, Hoover worked in the gold mines of Nevada, then took his skills and energies further afield, first to Western Australia and then to the rest of the world. Having been raised to disapprove of worldly pleasures, he found the fleshpots of London and the rest of Europe deeply distasteful, and developed a lasting distrust of the Old World's mores, manners and above all inefficiencies, for which he had little patience. In China to study the anthracite mines of Tientsin in 1901, he found himself caught up in the Boxer Rebellion. His sympathies were entirely with the rebels: 'The constant encroachment by the European empires – Britain, Russia, Germany, France – on the independence and sovereignty of China had at last touched off hidden mines in the Chinese soul,' he wrote in his memoirs. And when the uprising was finally put down after a month of savagery, he did his best to limit reprisals by the European, and especially the British, forces and used his authority to prevent some executions.[1] Appalled by what he saw in Tientsin, he harboured a contempt for the ways and people of the Old World which never left him.

Hoover's achievements as a mining engineer, efficiency expert and innovator soon brought him a worldwide reputation. In Broken Hill, New South Wales, he invented a method of extracting zinc from slag heaps of lead and silver; at Kyshtim in the Urals he reorganised the copper and iron mines; in Turkestan, he designed and built railways and smelters. He took his skills to Africa, China and Central America. By 1914, his company had branches in San Francisco, New York, London, Melbourne, Shanghai and St Petersburg, and he had accumulated a considerable personal fortune without sacrificing any of his Quaker principles.

When the Great War broke out, Hoover was in London, where he put his managerial expertise to good use by organising the return to the United States of some 100,000 stranded American tourists, a self-imposed task which, as he wrote later, 'set him on the slippery road of public life'. Having discovered the joys of public service, he chose not to return home himself. A fellow American engineer who arrived in London from occupied Belgium reported that as a neutral he had been able to cross German lines with the money to buy 2,500 tons of food for the starving city of Brussels. The Belgian people were trapped between the German occupation and the British naval blockade, intended to stop supplies of food and materials reaching Germany by sea. Deeply affected by their plight, Hoover recognised a vital humanitarian task that he was equipped to carry out, and threw himself into it with all his usual confidence.

In less than a month, Hoover had set up the Commission for the Relief of Belgium (CRB), the largest single enterprise ever undertaken by a private citizen or organisation. 'I was not bothered over administrative matters such as the purchase and overseas shipment and internal transport of large quantities of materials,' he wrote later. 'Any engineer could do that. But there were other phases for which there was no former human experience to turn to for guidance.'[2] These 'other phases' included patient negotiation with both sides to permit CRB ships to pass unharmed through the Allied blockade and the German U-boat menace, and countless cross-Channel trips, fighting seasickness on old Dutch steamers ploughing through heavily mined waters.

Remaining doggedly unaligned, Hoover's commission became to all intents and purposes a separate power with diplomatic privileges, issuing its own passports, flying its own flag and briefing its own envoys. With a monthly budget of $25 million, all raised privately in America, the CRB fed nearly ten million people on a regular basis, providing midday meals for 2,300,000 children. By the time it closed in 1919, it had spent close to $1 billion. But by then, Hoover was back in the United States, having been forced to return after Germany's declaration of unlimited submarine warfare in February 1917 and the immediate torpedoing of three CRB ships. With America's entry into the war, he left the administration of the commission in the hands of neutral Dutch and Spanish officials.

Back in Washington, President Wilson enrolled Hoover in his War Council as Food Administrator, probably the only role he was able or willing to fill, as a committed pacifist. In this position, he was said to regard himself as the second most important and best-known man in America, after the President, whom he saw two or three times a week and who discussed general policy with him and was very much influenced by his advice.[3] This included a vehement argument against forming any political alliance with the Europeans he so despised, and calling for US military forces to be strengthened so that America could control the peace settlement at the end of the war, overruling the French and British whom he did not trust.

To build up food reserves, Hoover ran a great campaign to persuade the American public to avoid waste and economise on consumption, so successfully that a new verb was coined: to 'hooverize'. Food production, meanwhile, was increased by guaranteeing prices to farmers, with the result that, by the end of 1918, the American food surplus was estimated at three times the amount that could be exported in an average pre-war year, much of it perishable. Believing that the war would run well into 1919, Hoover crammed supplies into the warehouses of the Atlantic ports, ready to feed the expected huge American Expeditionary Force in France. He also found himself increasingly responsible for supplying the European nations whose agriculture and trade had been severely damaged by the war – France, Britain, Italy and the neutral countries.

When peace arrived, Hoover was the natural, indeed virtually the only, choice to tackle the immense food problems facing Europe, with its agriculture devastated, its distribution systems in chaos and its national economies in ruins. In his Armistice address to Congress, Wilson stressed the dangers of the situation: 'Hunger does not breed reform; it breeds madness and all the ugly distempers that make an ordered life impossible,' he said. He did not need to spell out what he meant by 'ugly distempers', everyone understood only too well. There was no dissenting voice when he instructed Hoover to sail at once for Europe, to organise a relief programme that he described as America's 'second intervention'.

Some American officials were concerned that Hoover would be too abrasive, too impulsive, and too undiplomatic for the job – while running the CRB he had been known as the rudest man in London, and he made no secret of his intention to run his new show exactly as he wanted, to suit himself and America, without reference to the Europeans. Before the war ended, he had pointed out to the President that 'some members of the Allied Food Council are putting forward suggestions for international control of world distribution of food after peace . . . Stay clear of this.' Britain, France and Italy had indeed begun drawing up a plan for pooling credit, food, raw materials and ships for reconstruction and relief under an Allied board based on the existing Allied Maritime Transport Council. Sir Maurice Hankey, the British Cabinet Secretary, had even suggested that this might form a basis for the League of Nations. Hoover was having none of this: 'We will have the dominant supplies and my own view is that we should maintain a complete independence.'[4]

With the coming of peace, Hoover reiterated his doubts and concerns. Alongside his desire to promote American economic interests, he was determined not to allow the Allies to use food supplies, the bulk of which he would be providing, to blackmail the Central Powers into accepting peace terms: 'The United States would not countenance the use of food, medicines and clothing, for political pressures,' he insisted, perhaps a touch naively. He cabled a long note to Colonel House in Paris, telling him that 'this government will not agree to any program that even looks like inter-Allied control of our economic resources'; American aid, he said, 'will revolve around complete independence of commitment to joint action'. The note was so blunt that the State Department asked House not to let any of the Allies see it.[5]

Hoover dashed over to Paris to consult with House, and within twenty-four hours they had agreed a plan, which Hoover had prepared during his transatlantic voyage, for 'the relief of the civilian populations of the European countries affected by the war'. This proposed the creation of the office of Director General of Relief, which 'must be held initially by the United States Food Administrator', who would report directly to the Supreme War Council. Wilson rubber-stamped the plan, and Hoover went ahead with setting up his agency, with its headquarters on the fashionable Avenue Montaigne. As he did so, the first American ships were already arriving at neutral ports, laden with supplies. 'By the opening of operations,' he recalled in his memoirs, 'I had done away with the pool and Allied control of American resources in one act.'[6]

Before anything could be done, Hoover had to find out exactly what was needed. Again without reference to the Allies, he sent American 'mission specialists' into Central Europe to investigate and report on the situation. When House wanted to consult the British Foreign Office, Hoover slapped him down. 'Do nothing else,' he ordered. 'That is, simply inform them.'[7] The food dictator was starting as he meant to go on.

The Europeans naturally objected to Hoover's approach, even without seeing his blunt note. They suspected that, as Lloyd George put it, Hoover would become the 'food dictator of Europe', that the Americans were intent on unloading their vast food surpluses, seriously undercutting European and empire producers, and that American businessmen would seize the opportunity of moving into Europe, all of which was true but unavoidable. John Maynard Keynes, Britain's Chief Economic

Adviser to the Treasury, however, saw the possibility of gaining some advantage from the situation. 'The whole position is rather an extraordinary one,' he noted hopefully, 'as the immense surplus of pig products for which the Americans have to find a market . . . exposes them to pressure from us. The underlying motive for the whole thing is Mr Hoover's abundant stocks of low-grade pig products at high prices which must at all costs be unloaded on someone, enemies failing allies. When Mr Hoover sleeps at night visions of pigs float across his bedclothes.' Whether or not it was through British pressure, Keynes soon found a way in which Britain could profit from Hoover's problem: 'It has been suggested by the Americans,' he wrote, 'that we unload on Germany the large stocks of rather low-grade bacon which we now hold and replace these by fresher stocks from America which would be more readily saleable.'[8] Altruism was clearly not to be the driving force behind the relief operation.

Hoover calculated that in the twenty-eight countries of Europe there were some 400 million people, of whom 200 million were in imminent danger of starvation. The three major European Allies and four minor ones had ships and would be able to obtain credit to buy food from the United States, Canada or the southern hemisphere, where there were surpluses. In addition, there were thirteen neutral states, which had actually made money out of the war. All these could be called on to help. Those in need of that help included the thirteen liberated countries, most of which were destitute and under threat from the Communists, and the five enemy countries – Germany, Austria, Hungary, Bulgaria and Turkey – which had some gold reserves but no ships, and which were also threatened by Bolshevism.

Even when there were stores of food, the breakdown of the transport system made distribution impossible. Locomotives and rolling stock were halted by lack of lubricants: Oswald Garrison Villard, the editor of the New York *Nation*, reported from Germany that if lubricants were not provided, there would be no trains running at all within six weeks.[9] Those that could move were held up by disorder and international squabbling at the new frontiers: in Czechoslovakia, Austrian troops had removed all the railway freight cars they could take as they withdrew, and the Italians were demanding the remaining locomotives and wagons, and sealing the new country's borders until they got them.

Missions from Britain and France joined Hoover's agents in reporting on the desperate situation throughout much of Europe. 'Hell has been to this place,' an American military representative reported to Hoover from Vienna. 'It is still here. Twenty-five per cent of the children in this town have died in the last two months ... We can count food in calories, but we have no way to measure human misery.'[10] The city was entirely without meat for four consecutive weeks. More children were dying than were surviving: in 1914 births had exceeded deaths by 10,000, now there were 20,000 more deaths than births. A Swiss doctor, visiting an institution for destitute children, found it filled to five times its normal capacity. He broke down and wept at what he saw. 'The appearance of the children was terrible,' he reported. 'Their heads looked disproportionately big (owing to their stunted bodies), black rings round their eyes, the eyelids red and ulcerated.' Infants, he said, were given one half-litre of milk a day, and a syrup made from boiled-down turnips; children over the age of one were fed on turnips and cabbage. There were no coffins for those who died – 'the lucky ones', he called them – but boxes were used when they were available.[11]

After centuries of dominating Central Europe through the Habsburg Empire, Austria was reduced to a small, impotent and unimportant country of about eight and a half million people when Hungarians, Czechs, Slovaks, Poles, Slovenes and Croats claimed their independence at the end of the war. Separated from its hinterland, the Austrian remnant was suddenly deprived of its supplies of both food and raw materials, and the market for its manufactured goods, cut off, said one Viennese newspaper, as if by the blow of an axe.[12] Any food and materials bound for Austria were rotting in rail yards, trapped by the chaotic state of transport and borders closed by politicians and local wars. In normal times, there could be few countries less likely to succumb to Bolshevism than Austria, but these were far from normal times.

While rural Austria remained resolutely conservative, under the sway of the Catholic Church, at least one-third of the population lived in Vienna and the majority of these, a combination of intellectuals and workers, were solidly Socialist, as were many in other towns and cities. Nevertheless, at the end of the war, the deputies from the German-speaking areas had laid aside their differences and set up the 'Provisional National Assembly of the Independent German-Austrian State', with Social Democrats and the Catholic-Clerical Party joining forces in a coalition government. Their powers, however, were strictly limited by the situation, and much of their authority was challenged on the one hand by Communist agitators seeking to link Vienna with Munich and Budapest, and on the other by militias or home guard, the Heimwehren, formed by peasants and villagers banding together to protect their crops, homes and shops from marauding ex-soldiers, newly released prisoners of war and hungry predators from the starving cities. Other groups were formed to defend the country's southern borders against attacks by the new Yugoslav Army. Although the Heimwehren initially had no political affiliations, they soon developed an anti-Socialist and increasingly right-wing slant in response to 'Red Vienna''s attempts to commandeer food stores from the villages and extend its political control over the traditionally conservative and heavily Catholic countryside.

For Austria, 1919 had started badly, and continued to deteriorate throughout the cold spring. In January Colonel Cunninghame of the British Officers' Commission reported: 'Outwardly it is calm, inwardly there is a great deal of seething. Not related to theoretical Bolshevism, but to conditions approximating to destitution and despair.' A few weeks later, another British officer wrote: 'When I left Vienna on Feb 16th there was sufficient flour to last for one week. British doctors visiting the hospitals report the mortality there is very high on account of the scarcity of meat and milk . . . Bolshevism and Food are running a great race at present and the former is gaining ground.'[13]

By March, it was clear that the official rations were not enough to support even a meagre existence, even when people could get them. Markets were bare. There was no meat, or eggs or fat anywhere. In Linz, capital of Upper Austria, thousands of people, maddened by hunger, plundered food shops, stripping them of their few remaining supplies. In Vienna, children ate coal dust to dull the pangs of hunger, while in the official relief kitchens sawdust and wood shavings were mixed with the gruel to bulk it out. Men and women aged over sixty volunteered to commit suicide so that the children might have more to eat. Left-wing extremists staged demonstrations and mass meetings attended by great crowds from all classes of society, demanding the overthrow of the government. Attitudes in the cities towards Bolshevism visibly changed. 'Starving and facing political chaos,' the New York Times reported, 'the people ask "Can Bolshevism be any worse?"'[14]

Somehow, however, the attractions of Bolshevism failed to attract the Austrians, maybe because they were too aware that their only genuine hope of food supplies lay with the United States and the Allies. Local

Communists, aided by agitators sent from Hungary, tried to rouse the population: in April they organised a demonstration of 20,000 unemployed workers, returned prisoners of war and disabled ex-servicemen to march down the smart Prater to the parliament building, the Reichsrat, under red banners. A sailor shinned up a lamp post and shouted 'We are hungry' several times at the top of his voice. Someone raised the red flag up the official flagstaff; others tied red bows round the necks of pseudo-classical sculptures and draped a red cloth over a statue of the late Emperor Franz Josef. When a deputation was refused entry to the Reichsrat, they smashed windows and broke down the door. Mounted police drew their sabres and charged, half-heartedly. More police fired indiscriminately into the crowd, provoking a great cry of 'Murderers!' A passing coal cart was overturned to make a barricade; lumps of coal were hurled through the windows of the Reichsrat – but more of it vanished into pockets and aprons, to be taken home for fuel. Rioters siphoned petrol from the tanks of deputies' cars and used it to set fire to the building, chanting 'What do we want with a parliament?' and 'All power to the Soviets! We're all Bolsheviks now!' A veteran who had lost both his legs danced round the flames on his crutches, grinning maniacally as he sought vengeance on those who had sent him to war.

But this was still Vienna, not Budapest or Petrograd or Moscow. When a detachment of the new army, the Volkswehr, appeared, its officers were able to restore order without force, using only firm persuasion to calm the crowd. 'Comrades, don't push.' 'Comrades, give way, please.' 'Comrade, if you don't mind, will you please step over this railing?' And the comrades agreed. The fire was put out. The demonstrators dispersed, after hacking the flesh from the carcass of a police horse that had been shot during one of the charges. Within minutes only the skeleton and the saddle remained. Alongside it were the naked corpses of five dead demonstrators, stripped of their clothes by needy comrades. So ended the revolution in Vienna, its failure encapsulated in one question that had silenced the inflammatory diatribe of an agitator from Hungary: 'If Vienna makes a revolution, can Budapest send us twelve trains of daily bread?'[15]

In Poland three million Jews and a million children were starving to death and hundreds of thousands of people there and in Lithuania had as their only daily meal a bowl of so-called soup with one-third of one potato in it. When one of Hoover's investigators in German Bohemia asked forty-seven schoolchildren what they had eaten for breakfast, twelve said they had had nothing, thirteen had had only ersatz black coffee, four ersatz coffee with milk. The rest had breakfasted on wild herbs gathered in the fields.

Germany alone needed 200,000 tons of wheat per month and 70,000 tons of meat to avoid famine. Berlin before the war had slaughtered an average of 6,000 cattle a week and 25,000 pigs. In the spring of 1919, the figure had fallen to 700 cattle and 17 pigs. Eight hundred people a day were dying from deficiency diseases in Germany as a whole; in Berlin, during the first months of 1919, 30 per cent of babies died within a few days of birth, while in Düsseldorf, where the milk shortage was especially severe, the figure was a staggering 85 per cent. A British journalist, Henry Nevinson, recorded his horror at the sight of rows of skeletal infants in a Cologne hospital: 'They had no weight, no growth, no sense. Their limbs were as thin as sticks, shapeless and boneless.' The French had requisitioned large numbers of cows as reparations, leaving only those capable of producing unwholesome milk, and even where there was some milk, babies cold not drink it since there was no rubber for the teats of the bottles. Konrad Adenauer, the future German Chancellor who was then Burgomaster of Cologne, commented: 'We are too exhausted even to hate.'[16]

In Czechoslovakia, too, a million children were without milk; in industrial districts 50 per cent of babies were stillborn. In one Czech mining town, 116 out of 163 children born in 1918 had already died of tuberculosis by the spring of 1919. In Prague, meat, rice, coffee and tea had completely disappeared. At the beginning of February, no flour had reached the city for two weeks. There was no soap, leather, cotton or wool to make clothes. The mortality rate among children under fourteen years of age had risen to 40 per cent during the past year; among childbearing women it had grown from 3 to 34 per cent. The *New York Times* reported that 'Factories are stopped, houses unheated, the streets dark, the shops shut at sundown, and there is no public safety'. The hardships were not confined to workers' quarters. A British doctor reported on conditions in the normally affluent middle-class areas of the city:

I saw young girls emaciated to the bone, ill of various maladies, but principally of lack of proper food. Their place would naturally be in hospital, but in Prague the vast extent of misery precludes further reception in hospital of anyone except extreme cases. I saw men trying to work by sheer will-power, their muscles no longer supporting the task ... I saw families with eight or nine children in one room, living on black bread and imitation coffee furnished by the state.

Only in one instance did I see anything that suggested linen or cotton cloth. That was in a tiny room in which dwelt a mother and eight children. Its glass door had one pane missing, but everything was scrupulously clean and in order, and on the bed a snow-white sheet as the only covering – a relic of past well-being.[17]

Colonel Henry W. Anderson, head of the American mission to the Balkan States, reported that 'all the Balkan peoples just now are in a state of moral exhaustion and demoralisation brought about by the terrible privations they have had to undergo through war and revolution'. But the state in the greatest need of help, he said, was Romania: 'The Germans have taken everything there – food, clothing and household utensils. Small children can be seen walking the streets in bitter cold with only flimsy stuff to cover them, their limbs black and blue with cold. There are fifty thousand orphans in Romania.'[18]

In Bucharest, people were struggling to survive on sauerkraut and onions, when they could get them, and 'marmaliga', a mixture of corn-flour and water which an American correspondent described as similar to 'the food ordinarily given in America to poultry'. Five Red Cross canteens and six city council kitchens fed 8,500 people a day – wives, widows, children and orphans of Romanian soldiers, and crippled veterans who could drag themselves to get the food. The reporter found entire families living in mud huts or crammed into single, often window-less rooms: 'I found the children dressed in shirts. They had neither drawers, shoes nor stockings. Two barefoot children, living with their barefoot mother, had not eaten for twenty-four hours. There was no wood in the house and no money to buy bread. The children lay upon the bed sick from cold and hunger.'[19] Many Romanian babies were born without hair or fingernails, and few survived for more than a few hours. One of Hoover's agents reported that the Romanians were 'the most starved-looking people I have seen in Europe. The women and children for the most part are without shoes and stockings and everyone had patched ragged clothes ... All of them complained that their chil-dren had died for lack of food ... I visited many homes or hovels ... I found no food ... Cattle, pigs, even dogs are about half their normal weight.'[20]

General Greenly, head of the British Military Mission in Romania, urged the War Cabinet in London to give substantial support 'to enable Romania to defend her frontiers and to resist internal Bolshevism'. He called for a credit of £500,000 to buy railway material, and another of over £400,000 to buy military stores and animals, plus the use of British shipping to transfer material and stores. There was no mention of food supplies in his report, nor in the Cabinet discussion of it. Austen Chamberlain, the Chancellor of the Exchequer, grumbled at Britain's taking on the whole burden, and did not see why it could not be shared among the Allies. Lord Curzon, the acting Foreign Secretary, pointed out that the danger was acute, and that Romania was 'the sole outpost remaining to us in the East of Europe'. Churchill said there was no time to wait for a decision from Paris. 'The Bolshevik armies are pressing right on the Romanian frontier,' he said. 'Hungary, whom we thought we had crushed, has, according to the latest reports, once more assumed a hostile attitude towards the Allied Powers, this time in Bolshevik guise.'[21] Fighting the Bolsheviks was still seen as more important than fighting famine.

The enormous task of feeding Europe's starving millions was made even more difficult by the fact that the Allies were still enforcing the blockade. The relief supplies already shipped across the Atlantic for Germany and Austria were stuck in neutral ports, awaiting clearance. Hoover was incandescent with rage – he had been fighting the blockade since 1914, and wanted it lifted immediately, declaring that it no longer served any military purpose. 'Up to date,' he complained to the American Peace Delegation, 'not a single pound of food has been delivered to Germany. The uses to which the blockade is being put are absolutely immoral. I do not feel we can with any sense of national dignity and honor continue to endure this situation . . . I wish solemnly to warn the Conference as to impending results in the total collapse of the social system in Europe.'

The French were unmoved by such arguments. Clemenceau and Foch were still adamant in maintaining the blockade and making Germany suffer until the peace treaty had been signed. But the *Echo de Paris* recognised a dilemma linked with the threat of Bolshevism: 'If a state of order exists in Germany, her influence over Russia will be strengthened. If order is absent, revolution will be encouraged and may spread to France.' But it was not only Germany that was suffering from the effects of the blockade: the shortage of raw materials was keeping factories closed and exacerbating unemployment everywhere in Central

Europe. In Vienna alone, 100,000 men were idle, a figure that with their women and children meant that maybe half a million people, a quarter of the city's normal population, were living in misery.

In his battle against the blockade, Hoover found unlikely allies. Socialists everywhere were indignant at what they saw as unfeeling governmental cynicism and lack of humanity. Britain's trade-union-owned newspaper, the *Herald*, demanded: 'Has the Labour Party given a thought to those millions of starving and workless? Has the Triple Alliance [of British unions] dreamed of using a little of its strength to demand that the blockade be lifted? If faith in the Socialist International is to live, British labour must act. Our capitalists have "locked out" the workers of Central Europe. The cruel policy is nothing but a move in the game to capture the world's markets. The League of Nations is a ghastly mockery while this wickedness continues.'

Robert Smillie, the Scottish Secretary of the Miners' Federation of Great Britain, turned his attention to the suffering imposed on the starving children: it would have been more merciful, he said, to have turned the machine guns on them.[22] His words had little apparent effect in official quarters. When the founder of the Save the Children Fund, Miss Eglantyne Jebb, displayed a picture of an emaciated 'enemy' child, she was arrested and imprisoned under the Defence of the Realm Act. Undeterred by this, or by the ravings of the diehards, groups of British women responded to appeals from Germany and sent thousands of rubber teats to help save more babies from dying of starvation.

As a good Quaker, Hoover was driven by humanitarian principles in his fight against the blockade and the wicked Allied governments. But he also had solid business reasons, too. While he could not start distribution, stocks of American pork were stuck in overflowing warehouses, going nowhere. It had taken all his powers of persuasion to stop the British, French and Italian governments cancelling their orders. If the blockade continued much longer, many American farmers faced ruin, which could knock on through country banks and business in general and cause serious damage to the national economy. He tried to find a way round by having the northern neutral states – Holland and the Scandinavian countries – take the food and barter it for German products, but the Allies vetoed this. It began to seem as though the stalemate would go on until the Peace Treaty was signed, which could be weeks away.

Even if the treaty were signed next day, there would still be another problem that had to be solved before shipments could get under way:

who was going to pay? The American public and Congress were starting to feel that they had done enough in helping to win the war, and were not inclined to pay for the peace, or to get further involved in Europe's shaky finances by extending more credit. The Germans, it was felt, could be made to foot the bill for their own rescue package – they still had some gold and other assets – but most of the other needy nations were destitute. Wilson came to the rescue in February with a cabled message from the *George Washington* in mid-Atlantic: 'Food relief is now the key to the whole European situation and to the solution of peace. Bolshevism steadily advancing westward, poisoning Germany. It cannot be stopped by force but it can be stopped by food.' The reference to Bolshevism did the trick. Congress approved a grant of $100 million to provision Europe; a few days later, the House of Commons agreed to grant the equivalent of $65 million.

With the money promised, Hoover could start setting up the machinery of relief, opening offices in thirty-two countries ready to go into action as soon as the blockade was removed. To his fury, the Allies showed no inclination to lift it: Germany had only signed an armistice, not a peace treaty, was technically still at war with them and in theory liable to start fighting again if negotiations failed. They had always considered the blockade to be a legitimate weapon of war intended to bring their enemies to their knees – the Germans, after all, had pursued their own version with their U-boats – and were reluctant to lower their guard now. It was the same lack of trust that was holding back demobilisation – and yet both Britain and France were conscious of a greater danger that was being aggravated by hunger and hardship.

At the beginning of March, the *Manchester Guardian* sounded a solemn reminder:

Hunger is the parent of revolution, and whatever promotes hunger promotes revolution. That is precisely the process in which we are now engaged. We are not only maintaining the blockade of Germany, we have increased its stringency ... Of course if the object be to inflict the maximum of suffering on Germany, to ruin her industries as she has ruined some of those of Belgium and of France, and to kill off the old and the very young, as she has in some cases been guilty of doing, that may be a rude kind of justice, also on a pre-Christian model. But then good-bye to indemnities. Good-bye also to the hope of order in Central Europe. Welcome to revolution and to the dissolution of order over a large part of Europe.[23]

Two days later, Winston Churchill told the House of Commons:

At the present moment we are bringing everything to a head in Germany: we are holding our means of coercion in full operation or in immediate readiness for use. We are enforcing the blockade with rigour. We have strong armies ready to advance at the shortest notice. Germany is very near starvation. All the evidence I have received from officers sent by the War Office all over Germany shows, first of all, the great privations which the German people are suffering; and secondly, the danger of a collapse of the entire structure of German social and national life under the pressure of hunger and malnutrition. Now is therefore the time to settle. To delay indefinitely would be to run a grave risk of having nobody with whom to settle, and of having another great area of the world sink into Bolshevist anarchy. That would be a very grave event.[24]

Almost immediately, Lloyd George took up the cause, and on 8 March he used all his political guile in addressing the Council of Ten. The meeting got off to a promising start by browbeating a reluctant Italy into agreeing that the blockade could be lifted in the Adriatic, allowing 80,000 tons of food that Hoover had stored in Trieste to be forwarded to Austria, to be followed by regular deliveries of 3,000 tons a day. Only after various bits of routine business had been dealt with did the discussions turn to food for Germany. The French had already been persuaded to agree in principle to a British proposal that Germany could be supplied with food until the next harvest, provided they paid for it. It was how they were to pay for it that was still causing trouble. The Germans had gold, but the French insisted that this must only be used to pay reparations for the enormous damage which the Germans had wreaked on France during the war.

With the meeting in danger of getting bogged down in endless wrangling, Lloyd George took the stage, starting with an emotional attack on the effects of the blockade. So far, he said, not a single ton of food had been sent into Germany, while hundreds of thousands of tons were lying in Rotterdam, waiting to be carried up the waterways. The German fishing fleet had even been prevented from going out to catch a few herrings. British military officials throughout Germany, he went on, were reporting that every day the lack of food was increasing sympathy for the Spartacists. 'As long as the people were starving,' he said, 'they would listen to the arguments of the Spartacists, and the Allies by their actions were simply encouraging elements of disruption and anarchy.'

Using a highly emotive analogy, he said it was like stirring up an influenza puddle next door, 'and if Germany went, and perhaps Spain, who would feel safe? As long as order was maintained in Germany, a breakwater would exist between the countries of the Allies and the waters of revolution beyond. But once that breakwater was swept away, I could not speak for France, and I tremble for my own country.'[25]

Clemenceau roused himself to interpose that no promise had been made in the Armistice to feed Germany. 'As for Bolshevism,' he added, ignoring the fact that at that very moment Spartacists and Freikorps were tearing Berlin apart with bullets and shells, 'the Germans were using it as a bogey with which to frighten the Allies.' However, he conceded, his government would be guided by humanity, and Germany must be fed, subject to certain conditions.

It seemed that Clemenceau was finally softening. And at that critical moment, Lloyd George played his ace. A messenger entered the room and handed him an envelope, which he proceeded to open with a flourish before the eyes of the assembled statesmen, for all the world like a conjuror performing a magic trick. He drew out a telegram, which he scanned quickly and then read aloud. It was from General H.C.O. Plumer, commander of the British Army of the Rhine, telling him that: 'Food must be sent into this area by the Allies without delay.' The morale of his troops, Plumer said, was being badly undermined by seeing women and children starving. 'The continuance of those conditions is unjustifiable,' Plumer went on. He could not be responsible for the troops 'if children were allowed to wander about the streets half starved. The British soldiers would not stand that.' They were refusing to continue to occupy a territory in order to maintain the population in a state of starvation. His men were already sharing their rations with German civilians, he said, and he demanded an immediate supply of food to Cologne, which he would distribute from army headquarters.

The arrival of the telegram at that critical moment was not fortuitous, of course. It had been carefully stage-managed by Lloyd George, always the master showman, who had arranged with F.C. Tiarks, a director of the Bank of England who was acting as a commercial consultant with the army of occupation, to have it sent. And he had planted his good friend Lord Riddell in the antechamber outside the door to the conference room to make sure it was delivered at precisely the right moment.[26]

Lloyd George's *coup de théâtre* worked. Clemenceau was moved to agree that food should be sent, and even reluctantly accepted that the Germans might buy part of it with her gold. He still insisted, however, that the Germans must first hand over their merchant ships to the Allies, at least until the final terms of the Peace Treaty had been settled, to ferry it across the Atlantic – Allied shipping capacity had been drastically reduced by Germany's ruthless U-boat campaign. Surrendering their ships had always been a sticking point with the Germans, both as a matter of national pride and out of fear of the reaction of German sailors, but faced with the ultimatum 'no ships, no food', they finally capitulated and the deal was done. The ships would be used to transport American and Australian servicemen home, returning laden with food. To pay for it, Germany would be allowed to raise some $500 million by exporting coal, potash and other commodities, by using existing credits in neutral countries, and finally, as a last resort, by dipping into her gold reserves. In return, she would get 300,000 tons of food a month, until the autumn harvest. 'So,' the *New York Times* announced, 'the big obstacle to taking care of the Central Powers and staving off Bolshevism is removed. Herbert C. Hoover is satisfied and ready to proceed with his work.'[27]

Hoover was indeed ready – he had been chomping at the bit for weeks and wasted no time now in setting the organisation he had built up into motion. The first shipments of food left Rotterdam for Germany on 18 March. Because Congress was still imposing some restrictions on American appropriations, Hoover arranged for the British government to buy $10 million worth of foodstuffs from the American Grain Corporation, to be turned over to him for distribution in Vienna, with similar measures in other parts of the old Austro-Hungarian Empire. And to make sure that the food would get through, the Supreme Council gave him control over all the railways of the old empire, with a mandate to demand locomotives and rolling stock from all five of the new states into which it had split. The relief trains, it was ordered, would 'run over all lines without political or military interference', under the control of 1,500 engineers and other technicians, seconded from the US Army by General Pershing. Food, clothes and medical supplies began moving into the hardest hit areas, unhindered by tricky decisions on how the states would pay for them – the council appointed a four-man inter-Allied committee to sort this out.

Hoover's relief organisation grew fast. Its soup kitchens were soon feeding millions of children. It set up its own telegraph network,

stretching from Helsingfors (Helsinki) to Constantinople (Istanbul), with
main stations at Paris, Berlin, Prague, Warsaw and Vienna. It ran mines
as well as railways, distributing coal alongside food, to fight cold and
unemployment, feeding factories as well as people. It waged war on
typhus with experts borrowed from the Red Cross and the US Army
Medical Corps, and commandeered delousing equipment from all the
armies, including the German, attacking lice with tons of soap, thousands of hair clippers and special baths manned by American soldiers.
Travellers who did not have a certificate of delousing were forcibly
disinfected. It was a massive operation, and so successful that by summer
Hoover, with his usual bluntness, could announce that America had
done enough and the Europeans could look after themselves, an opinion
with which an increasingly isolationist Congress wholeheartedly agreed.
American aid and loans were severely reduced. But they, and he, had
done their job and had undoubtedly struck a massive blow in the battle
with Bolshevism.

# VI

## 'KILL THE BOLSHIE, KISS THE HUN'

BERLIN had been brought under control with the smashing of Spartacus, but other parts of Germany were still racked with revolutionary upheavals during the spring of 1919. There were more strikes in the Ruhr; in Saxony the War Minister, Herr Neuring, was thrown into the River Elbe at Dresden, and shot dead as he tried to reach the bank; Bremen and Hamburg still seethed, and seamen refused to crew ships bringing in Allied food relief; there were separatist revolts in Oldenburg and East Frisia; the workers' and soldiers' councils in Rhine-Hesse, Oberhessen, the Palatinate, Hesse-Nassau and Württemberg voted to amalgamate in a breakaway Hessian Soviet Republic. But to the outside world the most serious problems were once again in Munich.

The Bavarian Landtag was finally reconvened on 17 March, and a former schoolteacher, Johannes Hoffmann, was elected Minister-President. Hoffmann legitimised his new government with the ritual invocation of the spirit of his martyred predecessor: 'The political act which Prime Minister Eisner wanted to undertake on 21 February is now accomplished.'[1] Nobody knew what he meant, but it sounded good and could at a pinch be taken as meaning that parliamentary government had been re-established and a line drawn under the events of the recent past.

A tall, erect, dark-haired man in his mid-fifties, Hoffmann was a more imposing figure than Eisner, and commanded respect from a wider range of Socialists. He was a Majority Social Democrat, but from the slightly more radical wing of the party, and had served as Minister of Education and Culture under Eisner, when he had opposed the involvement of the Catholic Church in Bavarian schools. But although he was anti-Catholic, he was also against Communism. 'Every revolution has two enemies,' he famously told a series of open meetings in five of Munich's great beer halls on 19 March. 'One stands to the right, the other to the left.'[2]

Hoffmann approached his immense task soberly and with admirable reason, and would surely have had every chance of bringing some sense to the chaotic situation had it not been for three factors that were entirely beyond his immediate control. The first was the weather. The first two weeks of March had been unseasonably warm, raising hopes of good agricultural harvests that would help to ease Bavaria's critical food shortages. But in the second half of March a severe cold spell hit the state; by the beginning of April, Munich was buried under twenty inches of snow after the heaviest falls for years and the situation was rated as 'catastrophic'. Coal stocks were almost exhausted, and fuel rations had to be cancelled. The bad weather brought industry and commerce to a halt, imposing further strains on an economy that was already in a parlous state: unemployment in Munich was approaching 40,000, and the city itself was so deeply in debt that state bureaucratic and postal officials were refusing to accept its own emergency currency. Cold, hungry, short of work – the citizens could hardly be blamed for feeling disgruntled.

The second factor was the new constitution being drawn up in Weimar, which threatened to strip Bavaria of most of its cherished privileges under a highly centralised government. Since the foundation of Bismarck's Second Reich in 1871, Bavaria had enjoyed not only its own monarchy, but also its own military command, diplomatic corps, post and telegraph service, transportation system, and taxation arrangements, especially beer and brandy taxes, without which it could have no financial independence. The new constitution threatened to remove all these and leave the state subservient to the national government in Berlin, which would be dominated by the hated Prussians. When Hoffmann refused to go to battle to defend Bavarian sovereignty and sought to find a compromise, he provoked the anger of the people, and finally lost the support of the Bavarian People's Party (BVP) and the Catholic middle classes.

There was a strong popular feeling across all classes for secession and a possible link-up with Austria to form a southern Catholic state that would be a counterweight to northern Protestant power. A constituent assembly in Vienna had just voted by a massive 98 per cent in favour of Anschluss, the integration of Austria into the German Reich, and although this had been vetoed by France the vast majority of Bavarians, of every political persuasion, supported it. Hoffmann's authority was seriously damaged. Comparing him with Eisner, the *Bayerische Kurier* complained that 'even the Jew from Berlin' had been a better Bavarian than Hoffmann.[3]

The third factor was Hungary. Just as it seemed that the Bavarian Spartacists might be subdued and some semblance of order restored, news arrived that galvanised them into fresh action: the Bolsheviks in Hungary had overthrown the government and set up a full-scale soviet republic. 'The news from Hungary hit Munich like a bomb,' wrote Erich Mühsam, the anarchist leader who had kidnapped Auer in December.[4] It was the first soviet regime at national level outside Russia, and it proved that it could be done. Its leader, Béla Kun, called on Bavarian radicals to follow his example. Meeting in Augsburg, Zentralrat Councils members answered his call and voted overwhelmingly for a Bavarian soviet republic, with a programme of full socialisation, and an alliance with the soviet governments of Hungary and Russia. They also ordered the inevitable general strike, if Hoffmann refused to accept or at least to negotiate on their demands. However, when Niekisch and his fellow delegates arrived in Munich next morning, they found that Hoffmann was not there – unaware of the Zentralrat's decisions he had left on the overnight train for Berlin to confer with Scheidemann.

Suddenly, Munich was plunged back into anarchy. The beer halls were packed with mass meetings of workers, the unemployed and soldiers – who passed the only significant resolution, declaring that in the event of a general strike, the Munich garrison would side with the striking workers and offer no support to the government. Machine guns were installed around the Landtag, but no one was sure who had ordered them or whether they were there to protect the deputies or to prevent their meeting. In the Löwenbräukeller Niekisch spelled out the Augsburg resolution in language guaranteed to send shivers down any bourgeois spine: 'Elimination of parties, union of the entire proletariat, proclamation of a soviet republic, and brotherhood with the Russian and Hungarian proletariat. And then no power on earth will be able to prevent the immediate execution of full socialisation.'[5]

On 6 April, an assorted group representing most of Bavaria's left-wing parties and organisations – but not, significantly, the Communists – met in the unlikely surroundings of the Queen's bedchamber in the

Royal Palace and proclaimed a *Räterepublik*, a soviet republic, under the leadership of a twenty-five-year-old bohemian poet called Ernst Toller. Fresh placards declaring 'Bavaria is a Socialist Republic' appeared on all the street corners of the capital. The Hoffmann government fled Munich for the safety of Bamberg, just as the German National Assembly had fled Berlin for Weimar.

News of the Toller coup in Munich was welcomed by the Comintern as a sign that things were moving in the right direction. From Moscow, Zinoviev cabled an enthusiastic if over-optimistic message: 'We are deeply convinced that the time is not far off when the whole of Germany will be a soviet republic. The Communist International is aware that you in Germany are now fighting at the most responsible posts, where the immediate fate of the proletarian revolution throughout Europe will be decided.'[6] The Bavarians were less sure. The Toller *Räterepublik*, immediately dubbed the 'Schwabing Soviet' by the residents of Munich after the city's louche artistic quarter, and the 'Pseudo Soviet Republic' by the Communists, who refused to take part in it, lasted for just seven chaotic and sometimes comical days.

'Comrades!' Toller addressed the bewildered population, 'You do not know what a Soviet Republic means. You will tell it now by its work. The Soviet Republic will bring the new order.'[7] The new order was defined in a continuous stream of ludicrous pronouncements, proclamations, regulations, orders and counter-orders with no consideration for how they were to be carried out. Banks and large industrial concerns were to be nationalised, farms collectivised. Restaurants and cafés were closed – except for the Stefanie in Schwabing, the favourite haunt of poets, artists and intellectuals, which had been the cradle of the latest revolution and was now its headquarters. Foodstuffs were to be confiscated – government troops raided bourgeois homes to make sure they were not hoarding any. The proletariat was to be armed and the bourgeoisie disarmed. A Red Army was to be formed. Universities were to be run by the students, and professors stripped of their titles. The press was to be subject to censorship by a board consisting entirely of Schwabing literati, and newspapers were forced to print the poems of Hölderlin and Schiller on their front pages. 'Legalistic thinking' was banned and revolutionary tribunals set up in place of law courts, to root out counter-revolutionary activities. All rents were to be frozen, and unused lofts handed over to artists for use as studios. And so the list went on.

The commissars, as ministers of the new government were labelled, went their own ways. Eisner's friend Gustav Landauer was appointed Commissar for 'Propaganda, Education, Science, Art, and a few other things', as he put it on a picture postcard of himself which he sent to another friend. 'If I am allowed a few weeks' time,' he went on, 'I hope to accomplish something; but there is a bare possibility that it will be only a couple of days, and then it will have been but a dream.'[8] Landauer was an archetypal dreamer: it was he who had proposed the motion in the Queen's bedchamber for a soviet republic, saying it would 'signal the dawn of a new era of universal peace and noble humanity'. His fellow commissar, for Foreign Affairs, Dr Franz Lipp, was something else entirely. When he received a congratulatory message from Lenin and the Russian Foreign Commissar, Georgi Chicherin, asking about the revolution and how it was progressing, he replied to Lenin that the Bavarian proletariat was 'as firmly joined together as a hammer' but complained bitterly that 'the fugitive Hoffmann has taken with him the key to my ministry toilet'.[9] To make sure his complaint was widely registered, he sent a copy of his telegram to the Pope, addressing him as a close friend with the intimate 'du'. The Pope did not respond. Lenin did, asking for more specific details about the revolution, but studiously avoiding the matter of the locked toilet. When he found out about Lipp's correspondence, Toller decided to check his credentials and discovered that he had only recently been discharged from an asylum for the insane. He was 'kindly but firmly' removed from office.

Hoffmann, meanwhile, was gathering his government's strength in Bamberg, applying pressure on the capital by stopping its food supplies from loyal Bavarian farmers and cutting telephone, postal and rail services, while the central bank in Berlin suspended all money transfers to Munich. Sensibly declining Noske's offer of federal government troops, he relied instead on building up a local Bavarian militia to march on Munich, where his Republican Security Force still held the central rail station.

On Palm Sunday, 13 April, Hoffmann's Security Force took Toller's men completely by surprise with a dawn attack, arresting most of the leaders of the soviet and imprisoning them in the station. A fresh set of placards appeared on the streets declaring that the *Räterepublik* was finished and the legitimate government restored. Any rejoicing, however, quickly proved to be premature. While the Security Force barricaded itself in the station, waiting for support from Hoffmann which never

arrived – their courier had been intercepted while trying to cross Red
Army lines – heavily armed Communist soldiers marched into the city
and attacked them. The battle lasted for five hours before the Security
Force troops escaped by train through the rear of the station, having
lost more than twenty dead and a hundred wounded.

The Schwabing Soviet, however, had been destroyed, as hard-core
Communists seized power, proclaiming a second *Räterepublik* under
Eugen Leviné, a Russian-born agent sent by the Communist Party in
Berlin with Moscow's backing to put some steel into the Bavarians.
Gone was the airy romanticism of Toller and Eisner. In its place Leviné
and his supporters began a reign of terror in Munich that matched
those in Russia. Toller was released from prison and given command
of the 'Red Army', which defeated a force of Hoffmann troops at
Dachau, a quiet little market town about ten miles from the city, the
site of the mill providing the paper for the regime's currency.

Hoffmann had been desperately trying to recruit Freikorps to march
on Munich, appealing unashamedly to their Bavarian patriotism:

Bavarians! Countrymen! In Munich there rages a Russian terror, directed by
alien elements. This insult to Bavaria cannot be allowed to last another day,
another minute. All Bavarians must play their part, regardless of party . . . You
men of the Bavarian mountains, Bavarian plains, Bavarian forests, rise up as
one, gather in your villages with weapons and equipment, select your leaders
. . . Munich calls for your aid. Step forward! Now! The Munich disgrace must
be wiped out. This is the honourable duty of all Bavarians![10]

The response was immediate yet worrying for a good Socialist.
Hoffmann's call naturally appealed to men who were ultra-nationalist
and anti-democratic. Many were rabidly racist. Many were militantly
monarchist, eager to restore the old order, like Major General Franz
Ritter von Epp, a former commander of the Bavarian Life Guards, who
led the Freikorps Oberland but was still a serving officer in the regular
army – he would be appointed commander of all infantry forces in
Bavaria when things finally settled down. His adjutant was a much-
decorated thirty-one-year-old war hero, Captain Ernst Röhm, another
serving officer, who would find notoriety as the mentor of Adolf Hitler
and Heinrich Himmler and as the first chief of the Nazi storm troopers.

As tough as these men were, however, there were not enough of them
yet to take Munich, and with reports of increasing brutality and hard-

ship in the city, Hoffmann could not afford to wait until they were ready. After the debacle at Dachau, he was forced to turn to Noske in Berlin for help. Noske's response was prompt and ominous: 'The Munich insane asylum must be put in order.' He authorised 20,000 regular troops to move into Bavaria under the command of the Prussian Major General von Oven to see to it. Some 7,500 of the troops actually arrived, and were assembled on the army training ground at Ohrdurf in Thuringia, the state immediately to the north of Bavaria, where they were joined by 3,750 men from Württemberg and about 22,000 Freikorps and Volkswehr men from northern Bavaria, making a fully-equipped force numbering almost 35,000.[11]

Von Oven's force moved on Munich towards the end of April, and by the 29th had the city surrounded. The Red government began to fall apart amid growing anarchy. Toller resigned as commander of the Red Army, and was replaced by a young sailor, Rudolf Egelhöfer, who appealed for support from the regular troops of the Munich garrison. Among those troops was Corporal Adolf Hitler, who was actively involved in the soldiers' councils, where he was enjoying his first political position as his battalion's deputy representative, elected as a Social Democrat supporting Hoffmann. At the meeting called to discuss Egelhöfer's appeal, he is said to have leapt on to a chair and made a speech exhorting his fellow soldiers to refuse: 'We are not revolutionary guards for a lot of carpetbagging Jews!' Interestingly, he did not ask them to fight against the *Räterepublik*, but to stay neutral in the coming battle, which they did.

The battle for Munich was brief but bloody. The Spartacists alienated everybody by murdering ten hostages they had been holding, among them the beautiful Countess Hella von Westarp, secretary of the right-wing, *völkisch* Thule Society – a grave mistake, since this gave the counter-revolutionaries a wonderful excuse for righteous indignation and vicious retribution. At the same time, von Oven's advancing White Army came upon a camp holding some fifty Russian prisoners of war, whom they slaughtered without thought. This was only the beginning. As the army and Freikorps moved into the city, they killed hundreds of people, many of them entirely innocent, and the Reds did the same, while Hitler and his comrades sat in their barracks and did nothing. Order was eventually restored, but the situation in Munich was still volatile, and remained so for the next four years, as it did in Berlin and the rest of Germany.

*

The Hungarian coup, which had so excited the Munich revolutionaries, created the only Communist regime outside Russia that was able to hold on to power for any length of time during that era. It was also the only Bolshevik takeover that was entirely bloodless – though it more than made up for that omission later. On both counts, it caused a great deal of anxiety among the Western powers, who naturally feared that it could prove to be what we would now call the first domino. There was, in any case, almost universal distrust of Hungary, which had even fewer friends than Russia or Germany and was hemmed in on all sides by rapacious neighbours. The British diplomat, Harold Nicolson, spoke for many when he wrote later that he regarded 'that Turanian tribe with acute distaste. Like their cousins the Turks,' he continued, 'they had destroyed much and created nothing . . . For centuries the Magyars had oppressed their subject nationalities. The hour of liberation and retribution was at hand.'[12]

The dual monarchy of Austria-Hungary had been a vital component of the Central Powers, and although the union had been formally dissolved in October 1918, both partners were treated as enemy powers, unlike the Romanians or the Czechs, Slovaks and Yugoslavs, who could claim to have been dragged into the conflict against their will by their former imperial rulers. Only the Italians were sympathetic – and that was because they had their own quarrels with the new Yugoslavia and hoped to use the Hungarians against the Slavs. The British and Americans were decidedly cool; the French, whose troops made up the bulk of Allied forces in Central Europe, were actively hostile, encouraging the Serbs to move north and take over Croatia, the Czechs to take over Slovakia, and the Romanians to move into Transylvania, which represented almost half of the old Kingdom of Hungary.

In the face of international hostility and the bitterness of defeat, Hungary grew increasingly radical. Although the country's fertile wheat plains gave it protection against the outright starvation threatening Germany and Austria, the Allied blockade caused severe shortages of other foodstuffs and commodities and an almost total lack of coal and raw materials that brought industry to a halt. This fuelled mass unemployment which added to the general unrest. This in turn was played on by prisoners of war returning from Russia with glowing accounts of the great revolution, and by Bolshevik agitators led by a thirty-two-year-old former lawyer and journalist called Béla Kun.

Béla Kun was not the most attractive of men – Harold Nicolson described him as 'a little man of about 30: puffy white face and loose wet lips: shaven head: impression of red hair: shifty suspicious eyes: he has the face of a sulky and uncertain criminal'.[13] The son of a drunken Jewish notary in a tiny village in Transylvania and himself a qualified lawyer, Kun had made a name before the war as a radical journalist. He had been converted to Bolshevism while a prisoner of war in Russia, played an active part in the October Revolution and quickly achieved a leading role in the international movement, becoming a member of the Central Committee of the Bolshevik Party. Provided with fake papers and gold worth an estimated 20 million crowns, he returned to Budapest in November 1918, to found the Hungarian Communist Party and foment revolution.

By the new year, foreign correspondents described Budapest as being like a city built over an active volcano. 'The Russian epidemic of Bolshevism,' reported the *New York Times*, 'has reached the virulent stage. Famine and freezing are its active allies. New Year's Eve was celebrated with riot and murder in the city's streets.'[14] The trouble had been sparked by the closure of one of Kun's revolutionary newspapers by the newly appointed Army Minister, Count Alexander Festetics. It began in late afternoon with an attack on the barracks of the First Honved Infantry Regiment by a mob of soldiers and students firing 'hundreds of shots' through the windows, and hurling cobblestones torn up from the street. This attack was seen as the signal for a general outbreak of violence throughout the city, with calls for a Communist regime. The insurgents marched through the city to the military deten-tion barracks and demonstrated for the release of the prisoners. At the same time, Kun, who was under arrest in the jail at the time, tried to incite a riot, but failed when the guards slammed and locked the gates and drove the prisoners back into their cells with point-blank rifle fire. Festetics, who had only been in office for a few hours, ordered loyal troops and police to the trouble spots, and the situation was quickly brought under control. Kun was released after a couple of hours, nobody was sure on whose authority. He then issued a public threat that 'in the event of further opposition to the Bolsheviki by the loyal forces in the city, Budapest would be invaded by thousands of Bolsheviki from the surrounding districts', a piece of meaningless bluster that was still enough to start a panic that there was about to be a wholesale massacre.[15]

The rebels had been too few to succeed: only some 2,000 out of a total garrison of 20,000 had responded to Kun's call. But the situation remained volatile, and a week later Festetics's men discovered a Bolshevik plot to seize control of the flotilla of monitors – heavily armed, shallow-draught warships – that was lying on the River Danube at Budapest. Kun had promised the sailors of the Danube Fleet vast sums of money if they would support his cause and train their guns on the city. For some reason – presumably because his popular support was too great – Kun was allowed to remain free and active. Only after leading another failed Communist revolt on 20 February, two days after Clemenceau was shot and the day before Eisner was assassinated in Munich, was he finally locked up.

Even with Kun behind bars, the threat of a Bolshevik takeover continued through spring, exacerbated by a growing resentment at international attitudes. The final trigger came when the peacemakers in Paris decided to give Romania a large swathe of Hungary proper, and ordered the Hungarians to withdraw all their troops from the border region. Bitterly disappointed at the treatment his country had received, the President, Count Michael Károlyi, was forced to resign on 21 March. He had been in office since the end of October 1918, when the first revolution, led by a national soldiers' council, had unseated King Karl, and he had proclaimed the First Hungarian Republic on 16 November.

Although he was one of the richest aristocrats and landowners in Hungary, the liberal Károlyi had tried to introduce the sweeping reforms needed to change the country from a semi-feudal oligarchy into a modern, democratic state. On 5 February he had announced the distribution of all his landed property to the peasants, in line with a new law he had guided through the National Assembly. For five months, he managed to steer a difficult course between the forces of the right and the left, each of whom accused him of being too soft on their opponents. Both sides came together, however, in charging him with being too soft on the Allied peacemakers. His government resigned, and when he announced that he intended to appoint a Social Democrat government in its place, the Communists seized their opportunity and presented him with a proclamation already drafted in his name declaring that: 'In the face of this Peace Conference decision, I, the Provisional President of the Hungarian People's Republic, appeal to the world proletariat for assistance and transfer all power to the proletariat of the Hungarian people.' When Károlyi refused to sign this, it was printed without his knowledge in the official gazette – which was how he learned that he had 'resigned'.[16] For his successor, the Socialists turned immediately to the Budapest jail, where Béla Kun was incarcerated. They offered him not just his freedom, but power. Next day, newly released, he declared Hungary a soviet republic. No one objected, not a shot was fired. For once, Bolshevism had arrived without a fight.

Having first taken the precaution of contacting the Soviet Russian government to seek a military alliance – or, in other words, the protection of Trotsky's Red Army – Kun set about putting his revolutionary ideas into practice at once. All large agricultural estates and industrial enterprises employing more than twenty-five people were socialised; church property was confiscated; priests were only allowed to remain so long as they used their pulpits to preach support for the government; members of religious orders were forced to work in hospitals or other humanitarian institutions; schools were reorganised to emphasise the teaching of science and the principles of Socialism, with compulsory baths and sex education for children. Titles were abolished. Rural food stores were requisitioned to feed the starving capital. The Soviet political structure of soldiers', sailors' and workers' councils was imposed, and the whole of the judicial power of the state put into their hands, with special revolutionary tribunals to try political cases – it was all following what had become a familiar pattern elsewhere.

The Comintern received the news of the Hungarian 'revolution' with great jubilation. Zinoviev, Serge and Mazin hurriedly published a 'Manifesto to the Workers and Soldiers of All Countries'. 'Comrades!' it announced. 'In Hungary all power has been transferred to the working class ... Gritting their teeth, the Hungarian bourgeoisie had to yield ... The Entente imperialists burned their fingers. Their rapacious pressure only hastened the birth of the Socialist Soviet Republic ... When the Hungarian bourgeoisie thus confirmed their inability to save their country from ruin they gave clear proof that their historic role has been played out, and that their gravedigger, the proletariat, has come to take their place.' When the immediate fate of the proletarian revolution in Munich, as in Berlin, was decided by the Freikorps, Zinoviev was silent. But he could, at least for the moment, find some consolation in Hungary.

The Western Allies were seriously alarmed by the events in Budapest. On 22 March Colonel House noted in his diary: 'From the look of things the crisis will soon be here ... Bolshevism is gaining ground everywhere. Hungary has just succumbed. We are sitting upon an open powder magazine and some day a spark may ignite it.'[17] Lloyd George shared his fears. In a confidential memorandum circulated among Peace Conference delegates, he warned of what he saw as the greatest danger facing the West:

If Germany goes over to the Spartacists it is inevitable that she should throw in her lot with the Russian Bolsheviks. Once that happens all Eastern Europe will be swept into the orbit of the Bolshevik revolution, and within a year we may witness the spectacle of 300 million people organised into a vast Red Army under German instructors and German generals, equipped with German cannon and German machine-guns and prepared for a renewal of the attack on Western Europe. The news which came from Hungary yesterday shows that this is no mere fantasy.[18]

Wilson, too, stressed the urgency of the situation. Exhausted from trying to catch up on a month's work after his return from America, and suffering from the effects of a persistent cold and increasingly serious headaches, he was on the verge of a physical and mental breakdown. But when, on the following day, his physician, Rear Admiral Cary T. Grayson, pleaded with him to slow down, his reply was revealing and, coincidentally, an unconscious echo of Lenin's words to Arthur Ransome: 'Give me time,' he said. 'We are running a race with Bolshevism, and the world is on fire.'[19]

When it came to dealing with the new Communist state, however, the Allied firefighters were in some confusion. Clemenceau wanted to reinforce the Romanians and let them loose on the Bolsheviks in both Russia and Hungary. Foch, belligerent as ever, advised that they should forget Russia, which was already a lost cause, and use Romania to smash Hungary and so prevent a solid Bolshevik front in Central Europe. Wilson dithered, after his initial shock, but was firmly opposed to military intervention: 'It was important,' he said, 'to avoid an excessively hard attitude which would push one country after another into Bolshevism. The same danger existed in Vienna; should we have to trace a line of demarcation [for Austria], Vienna might answer by throwing herself into Bolshevism.' Studiously avoiding any prejudgement of the new Hungarian regime, he speculated that it was probably nationalist. 'It is a soviet government,' he suggested ingenuously, 'because that is the form of revolution which is in fashion; and there may well be different species of soviets.'[20]

Lloyd George had equally serious doubts about military action: 'Let's not deal with Hungary as with Russia,' he counselled. 'One Russia is quite enough for us.' He proposed sending someone they could trust to Budapest, someone such as the South African leader, General Jan Smuts, to talk to Kun and report back on him and his regime. The others agreed, but on Clemenceau's insistence they also agreed to send military supplies to Romania at the same time.[21] While Smuts's mission was ostensibly to fix an armistice line between the Hungarians and Romanians, the real idea, said Harold Nicolson, who accompanied Smuts as a Foreign Office adviser, was 'to see whether Béla Kun is worth using as a vehicle for getting into touch with Moscow'.[22]

Smuts left Paris for Budapest in a sleeper car attached to the new Paris–Bucharest train on the evening of 1 April, All Fools' Day, with a small band of aides, changing to a special train in Vienna. In Hungary, this was greeted as a sign that the Peace Conference was ready to recognise the new soviet regime. Greatly excited, Kun ordered a vast amount of red velvet to drape all the buildings on the route from the railway station to the Hotel Hungaria, 'the Ritz of Buda Pest', paying for it by selling the last of Hungary's dwindling assets, its fat stocks, to Italy. Smuts rather spoiled the party by refusing to leave the train, insisting that Kun come to him and holding the talks in the dining car, though it would have to be by candlelight, since the power had failed. The talks did not go well. Smuts offered a formal meeting in Paris; Kun demanded that any such meeting be held in Vienna or Prague. Kun wanted Smuts to offer recognition and to order the Romanians out of Transylvania. Smuts was not prepared, or able, to do either. He presented Kun with a draft agreement for the occupation by the Allies of a neutral zone between Hungary and Romania, with the promise that if he accepted it they would raise the blockade. It was clear that Kun longed to accept this – signing such a document would imply official recognition of his regime. But he was 'suspicious and afraid'. He took it away with him, saying that he must consult his Cabinet, which meant, Nicolson noted, that he had to consult Moscow.

The Spanish and Swiss consuls visited the train and reported that the Red guards were getting out of hand in the city, that the prisons were packed and there was fear of a massacre. They reiterated what everybody was saying, 'namely, that Béla Kun is just an incident and not worth treating seriously'. This confirmed the impression that Smuts had already gained, and by the end of the second day he had concluded that Kun was a stupid man whose government would not last long, and that there was no point in any further talks. He was determined to break off negotiations that very night, although the Hungarians were expecting to make an appointment for a further meeting the next day. 'Well, gentlemen,' he said, conducting Kun and his delegation 'with exquisite courtesy' back on to the platform and shaking hands with them, 'I must bid you goodbye.' And with that, he stepped back inside, nodded to his ADC, and saluted as the train began to move, gliding off into the night and leaving, as Nicolson recorded, 'four bewildered faces looking up at us in blank amazement'.[23]

On the return journey to Paris, Smuts's special train stopped in Prague and then Vienna, where Nicolson and fellow diplomat Alan Leeper walked to the British Embassy. 'The people are delighted to see us,' Nicolson noted in his diary. 'They think it means food somehow and protection against Bolshevism. A knot of people follow us about, "Gib uns zu essen . . . (Give us food)," an old man exclaims. Poor souls!'[24] When the train continued its journey, an additional coach had been attached containing the Archduke Maximilian, fleeing from what he feared would shortly be a Bolshevik Austria.

During most of March and April, the peacemakers in Paris were naturally preoccupied with finalising the main treaty with Germany, which for everyone's sake needed to be signed as soon as possible. But there were many other aspects of the peace to be dealt with, too, not least the drawing of new frontiers in Central and Eastern Europe and the creation of new states from the wreckage of the Ottoman Empire in the Middle East. These would all be covered by additional treaties with Austria, Hungary, Bulgaria and Ottoman Turkey, which all clamoured for the attention of the statesmen and their officials. And there was always the business of creating the League of Nations and its attendant International Labour Organisation, which still dominated Wilson's thinking.

Meanwhile, upheavals and unrest continued in various other parts of the world. The Russian civil war raged on, in all its messy complexity, with the fortunes of each side ebbing and flowing across the immense spaces of the old tsarist empire. During the spring and early summer of 1919, it seemed from the outside that the Whites, in their various guises and under their various leaders, were gaining the upper hand with a number of spectacular successes. Just before the spring thaw turned the roads into a sea of mud, they managed at last to coordinate their efforts into a great attack on three fronts, advancing from the east, north and south. By mid April they had driven the Bolsheviks back out of 300,000 square kilometres. But that proved to be the high point: Trotsky's Red Army was steadily building its strength and cohesion, and began regaining the lost ground throughout the year.

The Allies were anxious to withdraw their intervention forces from Murmansk and Archangel, but could not do so until the sea ice had broken up; the ice on the rivers, however, had already thawed, allowing Bolshevik monitors to sail up them and attack the British, American and French troops, who were all growing increasingly weary and mutinous. It would be June before they could be withdrawn, but Churchill aimed to 'raise the morale of our men out there by promising them definitely in a message direct from me that they will either be relieved by volunteers from England or withdrawn altogether as soon as Archangel is open'. He ordered the General Staff to start organising a force of 5,000 or 6,000 volunteers 'who could be sent if necessary to extricate these North Russian expeditions'. Were there 5–6,000 men available to be formed into special battalions? he asked, adding: 'There is no need to tell these men where they are going at this stage.' [25]

At the same time, the War Cabinet took a firm decision to pull out of the Caucasus and the Caspian, 'as soon as possible', leaving those areas to the Italians and White Russian forces under General Denikin. Britain should 'make it up to Denikin', Churchill wrote to Lloyd George, by sending him arms and munitions and an advisory mission of officers and sergeants, 'which may if necessary amount to 2,000 in all of technical assistants and instructors'.[26]

The British and American mutinies in north Russia were little more than grumbles to relieve the men's boredom and discomfort. Those in the Ukraine, however, among French troops and sailors, were more serious – and more political. The French had landed a division of 10,000 men, mostly colonial troops from Algeria and Senegal, in the great southern port of Odessa, the Marseilles of the Black Sea, on 18 December 1918. The Greeks sent two divisions, numbering 30,000 men; the Poles a 3,000-strong brigade; the Romanians – next-door neighbours with one eye on self-preservation and the other on possible territorial gains – an army of 32,000. Denikin, meanwhile, had 15,000 White Russians in the area. In all, some 90,000 men controlled a strip of territory fifty miles deep along the Black Sea coast from the Romanian border to Kherson on the River Dnieper. Equipped with tanks, armoured cars and airplanes, such a force should have been able to dominate much of southern Russia, but the troops were badly led and had little stomach for the campaign. A series of daring raids by the Red Cavalry, plus attacks on their right flank by Ukrainian anarchists, quickly forced them back into a small enclave around the port, where the anti-Semitic Denikin's White forces succeeded in antagonising the local population and the French troops by their brutality as they massacred Jews by the tens of thousands – Odessa was a big, opulent city with a famous Jewish ghetto, the Moldavanka, whose gangsters ran the docks. French troops were further demoralised by Bolshevik propaganda: Bolshevik agents got at them in cafés and cabarets and worked them up against the Russian tsarists for whom they were fighting. The Bolsheviks also brought out a daily news-sheet in French, which appeared in all the barracks, spreading often false news, as did a regular stream of wireless broadcasts: there was no French radio station powerful enough to relay news from France, and French ships only received very irregular messages from Paris.

By the end of March, relations between all the miscellaneous forces in and around Odessa had become totally impossible. The city was without food and in a state of virtual anarchy. Unable to get any sense out of the Russians or to rely on their own men, the French decided they had had enough and began pulling out, without consulting Denikin. The last of their troops embarked on 5 April, singing the 'Internationale' as they marched to the ships, and sailed for home, taking with them 10,000 of Denikin's men and 30,000 Russian civilians, who had managed to fight or bribe their way on board the ships. They destroyed all the military stores and equipment they could not take with them, preferring to blow them up or dump them in the sea rather than leave them for Denikin.

Shortly afterwards, the few French and Greek troops in the nearby Crimea left after a brief armistice with the Reds, during which the British Navy took the opportunity to evacuate the surviving members of the Russian royal family. In Sevastopol, French soldiers deserting from the forts joined a procession of sailors in a march to the town hall, where the chairman of the Revolutionary Committee, who spoke fluent French having worked at the Galeries Lafayette in Paris, thanked them for their support. When Greek troops opened fire on them, the

French shelled the Greek flagship until they stopped. French sailors raised red flags on their ships, imprisoned their officers and put to sea as a sign of unity with the Bolsheviks, threatening to turn their ships over to the Reds if their demands were not met for better conditions, an end to intervention and a rapid return to France and demobilisation. To complete the French humiliation, André Marty, the founder of the French Communist Party, led a mutiny in their Black Sea Fleet two weeks later, thus ensuring that any further intervention in the area was out of the question.

Herbert Hoover, who like Wilson still believed that Bolshevism was entirely the result of hardship and hunger and could be 'cured' if these conditions were alleviated, put forward a plan to calm the Bolsheviks down by sending food shipments. Once they were well fed, he reasoned, the Russian people would come to their senses and eschew radicalism. Wilson took up the idea, and even managed to persuade Lloyd George to support it. Their plan was to let the Bolsheviks know that if they stopped trying to export their revolution then America and Britain would provide Russia with substantial help. Knowing that the French would never agree, and that he could therefore never present it as an Allied scheme, Hoover proposed that it should be run by a respected figure from a neutral country. He suggested Fridtjof Nansen, the famous Norwegian Arctic explorer, 'a fine rugged character, a man of great physical and moral courage', who as it happened was already in Paris hoping to find a role in the League of Nations.[27]

In mid April, the Council of Four – America, Britain, France and Italy – approved the plan.[28] It was agreed that a group of neutral countries would collect food and medicines for Russia, which they would deliver if the Bolsheviks arranged a ceasefire with their enemies. But when Nansen tried to send a telegram to Lenin informing him of this, the French refused to allow him to use their lines, suspecting that British, American and even German interests were trying use the scheme to gain concessions in Russia. The British also refused him, afraid that their involvement might be seen as recognition of the Soviet regime. Eventually, Nansen managed to send his cable from Berlin.

When Lenin saw the telegram, he advised Chicherin and Litvinov to use the proposal '*for propaganda* for clearly it can serve *no other* useful purpose'. He told them to be 'extremely polite to Nansen, *extremely insolent* to Wilson, Lloyd George and Clemenceau' in their reply. They did just that, while refusing categorically to consider a ceasefire unless there was a proper peace conference. Hoover's scheme was buried; there was to be no more talk of humanitarian aid to Russia.[29] Churchill had a different slant on the problem and suggested another, simpler, solution: 'Feed Germany; fight Bolshevism; make Germany fight Bolshevism.' When Violet Asquith, daughter of the former Liberal Prime Minister, asked him 'What is your Russian policy?' he replied even more simply: 'Kill the Bolshie, Kiss the Hun.'[30]

During the spring, Spain and Italy contributed to the political and industrial strife that was still plaguing Western Europe. In Barcelona, already notorious as the most turbulent city in Spain if not the whole of Europe, Catalan nationalism added to a revolutionary movement for workers' control made a lethal mixture. The anarcho-syndicalists of the Confederation of Labour (CNT) aimed to end both capitalism and rule from Madrid, to create a Catalan Workers' Republic. In August 1917 they had joined with the Socialist General Union of Labour (UGT) to organise a general strike in the city, but had been machine-gunned into submission, leaving seventy dead, hundreds of wounded and some 2,000 prisoners. Unbowed, the CNT had spent 1918 regrouping and rebuilding its strength, and in the spring of 1919, encouraged by the revolutions elsewhere, it was ready to try again, this time with the aid of hired professional gunmen, *pistoleros*. With the employers hiring their own *pistoleros*, the lines were drawn for a bloody trial of strength between capital and labour.

The CNT bore a marked resemblance to the IWW in America, but with the added spice of anarchism. Its various branches were loosely linked in a regional and national federation, but its philosophy was so opposed to any form of organised bureaucracy that it employed only one paid official, and had no strike or benefit funds. Nevertheless, when the strike call went out in February, all 100,000 CNT workers in Barcelona downed tools, walked out and stayed out for a whole month, with not a peseta of strike pay among them. It was a truly remarkable example of workers' solidarity. Also remarkable was the fact that although thousands were arrested and given heavy sentences, there was very little violence.

The strike in Barcelona ended in an uneasy truce, but by then the revolt had spread to other parts of Spain. There were major strikes in Seville and Granada in the deep south, and in Andalusia the peasants of the great semi-feudal estates flocked to join the CNT and began demanding increased pay and the provision of work for unemployed day labourers and ruined smallholders 'until such time as the land was handed over to peasant syndicates, to be worked by them in common'. Big Bill Haywood's Wobblies would have been proud of their Spanish brothers, who had their own anarchist newspapers in more than fifty Andalusian towns. The grandee estate owners panicked at what they saw as Bolshevism invading their lands, capitulated to the peasants' demands, and fled to the safety of their city mansions.

Reactions outside Spain were equally alarmist. 'A wave of Bolshevism is passing over Andalusia,' a correspondent of the Paris *Temps* reported. 'At San Luccar a few days ago agricultural workers burned their barns to show their discontent at inadequate wages.' In London, *The Times* waxed more lyrical in its description. Anarcho-syndicalism, it reported, had not only 'yoked the political aspirations of Catalan home rule to the fiery chariot of Bolshevism' but was making a serious attempt to capture the whole country. The mention of a Bolshevik connection was enough to persuade the British government to provide a loan of £3 million, to help the Spaniards fight the Red menace.[31]

Italy in 1919 suffered from most of the common problems of post-war Europe, plus several that were exclusively her own. The food situation at the start of the year had been so bad that the American Red Cross had had to send relief shipments of spaghetti to southern Italy. In the cities of the north, meat was virtually unobtainable and the quality of bread, already much poorer than in France or Britain, was reduced still further to preserve the scarce stores of wheat. A severe coal shortage forced the prefect of Rome to issue a decree limiting the use of gas to eight hours a day. Industrial unrest grew, aggravated by mass unemployment and rising inflation: in the late winter and early spring, Rome, Milan and Genoa were shaken by a series of strikes by printers, dockers and postal, telegraph and telephone workers. The Italian Socialist Party grew more militant, and voted to pledge its allegiance to Lenin's Third International, raising fears of a link with the Bolsheviks in Hungary. But its growth was hampered by a lack of charismatic leadership – which the Italian people found elsewhere – and an upsurge of nationalist fervour stemming from bitter resentment.

The war had proved disastrous for Italy, which had emerged with a vast national debt, 578,000 men killed and perhaps twice that number

wounded. But when they presented the bill for their services at the
Peace Conference, the Italians discovered it would not be met. They
had been lured into the war by Britain and France in 1915 with the
secret Treaty of London, promising them territory including the southern
Tyrol, Rhodes and the Dodecanese Islands, and parts of Bosnia. This
would have transferred from Austrian to Italian rule some 1.3 million
Croats, just under a quarter of a million Germans, the whole Greek
population of the Dodecanese, plus numerous Turks, Albanians and
others. It had been a generous offer, as it had needed to be to outbid
Austria's promise of territory along the Dalmatian coast to bribe Italy
out of the war – but then it is always easy to give away other people's
property, especially when it belongs to a defeated enemy. The problem
was that the offer had been made on the assumption that the Austro-
Hungarian Empire would still exist at the end of the war; there was
no thought of the creation of an independent Yugoslavia. The offer had
also been made some three years before Wilson enshrined the principle
of national self-determination in his Fourteen Points, outlawing the idea
of transferring whole populations into the control of a foreign power
without their consent and at the same time condemning secret treaties.

The Italians refused to accept that the Treaty of London was no
longer valid, and demanded payment in full, to the fury of the Allied
leaders. Wilson objected to Italian demands for 'almost the whole of
the Dalmatian coast and practically all the islands of the Adriatic',
rejecting their argument that many parts of the newly freed Balkan
States were populated by citizens of Italian origin who wished to be
reunited with their motherland.[32] He remained unimpressed by this:
during his visit to Rome at the beginning of the year he had commented
sarcastically that recent waves of immigration had made New York the
largest Italian city in the world – he hoped Orlando's government was
not going to claim that along with the whole of the Dalmatian coast!
He went so far as to accuse the Italians of being imperialists – which
they unashamedly were – but this had no effect. However, when he
appealed directly to the Italian people, over the head of Prime Minister
Orlando, to accept a frontier line that would include Trieste but stop
short of the port of Fiume (Rijeka) some fifty miles further down the
Adriatic coast, Orlando walked out of the conference.

Fiume had become a potent symbol for Italians, who took to the
streets and demonstrated against the peacemakers in Paris. It provided
a focus for their general discontent, and aided the growth of the new

Fascist movement, which had been created in Milan by Benito Mussolini, a former director of the Italian Socialist Party and left-wing journalist, who had moved abruptly to the right and now edited his own newspaper, *Popolo d'Italia*. In 1915, he had fostered revolutionary action groups, which he called 'Fasci', to agitate for Italy's entry into the war. 'Today it is War,' he cried, 'tomorrow it will be Revolution!'

In March 1919, alarmed at the rising tide of industrial unrest throughout Italy and the growth of militant socialism, and maddened by the reports from Paris that portended defeat for Italian ambitions, Mussolini revived his Fasci, assembling a disparate band of dissatisfied veterans, futurists, anarchists, criminals and clerks to form the Fascio Milanese di Combattimento, the Milanese Combat Fascio. He addressed its first general meeting on Sunday 23 March, the day after Béla Kun took power in Hungary and, incidentally, on the same day that Wilson was finally making his first visit to the battlefields of northern France. The meeting was held in a small reception room belonging to the local Association of Merchants and Shopkeepers at Piazza San Sepulchro 9, in Milan. In the square below, a squad of armed *arditi*, tough former army commandos, stood guard, clearly indicating the violent nature of the new movement.

As well as promises to end the corruption and decay in Italian political life and to 'lay the foundations of a new civilisation', Mussolini also called for the abolition of the Italian Senate, universal suffrage, the granting of workers' rights and economic democracy. 'We are dynamic,' he cried, 'and we intend to take our rightful place, which must always be in the vanguard.' The Fasci would be 'organs of creativity and agitation that will be ready to rush into the piazzas and shout: "The right to the political succession belongs to us, because we are the ones who pushed the country into war and led it to victory."'[33]

By the middle of April, Fasci had been organised in Rome, Genoa, Verona, Parma, Naples, Turin, Padua, Trieste, Venice and Bologna, and a formal alliance had been declared with the 20,000-strong National Association of Arditi. They were soon flexing their muscles against the left. On 10 April the city government in Rome banned a mass meeting planned by the Italian Socialist Party in the Piazza Venezia, followed by a 'proletarian procession' to the Piazza del Popolo, to mark Lenin's birthday and to commemorate the murders of Liebknecht and Luxemburg. The Socialists responded by announcing that the march would go ahead anyway, and called a one-day general strike in protest at the ban. The demonstrations in Rome, heavily policed by cavalry and *carabinieri*, passed off relatively quietly, apart from one brief skirmish with a counter-demonstration of *arditi*. But four days later in Milan a demonstrator was killed in a clash with Fascists and police, and the Socialists called a general strike.

The Milan strike began peacefully on 15 April, with the usual mass meeting and procession. But when a group of Socialists chanting revolutionary slogans tried to carry their huge red flag into the centre of the city they were attacked by *arditi* and Fascists. In the ensuing battle, with revolver shots being fired by both sides, the Socialists came off worse, and were forced to retreat, with many injured. The Fascists then advanced on the offices of the main Socialist newspaper, *Avanti!*, where they were met by gunfire from the besieged staff. An army private guarding the entrance was hit and fatally wounded, whereupon the Fascists rushed the building, brushing aside the military guard, smashed the printing presses and torched the furniture and files. Four civilians were shot dead and at least thirty wounded. When police reinforcements finally arrived, they made over fifty arrests, mostly of Socialists. Mussolini, who had watched from a safe place, decided that this had been 'the first episode of the civil war', and noted with some satisfaction that the police held back when the victims of street violence were Socialists, and were reluctant to intervene. Nevertheless, he took the precaution of protecting himself with a personal guard of *arditi*, and turning the offices of his own newspaper into an armed fortress.

Mussolini was among the first to float the idea of a piratical expedition to seize Fiume for Italy. But he had a powerful ally and sometime rival in the author, playwright and war hero Gabriele D'Annunzio who had an even stronger flair for self-advertisement than Mussolini. D'Annunzio's literary reputation rested on three steamy, erotic novels published in the 1890s, numerous books of overlush poetry, and several overlong poetic dramas written between 1901 and 1904. His greatest creation, however, was undoubtedly himself. He saw himself as the last Renaissance man, a combination of artist and man of action, poet, lover and warrior, and lived his roles to the hilt. In spite of being short, bald and having what were described as 'unfortunate teeth', he became something of an international sex symbol, enjoying well-publicised affairs with actresses like Eleonora Duse (whom he married), Ida Rubinstein, the painter Romaine Brooks, and a string of aristocratic ladies.

In 1915, he had returned to Italy from self-imposed exile in France (where he had fled to escape his creditors) to urge his country into the war. Styling himself 'the Leader of Youth' – though he was then fifty-two – he brought with him 2,000 volunteers wearing Garibaldean red shirts supplied by a Paris couturier. During the war, despite his age, he joined a cavalry regiment, but also served in submarines and in the air, losing an eye but winning medals for bravery as he fought wherever and whenever he chose. Throughout 1919, he campaigned tirelessly for Fiume to be given to Italy, publishing inflammatory letters and articles in Mussolini's newspaper and plotting with various groups to seize the port, which indeed he did in September, ruling it like a medieval prince until it was declared an independent free city in December 1920, when he retired in high dudgeon after fruitlessly declaring war on Italy.

Inspired by Mussolini and D'Annunzio, the Fascists quickly rose to prominence in Italy itself during the summer and autumn of 1919. Within a short time, large tracts of the north of the country became ungovernable as they fought their left-wing and democratic enemies. The battle with Bolshevism became their main *raison d'être* as Communist-led strikes, riots, factory occupations and agrarian disturbances raised the real possibility of Red revolution. With the connivance of the government and the active backing of industrialists and landowners, Mussolini's black-shirted squads raided the headquarters of their political opponents, destroyed trade union offices, burnt down cooperative institutions, smashed left-wing presses, beat up Socialists with knuckledusters and blackjacks, and force-fed Communists on castor oil. This induced severe diarrhoea and dehydration, often resulting in death; sometimes, to ensure the dose was lethal, they mixed it with gasoline.

# VII

## 'RESPECTABLE PERSONS SHOULD KEEP INDOORS'

DURING the first four months of 1919, the influenza pandemic that had taken such an immense toll across the world finally petered out. It was replaced, however, with a new infection against which few nations were immune, and which was to prove far more long-lasting than the 'Spanish flu' and just as widespread. In South Africa, workers took over Johannesburg town hall in April and began to run the city. In New South Wales, a massive strike of Australian miners and seamen in support of an IWW-backed campaign for industrial solidarity under a single union turned into a trial of strength with government, the courts and existing unions which brought much of the country to a virtual standstill. In South America, Buenos Aires was still seething with discontent, and in Mexico government forces were hunting down the rebel leader Emiliano Zapata. Although Zapata was not a Bolshevik, he might as well have been, with his revolutionary slogan 'Land, liberty, and death to the landowners'. He was killed in an ambush on 10 April.

Revolutionary forces were at work in Egypt, too. Although these were nationalistic, aimed at removing the British who had occupied the country since 1882 to safeguard the Suez Canal, the insurrection was soon described by the British press as having 'developed into Bolshevism'. The trouble erupted when the British authorities arrested four leading nationalists for urging the Khedive, the puppet ruler of the country, to demand complete independence, and deported them to Malta. Strikes and demonstrations broke out all over Egypt, becoming increasingly violent as telegraph wires were cut and railway tracks torn up. Egyptian barristers in the courts went on strike. Looting and incendiarism was reported over a wide area, and a mob attacked a sugar factory at Hawamdin, south of Cairo.[1]

On 18 March nine unarmed British officers travelling to Luxor by train were beaten to death by a mob, their bodies stripped and dumped in the baggage van. The British imposed martial law, and sent General Allenby, the legendary commander who had defeated the Turks and earned his place in history by dismounting from his horse and entering Jerusalem humbly, on foot, to take charge. Allenby surprised everyone by releasing the nationalist leaders and allowing them to travel to Paris to canvass support at the Peace Conference. As it turned out, they had little success, but the British opened independence negotiations anyway, and agreed a constitution later in the year, which led on to full independence in 1922 but with Britain retaining control of the Suez Canal.

'The Russian Bolshevik Government for a long time has been organising an extensive propaganda for revolutions in China, India and Persia,' a *Washington Post* correspondent in London reported in January, 'and is now ready, as soon as the opportunity offers, to send agents with large sums of money to stir up trouble throughout Asia.'[2] There was certainly trouble for Britain in India, and here again the fear of Bolshevism fed into an already tricky situation. India had been plagued by revolutionary terrorism linked with the independence struggle since 1907. During the war, this had been covered by emergency powers under the Defence of India Act, but these powers had lapsed with the coming of peace. In 1918, a committee led by Sir Sydney Rowlatt, a justice of the King's Bench Division in England, had drafted legislation allowing the government to go on bypassing the normal procedures of law in dealing with 'activities prejudicial to the security of the state', that catch-all phrase beloved by all totalitarian regimes.

When the bill was presented to India's Imperial Legislative Council in February 1919, it was roundly and unanimously condemned as a denial of basic rights and civil liberties by the Indian members, almost all of whom were lawyers schooled in London's ancient Inns of Court. They were, however, outnumbered on the council by British members, and what became known as the Rowlatt Act was passed into law on 18 March 1919.

The timing of the Rowlatt Act could hardly have been worse. India was already seething with discontent from many different causes: there was disillusion with the meagre rewards being offered by Britain for

India's support during the war – some 1,440,437 Indian troops had served overseas, of whom more than 100,000 had been killed or wounded.[3] There were swingeing new taxes on excess profits; the changeover from a wartime to a peacetime economy had brought rampant inflation, widespread shortages, a disastrous slump in the textile trade, and a wave of industrial disputes with mill owners. India was particularly hard hit by the influenza epidemic, which claimed 12 million lives there, 20 per cent more than the entire death toll for all sides during the war; many Indians saw this as a cosmic indictment of Western civilisation and British rule. There were Hindu fears over a new marriage bill, which threatened traditional practices, and Muslim fears over the dismemberment of the Ottoman Empire, which threatened the holy places of Islam. The list went on and on.

In such an atmosphere, the Rowlatt Act provided a convenient focus for all the various grievances. The textile industry might have been in the doldrums, but the rumour mills were working overtime spreading the most horrendous stories. The anti-terrorist legislation in the Act would hardly affect ordinary Indians and few really understood what was involved, but it was seen as an insult to Indian honour, and defeating it became a matter of national pride. The young men of the Home Rule Leagues held protest meetings in various towns and cities, but these were local affairs, run by local leaders. They needed someone with enough weight and charisma to weld them into a national campaign. They found him in Mohandas Gandhi.

Gandhi was a London-trained Hindu lawyer, who had made his name fighting for the rights of Indian indentured labourers in South Africa, where he had lived for twenty-two years until he returned to India in 1915. Dubbed 'Mahatma' (Great Soul) by the famous Bengali poet, Sir Rabindranath Tagore, he had set up an ashram, a spiritual centre, in Ahmedabad, the principal city of his native Gujarat province, before setting off on a tour of India to get to know the people – and for them to get to know him. He had tried to avoid any involvement in politics, but had gradually been drawn into affairs that were increasingly political, before becoming a hero to India's masses through a series of campaigns on behalf of peasants and millworkers. During these, he developed the tactic of non-violent civil disobedience, *satyagraha*, with great success. But when he tried to apply the same idea to fighting the Rowlatt Act, the results were disappointing. He turned instead to an ancient Hindu process called a *hartal,* when people stopped work for a day, which they devoted to self-purification through fasting and prayer.

After some confusion over dates, Gandhi's general *hartal* was called for 6 April. It was taken up with varying degrees of success throughout India. In Bombay, where Gandhi himself led thousands in prayer and purification by bathing in the sea, 80 per cent of the shops closed, and in the United Provinces, the Punjab and Bihar, almost all large towns came to a standstill, though most people took no part in fasting, prayer or purification rituals. Almost everywhere, the *hartal* passed off peacefully, with Hindus, Muslims and Sikhs taking part in complete harmony.

The peaceful nature of the protest failed to assuage the British diehards in government, who found it hard to distinguish between a *hartal* and the Bolshevik weapon of choice, a general strike. The reactionary Lieutenant Governor of the Punjab, Sir Michael O'Dwyer, was not alone in believing that the *hartals* and the whole *satyagraha* movement were part of a revolutionary conspiracy which was about to raise the red flag all over India; the only way to deal with it was by the use of 'prompt force', before it got out of hand. When he heard that Gandhi was scheduled to pass through his territory on the train from Bombay to Delhi, O'Dwyer issued an exclusion order banning him from the Punjab, and had him taken off the train and put on the next one back to Bombay. The news of Gandhi's 'arrest' sparked protests and riots in Bombay, Ahmedabad and Delhi, which Gandhi did his best to stop. In Delhi, there was a new *hartal* lasting eight days, with little damage or violence except for a riot on 17 April in which two men were killed.

Worse trouble occurred in Lahore, capital of the Punjab, where a spontaneous *hartal* closed down the city within an hour of the news of Gandhi's arrest. It began quite peacefully, but when a number of protestors began heading towards the civil lines, the European quarter, O'Dwyer promptly sent troops and police with orders to drive them back behind the walls of the old city. When the students at the head of the crowd refused, explaining that their intentions were entirely peaceful and that they only wanted to show their sorrow at the Mahatma's arrest, the police opened fire at point-blank range. Eight marchers dropped dead. The rest scattered. Elsewhere, police confronted other crowds with less success, and before long the city was out of control. All police were withdrawn. O'Dwyer called on the local community leaders to exert their authority but no one would listen to them.

From 11 to 14 April, the only real power in Lahore was held by the fifty members of the People's Committee, elected at a packed meeting of Muslims, Hindus and Sikhs at the great Badshahi mosque. The very name 'People's Committee', with its overtones of Red revolution, was enough to horrify O'Dwyer. He sent in the troops, who broke up a meeting at the mosque then opened fire on demonstrators, killing ten and wounding twenty-seven. Martial law was proclaimed, and within a couple of days everything appeared to be back to normal.

Elsewhere in the Punjab, however, things were far from normal. In Amritsar, the holy city of the Sikhs, Muslims had been joining the Hindu celebration of Ram Naumi, the birthday of the semi-divine hero of Indian mythology, Lord Rama, when Hindus parade through the streets carrying statues of their gods anointed with ghee – clarified butter – and garlanded with flowers. The British found such a political show of unity between the three faiths alarming. On O'Dwyer's orders, Deputy Commissioner Miles Irving secretly arrested the city's two Indian leaders – a Hindu doctor who had served in the Indian Medical Service during the war, and a Muslim lawyer who was a member of Lincoln's Inn, a Cambridge graduate and a PhD of Munster University – and whisked them off to a secluded hill station a hundred miles away. Word of their disappearance quickly spread throughout the city, shortly before the news arrived of Gandhi's arrest. A great crowd began advancing on Irving's bungalow, demanding to know what had become of their local leaders.

According to the Indian version of events, the crowd was sorrowful and peaceful – the men had removed their turbans and shoes in the traditional sign of mourning. The British, however, saw the crowd as a menacing mob, which had thrown off its turbans and shoes to be ready for battle. Whichever is the correct version, a battle is what they got. As the masses marched through the city, their numbers growing all the time to an estimated 40,000, their mood became more excited and aggressive. Stones rained down on police and troops sent to head them off, and the troops opened fire. Three or four demonstrators were killed and several wounded, and in no time the demonstration had become a full-scale riot. The mob, now enraged, headed for the commercial heart of the city, where they destroyed the telegraph exchange offices, smashed and looted shops and burnt down the town hall, a Christian church and school, and two of the three European banks, murdering the managers and burning their bodies. During the day, as the violence raged throughout the city, a total of five European men and at least twenty-five Indians were killed. But what really inflamed

Anglo-Indian tempers was an attack on a white woman, an unpardonable offence in the eyes of the British male. Miss Marcia Sherwood, a respected doctor and mission-school supervisor, encountered a mob which knocked her from her bicycle, beat her up and left her for dead. A Hindu shopkeeper saved her life at the risk of his own, picking her up from the gutter and hiding her in his house.

One hundred and thirty terrified European women and children took refuge in a primitive fort under the protection of an inadequate force of British and Indian troops, aided by fifty men of the Gurkha Rifles whose train had fortuitously stopped at Amritsar. With all the telegraph lines cut, Irving managed to get a junior officer out on a light railway engine to fetch help, and military reinforcements started arriving at 11 p.m., under the command of Brigadier General Reginald 'Rex' Dyer, eventually bringing the number of troops in the city to a grand total of 1,200, still a pitifully small force to control an agitated population swollen far beyond the city's normal 160,000 by visitors for Ram Naumi and another Sikh and Hindu festival, Baisakhi, the solar new year, which fell that year on Sunday 13 April.

By that time, all was quiet again. An eerie calm hung over the wrecked city, lit by the flames of still-burning buildings. The fire had gone out of the demonstrations, but Dyer nevertheless persuaded Deputy Commissioner Irving to hand over control of the city to him. Dyer was a classic product of the Raj, whose attitude to political Indians made O'Dwyer look like a watery liberal. Dyer issued orders that 'no gatherings of persons or processions of any sort will be allowed. All gatherings will be fired on. Any persons leaving the city in groups of more than four will be fired on. Respectable persons should keep indoors.' He reinforced this message with announcements in all the main streets during Saturday, and again on Sunday morning, but despite his warnings, crowds of Indians from the surrounding countryside continued to pour into the city to celebrate Baisakhi by worshipping in the Golden Temple and bathing in its Pool of Immortality. There were also many who came to grab as much loot from the wreckage as they could carry away in their carts. Furious that his orders were being flouted, Dyer went back into the streets with another show of force and another proclamation, touring the city and distributing leaflets in local languages until 2 p.m., when the heat became totally unbearable and he was forced to retire.

Dyer had chosen to ignore reports that a meeting was to be held that afternoon in an open space known as the Jallianwala Bagh, confident that his authority would not be so openly flouted. However, when he received confirmation at 4 p.m. that a great crowd had gathered there and the meeting was definitely about to take place, he could ignore it no longer. Collecting a force of ninety men – all Indians and Nepalese Gurkhas – and two armoured cars, he ordered their British officers to stay behind: 'If there's anything to be done,' he told them, 'I'll do it alone.' Then he headed for the Jallianwala Bagh. The name literally means the garden of Jalli, but it was unlike any European idea of a garden. One Englishman remembered it as 'a piece of unused ground covered . . . by building material and debris and entirely surrounded by the walls of buildings'. Lying in the heart of the city barely 250 yards from the Golden Temple, it formed a rough rectangle measuring about 200 yards by 100 and containing three dusty peepul trees, a domed, broken-down tomb and a well. Estimates of the number of people crammed into the *bagh* that Sunday afternoon vary between 15,000 and 50,000, many of them Hindu and Sikh peasant families who had come in from the surrounding villages to celebrate Baisakhi and were camping there. Others had come to meet friends, gossip, play cards or dice, because that is what they normally did on Sunday afternoons. The densest part of the crowd was gathered around a wooden platform erected near the well, from which an assortment of politicians and poets were addressing them on the most recent iniquities of British rule and inciting them to murder the British.

Dyer arrived shortly before 5.15 p.m., and deployed his riflemen on a raised terrace with a clear field of fire over the entire square. Seeing the soldiers kneeling and raising their weapons to take aim, some of the crowd tried to run. But there was only one narrow exit open, and therefore little chance of escape. Even as the man who had been speaking, Durgas Dass, the editor of the Lahore Urdu newspaper *Waqt*, tried to calm the people, telling them the soldiers would not shoot, Dyer ordered his men to open fire and the first volley rang out from fifty rifles. When the troops tried to fire over the heads of the crowd, he ordered them to shoot straight and low, directing them to fire at those trying to escape the killing field as well as aiming where the crowd was thickest.

The shooting was as calm, deliberate and carefully aimed as target practice at the butts. It was broken only when the troops paused to reload their magazines. 'I fired and continued to fire,' Dyer later told the British government's official committee of inquiry, 'until the crowd dispersed and I consider this is the least amount of firing which would produce the necessary moral and widespread effect . . . If more troops had been at hand, the casualties would have been greater in proportion.' When he finally ordered his men to cease firing, they had used 1,650 rounds of .303 mark VI ammunition, killing an estimated 379 men, women and children and wounding some 1,200 more. Satisfied that he had achieved his purpose, Dyer ordered the troops to withdraw. Turning on his heel, he marched away without a backward glance at the carnage he had inflicted.

General Dyer was firmly convinced that he had saved the Indian Empire. In fact, he had signed its death warrant. The shooting at Jallianwala Bagh lasted just ten minutes, but in those ten minutes he had destroyed the trust in British justice and fair play that had been built up over one and a half centuries. He had shattered the myth of benevolent paternalism that had allowed a tiny group of barely a thousand British civil servants, backed up by as few as 15,000 British soldiers, to govern some 400 million Indians. As a result, what had been a desultory campaign by minority groups seeking home rule for India within the British Empire was transformed overnight into a vigorous, determined and popular national independence movement. The tide of revolution that was sweeping across the world in 1919 had reached South Asia.[4]

Gandhi wrote a sorrowful letter to Lord Chelmsford, the Viceroy of India:

It is not without a pang that I return the Kaiser-i-Hind Gold Medal granted to me by your predecessor for my humanitarian work in South Africa, the Zulu War Medal for my services as an officer in charge of the Indian Volunteer Ambulance Corps in 1906, and the Boer War Medal for my services as Assistant Superintendent of the Indian Volunteer Stretcher-Bearer Corps . . . I can retain neither respect nor affection for a government which has been moving from wrong to wrong in order to defend its immorality . . . The government must be moved to repentance. I have therefore ventured to suggest non-cooperation.[5]

The Bolsheviks in Moscow were delighted by this. The New Communist Manifesto had called for 'a series of risings and revolutionary unrest in all colonies', and Nikolai Bukharin, the party philosopher, had told the Eighth Congress of the Communist Party in March: 'If we propose the solution of the right of self-determination for the colonies, the Hottentots, the Negroes, the Indians, etc, we lose nothing by it . . . The most outright nationalist movement, for example, the Hindus, is only water for our mills, since it contributes to the destruction of English imperialism.'[6]

Dyer, like many other British officers and officials, was convinced that Gandhi and his associates were being manipulated by Moscow, and that the revolt in the Punjab had been timed to coincide with an invasion from Afghanistan. The Afghan dimension was not as far-fetched as it might appear – later in the year, Trotsky, baulked by lack of success in Europe, noted in a secret memorandum: 'There is no doubt at all that our Red Army constitutes an incomparably more powerful force in the Asian terrain of world politics than in the European terrain . . . The road to India may prove at the given moment to be more readily passable and shorter than the road to Soviet Hungary. The road to Paris and London lies via the towns of Afghanistan, the Punjab and Bengal.'[7]

The British had been obsessed for many years with the fear that Russia would invade India through Afghanistan. During the nineteenth century they had themselves invaded Afghanistan twice – catastrophically in 1838–42, and more successfully in 1878–80 – in efforts to safeguard the Indian Empire against Russia, and since the Second Anglo-Afghan War had controlled its foreign policy. The change of regime in Moscow had done nothing to reduce British paranoia – if anything it had increased it by adding a Bolshevik dimension. In September 1918, Lenin had sent his special envoy, Karl Bravin, to Kabul to open negotiations with the ruler, the Emir Habibullah, for Soviet–Afghan cooperation. On 20 February 1919, however, Habibullah was assassinated while on a hunting trip, possibly as a result of his dealing with Lenin, but equally possibly because of his long-standing friendship with the British which had earned him the enmity of the more extreme nationalist elements in Kabul.

Habibullah's second son, Amanullah, seized power on the death of his father. As soon as he had secured his position by the traditional method of purging his own family of anyone with political ambitions, he demanded formal recognition of Afghanistan as a sovereign state from Lord Chelmsford. And when he received no reply, he united the country behind him by declaring war on Britain and preparing for an invasion of India. Having heard that great nationalist revolts in the Punjab and elsewhere had weakened the defences of the Raj in the

North-West Provinces, he had leaflets distributed in northern India urging the Muslims to rise, tear up the railways, cut telegraph wires and kill the British. Seeking external support, he wrote a flowery letter to Lenin, 'the High-Born President of the Great Russian Republic', offering 'the friendly greetings of his friend Amanullah' and declaring that 'by raising the standard of Bolshevism he [Lenin] had earned the gratitude of the whole world'. His Foreign Minister, Mahmud Tarzi, also wrote expressing the hope that 'permanent friendly relations would now be established between the Bolsheviks and Afghanistan'.

Meanwhile, a self-styled Professor Barkatullah, a renegade Indian who had spent much of the Great War in Berlin, where he had been appointed Foreign Minister of a provisional puppet government of India, had arrived in Moscow claiming to be head of an Afghan delegation. An intercepted radio message to the Bolshevik Eastern Propaganda Bureau in Moscow asked the bureau to press Barkatullah 'to finish his promised pamphlet on Bolshevism in the Koran, and dispatch 100,000 printed copies in Persian, Hindustani and Arabic by special courier'.[8]

The Third Anglo–Afghan War began in April 1919, with an Afghan invasion of the frontier provinces of India, initially in a series of raids on soft and profitable targets such as caravans and bazaars by an army described as 'little more than a mob of bandolier-festooned rag-pickers'.[9] In response, the government of India ordered a counter-invasion, sending 3,000 troops under the command of General Dyer to reinforce the existing frontier forces, backed by aircraft – a flight of obsolescent Handley-Page bombers. Unable to gain enough altitude to fly over the mountains, they had to fly through the Khyber Pass, giving the Afghan riflemen the unique experience of firing down at them from above. They went on to bomb Kabul, the first airplanes ever seen by the city, claiming to have hit munitions factories and causing 'a large explosion'. One of the bombs, however, hit the Emir's harem, forcing the ladies to flee into the streets – which gave great offence to Afghan Muslims. A second raid on Jalalabad was reported to have damaged and set fire to several military buildings, and tribesmen in the Gandao Valley were attacked and scattered.[10]

Dyer may have been an appalling human being, but he was a competent and experienced general, and his professionally handled guns soon forced the Afghans to reconsider their position and request an armistice. The British were happy and somewhat relieved to end the war: 2,000 troops had mutinied in Rawalpindi when they discovered that they had, without their knowledge, 'volunteered' for duty in Afghanistan. Clerical staff in Poona downed pens in protest, and elsewhere motor transport units, composed of men long overdue for repatriation and demobilisation, also refused to accept their officers' orders. If the mutinies spread, the British authorities believed, their rule in India itself could be at risk. Although not defeated on the battlefield, thanks to Rex Dyer and their Handley-Page bombers, the British were routed at the conference table. The Afghans gained their independence from British India, with support from Soviet Russia – marking a notable advance in Bolshevik influence in the region.

# VIII

## 'THE MOST FRIGHTENED VICTORS
## THAT THE WORLD EVER SAW'

THE Soviet government in Russia could do nothing physically to help the radical cause in America, but it could and did provide support through its propaganda machine, funded by large sums of money. Karl Radek, executive secretary of the Comintern, boasted that the money Moscow sent to Berlin for the Spartacist revolution 'was as nothing compared to the funds transmitted to New York for the purpose of spreading Bolshevism in the United States'.[1]

The chief agent for spreading and coordinating Bolshevik propaganda in America was a German-born Marxist called Ludwig C.A.K. Martens, who arrived in the winter of 1918–19 with credentials from Soviet Foreign Commissar Chicherin empowering him to negotiate for the 'opening of commercial relations for the mutual benefit of Russia and America'.[2] Since the United States did not recognise the Soviet government, the State Department refused to have anything to do with him, but he stayed on in New York, setting up shop in the World Tower Building aided by Santeri Nuorteva, ostensibly his secretary but in fact one of the party's top propaganda experts. The two men worked closely with the Socialist left wing in America, and appeared often at rallies, enthusiastically supporting proposals such as 'We want an American Soviet'.

Although the Communist International claimed that the propaganda campaign was successful because 'many of the active Socialists have boldly confessed themselves Bolsheviks',[3] most of those who did so were already committed radicals: there was little sign of new converts being attracted in any significant numbers, nor of existing radicals being stirred into violent action. What the campaign did achieve was to alarm ordinary Americans and split the American Socialist Party into left- and right-wing factions, just as the Bolsheviks had split the Russian Social Democrats in the early years of the century. In the inevitable internecine struggle, the right wing, composed mainly of English-speakers seeking peaceful evolutionary change, refused to accept the Bolshevik programme for America. The left wing, composed mainly of immigrant Slavs, Hungarians and people from the Baltic States, made over-optimistic plans for an immediate revolution, issued its own manifesto and held a series of conventions; by late spring it had attracted some 30,000 supporters, about one-third of the total Socialist Party membership.

Even though they had little basis in reality, the exaggerated claims and bloodthirsty threats of the revolutionaries were seized on by newspapers eager to find sensational stories to replace war news. But the papers were concerned with more than boosting circulation figures: a large section of the press had its own agenda, guided by its owners – wealthy businessmen and industrialists who were determined to win back all the concessions they had been forced to make to organised labour during the war years. These men were also worried about any possible extension of government controls on the economy, particularly in railroads and mines, where unions were calling for nationalisation. In an effort to destroy the unions, the employers set out to discredit them as subversive, Bolshevistic and alien to American values. They started an open-shop campaign which they named the American Plan, claiming that it represented '100 per cent Americanism', and labelled the union shop 'Sovietism in disguise'. They issued a stream of derogatory press releases and took whole-page advertisements linking organised labour with Marxism. Their own most extreme publication, the *Open Shop Review*, described unionism as 'nothing less than Bolshevism' and 'the greatest crime left in the world';[4] even Samuel Gompers's conservative AFL was branded as a revolutionary organisation, while the IWW was seen as openly Satanic.

In such a situation, the activities of the Bolsheviks and their supporters were a gift to the American press. The *Washington Post*, for instance, still cashing in on the wartime demonisation of Germans, wrote: 'A revolutionary movement more deadly than anything this country has ever known is being organised in the United States, largely with German money and under the leadership of potential traitors at home and alien enemies abroad.' The *Post* demanded legislative action: 'REDS BEYOND

REACH,' its headlines shrieked. 'LAWS FAIL TO MEET PERIL. STATUTES TO COPE WITH MENACE MUST BE ENACTED BY CONGRESS.'[5] As the clamour grew, President Wilson, briefly home from Paris, responded by appointing a new Attorney General, A. Mitchell Palmer, to replace Thomas Gregory, who was returning to his private law practice.

Alexander Mitchell Palmer was a forty-seven-year-old Quaker born in Moosehead, Pennsylvania. After graduating from Swarthmore with the highest honours, he practised law in Stroudsburg, Pennsylvania, before being elected to the House of Representatives, where he was a noted supporter of such reformist causes as women's suffrage and trade union rights during his three terms between 1909 and 1915. He became vice chairman of the Democratic National Committee in 1912, when he was also chairman of the Pennsylvania delegation to the National Convention and was chiefly responsible for swinging its votes to Woodrow Wilson. Wilson repaid him for the important part he had played in ensuring his presidential nomination by offering him the post of Secretary of War, which Palmer graciously declined, pointing out that he was a Quaker and that 'the United States requires not a man of peace for a war secretary, but one who can think war'. Instead, Wilson appointed him to a judgeship on the United States Court of Claims, and then, in 1917, to the post of Alien Property Custodian, before giving him the Department of Justice, in which he was confirmed on 5 March 1919.

As a Quaker, Palmer was naturally opposed to the godlessness and violence of the Bolshevik creed. He was also, as a patriotic American, aware of the dangers emanating from the October Revolution, which he firmly believed had been managed 'by a small clique of outcasts from the East Side of New York'. But he was reluctant to subscribe to the growing hysteria by ordering disproportionate action: 'Because a disreputable alien – Leon Bronstein, the man who now calls himself Trotsky – can inaugurate a reign of terror from his throne room in the Kremlin; because this lowest of all types known to New York can sleep in the Czar's bed,' he asked, ' . . . should America be swayed by such doctrines?'[6]

From the start in his new role, Palmer signalled that he had not abandoned his liberal principles, or his ability to think clearly, by removing repressive measures imposed during the war. He released 10,000 enemy aliens from their parole, freed violators of wartime security and disbanded the American Protective League, which had been formed during the war to search out spies and disloyalty and whose 250,000 volunteer members were reluctant to abandon their vigilante activities. At about the same time, the fourteen Spaniards who had been arrested in New York for allegedly plotting to assassinate President Wilson on his return from Paris were released on a writ of habeas corpus: Federal Judge John C. Knox castigated the government prosecutors for holding them so long without warrants or a court hearing. On 10 March, when the Supreme Court upheld the convictions under the Espionage Act of the Socialist Party leader, Eugene Debs, and its General Secretary, Charles Schenck, Palmer considered recommending that President Wilson grant executive clemency for Debs; but Wilson was already halfway across the Atlantic and Debs had to wait until 1921 before being pardoned by a new president, Warren Harding, who invited him to the White House for Christmas.[7]

Palmer continued to speak of America as the haven of the oppressed, earning the condemnation of the xenophobic New York Times for his 'pre-Adamite sentimentality'. The Times was even more indignant when twelve of the alien radicals, brought east on the 'Red Special' for deportation after the Seattle strike, were released from Ellis Island because the government was finding it hard to prove that men who could not read had been influenced by the anarchistic ideas propounded in IWW literature. The Immigration Bureau, however, kept the Stars and Stripes flying high by insisting on prosecuting the remainder of the prisoners for 'many lawless things, such as attempting to set up a Soviet Government in the Northwest, of fomenting a strike that nearly verged upon rebellion, and of seeking to turn the minds of newly-arrived immigrants toward Bolshevism'. They had proved themselves unrepentant, said a government spokesman, by persisting in singing radical songs. Their defence lawyers countercharged that they were being persecuted because they had antagonised the powerful lumber barons of the Northwest. Even as their case was being heard, another train was heading across the country filled with aliens from San Francisco and Oregon bound for Ellis Island.

Despite Palmer's efforts to cool things down, the anti-Red neurosis continued to grow steadily during March and April. Ole Hanson did his bit to keep the pot boiling – and his personal profile high – by declaring that the Bolshevik menace was 'a peril we all must face and conquer. These alien enemies should not be tolerated. They should be deported as soon as they are found, or this nation will fail.'[8] And the *New York Times* added more fuel to the fire with the apocalyptic warning: 'BOLSHEVISM IN AMERICA IS PLANNING FOR THE FINAL STRUGGLE BETWEEN SANE SOCIETY AND ANARCHY.'[9]

In the US Senate, the Judiciary Committee unanimously approved legislation banning the display of red flags; the Mayor of New York proposed a draconian ban on all meetings in the city 'whose proceedings are conducted in a foreign language for the abuse of our government, or by or under the auspices of any persons who are not citizens of the United States'. Not to be outdone, the New York State legislature in Albany voted a budget of $30,000 for a full-scale investigation 'to learn the whole truth' about radical activities in the state, having received secret information that Bolshevik agitators with heavy financial support were making rapid headway. Even in sleepy New Hampshire, the governor, 'armed with the most drastic anti-Bolshevik law in the United States', vowed to 'rake the state with a fine-tooth comb' to find the Reds who were reportedly at work in two or three centres. And Vice President Thomas R. Marshall joined in by telling a Rotary Club meeting in Phoenix that if any naturalised citizen took up the Bolshevik cause, 'I would take away his naturalisation papers and send him to the farthest of the South Sea Islands.'[10]

Writing to Bernard Berenson, the financier, at his villa near Florence, columnist Walter Lippmann commented that the President's recent visit home had not done him much good, and that 'Frankly, people are very much annoyed at being neglected . . . The main interest here, however, is not what's going on in Paris at all – the people are shivering in their boots over Bolshevism, and they are far more scared of Lenin than they ever were of the Kaiser. We seem to be the most frightened victors that the world ever saw . . .'[11]

There was further alarm in America in mid April when communications on the East Coast from Maine to Connecticut were paralysed by a strike of 8,000 telephone operators employed by the New England Telephone and Telegraph Company. The operators, all well-educated women, were demanding wage increases from their current rates, which ranged from six dollars a week for novices to sixteen dollars after seven years, to a new scale starting at ten dollars a week and rising to twenty-two dollars after four years' service. Theirs was hard and demanding work, requiring intelligence, dexterity and stamina – it was not unusual

during busy periods for operators to faint at their switchboards – and
the women's demands were by no means unreasonable. Unfortunately,
that was not the view of the company, nor of the federal government,
which was involved since it had taken control of the nation's telephones
for the duration of the war. Postmaster General Albert Burleson had
consistently refused to recognise the rights of even temporary government employees to organise, and realising that the current dispute had
been chosen by the unions as a test case, he declined to intervene now,
even when asked to do so by the Massachusetts Republican Governor,
Calvin Coolidge.

The women formed pickets, dressed in their best clothes and wearing
Easter bonnets, and despite the inconvenience they were causing had
the sympathy of the general public, who had been shocked to learn
how little they were paid. They were quickly joined by male colleagues,
and within three days their numbers had grown to nearly 20,000 across
five states, putting over 630,000 telephones out of action and bringing
business to a halt. The company tried to break the strike in Boston by
using students from Harvard and the Massachusetts Institute of
Technology, but they were attacked by strikers and had to be returned
to their colleges in police vans for their own safety. In Providence,
Newport society ladies, accompanied by their maids, volunteered as
operators, but after a three-hour shift were exhausted and called taxi-
cabs to drive them home. The cab drivers sided with the strikers and
refused to pick them up.

'This town and state are with you,' Congressman James A. Gallivan
told a packed meeting of strikers at Boston's Grand Opera House. 'If
Congress were in session, Burleson wouldn't dare do this. He thought
you'd quit, but don't you do it.' Democratic Party officials in
Massachusetts appealed by cable to the President in Paris: 'Burleson
wrecking the party. Remove him and settle this strike.' Wilson refused
to intervene, saying he could not act intelligently from such a distance,
but Coolidge stepped in, threatening to take over the phone system and
run it under state authority. Finally, Burleson submitted to the clamour
and sent his deputy to negotiate. An agreement was quickly reached,
granting the women most of what they were demanding, and they went
back to work. The majority of people were happy with the result, but
the open-shop industrialists regarded it as a capitulation to organised
labour, and a dangerous precedent.

*

The great American public was unsettled by the strikes of spring 1919. But it was terrified by the bombs. The first, appropriately enough, landed on the desk of Mayor Ole Hanson in Seattle, on 28 April. Hanson, making the most of his new-found fame, was away at the time in Colorado on a Victory Loan tour, and the package was left on a table, where it leaked acid. When examined, it was found to contain an unexploded home-made bomb. 'The Saviour of Seattle' was unfazed, bravely accusing his attackers of cowardice. The incident would have been barely noticed, but next day a similar parcel bomb arrived in the home of a former senator, Thomas W. Hardwick of Atlanta, where it was opened by a maid. The explosion blew off both her hands, and severely burnt the head and face of Mrs Hardwick, who was standing nearby.

Now, the bombs made headlines, which were read by a clerk in the New York Post Office, Charles Kaplan, as he made his way home on the subway next day. Reading the descriptions of the packages, he realised with horror that he had set aside a pile of sixteen similar parcels for inadequate postage. He hurried back to the office, retrieved them and alerted the postal inspectors, who called in the police. The packages, each about seven inches long by three inches wide, bearing a Gimbell Brothers return address and a label marked boldly in red 'NOVELTY – A SAMPLE', did indeed contain bombs: a tapered glass bottle filled with a powerful acid and designed to break when the package was opened, allowing the acid to run on to three fulminating caps, to set off three sticks of dynamite. An alarm was circulated to all post offices, and a further eighteen bombs were discovered and disarmed, bringing the total of prominent citizens targeted for death to thirty-six.

The planned recipients of the bombs included Frederic C. Howe, Commissioner of Immigration at Ellis Island; Anthony J. Caminetti, Federal Commissioner of Immigration; Senators Lee S. Overman and William H. King, a bitter opponent of labour and a member of the Overman Committee; Oliver Wendel Holmes Jr, the Associate Justice of the Supreme Court who had rejected the appeals of Charles Schenck and Eugene Debs; Judge K.M. Landis, who had sentenced Victor Berger and Big Bill Haywood; Postmaster General Albert Burleson, who had not only fought the New England telephone operators but had also banned radical literature from the mails; Secretary of Labor William B. Wilson; the financiers John D. Rockefeller and J.P. Morgan; and

Attorney General Palmer. It was a strangely heterogeneous list, since several of the intended victims were noted for their liberal attitudes rather than any reactionary prejudices. But, they were all men in positions of authority and influence, involved with labour, immigration controls and anti-radical investigations.

The terrorists were never found, but anti-Red campaigners had a field day whipping the public into a frenzy. Hanson led the pack, declaring to an audience in Topeka: 'I trust Washington will buck up and clean up and either hang or incarcerate for life all the anarchists in the country. If the government doesn't clean them up, I will. I'll give up my mayorship and start through the country. We will hold meetings and have hanging places.'[12]

The postal bombs had been clearly intended to arrive around 1 May, and therefore were seen as part of a Bolshevik conspiracy to overthrow the US government, a suspicion that was enhanced when riots broke out around May Day parades and celebrations in several major American cities. May Day disturbances were something new to America, though they were almost traditional in Continental Europe. But in 1919, American radicals, taking as their theme the reconsecration of their lives to international Socialism, staged rallies, mass meetings and red flag parades, which quickly developed into fights with police and enraged citizens. In Boston, a riot erupted when police tried to stop an unauthorised Socialist red flag parade by 1,500 workers. Rocks were thrown, pistols fired, and knives used. One police officer was stabbed to death, and another three and a civilian were injured. As news of this spread to other areas of the city, crowds of angry citizens turned into mobs seeking vengeance, one of which demolished the Boston Socialist headquarters.

There were May Day riots in New York, too, where soldiers, sailors and civilians attacked Socialists, broke up their parades and smashed their offices. A gang of soldiers stormed the Russian People's House at 133 East 15th Street, forced a Socialist gathering to sing the 'Star-Spangled Banner' and seized all the literature they could lay their hands on. Later, about four hundred of them raided the new offices of the New York *Call*, where a reception for about seven hundred people was in progress. They smashed furniture, grabbed books and literature, and finally drove the reception guests into the street with such violence that seventeen of them had to receive treatment for their injuries.

Rough though the disturbances were in Boston and New York, it was in Cleveland that the worst violence occurred, with at least four major riots in different districts that turned into pitched battles. In one of them the situation was so bad that army trucks and a Victory Loan tank had to be used to separate the warring factions. All told, one person was killed and over forty seriously injured. The police made 106 arrests – all were Socialists, most of them aliens, but not a single anti-radical, either civilian or soldier. Though there were disturbances in several other cities, most of the press focused exclusively on these three, with claims that the riots might be 'dress rehearsals' for an imminent Red revolution.

In other parts of the world, May Day was celebrated with varying degrees of enthusiasm, and of violence. In Berlin, where in the past hundreds of thousands of workers had marched through the streets behind blaring bands, singing and chanting Socialist slogans, all was quiet. It was still a national holiday, but Noske had forbidden any demonstrations, and these days no one dared challenge Noske's decisions. 'Everything closed, even the restaurants,' moaned Harry Kessler. 'The impression is of a national day of mourning for the failed revolution.'[13]

The biggest celebration, naturally, was in Moscow, where Lenin addressed the annual parade in Red Square by claiming that 'In all nations, the workers have started on the path of struggle with imperialism. The liberated working class is celebrating its anniversary freely and openly, not only in Soviet Russia but also in Soviet Hungary.' Zinoviev echoed Lenin's sentiments in the May issue of the *Communist International* with an article enticingly entitled 'Prospects for the Proletarian Revolution'. 'The Third International already has as its members three Soviet republics – in Hungary, Russia and Bavaria,' he wrote. 'But nobody will be surprised if by the time these lines appear in print we have not three but six more.' In fact, he continued, the revolution was spreading so fast that one could predict with certainty 'that in a year's time, the whole of Europe will be Communist'.

Unfortunately for Zinoviev's prophecy, on that same May Day the Bavarian Soviet was entering its death throes as General von Oven's troops and Freikorps smashed through the Communist defences and began rampaging through Munich. Now there were only two Soviet republics. And the one in Hungary was under threat, from outside. A

week after General Smuts had steamed out of Budapest on his way
back to Paris, the Romanians had invaded Hungary with the tacit
approval of the French, claiming not only that they were acting in self-
defence, but also that they were intent on restoring order and removing
Bolshevism. They complained that for months past the Hungarian
government had been organising and subsidising a Bolshevik propaganda campaign in the villages of Romanian Transylvania, aimed at
provoking a nationalist uprising. Hungarian troops stationed there, they
said, were 'in a disorderly and undisciplined state', and had been 'systematically Bolshevised and allowed to pillage and terrorise the Romanian
villages and ill-treat those who avow Romanian sympathies'.[14] The
Czechs had then invaded Hungary from the north, with similar excuses.
Lloyd George was contemptuous of these blatant attempts to use the
Bolshevik bogey: 'They are all little brigand peoples,' he commented
disparagingly, 'who only want to steal territories.'[15]

The invasions were a lifeline to Kun, who was able to unite his
people under the nationalist banner. As the Romanians advanced on
Budapest, the Hungarian people rallied to defend their country and
their revolution. Volunteers from all classes rushed to join the newly
formed Red Army, and Italy happily sold them guns and ammunition.

Hungary's perilous situation did not deter Kun and his associates
from celebrating May Day with a grand carnival in Budapest, under
the direction of Interior Minister Tibor Szamuelly, the son of a Jewish
grain merchant who had been a prisoner of war with Kun in Russia
and who had been groomed alongside him to lead the revolution in
Hungary. Szamuelly called on Hungary's avant-garde artists, who had
embraced the revolution with the same enthusiasm as their brothers
and sisters in Russia, and they did him proud. Their posters were
superlative examples of modern, mainly expressionist, art exuberantly
affirming their liberation from the straitjacket of bourgeois convention.
Giant fists smashed through palace windows on to the dining tables of
the rich; marching ranks of barrel-chested soldiers called men to join
the Red Army; peasants in the fields knelt before an unearthly red star;
a grinning skeleton dangled over a drunken worker clutching a glass
of forbidden alcohol. And everywhere the revolutionary artist Michael
Biro's definitive image of a giant figure brandishing a hammer punched
home the message of working for the revolution.

In the city, they constructed triumphal arches, dancing booths and
a skating rink in the park. There was music everywhere as bands and

orchestras gave public performances in parks and squares and on bridges over the Danube. Streets were festooned in red. Buildings were painted red, as were cars and tramcars, lamp posts and the main railway station. A fifteen-foot high statue of Karl Marx was erected on Coronation Hill and one of Lenin thirty feet high in the park, while huge busts of Lenin and Liebknecht were placed in front of the House of Soviets. Thousands of troops marched through the streets to patriotic and Socialist tunes, cheered on by crowds waving red banners. There was a parade led by stars from the nationalised film studios, wearing the costumes from their favourite roles. The carnival ended with a mammoth fireworks display and the floodlighting of the main buildings in red.

Two days later, Kun's new Red Army went to war. Although unable to make much headway against the Romanians, they quickly drove back the Czechs and overran most of Slovakia. For the moment at least, patriotism was more important than politics in Hungary.

In Paris, where the Peace Conference was approaching a draft treaty, 1 May was marked by a one-day general strike. In their smart hotels the delegates were reduced to using candles to light their rooms, washing in cold water and walking up and down stairs rather than using the elevators. The weather was cold and wet – it had been snowing two days earlier – with a persistent heavy drizzle soaking the posters and placards giving the reasons for the strike:

> I strike to demand
> first, the eight-hour day;
> second, total amnesty;
> third, rapid demobilisation;
> fourth, a just peace and disarmament.
>
> I strike to protest against
> first, intervention in Russia;
> second, income taxes on wages;
> third, martial law;
> fourth, the censorship.

During the morning the streets were largely empty: Harold Nicolson thought that 'As a result, Paris resembles Edinburgh on Sunday . . . No taxis, tubes, theatres or (Thank God in heaven!) newspapers.'[16]

A massive demonstration planned by Socialists and labour leaders in the Place de la Concorde was not due to start until after 2 p.m., to allow time for lunch. In fact, the government had banned the demonstration, fearful that it might take a revolutionary turn, but the organisers refused to call it off, and around 20,000 working men and women, wearing buttonholes of red ribbons, gathered outside the Madeleine. At about 3 p.m. they set off, linking arms and marching down the Rue Royale singing the 'Internationale'.

When they approached the Place de la Concorde, the marchers found all entrances to the square barred by a cordon of provincial troops, behind which were cavalry and police. 'I shall never forget the sight of that black crowd coming down the street, waving its red flags at the moment it ran into the troops,' wrote Charles Seymour, the Yale history professor who was a member of the American delegation. 'It might have been Petrograd, or the Revolution of 1848, which started close to here and in very much the same manner.'[17] After a little pushing and shoving, the foot soldiers let the marchers through, but the mounted cavalry set about them, using the flat sides of their sabres but still drawing blood, while the police clubbed them with their rifle butts, beating them to the ground and kicking them as they fell. The workers retaliated with stones and pieces of metal and occasionally a revolver shot. A worker was killed near the Opéra, and another fatally wounded by a demonstrator's gun while making his way home. The battle raged for most of the afternoon, with American Red Cross ambulances racing around picking up the wounded, strikers and police alike. At the end of the day, the police recorded 428 wounded, a dozen seriously, as well as the two dead. The government claimed that it had stopped an incipient revolution; the Socialists charged the government with turning a peaceful demonstration into a battle with the police.

Next morning, when Mrs Wilson went for a walk, she saw no sign of the battle. The blood had been scrubbed and washed away, and life in the city returned to normal, as though nothing had happened. But the day after that, another would-be assassin was arrested outside Clemenceau's house. The young man, nineteen-year-old Raymond Cornillon, was found to be carrying a stiletto, a number of anarchist pamphlets, and a black flag inscribed 'Communist and Anarchist Federation of the Seine'. He admitted that he knew Emile Cottin, the man who had shot Clemenceau, but denied that he had intended to kill the Premier: 'I am not a murderer,' he claimed. 'I wished only to attract attention.'[18]

The May Day celebrations in Latvia were essentially a show of defiance by President Peter Stutchka and his Bolsheviks. Since the beginning of March, General von der Goltz's German Freikorps had been driving them back out of much of the country until little more than Riga and its immediate surroundings remained in their hands. And even that was under blockade by angry peasants, resisting the requisition squads that were trying to seize their produce. Nevertheless, the dreaded terror units in the city, reputedly led by a beautiful, club-footed young Amazon commissar riding a white horse and draped in a black velvet cloak, still went about their task of eliminating the bourgeoisie, herding them into the woods and shooting them in batches.

The Fête of the World Proletariat in Riga on 1 May was far less grand than its name suggested. A plywood Temple of Reason had been erected in the main square, lamp posts had been painted red and plaster statues of Marx, Lenin, Trotsky and Zinoviev imported from Moscow. Some streets had been renamed: Revolution Street, Karl Marx Boulevard, Third International Prospect. Damp and dismal weather did little to arouse any great enthusiasm, and almost doused the evening fireworks. Most of the crowds shivering in the rain as Stutchka made the obligatory speech lauding the coming world revolution were probably thinking more of the coming attack by General von der Goltz.

Goltz had been building up his forces since early February, when Freikorps had begun streaming in through the port of Libau (Liepaja). Attracted by the prospect of fighting and plunder, and especially the promise of land, demobilised soldiers had stormed the recruiting offices in Germany, eager for action against the hated Bolsheviks. Brutalised by four years of war, they were unruly and piratical – the flag of the Hamburg Freikorps was a skull and crossbones superimposed on the symbol of the ancient Hanseatic League; they grew their hair long and saluted only officers they knew and liked. Eighteen Baltic Freikorps were formed; they joined remnants of Goltz's old German Eighth Army, Polish mercenaries, a Russian émigré officers' corps and another German volunteer corps recruited in Russia.

By the end of February, Goltz's force numbered 30,000 – but it contained few Latvians. He was determined to prevent Karlis Ulmanis's legitimate Latvian government forming its own military force, doing his utmost to stop British arms shipments reaching them and blocking Swedish aid. He intended to become the military dictator of the region, and he was not prepared to tolerate any interference from local politicians. 'In Latvia, I alone have supreme command over all troops and military installations,' he announced as soon as he arrived. 'As the troops at the front, immaterial of what nationality, are solely under my command, so are military persons behind the front of whatever nationality – German, Lettish, Baltic or Russian.' His aim was not simply to set up a German grand duchy in the Baltic – which was precisely why the Germans had given the Baltic States their freedom from Russia in the Treaty of Brest-Litovsk – but to extend it into East Prussia and to be its ruler. And his ambitions did not stop there: 'Why not revive, under a new form in agreement with the Whites and under the flag of an anti-Bolshevik campaign,' he wrote, 'our old Eastern policy which was forgotten in August 1914?' And if that did not work, he had an even more cynical suggestion, with an ominous foreshadowing of Hitler's *Lebensraum* policy: 'Or why not work for an economic and political rapprochement with Russia, which, having massacred its intellectuals, needs merchants, engineers and administrators and whose frontier provinces, devastated and depopulated, might offer a fertile land for hard-working German peasants?'[19]

On 3 March, Goltz unleashed his troops, quickly driving the weak Bolshevik forces back to the Russian frontier. Within ten days, he had occupied most of Latvia and Lithuania, leaving only Riga and its environs as a treat for later. Setting up his headquarters at Mitau (Jelgava), a mere thirty miles from the capital, he gave his Freikorps a free hand to clear the rest of Latvia of Communists, a task that they undertook with great enthusiasm. Every day, in the main square of Mitau, suspects by the dozen were executed by German firing squads. In the port of Windau (Ventspils), the German military commander ordered all persons who had worked with the previous Bolshevik government to register with his police; the penalty for failure to register was death – but since most of those who did register were executed anyway, there was no great incentive to do so.

Watching Goltz's colonisation and subjugation of the Latvian people, the officers and men of the British Royal Navy's Baltic flotilla suffered agonies of frustration at being unable to intervene directly, partly because their orders from the government forbade it, and partly because they had neither the men nor the equipment for operations on land. No one felt the frustration more than the British Senior Naval Officer, Rear Admiral Walter Cowan, who had replaced Admiral Sinclair in January. Cowan was a small, highly energetic man who lived for two things: the navy and fox hunting – he was said to wear his yellow hunting waistcoat under his uniform while at sea. He had seen active service in many parts of the world; he had won the Distinguished Service Order at the age of twenty-seven, while commanding a gunboat on the upper reaches of the Nile, helping Kitchener to rout the Khalifa's Dervishes at Omdurman; he was mentioned in dispatches as an unauthorised naval ADC to Kitchener on land during the South African War, for which personal initiative the Admiralty deducted three years from his seniority; in the Great War he had begun by ramming and sinking a German U-boat near the Grand Fleet's anchorage at Scapa Flow, and had been in the thick of the action at the battles of the Dogger Bank and Jutland, where he was rewarded with the CB (Companion of the Bath). He was promoted to rear admiral in September 1918. When the German High Seas Fleet was escorted into Rosyth, his was the only glum face at dinner that night. Asked why he was looking so sad, his reply encapsulated his character: 'Nothing left to live for.'[20]

The posting to the Baltic offered Cowan the chance of fresh action against both the Germans and the Bolsheviks. He seized it with both hands. However, he soon discovered that those hands were tied by his orders, which said that his primary function was to 'show the British Flag and support British policy'. The Estonian and Latvian governments, he was told, had already been supplied with 10,000 rifles, plus machine guns and ammunition. He was only to supply them with more if he was reasonably convinced that the governments were stable and could control their armies and that the arms would not be used 'in a manner opposed to British interests, which may be summed up as follows: to prevent the destruction of Estonia and Latvia by external aggression, which is only threatened at present by Bolshevik invaders'. He was to have no dealings with the Germans, who were bound under the terms of the Armistice to withdraw from the former Russian provinces. And he was not to visit Riga or Reval without specific Admiralty authority, 'except that a destroyer may be sent for purposes of communication, and to acquire intelligence'.

It must all have seemed depressingly negative for a man of Cowan's temperament. But there was a bright spot, which offered him the hope of action: 'Whenever we are in a position to resist Bolshevik attacks by force of arms from the sea,' the orders said, 'we should unhesitatingly do so.' His predecessor, Admiral Sinclair, had already put British naval guns to good use in Estonia, and who knew what opportunities might arise in Latvia? Even better news was the instruction that he must treat armed Bolshevik ships operating off the coast of the Baltic provinces as 'doing so with hostile intent and treated accordingly'. That was more like it, though for the moment there were no Bolshevik ships at large as they were confined in their base at Kronstadt by the winter ice.

By the end of January, after Ulmanis had asked for German assistance, the situation had changed. The British government sent the Latvians another 5,000 rifles, together with fifty machine guns and five million rounds of ammunition; after learning that the Germans had pitched the previous consignment of five hundred rifles and ammunition into the sea to deny them to Latvian volunteers, Cowan stored the new weapons on a Latvian transport ship, the *Saratov*, in Libau harbour for safety until Ulmanis had recruited enough troops to use them.

On the same day, the port of Windau, only forty miles away, had been taken by Bolsheviks. Cowan was no doubt delighted when Ulmanis asked for a British ship to shell the Bolshevik positions. The Admiralty quickly gave permission, and Cowan sailed up the coast himself in his flagship and opened fire with his six-inch guns on the Bolshevik batteries guarding the harbour entrance. The batteries were destroyed, and the Bolsheviks fled. It was a timely reminder of British firepower and determination, which gave fresh heart to the Latvian people, and pause for thought to Goltz.

Goltz was so much the epitome of the Prussian general that he was almost a caricature: hard, brutal, ruthlessly pragmatic and arrogant to the point of insolence. But Cowan, though more mercurial, was not a man to be browbeaten or intimidated, and their relationship quickly became a battle of wits and wills, with a constant stream of minor aggravations and several potentially major incidents. After a German sentry, following orders of course, attempted to stop Cowan on shore, Goltz had the effrontery to issue the British admiral with a personal pass, which he calmly rejected with a firm but icily polite note. When British seamen began to share their rations with hungry Latvian children and set up soup kitchens on the quayside, Goltz had a large wooden barricade erected alongside the ships, with gates guarded by

armed German sentries, supposedly to protect the ships from harass-
ment by local people. Cowan watched the construction with interest,
but did nothing until he was assured the work was finished. He then
quietly moved the two ships involved further along the quay, beyond
the barricade, where they resumed their charitable activities.

On a more serious level, when the British reimposed their blockade
and refused to allow Goltz to import more German troops and arms,
he halted his advance on Riga, and sat back while the Bolshevik terror
in the city mounted; as the spring thaw had set in, he said, it would
be another three weeks before his troops could move. Meanwhile,
Stutchka executed more bourgeois, which suited Goltz's purpose
admirably, removing educated Latvians who might take part in government and administration. When Cowan told him that the blockade
would be lifted if he undertook not to hamper the recruitment and
organisation of a Latvian army, he refused and threatened to withdraw
his forces altogether, leaving the country defenceless against the
Bolsheviks. Cowan ignored this attempted blackmail. The blockade
remained, and Goltz sat tight.

When Cowan added a further consignment of 20,000 rifles, six
6-inch howitzers, twelve 18-pounder guns and twenty lorries to the
materiel stored on the *Saratov* for the Latvians, he discovered that Goltz
was planning to seize the ship and her cargo; he foiled this by sending
a destroyer to escort the *Saratov* to a safe anchorage in the outer
harbour, alongside two British cruisers. While this was happening, the
Latvian government asked for seven hundred rifles to be unloaded and
sent to their GHQ, in the forest about a mile away. The Germans did
nothing to hinder this – but almost immediately attacked and captured
the Latvian headquarters, seized the rifles, arrested the senior officers
and set fire to the building. Cowan obtained the release of the officers,
but it was now clear beyond any doubt that Goltz was not bothered
by the Bolsheviks, seeing them purely as a convenient excuse for moving
in and taking over Latvia, to further his own ambitions. Over the next
few weeks, he staged a series of clumsy attempts to set up a puppet
government, until he finally decided to move on Riga. And even then,
he was playing a cynical game; holding back his own troops, he left it
to a force of Balts, led by Baron von Manteuffel, to storm the city and
take their vengeance on Stutchka and his followers in an orgy of violence.
The Bolshevik threat to Latvia had been thwarted but, as was so often
the case elsewhere, the reaction proved to be at least as bad.

Cowan, meanwhile, had business elsewhere in the Baltic: the ice had finally melted, and the Red Fleet was reported to be moving out of its base at the island of Kronstadt, near Petrograd. According to his orders from London, Soviet ships must be regarded as having 'hostile intent and treated accordingly', something which the little admiral looked forward to with keen anticipation as he sailed deeper into the Gulf of Finland.

The final draft of the main Peace Treaty was printed and presented to the German delegation in Paris on 7 May. It was highly controversial, even to those on the Allied side: Hoover, Smuts and John Maynard Keynes, who had all received their advance copies at 4 a.m., were so disturbed by its harshness that they left their beds to pace the streets, meeting by chance and walking together to discuss what they had read. They all agreed that they would do whatever they could to modify the terms and point out the dangers.

The printed draft, some two hundred pages long – 440 articles contained in 75,000 words – was the first chance anyone had had to see the results of four months of deliberation. 'While I had known many of the ideas, agreed upon by committees, I had not before envisaged it as a whole,' Hoover wrote later. 'I was greatly disturbed. In it hate and revenge ran through the political and economic passages. Many provisions had been settled without consideration of how they affected other parts. Conditions were set up upon which Europe could never be rebuilt or peace come to mankind. It seemed to me the economic consequences alone would pull down all Europe and thus injure the United States.'[21]

Keynes also disapproved strongly of 'reducing Germany to servitude for a generation', which he later declared would be 'abhorrent and detestable, even if it did not sow the decay of the whole civilised life of Europe'. Shortly afterwards, he resigned and retired back to England, to express his condemnation in a book, laboriously entitled *The Economic Consequences of the Peace*, which would make his name. Lincoln Steffens, asked by William Bullitt and other disillusioned Americans for advice on how best to register their disapproval, said that having seen the Russian Revolution and this peace it was useless to try to fight for what is right under their system. He concluded that they should all 'labour to change the foundations of society as the Russians are doing'.

The German Foreign Minister, Count Brockdorff-Rantzau, received the draft treaty with an odd mixture of nervousness and arrogance. Tall, lean and supercilious, a toothbrush moustache emphasising his hatchet features, he remained seated as he refused to acknowledge his country's responsibility for the war and accused the Allies of murdering hundreds of thousands of non-combatants through the blockade, 'with cold deliberation after our adversaries had conquered and victory had been assured to them. Think of that when you speak of guilt and punishment . . .' Clemenceau sat silently livid; Lloyd George snapped his ivory paper knife into pieces and looked as though he was about to leap from his chair and punch Rantzau in the face – indeed, he later told his mistress, Frances Stevenson, that he had had the greatest difficulty in restraining himself from doing just that.[22] Wilson leaned back in his chair, his hands in his pockets, his face expressionless. On the way out, after Brockdorff-Rantzau and his colleagues had left, he told Lord Riddell: 'The Germans are really a stupid people. They always do the wrong things. They always did the wrong thing during the war. That is why I am here. They don't understand human nature. This is the most tactless speech I have ever heard. It will set the whole world against them.'[23]

On 9 May, the Germans gave the world further excuses for dislike and distrust when the murderers of Karl Liebknecht and Rosa Luxemburg faced a court-martial trial in Berlin's Moabit prison. The two principal defendants, Lieutenant Kurt Vogel and Captain Lieutenant Heinz von Pflugk-Hartung, arrived in court 'laughing, their chests decorated with medals. They gave the impression of going to a wedding rather than a murder trial.'[24] Pflugk-Hartung, charged with the murder of Liebknecht, was reported as being 'well-groomed, alert, had a clear and sparkling eye, and gave his evidence in an open and attractive fashion'; he was said to have made 'a very favourable impression on the court'. He said that 'he had taken quite a fancy to Liebknecht in the [Eden] hotel', and thought that 'for a Socialist he had interesting views and a good way of putting them'. Nevertheless, when he got into the car beside Liebknecht, whose head was streaming with blood after being clubbed with Private Runge's rifle butt, he drew his revolver and told him he would be shot if he tried to escape. He admitted that he had shot Liebknecht when he ran away after the car had been forced to stop because of a flat tyre. His evidence was accepted as satisfactory, and he was acquitted, 'with great applause at the verdict'.

Private Runge was partially excused, because someone at the hotel had called out, 'See that these swine do not reach the prison alive.' The person who had called out, who was not named, was said to be a civilian, and therefore not subject to a military court martial, though a hotel waiter swore that it was in fact Pflugk-Hartung. Either way, this was considered to lessen the blame attached to Runge, who looked so much of a criminal type that no one questioned why, after clubbing Liebknecht at one door of the hotel, he had been allowed to wait at another door to club Luxemburg. It was doubtful, the court thought, if his blows had actually proved fatal, and since he was probably mentally defective anyway, he was sentenced to two years' imprisonment.

Lieutenant Vogel apparently did not make such a favourable impression as Pflugk-Hartung, according to reporters, 'because he wore a monocle and had not the fine, open manner of the acquitted Captain-Lieutenant'. He said he had not needed to warn Luxemburg not to escape, because 'the poor woman was as good as dead', and claimed that some other officer had shot her through the head. He admitted, however, that he had had the car driven to the canal, into which he threw the body 'to save the honour of the Garde-Schützen-Division' – a strange excuse which, equally strangely, was accepted. While Runge had escaped a murder verdict because it was not certain that his blows had killed Luxemburg, Vogel escaped the same verdict because it was considered probable that she had died from those blows before he shot her. But, according to the reports, 'he gave his evidence in a shame-faced fashion, and so he was given a sentence of two years and four months imprisonment'.[25]

If left-wingers and liberals in Germany and abroad were incensed by the leniency of the sentences, they were even more furious a few days later when they learned that Vogel and a Lieutenant Liebmann, who had been sentenced to sixty days' solitary confinement for his involvement in the murders, had been allowed to escape. A friend, Lieutenant Lindemann, had simply arrived at the gates of Moabit prison in uniform, presented forged release orders for the two men, and had driven them away – the magic of militarism still worked. Using false passports, they crossed into Holland, from where they could not be extradited as their offences were considered political.

'So the only officer sentenced has escaped with the assistance of one of his comrades,' raged the Independent Socialist newspaper *Die Freiheit*. 'The camarilla of officers openly disregard all measures resulting from the revolution. They refuse to obey Government orders if the orders do not please them. Comrade Noske is a mere tool in the hands of the officers, who are openly preparing for a counter-revolution.'[26] The German government was certainly concerned at the growing influence of the militarists, a menace that was regularly discussed in Cabinet. But it was also aware of renewed danger from the left. After initially trying to suppress news of the escape, the government braced itself for a violent Spartacist uprising as a reaction to its handling of the case, and to the terms of the Peace Treaty. Berlin was expected to be the centre of the revolt, and measures were put in place to protect the Chancellery and the Foreign Office from attack.[27]

At the end of the month, while the furore over Vogel was still raging, Rosa Luxemburg herself put in an appearance. Her bloated body was discovered – some reports say that it floated to the surface, others that it was dredged up – in the Landwehr Canal, where divers had to prise it loose from a lock gate. Wary of Spartacist demonstrations, Noske ordered it to be taken to the military headquarters at Zossen, twenty miles south of the city, for safe keeping. The funeral was fixed for 13 June. It passed without incident as a long procession of 200,000 workers sombrely dressed in their best clothes and wearing red carnations in their buttonholes followed the coffin to the cemetery, where it was laid in a grave next to Liebknecht's. The route was lined with steel-helmeted troops in case of trouble. There was none. The placards carried by the mourners simply stated: 'Our Rosa – she was, she is, she will be again.'

# IX

## 'IN FORM IT IS A STRIKE ...
## IN INTENT IT IS REVOLUTION'

WHILE Rosa Luxemburg's murderers were cocking a snook at world opinion at the beginning of May, the next major outbreak of revolutionary neurosis was erupting in North America. This time, however, it was not in the troubled United States, but north of the forty-ninth parallel, in the mid-west of Canada. Winnipeg, capital of the province of Manitoba, lay on the prairies barely fifty miles from the frontier with the American states of North Dakota and Minnesota. Known as the gateway to the West, it had been primarily a fur-trading centre until the mid 1880s, when it became a hub of the Canadian Pacific Railway. Within a few years, Canada's other two transcontinental rail companies had joined the CPR, and all three established their repair shops, marshalling yards and roundhouses in and around the city, turning it into a boom town, heralded as the new Chicago with the potential to become a major manufacturing and marketing centre.

Immigrants who flooded into the prairie provinces in the early years of the twentieth century all passed through Winnipeg and many stayed on to take jobs in the fast-growing new industries, bringing with them a lively mix of international backgrounds, industrial experience and political ideologies. While the city remained a trans-shipment point and distribution centre for the thousands of new prairie farmers in the region, all was well. But as it moved into manufacturing it began to face problems. Despite its excellent rail connections, its distance from sources of supply and industrial markets meant transportation costs were high; the only way manufacturers could remain competitive nationally and internationally was by keeping labour costs low. This did not sit well with workers, particularly those from the great manufacturing areas of Britain, who were well schooled in trade unionism and the works of Karl Marx. These tough, strong-minded men sought to introduce their beliefs and knowledge into their new surroundings; they wanted their unions to negotiate fair wages to pay for decent living conditions, and to help bring about social change. They were faced with equally strong-minded, self-made men who had come to Manitoba to make their fortunes, and who took a very different view. To such men, unions were anathema; clashes were inevitable.

The conflict between capital and labour in Winnipeg extended beyond wage rates and working conditions. As long as the workers were poorly organised and represented they had little muscle, and the employers could keep a tight grip not only on the business life of the city, but also on its political life, free to run the city as they saw fit. This was something they were determined to hang on to at all costs. From the beginning of the century Winnipeg had been racked by a series of bitter strikes, as workers demanded union recognition and collective bargaining, and employers refused point blank to allow unions into plants and stores, using strike breakers, court injunctions and even armed militia to keep them out.

The war had brought added strains right across the country, with manpower shortages and the demands of a war economy exacerbating Canada's inherent problems, especially the antagonisms between Anglo-Canadians, French-Canadians and more recent European immigrants. Discontent reached a new peak in 1917, when the federal government of Prime Minister Sir Robert Borden controversially introduced conscription to squeeze more manpower into the armed forces before going on to win a blatantly rigged general election. In 1918, after the Russian Revolution, Borden succumbed to the universal fear by imposing strict press censorship, banning foreign-language publications, intercepting mail, deporting so-called troublemakers and putting in place an extensive network of undercover agents to spy on anyone who supported radical social change. In spite of – or maybe partly because of – these government measures, there were 169 strikes in 1918, more than during the three previous years put together, most of them in the west.[1] The federal government responded with regulations under the War Measures Act banning strikes in certain sectors of the economy, and outlawing a number of left-wing organisations, including the Social Democratic Party.

Although the dissatisfaction was nationwide, Winnipeg became its focal point. In spring 1918, there was a limited general strike after the city council had informed its employees that they did not have the right to strike for higher wages. Other workers came out in sympathy, and soon there were 7,000 strikers involved. The council capitulated, handing them an almost total victory, which had been made possible by the cooperation and mutual support of different unions working together, a lesson that was quickly taken to heart: a general strike could be an effective weapon when an individual strike had failed or was failing. Craft unions banded together in organisations such as the Metal Trades Council and Building Trades Council, linked together under the umbrella of the Winnipeg Trades Council, so that they could no longer be picked off one by one by the employers.

The end of the war brought the same tensions to Canada as it did to the rest of the Western world, with returning troops flooding the jobs market, inflation soaring and industry struggling to cope with a sudden switch to a peacetime economy. Canadians at home had worked long and hard to secure victory, while 60,000 men, about one in ten of all those in uniform, had been killed in action. Just as elsewhere, Canadians looked for reward in new hope, a new social order; and just as elsewhere, their hopes were dashed as they found themselves facing unemployment, depression and wage cuts. In this situation, radicalism began to flourish everywhere, but especially in the west. More and more traditional craft unions voted to merge into industrial unions, and more militant members were elected to local trades councils. The radicals made more and more inflammatory speeches at meetings and on street corners, praising the Russian and German revolutions, all of which were duly reported by undercover police agents. The North West Mounted Police (NWMP), the Dominion Police, the army and the Immigration Service all had agents monitoring radical activity – at some meetings, there must have been more agents than activists. They were recruited wherever possible from immigrants who could speak foreign languages and melt into ethnic communities, but their training was necessarily sketchy and they were naturally inclined to sensationalise their reports.

In London preparing for the Peace Conference, Prime Minister Borden coupled these reports with other intelligence that the Russians were smuggling large sums of money abroad, some of it to Canada, to fund a massive propaganda campaign. Telling his ministers back in Ottawa to be prepared for an organised effort to subvert the government in the new year, he appointed an old political ally, Montreal lawyer-financier Charles Cahan, as Director of Public Safety, with the responsibility of countering Red propaganda. Cahan went to work with a will, making speeches and writing pamphlets filled with apocalyptic warnings of 'incipient revolution raising its head with accompanying civil disorder and bloodshed'. He was backed up by the Commissioner of the Dominion Police, A.P. Sherwood, who publicly urged the government to continue its repressive measures 'until every Bolshevik idea shall be either stamped out or driven back to the home that gave birth to this dangerous form of madness'.[2]

In Ontario, police raided the offices of several banned organisations, seizing literature and arresting forty-four people. In Winnipeg, they arrested Michael Charitinoff, a newspaper editor, for possession of illegal literature, accusing him of being 'Lenin's ambassador to western Canada' and saying the Bolshevik leader had provided him with $7,000 to foment revolution. Judge Hugh John Macdonald, son of a former prime minister, found him guilty and sentenced him to three years in prison and a $1,000 fine.

Already gripped by blood-curdling accounts of what was happening in Russia and Europe, the general public was persuaded that the radicals were about to unleash a similar cataclysm in Canada. 'Is Bolshevism brewing in Canada?' demanded the popular *Macleans* magazine in its January 1919 issue. 'There is a bold, systematic and dangerous effort being made to lay the fuse of Bolshevism from one end of the Dominion to the other,' the article claimed, warning that labour radicals were plotting to seize control of all industry and to abolish the wage system. The article received warm praise from the Chief Press Censor, Ernest Chambers, who wrote to the magazine's owner, Colonel John Bayne Maclean, urging him to go on raising the alarm, which he gladly did.[3]

There were fresh alarms in March 1919, when representatives of the western unions met in Calgary, having despaired of being able to get their more traditional colleagues in the Trades and Labour Congress of Canada (TLC) to back more militant action. The TLC, which was affiliated to Samuel Gompers's conservative American Federation of Labor, refused to enter directly into politics, or to support industrial as opposed to craft unions. In Calgary, the rebellious western unions went even further, by agreeing to the formation of One Big Union (OBU) to represent all industrial workers, and committed to political action and social change. The OBU had long been the dream of the dreaded Wobblies, and to mainstream unionists, the government and the public it clearly meant Red revolution, an impression that the conference did little to dispel: its final resolutions endorsed Socialism, called for the abolition of capitalism, and applauded the Bolsheviks in Russia and the Spartacists in Germany. 'The Bolshevist spirit in its worst form lies back of the "Red" activities of last week's convention,' shrieked the *Calgary Daily Herald*. 'There is no place, no room for it in Canada.' Further east, the *Montreal Daily Star* solemnly announced 'Soviet Plotters Busy in Canada'.[4]

As the headlines grew ever more shrill and the police reports even more alarmist, the acting Prime Minister, Sir Thomas White, panicked. In mid April he cabled Borden in Paris that Bolshevism was now rampant in Canada, and especially in British Columbia. A revolution was about to take place, he said, begging Borden to get the British government to send a warship to Vancouver as a show of force. Borden sensibly refused. He did, however, agree to a proposal by Charles Hamilton of the NWMP to feed his secret agents' reports to the press, and for Chief Press Censor Chambers to orchestrate a counter-propaganda campaign involving the press, university professors, Canadian clubs, churches and movie-makers, using information of the 'right type' provided by his department. Chambers wrote to the presidents of several leading universities, asking them to make speeches or write papers exposing the fallacies of 'extreme red Socialism'. Charles Cahan, meanwhile, continued to speak and write about the Bolshevik threat, warning that an actual civil war was likely between labour and capital, which would need the army to intervene.

Cahan's predictions seemed increasingly justified as a wave of strikes hit every major Canadian city: teamsters, street railwaymen and metal-workers in Ottawa, shipyard workers in Montreal, and so on, but these were individual actions. When the anticipated general strike did eventually come – in Winnipeg, naturally – it was greeted as the fulfilment of a prophecy, the start of the Red Revolution. The government and the employers both asserted that the OBU was behind it, that it was the first test run of OBU tactics, and that defeating the strike would deal a knockout blow to the OBU. In fact, the strike had no direct connection with the OBU: it began as a simple labour dispute in the construction industry, over the old familiar demand for better pay. Since 1913, the cost of living had risen by at least 75 per cent, while building trades' wages had gone up by only 13 per cent. The workers wanted more; most employers were not unsympathetic, but they could only offer 50 per cent of what they wanted, claiming that any more would lead to bankruptcies. The building industry as a whole was in a bad way in Winnipeg. Half a loaf, they argued, was better than none. The union refused to accept this, and with negotiations deadlocked, called a strike for 1 May. That same day, the metalworkers voted to strike after their employers had refused to negotiate with the Metal Trades Council on wages and working hours.

Coincidentally, several other unions in Winnipeg were involved in disputes at that time. Strikes of telephone operators, police and street railway employees had only been narrowly averted at the end of April, so the general atmosphere was extremely febrile. When the metalworkers and builders asked for support at the regular weekly meeting of the Trades Council on 6 May, the response was immediate and positive. Individual unions balloted their members to ask if they were prepared to start a general strike in support of their comrades, and received an overwhelming vote of 'Yes'.

At 11 a.m. on 15 May, Winnipeg closed down. Ninety-five of the city's ninety-six unions were 100 per cent solid. Only the police union demurred. Factories, building sites and warehouses were deserted, streetcars stopped running, the mail went undelivered, newspapers, cinemas and restaurants closed, firemen left their stations, telephone exchanges were shut down, electricity workers left power generation and transmission equipment unattended, bread and milk roundsmen stopped delivering. At the waterworks a skeleton staff stayed behind at the request of the Trades Council to provide a meagre thirty pounds' pressure, enough to service single-storey dwellings. On the first day of the strike, 24,000 workers came out, a number that soon swelled to about 30,000. By the end of the month, they were still out and sympathetic strikes were taking place all over the country, involving over 80,000 workers in eighty separate strikes, mostly in the west, but some as far east as Nova Scotia.[5] Thousands of Great War veterans – 10,000 on one occasion alone – took part in marches in support of the strikers, which worried government officials who believed the situation could get seriously out of hand if veterans were to go over to the strike en masse.

Opposing the strike in Winnipeg was the Citizens' Committee of 1,000, a self-appointed group of business and professional people including individual members of such organisations as the Board of

Trade, the Manufacturers' Association and the Winnipeg Bar, who were convinced they were in the middle of an insurrection, what the *Winnipeg Free Press* called 'the Great Dream of the Winnipeg Soviet'. With the help of the militia they organised volunteers to run the utilities and provided a fleet of cars and trucks, standing ready at all times to move soldiers into position in case of trouble.

The General Strike Committee, fearful that any disorder would give the authorities the excuse to deploy the armed forces on the streets of the city, had asked policemen to stay at their posts to maintain public order and safety. The police complied, but this was not good enough for the Committee of 1,000 or the authorities, who were convinced that the police were under the control of or at least sympathetic to the strikers. The City Council demanded that all members of the police force should sign a pledge dissociating themselves from the Trades Council and promising not to take part in any future sympathetic strikes. Almost to a man, the police refused, and were sacked, to be replaced by some 1,800 newly recruited special constables, who were paid six dollars a day, a higher wage than the regular police. Inept and irrevocably hostile to the strikers, these untrained and often undisciplined men were soon involved in a series of violent incidents which did nothing to keep the peace or lower the temperature.

The Strike Committee was determined to avoid any confrontation or provocation, even forbidding peaceful picketing. 'The only thing the workers have to do to win,' the *Strike Bulletin* told them, 'is to do nothing. Just eat, sleep, play, love, laugh and look at the sun. There are those who are anxious for us to do something which would provide an excuse for putting the city under martial law. Therefore, once more, do nothing . . . WHAT WE WANT: (1) right of collective bargaining; (2) a living wage; (3) reinstatement of all strikers. WHAT WE DO NOT WANT: (1) revolution; (2) dictatorship; (3) disorder.'[6]

Although they had the examples of previous general strikes in Belfast and Seattle, the Strike Committee had not made plans for maintaining essential services such as garbage collection, and deliveries of staples like milk, bread and ice. At a meeting attended by representatives of the Committee of 1,000 and city officials, the owner of the Crescent Creamery Company, J.W. Carruthers, suggested that the problem could be solved if delivery wagons were issued with placards saying that the drivers were not scabs, but were operating with the permission of the Strike Committee. The new system worked well for a few days and conditions in the city were greatly improved; cinemas and theatres, which were allowed to reopen, followed suit by displaying the message WORKING IN HARMONY WITH THE STRIKE COMMITTEE. Opponents, however, including the mayor, complained that the placards implied that the Strike Committee had taken over the civic government. After a heated debate, the City Council decided by seven votes to four that the cards should be taken down. The Strike Committee complied the next day.

One of the most vehement opponents of the placards was Arthur Meighen, the federal Minister of the Interior, who rushed to Winnipeg shortly after the start of the strike, together with Gideon Robertson, the provincial interior minister. Robertson, a former labour man, launched into a furious attack on the OBU, charging that the strike was aimed at revolution and the destruction of the traditional craft union movement. Meighen weighed in with his own tirade in the House of Commons, revealing the government's fears: if unions were allowed to combine into larger unions, he asked, where was the logical end to the process going to be? Eventually there would be only one union capable of calling a tremendous strike which would bring anarchy to the country, 'the perfection of Bolshevism'. He described the Winnipeg strike leaders as 'revolutionists of various degrees and types, from crazy idealists down to ordinary thieves'.[7] The ministers had no authority over most of the strikers, apart from the postal workers, who were federal employees. They gave the postal workers three days to return to their jobs, and when they did not do so, fired them and replaced them with volunteers. Robertson gave a similar ultimatum to striking railway mail clerks, the provincial government did the same to its telephone employees and the city to its firemen, clerks and waterworks staff, all with the same results.

Previous general strikes – in Belfast, Glasgow, Seattle, Buenos Aires – had only lasted for a few days. But as days and then weeks passed, the Winnipeg strike remained solid, and showed no signs of collapsing. The government, City Council and Citizens' Committee of 1,000 prepared for battle. The usual Winnipeg detachment of twenty-seven Mounties was increased to 245 men, sixty horses, and four armoured vehicles with mounted machine guns. Army and militia forces were substantially reinforced, and stockbrokers, merchants, lawyers and real-estate dealers hurried to the military barracks each day for training with rifles and bayonets. All of this activity only served to strengthen

the strikers' resolve and build support for them elsewhere. When the
Trades and Labour Council in Vancouver heard that troops had been
sent to deal with the 'revolution' in Winnipeg, they voted for a sympathetic general strike. Fifty thousand workers came out on 2 June and
stayed out for a month, bringing industry and shipping to a halt. In
Toronto a general strike called for 30 May was less successful, but
shook the government nevertheless by showing that the unrest was not
confined to the west. Across the border, too, Americans were concerned.
'In form it is a strike that is on in Canada,' commented the *New York
Times*. 'In intent it is revolution.'[8]

The government in Ottawa, meanwhile, prepared to use the law
against the strikers. On 6 June a series of measures was put in place,
including amendments to the Criminal Code to allow the immediate
deportation of 'foreign-born persons who do not believe in or are
opposed to organised government'. This clause was aimed not at
European immigrants but at Americans: there was a strong belief, widely
reported in the press as fact, that the Winnipeg strike was a continuation of the Seattle action, financed and led by American Bolsheviks
who, having failed there, had crossed into Canada for a second try.[9]
Draconian prison sentences were set at up to twenty years for membership of 'unlawful associations', which were defined as those advocating
economic or political change by violent means – attending a public
meeting was considered acceptable evidence of membership. At the same
time, the section of the Code guaranteeing freedom of speech was
repealed.

In the early morning of 17 June, ten strike leaders were dragged
from their beds and hauled off to the nearby Stoney Mountain
Penitentiary, charged with seditious conspiracy. A further four were
arrested and charged later in the day. But still the strike continued, and
on 21 June a silent parade of pro-strike veterans ignored a ban on
demonstrations and marched down Main Street, to protest the arrests
and police violence. Encountering a 'black' streetcar with a volunteer
crew defying the strike, they smashed its windows and set it on fire,
at which point the Mounties arrived and charged them, swinging clubs.
The crowd responded with a hail of rocks and bottles. The Mounties
charged again. One rider was unseated, fell from his horse and was set
upon and beaten. The police charged again to rescue their colleague,
and began firing into the crowd, killing one demonstrator and wounding
several others. As the marchers scattered in panic, the militia arrived

and arrested more than eighty people. Armoured trucks with mounted machine guns patrolled the streets as 'Bloody Saturday' ended in virtual military occupation.

The strike was broken. The committee announced that it would send its people back to work if the government of Manitoba would appoint a Royal Commission to investigate labour conditions in the province. The Premier agreed, and the strike was officially called off on 26 June. It had lasted for an amazing six weeks, and had completely failed to achieve its objectives. The metalworkers obtained a reduction of five hours in their working week, but no pay increase; the building tradesmen got nothing. Many strikers lost their jobs, while others were taken back but lost seniority. Some policemen were taken back, but 403 postal workers, 119 telephone employees and 53 firemen were not. New civic employees had to sign oaths promising not to take part in any future secondary strike action. Eight of the arrested men eventually faced trial for agitating for a living wage, an eight-hour day and collective bargaining rights, which was declared to be seditious. One was sentenced to two years' imprisonment, five to one year, one to six months and one was found not guilty. Five of those convicted were later elected either to the Manitoba legislature or to the federal parliament. There was, however, one ray of light for Canadian workers arising from the Winnipeg strike. The Manitoba government honoured its promise to set up a Royal Commission to investigate the causes of the conflict, which recommended the establishment of a minimum wage, a standard eight-hour day, and some provisions for state-funded unemployment and health insurance, as well as pensions and recognition of the right to collective bargaining.

OBU membership climbed to some 500,000 during the strike, and this at a time when there were only some 380,000 trade unionists in the whole of Canada's workforce of over two million.[10] But it quickly dwindled again as traditional unions won recognition and improved contracts from relieved employers; radical syndicalism had been exposed as a failure. In the elections immediately following the strike, moderate socialist Labour candidates made sweeping gains.

The threat of Red revolution in Canada appeared to be over, but in the United States it was rearing its head again. For weeks, the Winnipeg strike had been given the full scare treatment in American newspapers, with stories of babies dying for lack of milk and the threat of plague because of a breakdown of sanitation services, but on 3 June it was knocked off the front pages by sensational home news. 'BOMB THROWERS RENEW TERRORISM', screamed the headlines. 'TERROR REIGNS IN MANY CITIES'.[11] The previous evening ten bombs had exploded almost simultaneously in eight different US cities. All but one of the explosions was outside a private home, though most of the intended victims were public figures: a federal judge in New York City; a municipal judge in Boston who had sentenced twelve radicals to jail for their part in May Day disturbances; a federal judge and the city's police inspector in Pittsburgh; the Mayor of Cleveland; a state legislator in Newtonville, Massachusetts; a silk manufacturer in Paterson, New Jersey; a prominent jeweller in Philadelphia, where the Catholic church of Our Lady of Victories was also badly shattered. None of the intended victims was seriously injured, but an innocent nightwatchman outside Justice Gott's house in New York was killed when he discovered the device on the building's steps and decided to investigate it.

In the most spectacular and newsworthy incident – an attempt on the life of Attorney General Palmer in Washington – one bomber blew himself up, but this was clearly accidental: since American anarchists and Bolsheviks believed in seeking paradise on earth, there was no place in their philosophy for the suicide bomber. 'The explosion took place about 11.15 o'clock,' Palmer reported. 'I had been in the library on the first floor, and had just turned out the lights and gone upstairs with Mrs Palmer to retire. I had reached the upper floor and undressed, but had not yet retired. I heard a crash downstairs as if something had been thrown against the front door. It was followed immediately by an explosion which blew in the front of the house.'[12]

Palmer was hurled across the room, showered with glass from the windows and narrowly escaping injury from the horns of an elk's head blown from a wall above him. The bomb ripped the entire façade from the house, and shattered his neighbours' doors and windows for a hundred yards along the fashionable R Street, NW. The Assistant Secretary of the Navy, Franklin D. Roosevelt, who lived opposite, had just closed his front door after putting his car away in his garage when the bomb exploded. He called the police, then hurried across the road to help his neighbour as he staggered out of the house, uninjured but severely shaken and, according to Roosevelt, regressing to his Quaker upbringing – 'He was "theeing" and "thouing" me all over the place. "Thank thee, Franklin" and all that.'[13] A few minutes later, Mrs Palmer emerged, also shaken but mercifully unharmed.

The bomber was not so lucky. His grisly remains were scattered across the front lawn: the lower part of a leg lay fifty feet from the front steps of the house, another leg a little further away, while other 'ghastly relics' were discovered as far away as S Street, on the next block, having been blown sixty feet into the air and a distance of at least seventy-five yards. One lump of flesh landed inside an open second-floor window of a Norwegian diplomat's house, another on Roosevelt's doorstep. Other body parts and shreds of clothing covered the pavement and trees and the fronts of houses. It appeared that the man, who had been wearing sandals with rubber heels, had been planting his bomb, packed with unstable nitroglycerine and contained in a dress suitcase, on the middle of the three heavy stone steps leading up to the Palmers' front door, but had slipped and fallen on top of it, setting it off and taking the full force of the blast.

The police recovered as much of the body as they could – the head was never found – and took everything to the DC morgue, where a pathologist tried to put enough fragments together to make an identification possible. The first clues came from a brown felt hat, battered but amazingly undamaged, which was found lying in the gutter. Its label was that of a Philadelphia hatter, De Luca Brothers of 919 South Eighth Street, and tucked into its band was a red railroad ticket from Philadelphia which had been punched at 6 p.m. that day, from which detectives surmised that the man had travelled from that city on the Baltimore and Ohio express, which had arrived in Washington at 9.15 p.m. They immediately recalled the bombings in Philadelphia on 30 December 1918, but could not make a direct connection between the two. The remnants of an Italian–English pocket dictionary found at the scene suggested that the man was probably Italian, which fitted the physical description they compiled of 'a swarthy man with dark hair and of slender build'. He had been wearing a cheap white shirt with green and yellow stripes, 'a collar of well-known make with a Chinese laundry mark', a (probably) black suit with green stripes, tan lisle socks and winter underwear. In his wallet was a picture of a young boy and a number of franked US, French and Italian postage stamps, presumably intended for the boy's collection. There was also a letter, written in French, which indicated that the dead man had only recently arrived in America from Europe on a French ship.

In spite of the many clues, the man's identity was never established. There was less of a mystery, however, about the purpose of his mission.

Near Palmer's front door, beneath a pile of leaves and branches, the police found about fifty pamphlets printed on pink paper measuring six inches by ten, entitled 'Plain Words.' Similar pamphlets were found at the other bomb sites. Their message could not have been clearer:

The powers that be made no secret of their will to stop, here in America, the world-wide spread of revolution. The powers that must be reckon that they will have to accept the fight they have provoked . . .

A time has come when the social question's solution can be delayed no longer; class war is on, and cannot cease but with a complete victory for the international proletariat.

. . . We have been dreaming of freedom, we have talked of liberty, we have aspired to a better world, and you jailed us, you clubbed us, you deported us, you murdered us wherever you could. Now that the Great War, waged to replenish your purses and build a pedestal to your saints, is over nothing better can you do to protect your stolen millions, and your usurped fame, than to direct all the power of the murderous institutions you created for your exclusive defense, against the working multitudes rising to a more human conception of life . . .

The jails, the dungeons you reared to bury all protesting voices, are now replenished with languishing conscientious workers, and never satisfied, you increase their number every day.

Do you expect us to sit down and pray and cry? We accept your challenge and mean to stick to our war duties. We know that all you do is for your defense as a class. We know also that the proletariat has the same right to protect itself. Since their press has been suffocated, their mouths muzzled, we mean to speak for them the voice of dynamite, through the mouths of guns.

We are not many, perhaps more than you dream of though, but are all determined to fight to the last . . . There will have to be bloodshed, but we will not dodge; there will have to be murder; we will kill, because it is necessary; there will have to be destruction, we will destroy to rid the world of your tyrannical institutions.

We are ready to do anything and everything to suppress the capitalist class, just as you are doing anything and everything to suppress the proletarian revolution.

. . . We know how we stand with you and know how to take care of ourselves. Besides, you will never get all of us . . . and we multiply nowadays . . .

Long live social revolution! Down with tyranny!

THE ANARCHIST FIGHTERS[14]

The bombs destroyed Palmer's liberal façade as surely and as instantly as that of his house. 'The outrages of last night indicate nothing but the lawless attempt of an anarchistic element in the population to terrorize the country and thus stay the hand of the government,' he declared next day. 'This they have utterly failed to do. The purposes of the Department of Justice are the same today as yesterday. These attacks by bomb throwers will only increase and extend the activities of our crime-detecting forces.'[15] Fitting actions to his words, he set about switching his department's stance from defensive to offensive, appointing William J. Flynn, former head of the Secret Service and one of the nation's most famous detectives, as the new chief of the department's Bureau of Investigation, with Frank Burke, manager of the Secret Service's New York office and a self-proclaimed Russian expert, as his assistant. To strengthen the assault on radicalism still more, he took on Francis P. Garvan, a veteran of the New York District Attorney's office, as Assistant Attorney General in charge of investigating and prosecuting radicals.

The new men went into action at once, mobilising every resource at city, state and national levels. Their agents made sixty-one arrests across the country in connection with the bombings, forty-five of them in Cleveland alone, including, bizarrely, all the students in an automobile repair class. But all those arrested were eventually released without charge, which did little to calm the nerves of politicians, judges and others who were considered to be at risk, or to reduce the clamour from press and public for results. Congress pitched in with a special appropriation of $500,000 to fund the search. Senator William H. King of Utah, a member of the Overman Committee, drew up a bill making it a capital offence to transport bombs in interstate commerce or to belong to an organisation favouring violent overthrow of the government. When Palmer advised the Senate Judiciary Committee that the wartime Espionage and Sedition Acts could no longer be used since hostilities had ceased, Senator Thomas J. Walsh of Montana read 'Plain Words' aloud in the Senate and then proposed a peacetime Sedition Act with penalties of a $5,000 fine or five years in prison, or both, for urging the overthrow of the US government, displaying the revolutionary symbols of international Socialism either in public or in private, or distributing anarchistic literature through the mails.

All the frenetic activity signally failed to produce the bombers. Conspiracy theorists soon speculated that they were being protected by powerful interests, to cover up the 'truth' that they were agents provocateurs planted by the government or by reactionaries who wanted to create a climate of terror that would justify the destruction of the radical labour movement in America. Others argued that the bombers' skill in evading capture clearly indicated that they were all part of a well-organised plot, masterminded by emissaries of international Bolshevism. The genuine emissary of international Bolshevism in New York, L.C.A.K. Martens, pooh-poohed this notion, saying that the bombings were far too clumsy and ineffective for that. Amid all the confusion, only one thing was clear: the bureau desperately needed better intelligence if it was to make any headway against the revolutionaries. Fortunately, there was already a man working in the Justice Department who had the answer, and who would eventually eclipse the three experienced investigators as the nation's foremost scourge of Bolsheviks and Communism. His name was J. Edgar Hoover.

The twenty-four-year-old John Edgar Hoover (no relation to Herbert C. Hoover) was an assiduous young man who lived for his work and truly believed that 'Commonism', as he called it, was the greatest evil in the civilised world. Born in Washington, the youngest of four children, one of whom had died of diphtheria at the age of three, Hoover had graduated from high school as class valedictorian but had been forced to turn down a scholarship to the University of Virginia in order to find a job to help support his mother; his father, who had worked for the Department of Commerce's Coast and Geodetic Survey overseeing the printing of charts and surveys, had suffered a nervous breakdown and been committed to a sanatorium. With the help of an uncle who was an attorney in the Justice Department, the young Hoover went to work as a file clerk at the Library of Congress, cataloguing new acquisitions. At the same time, he enrolled for evening classes in law at George Washington University, and after four years of unrelenting spare-time work graduated with honours as a Bachelor of Laws. A year later, in 1917, he obtained his master's degree and joined the Justice Department as an intelligence clerk in the newly formed war division.

Hoover's ambition on joining the Department of Justice was to become a government attorney and later, possibly, to open his own law office. But he soon discovered that he had found his true vocation, one which would occupy him for the rest of his life. He was assigned to the Enemy Aliens Registration section, where he was required to cooperate with the military and naval intelligence agencies in preparing evidence for the deportation of alien anarchists and revolutionaries. Within a short time, he had become the department's leading expert on the subject, and had extended his interest to cover native-born radicals, particularly the Wobblies of the IWW whom he both despised and feared, and whose leaders had been rounded up and prosecuted by the bureau late in 1917 for violation of the Selective Service and Espionage Acts.

Hoover's work in the registration section had brought him into contact with the then Alien Property Custodian, Alexander Mitchell Palmer, who had been impressed by his ability and single-minded devotion to duty. So after the bomb attacks in 1919, it was natural that Palmer, who had then taken over at the Justice Department, should turn to Hoover, promoting him to the position of Special Assistant to the Attorney General, charged with developing and coordinating information to be used to prosecute radicals, both alien and native-born. Hoover took to his new role so successfully that within a few weeks Palmer authorised him to set up and direct a General Intelligence Division (GID) in the bureau to spearhead the anti-radical campaign.

In his days as a file clerk in the Library of Congress, Hoover had learned how to handle the library's immense card catalogue system, and he now brought this skill to bear in creating his own card index to collate all available information on the country's estimated 10,000 Communists. He approached his task with such zeal that within its first hundred days, his division had compiled files on an astonishing 60,000 Americans, a figure that he would shortly increase to an even more astonishing 200,000 suspect individuals and organisations – which included the American Civil Liberties Union and 'liberals' such as Senator Robert La Follette, settlement house reformer Jane Adams, Assistant Secretary of Labour Louis Post, and Federal Judge George Anderson.[16]

Hoover's obsession for seeing red in even the most mildly liberal activities was matched and even outdone by the patriotic organisations that had blossomed during the war and which thrived on fear – they relied on it, indeed, for their very existence. Although the government-sponsored American Protective League had been disbanded at the end of the war, other patriotic societies were still as active as ever, switching their energies from the Germans to the new enemy, the Bolsheviks. The National Security League (NSL), founded in 1914, was financed by industrialists and financiers like T. Coleman DuPont, J.P. Morgan and

John D. Rockefeller. Its literature was circulated among schoolteachers, clergy, businessmen and government employees, constantly reiterating the basic theme: 'When you hear a man trying to discredit Uncle Sam – that's Bolshevism.' In 1919, the NSL held over a thousand meetings, with voluntary speakers in each town and active support from local chambers of commerce, the Boy Scouts and the Sons and Daughters of the American Revolution, reaching at least 375,000 people.

Vying with the NSL as the champion of one hundred per cent Americanism was the National Civic Federation, which had started out in 1901 with the aim of fostering closer cooperation between capital and labour, but which had for several years concentrated on targeting the IWW. It still had a few tame union representatives on its executive board – from conservative AFL unions, of course – but its main backers were steel magnate Judge Elbert H. Gary and department store tycoon V. Everit Macy. Its magazine, the *National Civic Federation Review*, edited by Ralph Easley, invented fantastic conspiracies and regularly warned of imminent revolution. During the late spring of 1919, it ran a series of alarmist articles on supposed Communist activities in schools, universities, the press, churches and organised labour, and led a campaign to root out disloyalty from textbooks on history and political economy.

The third main patriotic society, the American Defense Society, had been established in 1915 by Elon H. Hooker, founder of the Hooker Chemical Company at Niagara Falls, one of the first electrochemical plants in America. Its literature was even more rabid than the other two, constantly warning of the 'hundreds of thousands of Reds' ready and waiting to overthrow the government. It provided employers with small pamphlets denouncing Bolshevism, to be placed in the wage packets of their workers, and circulated the names of newspapers and periodicals such as the *Nation, New Republic, Public* and *Dial*, which loyal citizens should boycott. 'Recent outrages show that not enough has been done to check the spread of Bolshevism and anarchy of all kinds,' it declared in its bulletin of 9 June. 'It is obvious that the public has not been sufficiently alive to the impending dangers.'[17]

The three main patriotic societies had an influence far in excess of their combined membership of about 25,000. And as the American public absorbed their minatory message, other groups rushed to join the fight. The Elks, that most famous of American fraternal societies, rallied to the cause, declaring that its 600,000 members would enlist in the war against Bolshevism. At its national convention in Atlantic

City on 9 July it unanimously passed a resolution stating its position: 'Every Elk has taken a solemn obligation to support the Constitution and the laws of the United States. No man can be a Bolshevik and remain a loyal American citizen.' Frank L. Rain, the newly elected Grand Exalted Ruler of the Order, declared it was foolish to quibble over distinctions between anarchists, Bolsheviks and IWWs. All three, he said, were criminal associations of a similar stripe and should be handled as a unit. Much of their power for evil, he added, derived from what he called 'the polite or parlour Bolshevik', a type that he described as a 'soft-baked, maundering idiot with half digested radical theories, and a ball-bearing tongue'. The colleges, he said, 'had produced some particularly pernicious parlour Bolsheviki'.[18]

Two other organisations, representing two very different philosophies, contributed powerfully to the anti-radical crusade: the American Legion and the Ku Klux Klan. By far the more important was the American Legion, an association of ex-service veterans, which started in March 1919 with a meeting of American Expeditionary Force members in Paris. This was followed on 9 May by a caucus meeting in St Louis, which agreed the name and a constitution beginning with the preamble 'For God and Country we are gathered together' and declaring as its aim 'To uphold and defend the Constitution of the Unites States of America; to maintain law and order; to foster and perpetuate a one hundred per cent Americanism'.[19]

The press hailed the Legion's opposition to Bolshevism as 'one of the greatest forces for good this country has ever known' and agreed that it would 'keep all post war changes safe and sane'. The existing patriotic societies welcomed its arrival as a powerful ally: its members had been conditioned by army service and training to love the flag and all it stood for, and to resist anything that threatened it or even dared to criticise it in any way. They were especially hostile to Bolshevism, which they blamed for Russia's betrayal of the Allies at Brest-Litovsk and for keeping thousands of unwilling doughboys in uniform in Archangel and Vladivostok.

The Legion quickly became an important element in American society, with branches – 'posts' – in every town in the country. By autumn its membership had grown to 650,000 and would reach a million by the end of the year. Its magazine, the *American Legion Weekly*, regularly published inflammatory articles by Seattle's Mayor Ole Hanson, wildly exaggerating the amount of radical activity in the United States; it constantly called on all Legionnaires to fight 'Red autocracy' and to stage parades showing plenty of American flags as an antidote; it demanded jail sentences and deportations to wipe out the Bolshevik menace, pledging unfailing Legion support for such action by the government.[20] In such an atmosphere, it is hardly surprising that many Legionnaires were carried away by their emotions and took to vigilante action, running suspected radicals out of town, tarring and feathering aliens and brawling with Socialists. 'Leave the Reds to the Legion' became a national rallying cry.[21]

The Legion may have been overzealous in its Red bashing, and some of its patriotism may have been misplaced or overstated, but as an organisation it was basically sound and honourable. The Ku Klux Klan, on the other hand, was a dangerous conspiracy posing as great a threat to democracy as the Bolshevism it opposed. The modern Klan had been established in 1915 in Atlanta, Georgia, by W.J. Simmons, a fundamentalist preacher and former Methodist circuit rider, and at first grew slowly and locally. But in the heightened atmosphere of 1919, it began to explode across the South, through the states of Alabama, Mississippi, Georgia and Texas. It was essentially concerned with race, religion and nonconformity, but since its bible, the *Kloran*, was overflowing with statements of extreme patriotism, and its constitution spoke of 'conserving the ideals of a pure Americanism', KKK members had no difficulty in adding radicals to its standard list of targets – Catholics, 'niggers', Jews and foreigners. In the eyes of the Klan, all aliens were 'un-American' and 'agents of Lenin', Jews had not only caused the revolution in Russia but would do the same in America unless they were stopped, and Negroes had long since turned to Bolshevism. Catholics were suspect and un-American because they already owed allegiance to a foreign power. And organised labour, of course, was simply the tool of 'foreign agitators'. In 1919, in the Southern states of America, such doctrines struck a chord for many nervous whites, and had a considerable influence on public opinion. The Klan's growth at that time was both a contributory factor and a result of the burgeoning Red scare.

The anti-Red neurosis that was tightening its grip on America was by no means confined to the Deep South, or to the flag-waving veterans of the American Legion. The next outbreak was in the city and state of New York.

In the spring, a prominent lawyer and former intelligence agent,

Archibald E. Stevenson, had published a report stating that Bolshevism was rampant among New York workmen and calling for strong action to counter it, a demand that was supported by the influential Union League Club. In response, on 26 March the State Legislature had authorised the formation of a committee headed by Senator Clayton R. Lusk 'to investigate the scope, tendencies, and ramifications of seditious activities in New York', with funding of $30,000.

The Lusk Committee had been due to begin its inquiry on 1 July, but after the second wave of bombings Senator Lusk decided there was no time to lose and that it would start its proceedings on 12 June – which just happened to be three days before the US Senate's Overman Committee was due to publish its report. Radical propaganda, Lusk declared melodramatically, was 'no longer being carried on by a few half-demented anarchists, but is being handled systematically by shrewd, capable men and women . . . who have been so successful that today their followers and sympathizers in New York City are numbered by the hundreds of thousands'.[22] The fact that he had not even begun his investigations and had no evidence to back up such a statement was clearly less important than grabbing the headlines.

Lusk made sure of upstaging Overman again when his committee began its proceedings. As the members gathered in New York City Hall for their first meeting, twenty agents of the Justice Department and ten officers of the state police burst into the offices of the Russian Soviet Bureau in the World Tower Building, cut the telephone lines, served L.C.A.K. Martens with a subpoena and hauled him off to City Hall to face questioning. They then seized material from his office, carting away some two tons of literature and documents which the committee would sift for evidence. Once again, the newspapers ran the story under banner headlines, though some were concerned that in making the raid the committee had assumed powers that it did not legally possess. The liberal and radical press condemned both the raid and the way in which it had been carried out: the New York *Call* denounced the police as 'Black Cossacks'. Martens, who was questioned only briefly by the committee and then released, denounced his arrest as 'an outrage and an uncalled for insult to the people of Russia'.[23]

Lusk moved quickly to justify the raid, announcing that the seizures proved that there were at least fifty radical journals circulating in New York City alone, with an estimated weekly readership of some 500,000 potential revolutionaries. The evidence, he said, showed that Martens was the 'American Lenin' and that he had been receiving huge sums of money from Moscow to finance a revolution, preparations for which were well advanced. State Attorney General Charles D. Newton, who had been appointed chief counsel to the committee, backed him up by saying that the Soviet Bureau was the 'clearing house' for all radical activity in the United States, and that its prime task was the bolshevising of American labour.

The Overman Report, liberally laced with lurid though mostly apocryphal accounts of life in Russia under the Bolsheviks, was published on 15 June, and reinforced all that Lusk and the patriotic societies were saying. Two days later, Brigadier General Marlborough Churchill, head of the army's Military Intelligence Division, told the US Senate's Military Affairs Committee that his men were keeping an eye on the activities of all Reds and other radicals in all the large cities. He produced maps of New York 'charting the haunts of Bolsheviks, anarchists, and other extreme radicals'. These included not only houses and halls in the poorer districts of the East Side and near Washington Square and Brownsville, but also some of the best residential sections of Manhattan and Brooklyn, showing that 'the radical menace in this country was by no means confined to the proletariat, but that the "parlour group" was also to be feared'. General Churchill testified that 'investigation of disloyal persons' had been discontinued since the Armistice, 'but without going outside our proper sphere, we can keep track of those societies that are endeavouring to break down the morale of enlisted men and discharged soldiers'. There were, he warned, societies in the United States which were trying to form councils of soldiers and sailors similar to those in Russia.[24]

Lusk's men struck again on 21 June, with simultaneous raids on the headquarters of the Left Wing Socialists on West 29th Street, the East 4th Street offices of the IWW, and the Rand School of Social Science on 15th Street near Fifth Avenue, a college of higher education founded by the American Socialist Party in 1906 and named after Carrie Rand, a noted anti-slavery campaigner. Although the school was openly Socialist, it was in fact decidedly anti-Bolshevik. The raids were all low-key, carried out by state police in plain clothes and armed with search warrants. There were no arrests, and no violence. In the Left Wing Socialist HQ, the police found only a few men quietly playing cards, one of whom, a janitor, left his game to show them around the premises and watched as they confiscated documents, literature and mailing lists. In the IWW offices, too, there was only a handful of members present. The only excitement came when two of them had to be prevented from throwing themselves out of the window, fearful that they were about to be arrested and tortured by the 'Black Cossacks'.

The biggest and most important raid was on the Rand School, with fifty men under the direction of the lawyer Archibald Stevenson himself. To their surprise – and possibly disappointment – they met with no resistance and were allowed by the director, Algernon Lee, to carry out their search so calmly that classes were not disrupted. Lee, however, refused to open a large steel safe, which he said contained some Socialist Party funds, mailing lists and other documents, contending to Stevenson's fury that the contents of the safe were not covered by the search warrant. For the next two days the safe became something of a cause célèbre in the press. It was kept under close guard until a new warrant was obtained and the materials they wanted were seized by Stevenson's men.

On the same day as the events at the Rand School, the Russian Federation of the Socialist Party staged a mass meeting in Madison Square Garden, to protest against the raiding of Martens's office the previous week. The meeting attracted some 6,000 people, about half of whom were women and, according to the police and federal agents, more than 90 per cent of foreign birth, mostly Russian. It also attracted a number of government stenographers, who took down every word for the Justice Department. The meeting passed without any serious incident, apart from the arrest of two people who waved red flags and shouted for the downfall of the United States.

Among the speakers were several prominent Socialists, including Rose Pastor Stokes, a long-time activist who was out on bail after being sentenced to ten years' imprisonment for disloyal activities during the war. As fiery as ever, Stokes called openly for class war, and for One Big Union as the best means of bringing Bolshevism to America. She was supported by another member of the Socialist National Committee, C.E. Ruthenberg, who had organised the violent May Day demonstration in Cleveland and was facing a fifteen-year jail term for sedition. 'The time has come,' Ruthenberg declaimed, 'when we are ready to end the rule of the capitalist class in the United States . . . if the working class carry on our propaganda and agitate for revolution, we can sweep this government out of existence.' Speaker after speaker reiterated the same message, but the biggest reaction was for one Alexander Stoklitzky, who spoke in Russian and brought the crowd to its feet when he called for three cheers for the Bolshevik government of Russia.[25] It was all heady stuff, and although it was essentially nothing but empty rhetoric, it had the government agents scribbling furiously as they prepared their scary reports, which appeared to confirm the worst fears of Hoover, Lusk, Overman, Stevenson and their fellow doomsayers.

The Lusk Committee followed up swiftly with a series of sensational revelations based on the documents found in the Rand School safe. They showed, Stevenson claimed, that radicals were in control of at least a hundred trade unions, and that the school was conspiring with Martens and the Soviet Bureau to Bolshevise American labour. Perhaps more significantly, he introduced a new and highly emotive element by declaring that the documents indicated that radicals were using the school to target the black population with their propaganda, that they were planning to subsidise black orators, start black newspapers and play up injustices to the black race. All of this, Lusk and Stevenson said, proved that the school was the actual headquarters for American Bolsheviks who were intent on fomenting revolution.[26]

Alarmed by its own allegations – which were almost completely unfounded – the Lusk Committee moved to close the Rand School down, filing suit to have its charter revoked. On the basis of the Lusk disclosures, Governor Alfred E. Smith hurriedly appointed an extraordinary term of the State Supreme Court 'for the purpose of investigating acts of criminal anarchy'. Unfortunately, this would require firm evidence, which the committee simply did not have. Throughout July, the case was continually postponed while they struggled to assemble real facts, until eventually the court ran out of patience and threw it out.

Undeterred by its failure to nail the Rand School, the Lusk Committee went on pursuing its anti-radical crusade for the rest of the year, supported by the patriotic societies, employer groups, the Legion and the Klan. Support for the crusade came from many different quarters, among them the AFL, whose President, Samuel Gompers, feared the competition from radical labour to his traditional craft-union power base. In a statement to the Senate Judiciary Committee based on a report of conditions in the state of Michigan, Gompers rather surprisingly blamed prohibition for the growth of the IWW and other radical organisations there, which he said had reached a point where it had become a menace to the safety of the nation. He charged prohibition with 'aiding and abetting Bolshevism by oppressive legislation depriving the workers of their beer', and said that if beer was prohibited then wine cellars, too, should be forced to disgorge their stocks, in a 'bone-dry' policy for all. The present policy, he said, was breeding class hatred 'on an alarming scale'. The 'IWW-Bolshevist movement' in Michigan, he said, had failed until prohibition was introduced, since when the House of the Masses, the headquarters of the radicals in Detroit, had increased its membership to 21,800. He described the movement as 'a fierce form of radical IWW teaching and preaching, akin to the revolutionary Socialism of Europe. It is Socialism born of class division and class antagonism.' 'Oppressive legislation begets radical propaganda,' Gompers concluded dramatically, 'and should Bolshevist doctrines ever gain a foothold in this country, which God forbid, the prohibitionists will not be free from responsibility.'[27]

For all their shouting, Lusk and his allies failed to uncover a single genuine subversive conspiracy. They succeeded only in creating a climate of irrational fear, unfounded suspicion and blind intolerance.

# X

## 'BOLSHEVISM WILL LOSE ITS ATTRACTION'

THROUGHOUT June, the whole of Germany, both north and south, remained tense, uneasy and volatile as the fate of the Peace Treaty hung in the balance. The Allies were slow in responding to the German counterproposals, which had been delivered on 29 May, largely because they were falling out among themselves over the details, and this delay increased the uncertainty and gave the Germans more time to brood on what they saw as the injustices about to be heaped upon them. As the month wore on, it seemed increasingly likely that the German government would simply refuse to sign, plunging Europe into confusion once more. George Renwick in the *New York Times* spoke for many when he wrote: 'The horizon is heavy with the darkest storm clouds, and these may break into the lightning of war in the angry east when the final answer has been given, and it is hard to believe the deluge and chaos will not sweep over the rest of the country.'[1]

Refusal to sign the treaty could have only one result: the resumption of the war, bringing with it havoc, famine and total ruination, exactly the conditions needed by the radicals for a new revolution. On the other hand, if the government did sign, the army might rebel and refuse to support them any longer, allowing the radicals to bring in the revolution anyway. It seemed like a no-win situation. Noske banned all open-air demonstrations in Berlin, strengthened the Berlin garrison and posted troops to form a cordon all around the city. He also occupied several other important cities. Spartacus and the hard left were still very much alive, as was proved on 6 June, when there were riots and one-day general strikes in Berlin and Munich in protest against the execution in Munich of Eugen Leviné, one of the leaders of the Bavarian Soviet. A week later, Rosa Luxemburg's funeral passed off entirely peacefully, but the threat of violence still hung in the air. The Allied response to the German counterproposals was due to be handed over to Brockdorff-Rantzau and the German peace delegation that day, but was postponed until 16 June.

When the revised Peace Treaty was handed over in Versailles shortly before 7 p.m. that evening, the Germans' worst fears were realised. Their protests had gone largely unheeded, the changes were only minor – written over the original text in red ink to save time reprinting the whole thing. They were accompanied by a stiff note from Clemenceau – which had actually been written by Philip Kerr, Lloyd George's private secretary – accusing the Germans of failing 'to understand the position in which Germany stands today' and of behaving 'as if this were but the end of some mere struggle for territory and power'.

Any hopes the Germans might have entertained of being absolved of total blame for the war were soon dispelled. 'In the view of the Allied and Associated Powers,' the note continued, 'the war which began on the first of August, 1914, was the greatest crime against humanity and the freedom of the peoples that any nation calling itself civilised has ever consciously committed . . . Germany's responsibility, however, is not confined to having planned and started the war. She is no less responsible for the savage and inhuman manner in which it was conducted.' The note listed German war crimes: the rape of Belgium; the first use of poison gas; the bombing and long-distance shelling of cities for the sole purpose of reducing the morale of their opponents by striking at their women and children; the first use of submarine warfare, leaving great numbers of innocent passengers and sailors in mid-ocean far from succour at the mercy of wind, waves, and 'the yet more ruthless submarine crews'; driving thousands of men, women and children from their homes and into brutal slavery in German territory; barbarities practised against their prisoners of war 'from which the most uncivilised people would have recoiled'. It was a devastating indictment and was summed up in an equally devastating judgement:

The conduct of Germany is almost unexampled in human history. The terrible responsibility which lies at her doors can be seen in the fact that not less than seven million dead lie buried in Europe, while more than twenty million others

carry upon them the evidence of wounds and suffering, because Germany saw
fit to gratify her lust for tyranny by a resort to war.

The Allied and associated powers believe that they will be false to those
who have given their all to save the freedom of the world if they consent to
treat the war on any other basis than as a crime against humanity and right.

The Allies concluded that what they were proposing was 'fundamentally a peace of justice'. 'There must be justice for the dead and wounded,
and for those who have been orphaned and bereaved, that Europe might
be free from Prussian despotism . . . There must be justice for those
millions whose homes and lands and property German savagery has
spoliated and destroyed.'[2]

The German delegates were informed that there would be no further
discussion, the revised treaty was final. They were given three days to
reply, though this was later accepted as unreasonable, given that they
had been presented with only one copy, in French and English, which
would need to be translated and printed, and that it would in any case
take them until the next day to travel home. The deadline was extended
until 23 June. Brockdorff-Rantzau and his team collected their papers
and belongings and left for Weimar that night. They were provided
with a police escort for the journey from their hotel to the railway
station, but since there was a police strike in progress, the escort was
weaker than it should have been, and when they came under attack
from French spectators, the police made no move to protect them. Some
reports say that the crowd was provoked by German typists pulling
faces and taunting them; others say that heaps of stones, bricks and
sticks had already been piled up along the route. Either way, bricks
and stones hailed down on the cars as they passed, injuring several
members of the delegation, including the prominent Hamburg banker
Dr Karl Melchior, Minister Giesberts and a secretary, Frau Dorlblush,
who was hit on the head and knocked unconscious. Two French military drivers were both badly cut by flying glass.[3] The unfortunate Frau
Dorlblush never fully recovered from her head injury, and was later
paid a substantial sum in damages.

Clemenceau wrote at once to the Germans with a full apology for
'this reprehensible act', and dismissed the responsible police commissioner, but the damage had been done, enraging the delegation and
adding more fuel to the fire of public anger in Germany. A strike of
printers had deprived Berlin of newspapers for three days, apart from

*Vorwärts*, which had settled with its own print workers, so the city was awash with rumours and counter-rumours. However, on 17 June the *Berliner Mittagszeitung* appeared with a Reuter report containing the text of Clemenceau's note, and another midday paper, the *Neue Berliner (12-Uhr-Mittags)*, hit the streets with an enormous headline, 'ATTEMPTED MURDER OF THE GERMAN PEACE DELEGATION'. 'This all looks like a fresh war,' Harry Kessler commented gloomily in his diary. 'It was like 1914. And just as stiflingly sultry and sunny as it was then at the end of July.'[4]

In Weimar, the German Cabinet was deeply divided, with seven members in favour of signing the treaty and seven dead set against it, whatever the consequences. Leading the antis was Brockdorff-Rantzau, who informed the Cabinet that his delegation was unanimous in recommending that the government should refuse to sign, convinced that the Allies, and especially France, would not go through with their threats. He believed that they were bluffing and did not want to occupy Germany, and that if Germany called their bluff, they would negotiate seriously and make concessions. He believed that the Allies were divided, and that if the Germans stood firm the British and Americans would break with France, which had too many troubles of its own with the danger of a general strike looming.[5] This would, he believed, lead to a revolution, the overthrow of the French government and the collapse of the Peace Conference. All that Germany had to do was wait. As an added factor, Brockdorff-Rantzau and his supporters knew that the US Senate was about to debate a resolution by former US Secretary of State Philander C. Knox, now a Republican senator from Pennsylvania, to tear up the Peace Treaty by removing the League of Nations sections, and sign a separate peace with Germany immediately. 'Here,' commented the *New York Times*, 'is reason enough for German refusal.'[6]

Observers in Paris had noticed a marked change in Brockdorff-Rantzau's attitude when the French National Labour Federation announced provisional plans for a general strike to start on 16 June. This was postponed, but the miners began a national strike on that day, by which time Paris transport workers had already been out for a week, as had the metalworkers. As the miners began their strike, the transport workers ended theirs, but that same day the Executive Committee of the French Socialist Party met Italian Socialist and Labour leaders to organise a simultaneous general strike in France, Italy, Belgium and Britain. Its aim was nakedly political, especially in France, where

the Socialists believed the time was right for a revolution – in this
respect at least, Brockdorff-Rantzau was right. In the event, the plan
came to nothing. French public opinion was too strongly against it –
the National Union of Combatants, the French equivalent of the
American Legion, dropped 80,000 leaflets from airplanes over Paris,
warning that a general strike would be playing into the hands of the
Germans. The idea was knocked on the head once and for all when
the British and Belgian unions refused to have anything to do with it.
Nevertheless, Brockdorff-Rantzau still clung to his fanciful notions and
continued to argue for a defiant delay.

Leading the opposition to Brockdorff-Rantzau was the leader of the
Centre Party, Matthias Erzberger, his exact antithesis in every way.
While Brockdorff-Rantzau was the epitome of cold Prussian arrogance,
Erzberger was a cheerful southern Catholic, the son of a village postman.
Outspoken and pragmatic, he had made many enemies during the war
by championing a moderate, negotiated peace, and he followed the
same line now. Germany, he insisted, could not afford to start fighting
again. The treaty would place terrible burdens on the German people,
and might well provoke the right into trying a military coup, but it
offered the country the chance of survival. With peace, the economy
could begin to recover and unemployment would fall. 'Bolshevism,' he
said, 'will lose its attraction.' If they did not sign, the Allies would
occupy Germany's industrial heartland and cut the country in half from
the west while the Poles would probably invade from the east, and the
economy would collapse. 'Plunder and murder will be the order of the
day,' he forecast, with Germany breaking up into a 'crazy patchwork
quilt' of states, some under Bolshevik rule, others under right-wing
dictatorships.[7]

The premiers of the southern states of Württemberg, Baden, Saxony
and Bavaria – Hoffmann, once more, now firmly back in position –
arrived in Weimar on 18 June to join in the argument, fearing that they
might find themselves having to negotiate separate peace treaties for
each of their states. They found the town in a state of virtual siege:
shortly before midnight the day before, a gang of fifty Spartacist prisoners had escaped from the local jail and attacked the palace where
the Cabinet was meeting. They had been beaten off by guards with
machine guns, but the situation remained tense and Noske had flooded
the area with heavily armed troops.

Over the next two days, the Cabinet argued and agonised, but remained deadlocked. While it did so, the Allies in Paris were making their own preparations and proving Brockdorff-Rantzau wrong. 'If Germany refuses,' Clemenceau told his fellow leaders in the Council of Four, 'I favour a vigorous and unremitting blow that will force the signing.' The council instructed Marshal Foch to prepare for an advance into Germany with the forty-two divisions of French, British, Canadian and American troops that he had at his disposal. Troop concentrations were to be complete by Friday 20 June, ready for an immediate advance. General Pershing cancelled plans for the US Fourth and Fifth Divisions to return home in the near future and placed them on standby with the other three US divisions. The British Admiralty ordered all ships in German ports to stop unloading foodstuffs; Wilson quickly ordered all American ships to ignore this, but the Admiralty still detained a number of American steamers that were in British ports taking on food for Germany. The Royal Navy cancelled all leave, placed the Grand Fleet on war alert ready to sail for Germany at immediate notice, and dispatched twelve cruisers and a number of destroyers to Copenhagen, while the British airship R-34, armed with Vickers and Lewis machine guns but carrying no bombs, flew low over Hamburg, Wilhelmshaven, Friederichshaven, the Kiel Canal and along the German Baltic coast in a show of power. Foch established his war headquarters at Coblenz and set about forming a solid front from the Rhine to the Danube, with Polish and Czech troops ready to strike from the east and south. Britain would occupy the all-important Ruhr, containing Germany's richest industries, France would take over an area further south including Frankfurt, the Rhineland and Stuttgart, America would occupy the mainly forested and agricultural region around Kassel. Five hundred thousand men stood ready to start the invasion at 5 a.m. on Monday 23 June.

As the time grew nearer, the German ministers still failed to agree. On 20 June, Scheidemann, Brockdorff-Rantzau and four other ministers resigned, and the government fell. With no German government to take the decision or to sign the treaty, the Allies agreed to extend their deadline for another two days, while Ebert, who had been persuaded to stay on reluctantly, tried to form a new administration. Meanwhile, the military build-up continued, and so did the rumours.

In Scotland, Admiral von Reuter, the officer commanding the interned German Imperial Fleet, suddenly realised that the British battle squadron guarding his ships was no longer there. In fact, the British ships had left to conduct routine torpedo exercises, but Reuter assumed that their departure meant the Armistice had ended and the war was about to start again, confirming what he had read in German newspapers. In his opinion, he later claimed, this revived the general orders of the German Navy that no warship should be surrendered, but should rather be sunk, both as a point of honour and to prevent its being taken over and used against Germany.[8] He hoisted a prearranged flag signal and within minutes their skeleton crews had opened the sea valves and were taking to the lifeboats as ten battleships, five battle cruisers, ten light cruisers and forty-nine destroyers began sinking into the chill waters of the anchorage known as Scapa Flow. This was highly embarrassing for the British, though they had actually wanted to tow the German fleet out into deep water and sink it anyway. The French were even more furious – they had fewer ships than the British, and had planned to take their share of the German fleet into their own navy, as indeed had the Americans. Unaware of Reuter's reasons, the Allies regarded the scuttling as yet another example of German bad faith, and their attitude hardened still further. The Paris press screamed that France should demand additional reparations from Germany, and compensation for a broken obligation.

By the late afternoon of 21 June, as the final German ship was turning turtle in Scapa Flow, Ebert succeeded in forming a new government, with the forty-nine-year-old moderate Socialist Gustav Bauer as Chancellor. Bauer was a competent organiser and an expert on labour matters, uninspiring but not contentious, something that could hardly be said of the obvious first candidate, Erzberger, who was given the consolation prize of Deputy Chancellor and Finance Minister. The other obvious candidate, 'the Bloodhound' Gustav Noske, was also too controversial, and although disappointed agreed to stay on in his vital role as Defence Minister. His attention was needed at once in Westphalia, where the Spartacists were staging another uprising that required the declaration of a state of siege before it could be put down.

Next day, Sunday 22 June, the full National Assembly met and voted by 237 to 138 to sign, but with two reservations: Germany would not recognise that she was solely responsible for the war, and she would not hand over any individuals accused of war crimes – one of the many rumours floating around was that the Allies had a list of thousands of men, besides the Kaiser and Hindenburg, whom they wanted to try as war criminals. This was the message sent to Paris to the Council of

Three, as the Four had become since the Italians had withdrawn and Orlando had been booted out of office in Rome on 19 June for failing to win Fiume. The response was swift and unequivocal: 'The time for discussion has passed. [The Allied and Associated Powers] can accept or acknowledge no qualification or reservations . . .'

The war preparations continued amid increasing tension on both sides. When they received orders to return to France, British troops in camp in Surrey mutinied, formed a soviet and refused to salute their officers or obey commands they did not like. Two battalions of regular troops armed with machine guns were sent to put down the revolt, arresting four hundred soldiers and dispersing more than a thousand to other camps. In Germany, there were food riots in Mannheim, Hamburg and Berlin. In Kassel, Spartacists stormed the prison and police station, but were beaten back. In the early hours of Monday 23 June, the German government sent an official note to the Three asking for a further forty-eight hours to consider – the invasion was now due to start at 7 p.m. that day. Wilson, Lloyd George and Clemenceau were woken from their beds. Lloyd George was still suffering from a sore throat and could not go out, so the others gathered in his flat at 9 a.m. It took them less than half an hour to decide on their reply: it was 'not possible to extend the time already granted . . . to make known your decision relative to the signature of the treaty without any reservation'.[9]

In Berlin, the diarist Harry Kessler described the effect of this blunt message: 'Since the Entente has declined to accept our signature *under reservation*, the military leaders have announced their resistance to the government, the Centre Party has withdrawn its agreement to signature, and the government has decided to resign. This evening the ultimatum expires. The tension is terrific. Very oppressive weather. Counter-revolution, war, insurrection threaten us like a nearing thunderstorm.'[10] In desperation, Ebert telephoned General Groener at Supreme Command HQ and asked him where the army stood. Would Groener be able to defend Germany if the Allies invaded, or would it be useless to resist. After consulting Hindenburg, Groener told him he must sign and hope that once the deed was done sanity would prevail and the army would not revolt. In a fifteen-minute session, the National Assembly agreed.

The official message was delivered to Clemenceau, Wilson and Lloyd George in the study of Wilson's house in the Place des Etats-Unis at

5.30 p.m., a bare ninety minutes before the invasion was due to begin. Clemenceau opened the note and said with a deep sigh, 'We have waited forty-nine years for this moment.' The official signing was fixed for 28 June, in the Hall of Mirrors in the Palace of Versailles, five years to the day since the assassination of the Archduke Franz Ferdinand at Sarajevo, and forty-eight years since the end of the Franco-Prussian War, when the victorious King Wilhelm I of Prussia had been proclaimed Kaiser of a newly united Germany in that same room. Immediately the treaty was signed, with all the ceremony needed to complete the humiliation of Germany, Wilson and Lloyd George left Paris to give some much-needed attention to domestic affairs in their own countries.

For the moment, Germany was still in turmoil, with riots and strikes and isolated revolts in many towns and cities. In Berlin a strike by transport workers stopped all local trains, trams and buses for two weeks, but there was no violence. Although the workers' councils and Independent Socialists tried to use the strike as a springboard for a soviet republic, they met with little response. Most Berliners accepted the situation as nothing more than a passing inconvenience, getting about the city in good humour with the help of curious fleets of country carts and lorries with kitchen chairs and schoolroom benches for seating which appeared on the streets as enterprising owners cashed in on the situation.

There was more serious trouble in Hamburg, where Communists and Spartacists threatened to turn the city into another Munich. They stormed the City Hall, overwhelming government troops and capturing large quantities of rifles, machine guns and ammunition, with which they swept through the city, shooting and looting and releasing prisoners from jails. Under the leadership of a Committee of Twelve from the workers' and soldiers' councils, they tried to set up a soviet government, but this was short-lived. Noske moved fast to send in 40,000 troops and order was soon restored. Here, as elsewhere, the main problem was the food shortage, and as supplies flooded in with the final lifting of the blockade on 12 July, the heat rapidly dwindled.

Labour trouble was not confined to the cities: in the countryside of Pomerania in north-eastern Germany, agricultural labourers rebelled against their feudal Junker overlords, demanding higher wages and improved rights. When they tried to negotiate, the Junkers refused to acknowledge that their workers were anything but serfs, and used their influence with the military high command to have the whole region put under martial law. Troops occupied the great estates, forced the labourers back to work and arrested fifteen members of the executive committee of their union.[11] Once again, an uneasy peace had been imposed, and the threat of revolution had proved to be hollow.

By July the only Red regimes still surviving were in Russia itself, including the Ukraine and Belorussia, and in Hungary. In Hungary, however, the gloss was beginning to wear off the revolution. Since its mobilisation on 3 May, Béla Kun's Red Army had been successfully attacking the Romanian and Czechoslovakian invaders of Hungary, halting the Romanians in the north-eastern provinces, driving the Czechs back in the north, and occupying most of Slovakia. On 16 June they proclaimed the formation of the Soviet Republic of Slovakia, under the protection of the Hungarian Red Army, creating an enlarged gap in the cordon sanitaire which the Allies, and in particular the French, were trying to establish between Western Europe and Soviet Russia. The Allies would have been even more concerned, and the gap would have been even larger, had the Hungarians succeeded in their efforts to persuade their Austrian comrades to stage a coup in Vienna. Kun's men smuggled in vast sums of Russian money to finance a putsch, and there was some violence and bloodshed in the streets when police broke up a march of 6,000 Communist supporters, leaving seven dead and more than sixty seriously injured. But the Viennese Workers' Council refused to cooperate with the Hungarians, and a mass round-up of Austrian plotters on 14 June put an end to the attempt and to hopes of a Red Austria.

The Allied leaders in Paris, who had been preoccupied with finalising the German treaty and distracted by disputes with Italy over Fiume, woke up to what was happening, hurriedly announced new borders between Hungary and her neighbours, and ordered everyone to stop fighting immediately. The fighting went on regardless. The Hungarians said they would stop if the Romanians did; the Romanians said they feared simultaneous attacks from the Hungarians and the Russians, and perhaps even the Bulgarians, who they claimed were armed to the teeth, and mounted fresh offensives.[12] As they gained ground, Hungarian unity began to crumble. Disillusioned officers who had rallied to the defence of their country just a few weeks before began defecting to the White opposition in Vienna, or in Szeged, close to the Romanian border in the south-east, where French troops commanded by General Franchet d'Esperay, fresh from the debacle in Odessa, had established an enclave. There, under the protection of the French, who were determined to see an early end to the Hungarian Soviet Republic, a group of noblemen led by Count Gyula Andrássy set up a rival government and began forming a White Army of 'death battalions', under the command of Admiral Nicholas Horthy.

In Budapest, the bright revolutionary posters and the statues of Marx and Lenin were defaced and damaged. The Swiss Red Cross reported that children were dying like flies in hospitals that had no food, no medicines, no soap, no bandages, no bedlinen. The middle classes committed suicide by the score, in despair at having their savings confiscated, their homes invaded by slum families, and their furniture, including beloved grand pianos, chopped up for fuel, as were the trees in the city's parks. Unable to improve conditions, Kun fell out with the trade unions, who began to organise strikes in towns and cities.

It was in the countryside, however, that the real trouble started, as the peasants staged armed revolts against the attempted collectivisation of agriculture and the seizure of their crops. Conditioned by centuries of serfdom, they refused to believe that the revolution was anything but a temporary aberration in the natural order of things. They refused to fight except for their own land, which they would defend against everyone – including citified Bolsheviks. They refused to send food to the cities, and began blockading Budapest, adding to the problems caused by the international blockade, which the Allies announced would not be lifted until there was a new Hungarian government 'which gives some assurance of settled conditions'. Trying to buy off Clemenceau and the French, Kun reluctantly withdrew his army from Slovakia, and the short-lived Soviet government there collapsed.

Kun's withdrawal from Slovakia offended both the nationalists and the Budapest Soviet, though in fact his forces had been so weakened by desertions that he had had little choice. Under pressure from all sides, he at last resorted to the traditional Bolshevik tactic, the Red Terror, organised and carried out by Tibor Szamuelly, always more ruthless and fanatical than Kun, and the man chosen by Lenin to safeguard the revolution. Small, pale-faced and with jet-black hair, Szamuelly was described – admittedly by reactionary journalists – as 'sickly and undersized, with a diseased and degenerate air, a fiend who indulged in every form of vice as a matter of atheistic principle. If it was possible for the instincts of wild beasts to be found in human beings, they were to be found in Tibor Szamuelly. To hang and torture, to inflict pain, grief and spiritual agony on others, were the breath of life to him. He looked like the very spirit of the Inquisition as, haggard and of a corpse-like pallor, he walked among his robust, thick-set terrorists.'[13]

Szamuelly hated all so-called 'enemies of the people', by which he meant anyone who was not an urban industrial worker or a Socialist intellectual. But he reserved his greatest venom for the deeply conser-vative peasants and reactionary country folk, whose kind he blamed for the failure of the revolutions in Austria and Bavaria, and who had even threatened Lenin's Bolshevik Revolution in Russia itself. With a force of specially recruited paramilitary terror squads, he set out from Budapest in a vivid red-painted armoured train to deal with the obsti-nate peasants and counter-revolutionaries of western Hungary. He did not always have things entirely his own way: when he left the train, his car was fired on by rebels, and sometimes there were even pitched battles, including one with 3,000 peasants and townspeople armed with cannon, machine guns and rifles, who were defeated with nearly a hundred killed. But more often the villagers were armed only with scythes and pitchforks, and were easily put down. After each fight, Szamuelly selected a number of rebels to be publicly executed as an example to others; *The Times* described him as 'smiling and smoking while his victims were breathing their last'. Once again, Western readers shuddered with horror at the beastliness of the Bolsheviks.

In mid July, Szamuelly was ready to turn his terror squads loose on the Budapest bourgeoisie, but Lenin called him to Moscow for emer-gency talks. While he was away, the Romanians began a fresh attack. As they advanced on the capital virtually unopposed, announcing that they were determined to suppress the 'godless Bolshevik regime', the divided Hungarian Army collapsed, and with it the revolution. On 1 August, in a tearful speech, Kun submitted to a demand from the Central Workers' and Soldiers' Council that he should resign and hand over to a Social-Democratic government. He and his Cabinet fled to Vienna under an Allied safe conduct, but Szamuelly, hurrying back from Moscow, was arrested at the Austrian border and blew his brains out. The board of management of the local Jewish cemetery refused to allow his body to be buried there. Kun moved back to Moscow, where he became involved in bitter internecine squabbles with the other members of the Hungarian party and was fired from its Central Committee. After being employed in a variety of jobs for the Comintern

he was eventually restored to favour and was given the ultimate honour
of being made a member of the Executive Committee of the Comintern
itself, alongside giants like Bukharin and Stalin. In 1937, however, he
became a victim of Stalin's purges and was sent to a labour camp,
where he died or was executed in 1938.[14]

The Hungarian Soviet Republic had lasted just 133 days. A series of
weak, short-lived governments followed, until the Romanians finally
withdrew from Budapest, carrying as much loot as they could lay their
hands on, and Admiral Horthy took power as 'Regent' of a restored
kingdom without a monarch. As in Munich and Riga, the Red Terror
was replaced by a White Terror that was infinitely worse, as anti-
Bolshevik gangs rounded up anyone who could be accused, rightly or
wrongly, of having Communist sympathies, beating, torturing and
murdering them in an orgy of proto-Fascist reaction. Horthy remained
in dictatorial power until 1944.

In Russia, the civil war still raged back and forth across the vast territories of the former tsarist empire. Although the Whites were still
recording victories, there were clear signs that overall the Reds were
slowly but surely gaining the upper hand. The ill-judged and ill-executed
Allied intervention in north Russia was coming to an end as the Allies
stepped up their preparations to withdraw from Murmansk and
Archangel. The Americans started to evacuate their troops on 3 June,
and would be gone completely by the end of July. The British, meanwhile, brought in two brigades of so-called volunteers, regular soldiers
to relieve and replace the last of the conscripts and to organise and
cover the evacuation of men and equipment. Although they were
supposed to be there for purely defensive purposes, they were involved
in several savage attacks on Bolshevik forces during the rest of the
summer, aided by RAF aircraft and an Australian company which broke
the enemy line in front of them with a bayonet charge, as they tried
to set the White Russians in a strong position before they left. The
evacuation went smoothly: the last British troops left Archangel on 27
September and Murmansk on 12 October. In the Far East at Vladivostok
all the Allies – apart from the Japanese, who had their own motives
for staying put – began making preparations for withdrawal.

Mainly on the insistence of Churchill, whose hatred of Bolshevism
and all it stood for remained as strong as ever, Britain was still providing
aid to the White Russian generals in the form of arms, equipment and

small teams of military advisers, but Lloyd George and the rest of the government no longer wanted any direct involvement.

There was, however, one area where Britain was still very much involved. Lenin and Trotsky had failed in their efforts to export Bolshevism to Europe, or to cling on to the breakaway border states. The nationalist governments had survived in Latvia and Lithuania, where the main threat to their independence now appeared to be from Goltz and the German Balts rather than the Bolsheviks, but Estonia was still in serious danger of attacks by the Red Army. As the head of a British diplomatic mission, Stephen Tallents, reported:

In Lithuania and Latvia I found German troops in complete occupation, and these cannot be withdrawn without effective substitution unless both countries are to be resigned to the Bolsheviks. Estonia is free of Germans and shows a much stronger national spirit, but she is more hardly pressed by the Bolsheviks. The presence of many Russian refugees, coupled with the nearness of Kronstadt and Petrograd, leads the Bolsheviks to regard an independent government in Estonia as a special menace. The military activity of the Germans in Latvia and Lithuania tends to strengthen the Bolshevik threat to Estonia, as it prevents the Red armies from advancing towards East Prussia.[15]

Britain was not in a position to offer Estonia military aid on land, apart from arms, equipment and advice, for which it sent a military mission under General Sir Hubert Gough, who had commanded the British Fifth Army in France. Gough's brief was to study the situation and recommend the best ways in which the Baltic States could defend themselves against both the Bolsheviks and Goltz's Germans. After taking Riga from the Bolsheviks, Goltz had moved north with a division of 12,000 German troops and a strong force of Balts and German volunteers calling itself the Baltic Landeswehr, with the aim of subjugating Estonia. Armed and equipped by Britain, the Estonians routed the invaders and advanced towards Riga. By 1 July, they were within ten miles of the Latvian capital, before Gough and Tallents persuaded them to halt and imposed a general armistice.[16] Goltz was ordered to leave Latvia immediately and return to Germany.

Tallents then removed the German commandant from his position in Riga and appointed himself temporary Civil Governor until Premier Ulmanis could return and take over a restored Latvian government. To make sure the Landeswehr concentrated its energies on fighting the Bolsheviks, Tallents removed its German commander and replaced him with a twenty-seven-year-old British lieutenant colonel, the Hon. Harold Alexander, DSO, MC (later Field Marshal Earl Alexander of Tunis), who had at one time during the war been the acting commander of the Fourth Guards Brigade, despite his youth. Alexander thus found himself commanding a German–Balt force of brigade strength, whose officers were almost entirely composed of his former enemies, which he achieved with great success, quickly earning their respect and loyalty. At Gough's behest, the reformed Landeswehr lined up alongside the Latvian and Estonian armies to drive the Bolsheviks out of their countries during the rest of 1919 and early 1920.

At sea, Admiral Cowan and his Royal Navy force enjoyed a summer of high activity against the Red Fleet in the Gulf of Finland. Cowan supported Estonian forces by shelling Red Army positions and preventing Bolshevik amphibious landings, engaging enemy ships whenever they could be enticed out of the safety of the great naval base on Kronstadt, the island fortress guarding the approaches to Petrograd. Kronstadt's defences were formidable, with extensive and lethal minefields, powerful shore batteries and underwater obstacles. But Cowan's difficulties did not end there: the Bolshevik Baltic Fleet, which included battleships and heavy cruisers, far outnumbered and outgunned his own light force. Cowan knew all this, of course, and typically relished the challenge. What he did not know was the state of mind of his enemy. According to the official Soviet history of the period:

In view of the importance of the defence of the sea approaches to Petrograd, the Soviet Command paid special attention to strengthening the Baltic Fleet. At the end of May the agent of the Council for the Defence of the Republic, Stalin, arrived at Kronstadt. The Commandant of the fortress and the chief of the Naval Base were placed under the command of the Revolutionary War Soviet of the Baltic Fleet, and the maritime sector of the Front was placed under the Commandant of the fortress. The Fleet's responsibility for the defence of Petrograd was thus increased. At the same time political workers were assigned to the ships, their crews checked, and the hostile and corrupt elements expelled and replaced by fresh men.[17]

Clearly, any action by Cowan's ships could be met with stiff, even fanatical resistance. His force was strengthened by the arrival of reinforcements at the end of May, including two more light cruisers – one to replace his flagship, which had struck a mine and been forced to return to the UK – a flotilla of submarines and their depot ship, the rest of the First Destroyer Flotilla, three minesweepers and a large fleet oiler, which struck a mine but still managed to struggle into harbour with its cargo intact. The reinforcements helped to improve the balance of numbers, but the Russian battleships and heavy cruiser still gave them superior firepower and range. Nevertheless, Cowan set about luring the Russian ships far enough out of Kronstadt to bring them into action.

With the approval and support of the Finnish government, Cowan established a new operational base for his ships in Biorko Sound, a large anchorage on the coast of Finland, only thirty miles from Kronstadt and less than twenty from the northern end of the mine barrage, from which he could move quickly against any Russian ships that ventured out into open water. The Finns had torpedo boats and minesweepers based there, which they placed at Cowan's disposal. The first encounters ended disastrously. Two engagements between British and Russian destroyers supported at long range from behind the barrage by the battleship *Petropavlovsk* were inconclusive, but as the British destroyers broke off, one of the two submarines on patrol attempted a torpedo attack. The torpedoes missed their mark, the submarine broke surface and before she could submerge again the Russians opened fire and scored a direct hit which tore through her pressure hull and sent her to the bottom with the loss of all hands.

Further skirmishes, in which Russian ships either remained behind the protective minefields or slipped out and back for lightning attacks, added to Cowan's frustration. Relief came in the shape of Lieutenant Augustus Agar, commander of a Royal Navy detachment of two forty-foot coastal motorboats (CMBs) to be used to ferry secret agents and couriers to and from Petrograd to maintain contact with the master spy Paul Dukes, otherwise known as Agent ST25, Britain's major source of intelligence in Russia since the closure of the embassy after the revolution. Agar decided to set up his base secretly in Terrioki, a village near the Finnish frontier which had previously housed the St Petersburg Imperial Yacht Club, some thirty miles east of Biorko and only twenty-five miles by sea from Petrograd. To avoid attracting attention by sailing his boats along the Finnish shore from the naval base at Hango, near Helsingfors (Helsinki), Agar visited Cowan to ask for a ship to tow them to Biorko, from where they could make their way quietly to Terrioki. Cowan agreed, but at the same time saw another use for the CMBs. Not only were they extremely fast, with a top speed of thirty-six knots, but they also had a very shallow draught, barely two feet nine inches, which meant they could ride unharmed over mines, which were sunk to a depth of six feet, and even the sunken breakwaters, which were about three feet below the surface. In theory, therefore, they should be able to penetrate the harbour at Kronstadt, armed with torpedoes, which Cowan provided.

On 13 June, Agar heard that the garrison in Krasnaya Gorka, the principal fortress on the southern side of Petrograd Bay, and its satellite, Grey Horse Battery, had mutinied. This created a serious situation for the Bolsheviks, since both Kronstadt and the rear of the Red Army's front on shore were now within the field of fire of the fortress guns. If Kronstadt fell, Petrograd would be at the mercy of an Allied attack from the sea. On 16 June, the Soviet commander ordered his ships to bombard Krasnaya Gorka from behind the minefields, where he believed they could not be reached by Cowan's force. The two battleships, *Petropavlovsk* and *Andrei Pervozvanny*, emerged from Kronstadt and started their bombardment. They were observed by Agar, returning from a successful courier trip, who roared at full speed to Biorko to report to Cowan. With the admiral's permission and encouragement, he sailed his two boats from Terrioki that night to attack the Bolshevik ships, but had to abort his mission when one of the boats struck a submerged object, probably a dud mine, broke a propeller shaft and had to be towed back to base. Next morning, to Agar's great disappointment, the two battleships returned to the safety of Kronstadt.

The battleships were, however, replaced by the cruiser *Oleg*, which took over the bombardment, and Agar decided to attack her with his single boat that night. Crewed by Sub Lieutenant J. Hampsheir and Chief Motor Mechanic M. Beeley, Agar threaded his boat through the screen of destroyers surrounding the *Oleg*, only to find that the torpedo's discharge cartridge had been accidentally fired and needed to be reset. After many agonising minutes, the job was done. Agar put on speed, cleared the destroyers and fired the torpedo, 'as if it were an ordinary practice run'. Then he turned and made for the Estonian coast, 'hoping to mislead the enemy as to where we had come from. Within a minute, there was a thick column of smoke from the *Oleg*. Flashes came from all directions, the forts, the destroyers, the ship itself, which were followed by splashes as the shells threw up columns of water soaking us to the skin. We were not far from Krasnaya Gorka when we turned north towards the Finnish shore at 35 knots.' They reached Terrioki shortly after 3 a.m. The whole operation had taken less than four hours.

The *Oleg* sank in twelve minutes, with the surprisingly small loss of only five men.[18]

On Cowan's recommendation, Agar was awarded the Victoria Cross 'for conspicuous gallantry, coolness and skill in penetrating a destroyer screen, remaining in close proximity to the enemy for twenty minutes while his torpedo was repaired and then successfully completing an exceptionally difficult operation in far from ideal weather conditions, finally escaping notwithstanding heavy fire from enemy warships and forts'. Hampsheir was awarded the DSO, and Beeley the CGM.[19]

Although Agar had sunk the *Oleg*, his exploit had been too late to save Krasnaya Gorka which had been recaptured by the Bolsheviks and reinforced by Stalin, along with the other forts around Kronstadt. But Cowan had been impressed by the CMBs' action and quickly saw the possibilities they raised of attacking the Red fleet within Kronstadt. While Agar and his boats went back to their secret agent courier role, the admiral called for reinforcements, which the Cabinet reluctantly – apart from Churchill – approved, together with a lifting of the ban on offensive action. These included not only a flotilla of eight larger CMBs, but also three cruisers, half of the Third Destroyer Flotilla, minesweepers and minelayers, and most significantly an aircraft carrier, the *Vindictive*, a converted heavy cruiser armed with four 7.5-inch guns and carrying twelve aircraft. By the time *Vindictive* arrived, work was well advanced on the construction of a rudimentary airstrip at Koivisto and a seaplane mooring at Biorko, so she was able to put her airplanes ashore and return to Copenhagen to collect of fresh batch of machines which had been ferried out from Britain by the carrier *Argus*.[20]

Initially, the aircraft were employed for reconnaissance and anti-submarine operations, with the occasional bombing and strafing run over Bolshevik land forces battling with White Russians and Estonians. But from the end of July they began bombing ships and shore facilities inside Kronstadt itself, though these were mainly of nuisance value since the bombs were generally too small to cause any serious damage. As the raids continued, so Bolshevik anti-aircraft fire became steadily more practised and more effective, but at the same time the British airmen were gaining valuable experience. Cowan's plan was for them to make diversionary attacks and draw enemy fire while the CMBs crept into the harbour and went about their business, something that called for as much coolness and courage from the RAF pilots as it did from the Royal Navy crews of the CMBs.

In the early hours of 18 August seven CMBs slipped out of Biorko Sound and rendezvoused with Agar, who led them to the harbour entrance while the RAF aircraft started their bombing runs from various directions. With Bolshevik searchlights and gunfire concentrated entirely on the aircraft, the CMBs entered the harbour unseen, and picked out their targets. Their main problem was that the harbour was crowded and the boats could only fire their torpedoes when they were at top speed. Nevertheless, they struck hard, sinking a submarine depot ship and one battleship, and seriously damaging the other battleship before withdrawing. By then, of course, the Bolsheviks were well aware of their presence, and threw everything at them. In spite of the valiant efforts of the RAF pilots to provide cover and diversion, three of the seven CMBs were destroyed, four British officers and four men were killed, three officers and six men taken prisoner. But the cost to the Bolsheviks was far greater. Although they continued to mount sporadic individual attacks wherever possible, and inflicted some casualties, they had only a handful of destroyers and submarines with which to oppose the British Navy, which established complete control in the Baltic until December 1919, when the ice forced it to leave.[21] The British naval force had played no significant part in the Russian civil war, or the Allied intervention, but it had been immensely important in helping the Baltic States, and to a lesser extent Finland, to resist the advance of Bolshevism and establish their freedom.

# XI

## 'IT HAS THE TAINT OF BOLSHEVISM'

THE first half of 1919 had been dominated by revolution, both real and imagined. By July, most of the danger had passed, but the fear remained, and would do so until well past the end of the year, based on the strikes and industrial unrest that were rampant almost everywhere. France teetered once more on the edge of a national general strike through the month. In Italy, where Orlando's government had collapsed on 19 June – 'dropped to the ground like an empty sack' as one commentator put it[1] – a continuous wave of disorder swept across the country, with general strikes in Milan, Naples, Verona, Genoa and Turin, and riots in every major city, mainly in protest at low wages and the high cost of living. Elementary-school teachers and even some village priests walked out of their jobs, while in Rome waiters shut down every restaurant, inn and café in the city, apart from small family-run establishments. In towns and cities, people formed themselves into 'chambers of labour', similar to workers' councils, which forced shopkeepers to reduce food and other prices by 50 per cent and sent representatives wearing black or red armbands depending on whether they were Republicans or Socialists, to take control in smaller towns and villages. Anyone who resisted was badly treated, and there were many injuries and several deaths in the widespread disturbances that ensued.[2] Adding to the confusion, there were violent demonstrations organised by Mussolini against the new government of Francesco Nitti, a liberal whom the Nationalists despised for his opposition to the war. On 1 July, Mussolini reacted to the left-wing activity by publishing his Fascist manifesto: at the time its importance seemed negligible, with few people realising that it was setting out the scenario for the next twenty-five years of Italian political history.

On the other side of the world, Australia was hit by a seamen's strike that had started some weeks before in Queensland but had now spread to New South Wales, Victoria and South Australia. Virtually all the shipping in the harbours of Melbourne, Sydney and Adelaide was tied up; interstate trade was halted, stopping supplies of flour and wheat to Queensland. Food prices rocketed to unheard-of levels, putting such staples as eggs, vegetables and butter beyond the reach of the masses, while the cost of clothes and soap were prohibitive. The most serious effect, however, was the shortage of coal which led to electricity and gas supplies being restricted to a few hours each day: Melbourne, where the gas company's reserve was down to one week's supply, faced the possibility of a complete shutdown of gas and electric light and power, and both there and in Adelaide tram and train services were severely curtailed. The effects also spread far beyond Australia's own shores – with no regular shipments of frozen meat from down under, Britain's butchers faced a shortage of lamb and mutton, which forced up prices. The deadlock in Australia continued through all of June and most of July, with no softening of attitudes – when the president of the Seamen's Union was threatened with deportation, he welcomed it, saying he would then be able to start a maritime strike in England.[3] The strike finally ended on 2 September, when the Australian government called a round-table conference. It had lasted four long months.

In Britain, the biggest strike of the year started in Lancashire on 23 June, when 450,000 cotton workers brought the mills to a halt for eighteen days over a pay claim. They succeeded in reducing their working week from fifty-five and a half hours to forty-eight, with a wage rise of 30 per cent, a notable victory. The millworkers' battle was a straight fight for better pay and conditions. While they were still out, however, the annual conference of the Labour Party, held in the Lancashire seaside resort of Southport, was debating whether it should support strike action for political ends by the Triple Alliance. Robert Williams, General Secretary of the powerful Transport and General Workers Federation, and miners' leader Robert Smillie wanted a great strike immediately, to force the government to end conscription and all interference in Russia and release conscientious objectors and other 'political prisoners' from jail. But the majority believed that they could achieve their political aims by using political weapons – the Labour Party had after all been formed in 1900 as the unions' political arm. They argued that strikes for political purposes were unconstitutional, and that 'industrial weapons should be reserved for industrial purposes'.[4]

The principle of separating industrial and political aims was soon put to the test. The final report of the Sankey Commission on the coal mining industry had been published on 23 June. Its opening words were unequivocal:

I recommend that Parliament be invited immediately to pass legislation acquiring the coal royalties for the State and paying fair and just compensation to the owners. I recommend on the evidence before me that the principle of State ownership of the coal mines be accepted.

Realising no doubt that his proposal might sound dangerously radical, Mr Justice Sankey later in the report stressed that it was strictly a one-off:

Coal mining is our national key industry upon which nearly all other industries depend. A cheap and adequate supply of coal is essential to the comfort of individuals and to the maintenance of the trade of the country . . . Coal mining occupies a unique and exceptional place in the national life, and there is no other industry with which it can be compared.[5]

It looked as though the miners had won. But the commission had been made up of six miners' supporters (three union officials led by Robert Smillie, and three Fabian intellectuals) and six capitalists (three coal owners and three 'independent' industrialists), and Sankey's report reflected only the unanimous views of the union side. Five out of the six capitalists were dead set against nationalisation and one, Sir Arthur Duckham, came up with an elaborate scheme of his own for a profit-sharing trust. Lloyd George initially pledged to accept Sankey's report 'in spirit and in letter'. When it came to acting upon it, however, he pointed out that Sankey had based his findings 'entirely on the expectation that there will be increased harmony between employer and worker in the mines. But since Mr Justice Sankey penned that report two or three things have happened which I think would have induced him to change his mind at the time.'[6]

What might have changed Sankey's mind was a major strike in the Yorkshire coalfields, starting on 21 July, in defiance of the miners' national federation which had agreed to continue negotiations on all outstanding disputes as long as the men remained at work. There were several smaller strikes going on at the time in different parts of England, Scotland and Wales, but these were generally confined to individual collieries and concerned with local grievances. The Yorkshire stoppage involved more than 150,000 men and was unmistakably political, since it was against the government, which still controlled wages under wartime regulations. It also had a disastrous effect on other industries, putting 50,000 men out of work almost immediately – 30,000 of them in the Bradford woollen trade alone – as their factories and mills were forced to shut down by lack of fuel.

The Yorkshire miners were looking for wage increases of up to 16.6 per cent, to compensate them for reduced income from piece rates after working hours were cut from eight to seven hours a day; the government prohibited any rise of more than 12 per cent. Such an impasse was a perfectly normal basis for a strike, but the Yorkshiremen wanted more. They wanted immediate nationalisation of their industry and a say in how it was run – it had been nearly a month since Sankey had delivered his report, and the government had done nothing. It was ironic that the miners' action demolished Lloyd George's theory that nationalisation would produce industrial harmony, on the grounds that although men could be asked to strike against an employer who was making a profit, they would not strike against the state, 'which has only the common interest of all to look after'. The Yorkshire strike, said Lloyd George, 'was a direct strike against the government'.[7] The press agreed: 'This is not an ordinary trade dispute,' the *Scotsman* thundered. 'It is clearly the doing of implacable fanatics bent on nothing less than the destruction of the present order of things. It has the taint of Bolshevism.'[8] Lloyd George seized on the excuse to renege on his promise and throw out the Sankey report altogether.

Within days, the number of strikers in Yorkshire had risen to 200,000, as they were joined by men responsible for operating the pumps that prevented pits from the constant danger of flooding. Once a pit was flooded, it was finished, and could never be reopened, so it was usual during a strike for men operating the pumps and other basic safety maintenance to keep working. The government responded by sending in naval stokers, men used to manning ships' pumps, to take over, with troops to protect them. The troops were not needed: only the most diehard strike leaders considered the sailors as blacklegs. Most men and their communities welcomed them, knowing that without them they would have no jobs to go back to when the strike was over.

The Yorkshire miners held out for five weeks, during which they were joined by relatively small numbers of miners in Scotland, Derbyshire, Kent, Leicestershire and South Wales, until they reached a compromise settlement that was accepted in all the coalfields on 18 August. The miners returned to work, the stokers returned to their ships, the prospect of coal nationalisation was returned to the closet – it would have to wait until after the Second World War for a Labour government to bring it out again and put it into effect.

While the miners were out, Liverpool dockers were also on strike, paralysing the port and holding up literally hundreds of ships, and at the same time bakers in London and elsewhere stopped supplies of bread for over two weeks. The strike which really rocked Britain, however, and which for many, including the government, had more ominous and sinister elements, was called by the National Union of Police and Prison Officers (NUPPO) on the evening of 31 July. This was the culmination of six years of discontent among policemen and women, dating back to October 1913, when their newly formed union had been banned. The then Commissioner of the Metropolitan Police, Sir Edward Henry, had announced from the start that any officer joining the union would be instantly dismissed, and in 1916 this threat had been extended to cover anyone even attending a union meeting. Despite this, the union continued to exist clandestinely; when a meeting was raided by military police in February 1917, the single men present held the door shut while their married colleagues with families to support escaped through a rear window. Forty men had their names taken, fourteen of whom were dismissed from the force while the others were heavily fined.

In August 1918, Police Constable Tommy Thiel was dismissed for organising the union in provincial forces. The NUPPO executive promptly demanded his reinstatement, together with better pay and recognition of the union. At the same time, it suspended a no-strike clause in its constitution and called a strike to begin at midnight on 29 August. Although the union officially had only forty-seven paid-up members in London, 10–12,000 of the Metropolitan Police's 19,000-strong force came out. A mass meeting was held at Tower Hill, thousands of new members joined the union, and the London Trades Council voted to offer support by every means within its power.

Shaken by the strength of support for the strike, Lloyd George was quick to intervene, inviting the chairman of the unrecognised NUPPO to meet him in Downing Street on 31 August. The meeting was interrupted by news that the troops standing guard outside were fraternising with the striking police and declaring that they would refuse to obey any order to clear them from the street or to act as strike breakers. Pragmatic as always, Lloyd George gave way with good grace, raised the pay increase already offered by the Home Office, reinstated Thiel and twenty or so others dismissed for union activity, and even introduced a widow's pension. The men returned to their duties a mere forty-four hours after they had stopped work, celebrating their victory. But they had not won official recognition – the demand that had been at the heart of the dispute. Lloyd George cannily bought time by telling them that 'the government could not recognise a union for the police *in wartime*', leaving them to infer that it would do so after the war, though of course he had no intention of doing any such thing. Justifying this years later, he wrote: 'This country was nearer to Bolshevism that day than at any time since.'⁹

Sir Edward Henry was made the scapegoat for the strike. He was replaced as Commissioner by General Sir Nevil Macready, a distinguished soldier with a reputation for strict discipline who had commended himself to Lloyd George by the way he had restored order in the Welsh town of Tonypandy during a miners' strike in 1910, using troops with fixed bayonets. After the Prime Minister's capitulation, Macready was unable to prevent the continued growth of NUPPO, which reached a national membership of 55,000 by the summer of 1919, and was even forced into making further concessions. But on 30 May, with industrial unrest increasing in the country, he issued an order that any officer or man failing to report for duty, even under the threat of intimidation, would be dismissed with the loss of all pension rights, and would never be allowed back. The union's reaction – after one of its divisional secretaries gave in and resigned – was to ballot its members on strike action. The result was a massive majority – 48,863 for, 4,324 against – in favour of a strike.¹⁰

The government moved swiftly to draw the union's teeth with a bill in Parliament that offered substantial concessions on pay and conditions, and the introduction of democratic representation through a national Police Federation, a union in all but name. The sting in the tail was that police officers were forbidden from membership of any other labour organisation, which meant a death sentence for NUPPO. When the government refused to negotiate on this, NUPPO went ahead with its strike call, on 31 July.

The government's sweeteners ensured that the strike was not a success. On the first night only 240 men walked out in London, a number that rose to 850 the next day, mostly in the East End, and peaked at 1,081. In Birmingham a mere 112 policemen struck, but in Liverpool more than half of the city's 1,860 policemen stopped work. Unlike London, which stayed calm, Liverpool was torn by serious rioting, with looters helping themselves to the contents of shops, particularly clothing, jewellery, groceries and boots and shoes. They repeatedly plundered warehouses in the docks, until the government sent two Royal Navy destroyers and a cruiser to patrol the Mersey. Soldiers sent to keep order on the streets refused to fire on the looters, saying that they were not there to break the strike. But when a crowd outside St George's Hall tried to take the rifle from a sentry, he fired into the air, bringing a squad rushing to his defence. They fixed bayonets and charged when the mob attacked them with pickaxe handles, while soldiers elsewhere in the city were forced to fire over the heads of rioters in self-defence. The violence burnt itself out after three days and nights. After seven days, the strike fizzled out everywhere – despite brave words of support, no other unions came out in sympathy. Most of the strikers were ex-servicemen, all were dismissed, none were reinstated – the Home Secretary, Edward Shortt, said there were more than 2,000 applicants waiting for their jobs. It was the last time police in Great Britain ever stopped work.

President Wilson arrived back from Paris on 8 July to a nation still recovering from the fear of a great Bolshevik-led uprising which had been forecast for Independence Day. Since the spring, many radicals and liberal labour groups had been talking of a nationwide general strike to force the release of Thomas Mooney, a construction worker and radical agitator who had been convicted – unjustly, his supporters claimed – for his alleged part in a bomb explosion that had killed nine people and wounded another forty during a San Francisco Preparedness Day parade in July 1916. The death sentences on Mooney and his supposed co-conspirator, Warren K. Billings, had subsequently been commuted to life imprisonment, but the two men, and particularly Mooney, had become symbols of injustice to the working class. Although the AFL was opposed to the idea of a strike, it was felt that individual unions might support it, as there was considerable sympathy for Mooney among members, who saw him as a victim of anti-union prejudice.

The Mooney general strike was planned for 4 July, and as Independence Day approached radical propaganda grew alarmingly, while the non-radical press was filled with horror stories about what was to come. Remembering Seattle and Winnipeg, the general public had no difficulty believing that a new general strike on a massive scale was possible, or that following the recent bombings there would be murder and mayhem. In New York City, 11,000 policemen and detectives mounted a twenty-four-hour watch on federal, state, county and city buildings and installations, and on the Stock Exchange and the homes of prominent citizens. Hundreds of special deputies were sworn in, and all public meetings banned for the day; the city even refused to allow the American Defense Society to hold its Independence Day rally at Carnegie Hall in case it incited both radicals and patriots to violence.

The picture was the same in other cities and regions. In Chicago, the entire police force was put on alert, backed up by a thousand volunteers and two companies of the Fourteenth Infantry. In Boston, the Federal Building was guarded by thirty fully armed soldiers; in Philadelphia the streets were literally 'filled with policemen'. Federal agents were stationed thickly across the Pacific Northwest to forestall a rumoured uprising by Wobblies, and hundreds of known or suspected Reds were rounded up and imprisoned for the day to keep them out of trouble. But when the day itself came, nothing happened. There was no strike, no bloodshed, no bombings – the only explosions were from festive fireworks.[11] To save face, the press and the patriotic societies claimed that the Reds had been deterred by the massive show of strength, an explanation which a large part of the public was happy to accept. The distrust of organised labour was deeply felt, exacerbated by an epidemic of strike fever that continued during the whole of July. Forty thousand seamen all along the Atlantic and Gulf coasts tied up shipping for three weeks, machinists came out in Chicago, where 100,000 construction workers were locked out, bakers and telephone operators in St Louis, elevated-railway employees in Boston and even government airmail pilots who wanted safer planes after a number of crashes, all stopped work.

The President, preoccupied with trying to steer the Peace Treaty through Congress against determined opposition, did little to calm the industrial turmoil. Although he had always believed that politics and big business should be separate, he had sent the chairman of the Democratic National Committee, Homer S. Cummings, on a two-month fact-finding tour of the country to examine the causes of high prices in food, clothing and other necessities, which he rightly blamed for most of the strikes. But when Cummings delivered his report, towards the end of July, Wilson handed it over to Attorney General Palmer with instructions to consider introducing legislation for some form of price control.

Palmer called a conference of Cabinet members and officials, including the Director General of the Railroad Administration: the rail unions were threatening to call a massive strike in the autumn, citing the cost of living as their reason for demanding a huge hike in wages. This was worrying enough, but what was even worse was that they were also pushing for the US government to buy the railroads, which it had seized during the war, and operate them under a plan drawn up by Glenn R. Plumb, a counsel for the railroad brotherhoods. Under the Plumb Plan, the railroads would be operated by a corporation of fifteen men, five representing the public, five management and five labour, with profits divided between the government and managerial and classified employees.

The Plumb Plan generated a great deal of support, and a great deal of hostility. By August, when a bill embodying the plan was introduced to Congress, Plumb claimed that there were roughly eight million workers who were fighting for it and that if it was not adopted there would be serious trouble. The railroad companies mounted a powerful counter-attack, with an emotive advertising campaign calling the plan the first step along the road to Bolshevism, while the general press warned that banks, natural resources and public utilities would be the next targets. The charge of Bolshevism was enough to scupper the bill: some Congressmen thought the plan 'might well have been formulated by a Lenin or a Trotsky', and others described it as 'a bold, bald, naked attempt to sovietize the railroads of this country'.[12] It was duly defeated.

Unabashed by the collapse of its case against the Rand School, the Lusk Committee went on collecting 'evidence' and continuing its anti-radical campaign at full blast. One of its most worrying charges was that radicals were systematically indoctrinating black Americans, in an attempt to undermine their loyalty. This view was enthusiastically endorsed by

J. Edgar Hoover as he busied himself with building his mammoth card index and compiling incriminating dossiers. One of his special file categories was marked 'Negro Activities'; since early in the year he had been monitoring the black leader Marcus Garvey and other activists in the growing black nationalist movement. He described Garvey as 'one of the most prominent negro agitators in New York', believing that his paper, *Negro World*, 'upheld Soviet Russian rule' and engaged in 'open advocation [*sic*] of Bolshevism'. He had some justification for this: in July, for example, writing about Bolshevism, the *Negro World* told its readers that it was their duty 'to avail themselves of every weapon that may be effective in defeating the fell motives of their oppressors', while the *Challenge* naively claimed that 'Bolshevism is not bad . . . Sovietcy takes away nobody's freedom. It gives a larger freedom.'[13] Hoover recommended that 'something must be done to the editors of these publications as they are beyond doubt exciting the negro elements of this country to riot and to the committing of outrages of all sorts'.[14]

When racial unrest erupted in the summer of 1919, it was inevitable that Bolshevism was seen as a prime cause: 'REDS TRY TO STIR NEGROES TO REVOLT' was one typical headline, while the *New York Times* averred that 'Bolshevist agitation has been extended among the Negroes'.[15] Racial trouble was simmering in various parts of America, but it finally boiled over in Washington DC, in July. For a month, the nation's capital had been in the grip of a crime wave, which included a series of attacks in the street by black men on white women. Little had been done about it, and tensions had risen steadily until, shortly after 10 p.m. on 18 July, two black men were seen to accost and jostle a white woman, nineteen-year-old Mrs Elsie Stephanick, who was walking home along D Street in the south-west quarter of the city after working a late shift at the Bureau of Engraving and Printing. The men were chased off by several of her colleagues and a group of sailors and marines who, on learning that Mrs Stephanick's husband was a serving soldier, decided to exact retribution on his behalf. Next day, they spread the word to other servicemen that 'the boys were going to avenge the attack on Mrs Stephanick tonight', and that 'if they wanted to see action they should fall in at Ninth Street and the Avenue between 10 and 10.30 o'clock'.[16]

More than four hundred servicemen, mostly in uniform and carrying revolvers or clubs, answered the call. They were joined by about three hundred civilians, who armed themselves with pieces of wood from lumber yards along the way. They found one of the men who had attacked Mrs Stephanick, and prepared for a lynching, but he escaped and barricaded himself in his house. The frustrated mob hurled bricks and pieces of wood at the house, and at any black people they could see, before the police finally intervened, broke up the crowd and sent them home.

The attacks started again next evening as a mixed mob of white soldiers and civilians swarmed along Pennsylvania Avenue, beating up any black person they saw, dragging them from cars, buses and streetcars, even outside the gates of the White House itself, where President Wilson languished in bed suffering from an acute attack of dysentery. Things quietened down when the soldiers had to return to barracks for their Sunday midnight curfew, but there was much talk of meeting again on the Monday night 'to *really* clean up the black districts'.

By the next evening, however, the black population was ready to fight back. They had spent the day arming themselves – police estimated that at least five hundred revolvers were sold in the city that day, and those unable to buy guns in the District had piled into cars and driven to Baltimore. By evening the atmosphere was electric, yet the city police commissioner refused to make preparations apart from warning law-abiding citizens to stay indoors. The military authorities, at least, had wisely confined all soldiers to camp, and as trouble brewed sent a detachment of cavalry from Fort Myer to confront and disperse a mob of a thousand whites marching through the city. Frustrated, the mob turned back and surged to the downtown area, attacking any blacks they encountered. Two black men were shot down and killed after using their weapons to defend themselves. But this time the blacks retaliated, with heavily armed gangs roaring through the city in high-powered cars, shooting as they went. The battle raged till dawn, leaving four people dead – two blacks, a white civilian and a policeman shot by a seventeen-year-old black girl – and at least two more dying, while hospitals treated hundreds of cases of gunshot wounds, broken bones and lacerations. Three hundred rioters were arrested. It had been the bloodiest night in the city since the Civil War.

Next day, finally, the President called the Secretary of War, Newton D. Baker, and ordered him to put a stop to the trouble. Baker sent more than 2,000 fully armed federal troops into the city to restore order, which they did, aided by torrential rain that kept people of all colours off the streets.

The violence in the capital was over for the summer. But within days it erupted again, and far more seriously, in Chicago. Washington in 1919 was still very much a Southern city with a preponderantly black population and regular underlying racial tension, but Chicago was a tough northern metropolis, where the tensions were political and industrial as well as racial. The city on the shores of Lake Michigan had a history of union militancy, particularly in mass production industries such as steel, meat packing, ready-made clothing and agricultural equipment, and in 1919 recorded more strikes than any other city apart from New York. Almost every day through that long, hot summer there was another strike – at Argo's Corn Products Company, the Crane Company, International Harvester, all the major packing houses and steel mills. While labour in the rest of the country ignored the Mooney general strike call, in Chicago 100,000 men stopped work for twenty-four hours.

The race issue in Chicago was complicated by several factors but mainly by the simple need of workers to protect their jobs and the improvements in wages and conditions which they had wrung from employers during the war. The war, with its unprecedented opportunities for work, had attracted some 50,000 Southern blacks to Chicago between 1916 and 1919, a huge and indigestible influx. The general migration from the South had started some years earlier, but the new arrivals meant that the black population of Chicago had more than doubled since 1910,[17] bringing fierce competition for jobs and above all for housing. A five-mile swathe running through the heart of the south side became known as the Black Belt, containing the greatest concentration of African Americans outside of New York's Harlem. It also contained much of Chicago's vice, as corrupt city politicians allowed the underworld to operate unhindered through saloons and cabarets whose white gangster owners sheltered behind black frontmen, openly flaunting prohibition, which came into effect on 30 June. Mixed crowds ignored the city's 1 a.m. closing time and drank till dawn in the 'black and tan' nightclubs, dancing the shimmy to the sound of black jazz musicians, who had themselves made the journey north from New Orleans in search of employment.

As more and more migrants arrived, the Black Belt expanded into choice residential districts, creating great resentment among white homeowners, who tried to drive out blacks with mob violence, bombings and murder. This resentment followed blacks into the workplace, deepening the existing antipathy which stemmed from employers' pre-war use of migrant black labour to break strikes. As industrial recession struck in the spring of 1919, the competition for jobs increased, and although most blacks had obtained their jobs honestly and were the first to be fired, white suspicions remained and the atmosphere became increasingly charged.

On Sunday 27 July, a seventeen-year-old black boy called Eugene Williams was swimming in the lake from the 29th Street beach, which had long been informally divided into black and white sections. Using a railroad sleeper as a float, Eugene drifted across the 'line' between the two sections. White bathers immediately began shouting and throwing stones at him, one of which hit him on the head. He let go of the sleeper, swam for a few strokes, then sank beneath the water and drowned. Enraged blacks were further infuriated when a policeman on duty refused to arrest the white youth who had thrown the stone, claiming that he could not identify him in the crowd. They rampaged along the beach, fighting and brawling, beating up whites, seeking revenge.

Next day, the whites struck back. There was talk of 'cleaning up' the stockyard districts, and at the end of the working day gangs swooped on black workers as they made their way home. Blacks walking on the streets were set upon. A gang of fifty white men dragged a black man and two black women from a streetcar and beat them unconscious. A white motorman was hauled out of his cab by blacks and stabbed to death, and a dozen streetcars were wrecked. The authorities stopped all streetcars and elevated railway trains in the area, forcing more people on to the streets on foot, and into danger. For five hours the Black Belt became a battleground as blacks and whites fought each other with guns, clubs, knives and razors. At 11 p.m. the police moved in in force, breaking up black crowds with guns and clubs. By the end of the evening, seven people had been killed – five black and two white – and more than forty seriously injured.

On the third day, rioting erupted again even more seriously, spreading out of the Black Belt and into the Italian district in the west and the affluent north side of the city, including the famous business district, the Loop, where two black men and one white were shot and killed. The situation was aggravated when 5,000 tramway workers repudiated a deal negotiated by their union leaders and went on strike for higher wages, tying up the city's transport and sending yet more pedestrians on to the streets. That night, in a series of pitched battles, another fourteen people were killed and over 150 seriously injured in stabbings, shootings and beatings. In one case a black man was shot to death, then petrol was poured on his body and set alight. Whites attacked the Provident black hospital, shooting at patients and staff and killing one man. The fighting continued even in the 'bull pen' in the city jail, when blacks and whites were locked up together.

A committee of black leaders and ministers issued a statement blaming the riots on bad feeling stemming from official indifference to the bombing of houses occupied by blacks, and the refusal by police to arrest those responsible for the drowning of Eugene Williams. They appealed to the Governor of Illinois, Frank Lowden, to send in troops, and he finally did so, over the heads of the police and city authorities, who refused to call for such help – the acting chief of police claimed that he was 'very pleased with conditions'.[18] Three thousand armed soldiers from the Fourth Regiment of the Illinois National Guard were sent to patrol Chicago's streets on 31 July, with another 3,000 men in reserve, and the fighting gradually died down, though there were still a number of ugly incidents. That night, both sides turned from street fighting to arson, with thirty-six fires reported as they tried to burn each other out. Blacks were blamed for the mysterious burning of forty-nine houses in Back of the Yards, which left 948 people, mainly Lithuanians, homeless.[19]

By morning, an uneasy peace had returned and Chicago could start counting the cost of five days of bloody conflict. Thirty-eight people – fifteen whites and twenty-three blacks – had been killed, and 537 seriously injured. The city authorities had to rush in emergency food supplies to the Black Belt, where arson, looting and shooting had brought the population close to starvation. A grand jury was empanelled to investigate the riots, but went on strike when the state's attorney insisted on seeking to indict only black rioters. Meanwhile, the Chicago City Coroner ruled that Eugene Williams had not been struck by stones, but had simply drowned. The white youth who had finally been arrested for his murder was released.[20]

As summer moved into autumn, there was further racial violence in different parts of America: two blacks died during two days of rioting in Knoxville, Tennessee, at the end of August, and four weeks later federal troops were called out to restore order in Omaha, Nebraska, after a mob burnt down the new courthouse, overpowered the mayor and almost beat him to death when he tried to stop them lynching a black prisoner accused of robbery and raping a white girl. Besides the

24. Intervention in the Russian Civil War cost many American and Allied lives. Here, German prisoners in Vladivostok manhandle flatbed rail trucks carrying the coffins of seventeen US servicemen killed fighting the Bolsheviks in Siberia.

25. Bolshevik agitation was blamed for race riots in Chicago in July 1919, with National Guardsmen called out to keep order on the streets.

26. Steel strikers in Pittsburgh paraded the streets to raise public support for their cause.

27. Facing them were armed state troopers, ready for trouble, like these at Farell, Pennsylvania

28. The implacable faces of capitalist power: (*left to right*) Judge Gary, Governor Calvin Coolidge and John D. Rockefeller Jr, who led the fight against the unions in America.

9.–31. The workers' champions and bosses' bogeymen: 'Big Bill' Haywood, leader of the IWW; Samuel Gompers, of the American Federation of Labor; and Eugene Debs, Socialist presidential candidate, sentenced to a ten-year prison sentence for speaking against American involvement in the war.

32. Straw-hatted
members of American
Actors' Equity, seen here
on 45th Street, New
York City, darkened the
lights of Broadway in
the most decorous
and successful
strike of the turbulent
summer of 1919.

33. British coal miners
were led by their fiery
Scottish president,
Robert Smillie, in a
series of bitter strikes
that failed to deliver
their aims.

34. Eamon de Valera, seen here addressing a public meeting in Los Angeles on his US tour as President of Ireland's Dáil Éireann, was a thorn in Britain's side as a revolutionary leader, but had no communist connections.

35. Benito Mussolini (*left*), seen here with nationalist hero Gabriele D'Annunzio, founded the Fascist movement as part of the right-wing reaction to Socialist and Communist disturbances in Italy.

*Trotsky'll Get You If You Don't Watch Out!*

36.–37. The Great Red Scare inspired widely differing responses from America's cartoonists. While Fitzpatrick of the St Louis *Post-Dispatch* poured scorn on the Senate's fears, W. A. Rogers in the New York *Herald* suggested a more popular solution to the problem of radicalism.

38. Many of Palmer's supposedly dangerous aliens were innocent immigrants such as these workers attending English classes at night school in Chicago.

39. Police raids on suspect organisations were nothing if not thorough, as witness the result in this office of the Union of Russian Workers in New York, where they claimed to have found bomb-making chemicals.

40. The 'Red Ark', the SS *Buford* carried 249 deported aliens from New York to Soviet Russia

41. Nicknamed 'the Red Queen' by the press, Emma Goldman was an unrepentant anarchist and advocate of birth control, proud to be 'the first political agitator to be deported from the United States'.

prisoner, two other men were killed and twenty-three seriously wounded in the melee before the troops arrived.

The Knoxville and Omaha riots were individual incidents on a much smaller scale than those in Washington and Chicago, which were not repeated during the remainder of that year. Nevertheless, the suspicion remained that Reds were behind all the unrest: the *New York Times*, for instance, was quick to blame 'agitators among the negroes, supported by the Bolsheviki, the IWW, and other radical elements in the country' for supporting a campaign 'for self-determination for the negroes of all corners of the earth'. 'A negro newspaper,' the *Times* continued, said that 'the negro wants a Lenin and Trotsky to emancipate the black people of the earth.'[21] The Bureau of Investigation gave credence to the allegations, stating that it had information that Russian soviet interests were supplying funds for propaganda to stir up race hatred, and that 'IWW and soviet influence were at the bottom of the recent race riots in Washington and Chicago'.[22]

Although the race riots stole the headlines in July, industrial strife took over again in August, as railway shopmen, responsible for maintenance and inspection of trains, walked out at the beginning of the month for higher wages, severely disrupting both passenger and freight traffic from coast to coast. As the month wore on, other rail strikes halted subway and elevated lines in New York, and a sympathy strike in Los Angeles and southern California caused catastrophic losses to fruit and livestock in transit. Simultaneously with the wage strikes, the main brotherhoods stepped up their campaign for a government takeover of the railroads. Although the two issues were quite separate, it was only natural for the American public to see a connection between them and to suspect a Red plot, particularly when 20,000 union members staged a march in Portland, Oregon, coupling demands for joint ownership of the railroads and the withdrawal of the remaining US troops from Russia.

On a smaller scale, another stoppage that attracted great attention during August was that of actors, who walked out of New York's playhouses on the 7th, the first ever strike in American theatre. Working conditions for actors at the time were appalling, with unscrupulous producers and managers exploiting would-be stars in every conceivable way. Under the standard employment contract, actors were not paid for rehearsals for new shows, which usually took between four and six weeks for straight plays and up to three months for musicals, and had to buy their own costumes. They could be – and often were – fired without notice, or laid off indefinitely without pay but forbidden to take work elsewhere; more highly paid actors could be replaced by lower-earning understudies once a show had opened successfully; extra performances on Sunday evenings or public holidays were not paid for, and it was common for managers to cancel a Saturday evening perform-ance, deduct wages for the missed show, then put on an unpaid Sunday evening performance in its place.

Since 1913, performers had been represented by the Actors' Equity Association, a union which provided expert advice and sued theatre managers who broke contracts, as many of them regularly did. Between 1913 and 1919, the union obtained legal judgements of some $460,000 for its members. When the standard contract agreement expired in the early summer of 1919, the managers jumped on the open-shop band-wagon and refused to recognise Equity, or to submit to arbitration on the union's right to negotiate on behalf of its members. Faced with this blatant attempt to break the union and impose a one-sided settlement, the actors rebelled. Having first affiliated to the AFL, Equity called a strike.

In theatrical terms, the strike was an immediate smash hit. On the first night, twelve theatres, almost half of Broadway's first-class houses, went dark; incredulous managers, who had refused to believe that actors would ever abandon their golden rule that the show must go on, were forced to refund an estimated $25,000 to disappointed audiences. Next day, the union claimed 1,200 new members, bringing its total member-ship to 5,400, a tiny number when compared with the railroad broth-erhoods or the miners' unions, but highly newsworthy since it included 90 per cent of the biggest names in show business. When Eddie Cantor walked out of the starring role in the Ziegfeld *Follies*, Al Jolson refused to 'play the scab' and replace him. The illustrious Barrymore clan gave its concerted support. Ed Wynn, the comedy star of *Gaieties of 1919*, joined the picket lines outside theatres on 44th Street, drawing more crowds than the shows and persuading them with jokes and ad-lib humour to stay away. Emboldened by the actors' stance, chorus girls formed their own union, electing Marie Dressler as their first president; musicians and stagehands organised, too, and seriously considered staging a sympathy strike. By the end of the month, no fewer than twenty-five New York theatres were closed, the strike had spread to Boston and Chicago, and the producers had lost over $1 million.

It was the intervention of the stagehands that finally brought the end of the strike, when over four hundred of them joined striking performers on 28 August to close down the Hippodrome, reputedly the world's largest theatre. Two days later the Hippodrome's management broke ranks and signed new contracts recognising Actors' Equity and the new Chorus Equity Association. With Labor Day, the traditional start of the new season, approaching fast, and faced by the threat of sympathy strikes by musicians and electricians, the other managements followed suit, agreeing to almost all of Equity's demands. They saved face – and at least part of the open-shop principle – with an agreement that no actor would be forced to join Equity in order to work. The theatres reopened on 6 September.[23]

The actors' strike had been a landmark success for the principle of organised labour, but it is doubtful whether the general public appreciated this, knowing more about the glamour and rewards of the successful few and little if anything of the hardships and unfairness involved in what was always a precarious profession. To many, if not most, onlookers the high-profile strike was yet another example of the creeping Bolshevism that was afflicting America, and socially conscious stars could be seen as parlour Bolsheviks. That would most certainly have been the view of J. Edgar Hoover, who had by then been authorised by Attorney General Palmer to establish a new General Intelligence Division in the Bureau of Investigation, under his own direction, to spearhead the anti-radical crusade.

As the players returned to the stage, Hoover was more concerned with other, more menacing events in Chicago, where the American Socialist Party's annual convention was embroiled in even more contentious factional infighting than usual. The left and right wings of the party had been battling for its soul ever since the Bolshevik Revolution in Russia, with the militants of the left demanding a policy of revolution now, and the moderates of the right clinging to their belief in democratic evolution. By May 1919, following the formation of the Comintern, the militants had become so strident and abusive that the National Executive Committee suspended from membership all those who adhered to the left-wing philosophy. Some 30,000 were affected by this, about one-third of the entire active membership of the party. Ninety-four delegates from twenty states attended a meeting of revolutionary Socialists in New York City on 21 June, where they decided not to form a breakaway party at once but to attempt to take over the whole party at the Chicago convention. In preparation for this, they declared their allegiance to the Third International and drew up a new, radical manifesto: 'The world is in crisis. Capitalism, the prevailing system of society, is in process of disintegration and collapse . . . Humanity can be saved from its last excesses only by the Communist Revolution.'[24]

By the time of the Annual Convention in Chicago's Machinists' Hall, the left wing had the support of some 60,000 of the Socialist Party's 100,000 members, but as usual they fell out among themselves, and split into two factions, native-born English speakers in one and foreign-language immigrants, mainly Russians, Latvians, Estonians, Lithuanians, Poles, Ukrainians, Hungarians and Yugoslavs, in the other. The English speakers' plan to take over the whole party never got off the ground; they were forcibly ejected from the convention before it had even officially opened. Victor Berger spoke for the rump of traditional Socialists when he announced: 'We are the party, the others are just a lot of anarchists.'[25]

The ejected group repaired to another room in the building, where they immediately declared themselves to be the Communist Labor Party. They were led by the journalist and Harvard graduate John Reed, former New York State legislator Benjamin Gitlow, and William Lloyd, son of the millionaire journalist the late Henry Demarest Lloyd, who had made his name on the *Chicago Tribune* with a series of exposés of capitalist monopolies such as Standard Oil and the railway cartels. Their manifesto stated that their new party was 'in full harmony with the revolutionary working class parties of all countries and stands by the principles stated by the Third International' and that it proposed 'the organisation of the workers as a class, the overthrow of capitalist rule and the conquest of political power by the workers'.[26]

The foreign-language rebels had nothing but scorn for the Communist Labor Party, which it regarded as a collection of bourgeois pretenders. They formed their own rival grouping, which they named simply the American Communist Party. Meeting in the IWW hall, which they called the Smolny Institute, after the Bolshevik headquarters in Petrograd, they drew up a programme based entirely on the Bolshevik Revolution and the aims of the Comintern: 'The Communist Party is fundamentally a party of action . . . the Communist Party shall keep in the foreground

its consistent appeal for proletarian revolution, the overthrow of capitalism and the establishment of the dictatorship of the proletariat . . .'

The two Communist parties drained the American Socialist Party of
about 75 per cent of its members. They also drew off about 2,000
Wobblies from the IWW, including many of its leading figures, such as
Earl Browder, James Cannon and Bill Shatov, who later went to Russia,
where he became one of the country's greatest railroad builders. Even
its founder, Bill Haywood, moved over, saying, 'Here is what we have
been dreaming about; here is the IWW all feathered out.'[27] He, too,
later left for Russia 'to observe Bolshevism in action' – and, incidentally, to escape the jail sentence under the Espionage Act, against which
he was appealing with little hope of success.

The formation of not one but two Communist parties in America was
enough to send shivers of excitement through J. Edgar Hoover and A.
Mitchell Palmer, and to reinforce their determination to scotch the
growth of radicalism in any and every way possible. In this, they had
the support of the majority of the Cabinet, where the strongest anti-
Bolshevik voice was that of the Secretary of State, Robert Lansing, who
had been issuing dire warnings against it since January 1918. On his
return from the Peace Conference, where he had been exposed to the
effects of Bolshevism in Europe, he was seriously concerned at seeing
the 'unrest and wide dissatisfaction at present conditions' in America,
and the growth of 'strong socialistic, if not Communistic sentiment,
which directly menaces our democratic institutions'. By August, he was
repeatedly urging the President to warn the public about the true dangers
of Bolshevism, and asking, 'I wonder how long we can tolerate the
radical propaganda which is being carried on in this country and is
teaching the laboring class to revolt against the present economic order?
How long can we go on in this way without a disaster?'[28]

Since his own return from Paris, Wilson had been totally preoccupied with his bitter battle with Cabot Lodge and the other opponents
of the Peace Treaty and the League of Nations. By late August he was
desperate with frustration at being unable to defeat Lodge and persuade
Congress to ratify the treaty; despite being tired and ill, he decided to
ignore his doctor's advice and go directly to the American people with
a grand tour of thirty cities in twenty-seven states, covering 11,000
miles by rail in twenty-seven days, starting on 3 September. Having
agreed to Lansing's plea to 'warn the country in some way that may

attract attention',[29] he seized on the Bolshevik threat as a valuable weapon in his struggle to win popular support: the treaty was vital, he asserted in his speeches, not only to save the world from further wars, but also to defeat Bolshevism. His Republican opponents, he said, were not Bolshevists, but he strongly implied that in their opposition to the treaty they were the dupes of Bolshevists.[30]

# XII

## 'NO TIME FOR MOLLYCODDLING'

WHILE President Wilson was dragging his exhausted frame around the western states, America was racked by two major strikes, one at the beginning of his gruelling tour, the other at its abrupt ending. The first was in Boston, where the city's police had been attempting for months to negotiate a badly needed pay increase, shorter hours and improved conditions. In May, the city had unilaterally granted them a rise of $200 a year, bringing the starting salary for a patrolman to $1,000 and the top wage for veteran officers to $1,600, out of which they had to buy their own uniforms and equipment. They were offered no improvement in hours or conditions, which were appalling: men worked seventy-three hours a week on the day shift, and eighty-three on night duty; their station houses were infested with rats and bugs, some were so crowded that men had to sleep two to a bed and share the same locker; and they had no independent channel for complaints about unfair treatment at the hands of superior officers.

Forbidden to join a union, the Boston police formed the 'Boston Social Club', a patently transparent cover, and set about organising themselves for the coming fight. In late July, Police Commissioner Edwin Upton Curtis, a conservative banker-lawyer and former mayor, declared: 'I am firmly of the opinion that a police officer cannot consistently belong to a union and perform his sworn duty . . . I feel it is my duty to say to the police force that I disapprove of the movement on foot.'[1] Undeterred by Curtis's disapproval, the Boston Social Club went ahead and applied to the AFL for affiliation, which was swiftly granted. Curtis's response was to insert a new clause in the department's rules and regulations: 'No members of the force shall join or belong to any

organisation, club, or body composed of present or present and past
members of the force which is affiliated with or a part of any organisation, club or body outside the department.' The only exceptions to
the rule were posts of the Grand Army of the Republic, United Spanish
War Veterans and the American Legion.[2]

In a number of other American cities, notably New York and
Washington, policemen had formed unions, and even affiliated with the
AFL, as indeed had firemen and other civic employees in Boston. In
most cases there had been no trouble, but at the beginning of September,
the commissioners in the District of Columbia issued a warning that
any policeman who joined an affiliated union would be dismissed. AFL
and union representatives played for time by starting federal court
proceedings, then appealed to President Wilson, who sent a telegram
from his train overriding the commissioners' order until he could look
into the matter personally when he returned to Washington.

Commissioner Curtis ignored Wilson's directive to his counterparts
in Washington, and charged the nineteen newly elected union officials
with insubordination. The union replied that any disciplinary action
against their officers would provoke a strike. Curtis set up a hearing
for the men – but since he was both judge and jury its impartiality was
questionable to say the least and it was hardly surprising when he found
them guilty. At this point, Mayor Andrew Peters stepped in, appointing
a citizens' advisory committee of thirty-four prominent Bostonians to
examine the dispute and search for a way of resolving it; meanwhile
the Commissioner was to delay passing sentence on the men for four
days, until Monday 8 September. Massachusetts Governor Calvin
Coolidge was asked to serve as an intermediary, but refused to get
involved. On the Sunday morning, the committee delivered its proposal,
which was acceptable to the counsel for the policemen's union: the
union would surrender its charter with the AFL, the nineteen organisers would be protected from punishment or dismissal, and independent
arbitrators would consider the men's grievances and wage demands.
The committee also delivered a copy to the Boston press, which gave
it almost universal approval.

The committee recommended that Governor Coolidge should be
consulted, and that a special conference should be held that day to
avert the approaching crisis. Coolidge, however, left town for the
weekend – ironically to be ready to speak at the state convention of
the AFL in Northampton, where he made no mention of the union

problems he was evading by his absence. Curtis, too, chose to be away from Boston over the weekend. When he returned on the Monday morning, he rejected the committee's report out of hand and summarily fired the nineteen men. That evening, nearly every member of the force attended a secret mass meeting to vote on a strike: the result was 1,134 in favour, and two against. Curtis refused to believe that more than a handful would actually strike – he assured Mayor Peters and Governor Coolidge that he had everything under control, and boasted to reporters 'I am ready for anything.'

At evening roll call next day, Tuesday 9 September, 1,117 of Boston's 1,544 cops left their posts. Commissioner Curtis's bold statement of being ready for anything proved to be totally false – in fact, he and the Governor had made virtually no preparations to cope with the strike, despite Mayor Peters's desperate pleas to Coolidge to have state troops standing by to patrol the streets. The Mayor himself was forbidden by law from calling out the guard until rioting had actually begun. Boston was thus left undefended against rowdies and criminals, guarded only by a few volunteer policemen. Coolidge's biographer, William A. White, gave a graphic description of what happened next:

Little knots of boys and young men began wandering through the streets. The old policemen were gone. Groups joined groups, at first hilarious, but acutely realising that no one would bother them. Under the street lamps, scores of crap games began to operate on the Common ... It was evident that the new police were not interested in crap games. This emboldened the gamblers. The mob grew noisy, also offensive. Its voice changed from a mumble to a nervous falsetto. Sporadically, little mobs broke apart and gravitated toward the larger mob instinctively ... By midnight the coagulating crowds had formed one raging mob, a drunken, noisy, irresponsible mob, without grievance, without objective; an aimless idiot mad with its own sense of unrestrained power. Someone threw a loose paving stone through a store window about one o'clock. The tension snapped. The mob was crystalized. It found its courage. Its desire took hazy form – loot! Sticks and bricks went whizzing into offices on second and third floors. By two o'clock, looting had begun.[3]

Bands of roughs began smashing store windows and helping themselves to whatever took their fancy – jewellery, cigars, clothing, footwear – stealing spare tyres from parked cars, attacking and robbing pedestrians. They stoned streetcars, threw rocks through the windows of police stations and pelted the volunteer policemen with mud. The

Provost Guard of the Boston Navy Yard was rushed into the city to help keep order, but it faced a hopeless task.[4]

In the morning, armed gangs began more systematic robberies, backing trucks up to the smashed windows of stores and loading them with loot in broad daylight. Secret Service agents watching the railroad stations recognised well-known criminals from other cities arriving on every train to join the bonanza. When volunteer policemen arrested about 150 looters, they were attacked by crowds and forced to release their prisoners. Mayor Peters, a Democrat who had supported the policemen's right to form an independent union but not to affiliate with the AFL, pressed Curtis to seek a solution through arbitration, and blamed the Commissioner's stiff-necked intransigence for the situation. When Curtis, with the support of his fellow Republican, Governor Coolidge, refused even to consider such a step, Peters took it upon himself to call out the Tenth Regiment of the State Guard to support the volunteer police. Stung into action at last, Coolidge mobilised the Eleventh Regiment. By evening there were 5,000 troops on the streets and in a series of violent clashes three rioters were killed and several wounded by rifle and machine-gun fire.

In other circumstances, the Commissioner's blank refusal to negotiate on any of the men's claims, particularly over recognition, would have been enough to trigger a general strike in sympathy by other unions. The Boston Central Labor Union had pledged its support in advance, and immediately after the walkout ordered a ballot by member unions on a general strike proposal. The proposal was defeated – after all the violence, public opinion was far too hostile to the policemen's cause. The policemen had given clear reasons for their strike: to protest against the arbitrary actions of Commissioner Curtis, to obtain the reinstatement of the nineteen sacked union leaders, and to force recognition of their union and its right to affiliate with the AFL. But inevitably, the press in Boston and elsewhere immediately labelled their action as 'Bolshevistic'. The *Boston Telegraph* set the tone with a resounding editorial:

The tumult and the disturbance of public order that have disgraced the city of Boston for the last two nights are but the foretaste of the bitter fruits to come if the people of Massachusetts crawl before the ultimatum of the American Federation of Labor . . . The challenge contained in that ultimatum is a challenge to straight Americanism. It must and it will be met, standing – regardless of the cost in life and treasure. For behind Boston in this skirmish with Bolshevism stands Massachusetts, and behind Massachusetts stands America.[5]

Other papers branded the strikers 'deserters' and 'agents of Lenin', and exaggerated the extent of the lawlessness in the city. The *Evening Transcript* printed pictures of looted stores and declared that the destruction on Tremont Street, opposite Boston Common, was worse than that on Nevsky Prospekt in Petrograd during the Bolshevik Revolution. Newspapers across America followed suit with blood-curdling headlines and ever more lurid stories liberally spiced with key words such as 'soviet', 'radical', 'chaos' and 'terror'. The *Philadelphia Public-Ledger* proclaimed: 'Bolshevism in the United States is no longer a specter. Boston in chaos reveals its sinister substance,' while the normally sober *Wall Street Journal* screamed, 'Lenin and Trotsky are on their way.'[6] In Congress, Senator Henry L. Myers of Montana solemnly warned that if something was not done 'the nation will see a Soviet Government set up within two years'.

Overwhelmed by the tidal wave of criticism, and with the city transformed into an armed camp, with machine guns and barbed wire protecting banks and public buildings, the Boston policemen realised that they had made a grave error of judgement. On the advice of Samuel Gompers, who had just returned from an international labour conference in Europe, their leader, John F. McInnes, told Governor Coolidge that his men were prepared to go back to work pending possible mediation. Curtis would have none of it. Echoing the action of Metropolitan Police Commissioner Macready in London, he announced that he would not reinstate any strikers, but would immediately recruit a whole new police force, whose members would be given a $300 a year pay increase. Coolidge backed the Commissioner. When Gompers tried to intervene on behalf of the policemen by charging Curtis with deliberately provoking the strike, the Governor replied with a crushing telegram: 'Your assertion that the Commissioner was wrong cannot justify leaving the city unguarded . . . There is no right to strike against the public safety by anybody, anywhere, at any time.'[7]

Newspapers everywhere in America seized on Coolidge's statement, especially its eminently quotable last sentence, and blazoned it across their front pages, turning him overnight from an undistinguished local politician into a national hero eclipsing Ole Hanson as the new champion in the fight against the Reds. They heaped praise on Coolidge and

Curtis for the stand they had 'so stoutly taken against the Bolshevists in their city', and for preventing 'the beginnings of Soviet government'.[8] It proved to be the first, albeit inadvertent, step on the road that would lead Coolidge to the White House.

The hysterical reaction to the Boston police strike was symptomatic of the fearful atmosphere of the time. These strikers were hard-nosed cops, mostly Irish-Americans who were more likely to say 'Hail Mary' than 'Long Live the Dictatorship of the Proletariat', and whose reflex reaction to radicalism was to reach for their nightsticks. At virtually any other point in American history it would have been ludicrous for anyone to imagine them as deep-dyed Red revolutionaries, but in the madness of 1919 anything was possible.

On the third day of the Boston police strike, the American public was shaken by news that the unions were planning a new strike on a much larger scale, this time in the steel industry. There were barely 1,500 Boston policemen, but there were more than 500,000 workers in the American steel industry, and as many as 70 per cent of them were recent immigrants from Russia and Eastern Europe, men who could readily be painted as having Bolshevik and un-American sympathies. Like the policemen, the steelworkers had a genuine case for better pay and conditions: the annual income for unskilled workers averaged $1,466, way ahead of the policeman's pittance but still $121 short of the recognised minimum subsistence level for a family of five, for an average working week of sixty-nine hours. For almost half the men, the working day had been extended to twelve hours, seven days a week, and twelve-hour shifts were often scheduled back-to-back, so that they were forced to work continuously for twenty-four hours.[9]

Unrest had been brewing in the steel industry for some time. In August 1918, twenty-four unions had gathered in Chicago and set up a National Committee for Organizing Iron and Steel Workers, with Gompers as honorary chairman, John Fitzpatrick as acting chairman, and William Z. Foster as secretary-treasurer. Foster, then thirty-eight years old, was famous – some would say infamous – as an agitator and industrial troublemaker, known to his friends as Bill and to employers as 'Red' Foster. Born into a poor labouring family in the slums of Philadelphia, after six years of schooling he had found his first job, and joined his first strike, on that city's streetcars, before taking off to work as a seaman on square-rigged sailing ships, and then in the building, mining, fertiliser and lumber industries and on the railroads, and had been involved in agitation wherever he went. With such a background, he was a natural recruit for the IWW and for Socialism, but abandoned both to devote himself to regular trade union activities, organising unskilled railroad workers and the meatpacking industry, before turning his energies to the steel industry. Foster was instrumental in setting up the National Committee and then directed a massive campaign to recruit and organise steelworkers in the face of fierce opposition from the company bosses: they banned union meetings, fired known union men and even kidnapped union organisers – including Bill Foster himself – and ran them out of town before they could talk to potential recruits. In spite of this, by the summer of 1919 he could claim to have 100,000 members and a union in every important mill town. The battle lines were drawn.

Facing Foster and the union, the steel barons were ready, even eager, for a fight, in support of the open-shop principle. Bolstered by the colossal profits they had made from the war, they knew that if need be they could easily afford to shut down the entire industry and starve their opponents into submission. Their standard bearer was Judge Elbert H. Gary, chairman of United States Steel Corporation, 'the commanding general of the largest industrial army in the world'.[10]

Gary had been a highly successful corporate lawyer in his native Illinois, then made his name as a judge when he presided over the trial in 1886 of a group of anarchists charged with killing a policeman by throwing a bomb into a crowded meeting in Chicago's Haymarket, during a previous period of industrial strife. Although there was a complete lack of evidence linking the men with the actual killing, Gary had sentenced seven of the defendants to death and one to the penitentiary, on the grounds that they had 'generally by speech and print advised large classes to commit murder', and that 'in pursuance of that advice, and influenced by that advice, somebody, not known, did throw the bomb that caused the death'.[11] Gary's firmness in handling the Haymarket case created an indelible impression on patriots such as the financier J. Pierpoint Morgan. When Morgan created the United States Steel Corporation through a series of mergers and acquisitions, he decided Gary was the right man to head the new company and bring order to the steel industry. Tempting him away from the law by offering him America's first $100,000 salary, Morgan appointed him chairman of the board. A devout Methodist and a teetotaller, handsome, grey-haired and dignified, Gary was described by H.L. Mencken as 'the Christian hired man'.[12]

Judge Gary, who had a whole town named after him when the company built it around a new steelworks in Indiana in 1905, professed to seek a 'community of interest' between employers and workers, and promoted the growth of welfare capitalism, providing company houses at low rents, loans to employees to help them purchase their own homes, and paying bonuses for 'long and faithful service'. In January 1919, in a brilliant PR move designed to pre-empt the unions in the struggle he knew was coming, he told his executives that management had an obligation to 'make the Steel Corporation a good place for them to work and live. Don't let the families go hungry or cold, give them playgrounds and parks and schools and churches, pure water to drink, every opportunity to keep clean, places of enjoyment, rest and recreation.'[13] Paternalism on this scale was designed, of course, to tie employees body and soul to the company, and many of the men, especially those who had served overseas during the war, resented being told that the company always knew what was best for them and their families – which ultimately boiled down to what was good for the company.

The Steel Corporation was undoubtedly a better employer than many, if not most, steel companies, whose workers were forced to endure living conditions that were appalling, in many cases consisting of 'mere unpainted shacks without running water or plumbing'.[14] But its benevolent paternalism applied only to skilled workers, while the mass of unskilled men, who had no bargaining power and no representation, were treated as casual labour to be hired and fired as it suited the company. However, these men, mainly immigrants from Eastern Europe known derisively as 'Hunkies', had changed with the war. Previously they had still related to the Old World, intending to return to their home villages as soon as they had saved enough money from menial, back-breaking work. But the war had stopped the two-way movement between the two continents, and by 1919 the revolutionary state of much of Europe made returning 'home' a much less attractive proposition anyway. Influenced by the great wartime Americanisation programmes designed to 'cement the people in our country into a homogeneous nation',[15] they had begun to see themselves as Americans, entitled to the equality and democratic freedoms for which the war had been fought. When the employers, freed from the restraints imposed by the National War Labor Board, began cutting wages and clawing back benefits they had been forced to grant their workers, including the right to organise, the workers flocked to join Bill Foster's crusade under the slogan 'Eight hours and the union!'

Most steel companies instantly fired any worker they found engaging in union activities, and made it impossible for labour organisers to get permits for parades or to hire halls, while local newspapers ranted against them and sheriffs and their men broke up any gathering with maximum force. The Mayor of McKeesport, near Pittsburgh, finally agreed after months of refusals, to allow meetings in halls, on condition that no speeches were made in foreign languages, and that Foster did not address them. But when a meeting was held, he had it broken up by police and the speakers arrested and thrown into jail, charged with riot. Bail was set at an exorbitant $3,000 each. Police in Homestead, a Carnegie Steel town seven miles east of Pittsburgh, jailed the legendary eighty-nine-year-old agitator Mary Harris 'Mother' Jones for telling a union meeting that 'we are going to see whether Pennsylvania belongs to Kaiser Gary or Uncle Sam . . . Our Kaisers sit up and smoke seventy-five-cent cigars and have lackeys with knee pants bring them champagne while you starve, while you grow old at forty . . . If Gary wants to work twelve hours a day let him go into the blooming mill and work. What we want is a little leisure, time for music, playgrounds, a decent home, books, and the things that make life worth while.'[16]

Judge Gary chose simply to ignore the unions. Any man in his employ was welcome to join a union, he said, but no one could make him recognise them or negotiate with them. He even refused to supply steel to any contractor who used union labour. So when Gompers, on behalf of the AFL, asked him on 20 June for a meeting to discuss conditions in the steel industry, he declined even to acknowledge the request. Under great pressure for immediate action, the National Committee balloted members of the steel unions, 98 per cent of whom voted in favour of 'stopping work should the companies refuse to concede . . . higher wages, shorter hours, and better working conditions'.

The companies reacted violently against the threat of a stoppage. On 26 August, drunken deputy sheriffs opened fire on a picket line of miners at West Natrona, Pennsylvania, who were involved in a local strike against the Allegheny Steel Company, killing one man. An organiser for the United Mineworkers, forty-nine-year-old Mrs Fannie Sellins, tried to intervene but was clubbed to the ground and shot. A deputy crushed her skull with a cudgel, and her body was dragged by the heels and flung into the back of a truck, along with that of the dead miner. There was no attempt to bring the murderers to justice. Another woman speaker was killed at Brackenridge, Pennsylvania, and although the man who shot her was arrested, he was released at once on bail of $2,500 – a notably lower sum than that demanded of the men jailed in McKeesport. In Hammond, Indiana, meanwhile, detectives hired by the steel company shot and killed four defenceless union men, and so intimidated witnesses that no one would come forward to give evidence against them.[17]

At the same time as Mrs Sellins was being murdered in West Natrona, a deputation of union leaders called at United States Steel's headquarters at 71 Broadway, New York City, and asked to see Gary. The Judge refused to meet them. Fitzpatrick and Foster handed over a letter asking him to agree to an arbitration conference, to avert the coming strike. He replied next day, saying that 'The officers of the corporation respectfully decline to discuss with you, as representatives of a labor union, any matters relating to employees.' When they asked him to reconsider, he refused.[18]

President Wilson, busy preparing for his grand tour, found time to appeal to both sides to hold back, and on 31 August declared in a Labor Day message that he would call an industrial conference in the near future 'to discuss fundamental means of bettering the relationship of capital and labor'. When Gary still refused to budge, Gompers wired the President, asking him to intervene and persuade the Judge to come to the table. Wilson sent his friend Bernard Baruch to talk to him, but Gary remained adamant. He would not talk to any trade union, even for the President of the United States.

There was clearly no way the strike could now be stopped, and on 10 September the National Committee voted that it should begin on the 22nd. They issued 200,000 copies of the strike call, in seven different languages, wrote a calm and measured letter to the President explaining their position, detailing their grievances and describing the background to the strike, and published a list of their twelve demands:

> Right of collective bargaining.
> Reinstatement of men discharged for union activities.
> An eight-hour day.
> One day's rest in seven.

Abolition of the 24-hour shift.

Increase in wages sufficient to guarantee American standards of living.

Standard scales of wages in all trades and classifications of workers.

Double rate of pay for all overtime, holiday and Sunday work.

Check-off system of collecting union dues and assessments.

Principles of seniority to apply in maintenance, reduction and increase of working forces.

Abolition of company unions.

Abolition of physical examination of applicants for employment.

Judge Gary retaliated by publishing his own letter to the heads of his subsidiary companies explaining his position: 'It is the settled determination of the United States Steel Corporation and its subsidiaries that the working conditions of their employees shall compare favorably with the highest standards of propriety and justice.' He claimed that 'large numbers of our workmen are not members of unions and do not care to be', and that the open-shop principle was 'of equal benefit to employer and employee',[19] something the employees found hard to accept. Gary's own boss, J.P. Morgan, certainly accepted it, however, applauding his action in a telegram from London: 'Heartiest congratulations on your stand for the open shop ... I believe the American principle of liberty deeply involved and must win out if we all stand firm.'

Gary received solid support from fellow autocrats like Henry Clay Frick, the man who in 1892 had hired a private army of three hundred Pinkerton detectives which had engaged in a thirteen-hour gun battle with strikers at Carnegie's Homestead mill in which seven workers and three Pinkerton men died. Frick's bloody suppression of the Homestead strike had halted union organisation in the steel industry, and it had never recovered. Although Frick had quarrelled with Carnegie in 1899 and resigned from the board, moving to New York to play golf and build up his art collection, his attitude to the unions had not softened. 'I am utterly opposed to collective bargaining and representation,' he wrote to John D. Rockefeller Jr, in 1919, 'and ready to close every mill.'

There was no mention of socialisation or nationalisation anywhere in the men's demands, but this did not stop the companies and the press tarring them with the brush of Bolshevism. This was only to be expected, of course, since several of the union organisers were well known for their radical views. Fitzpatrick, for instance, was liberally quoted as having said, 'We are going to socialise the basic industries of the United States,' and Foster's past connection with the IWW was a gift to his opponents. A pamphlet he had written on syndicalism during that period of his life, eight years earlier, was reprinted and circulated to newspapers and politicians across the country. In it, he had written: 'The wages system must be abolished. The thieves at present in control must be stripped of their booty and industry so reorganised that every individual shall have free access to the social means of production. . . . The syndicalist considers the State as a meddling capitalist institution . . . he is a radical opponent of "law and order", since he knows that for his unions to be "legal" in their tactics would be for them to become impotent . . . He knows that he is engaged in a life and death struggle . . . with him the end justifies the means.' And perhaps most damningly of all: 'The syndicalist recognises no rights of the capitalists to their property, and is going to strip them of it, law or no law.'[20]

It was useless for Foster to plead that he had moved on since he wrote those lines, that he had changed, that he and his colleagues had done everything possible to avert the strike, and that they had been brought to their present position by the obduracy of the employers. He was seen as a Red, and the fact that he was leading the National Committee was enough to damn the whole thing as a Bolshevik plot. If the conservative Sam Gompers and the AFL supported it, the argument went, they had clearly been taken in by the Bolsheviks. Newspapers like the *New York Times* regularly warned Gompers against the 'Red element' within the federation, declaring that they wanted the proposed strike not for wages and working conditions but for 'power, for control of the industry'. Some papers did castigate Gary for his refusal even to talk to the unions or to listen to the President: normally conservative papers like the *Chicago Tribune* and the Springfield (Mass.) *Republican* charged him with behaving like an 'extreme reactionary', whose actions would drive moderate unionists into the arms of the Reds. And the liberal press declared that he was totally in the wrong by trying to 'smash unionism'. But the critics were in the minority, and were countered by papers like the *Wall Street Journal*, which asserted that Gary was actually 'fighting the battle of the American Constitution'.[21]

The public in general may have bought the employers' line that this was a strike for political purposes, intended to undermine American democracy. The steelworkers did not. They were not deterred from their support for Foster or from their determination to strike for what they saw as their just demands. On 22 September an estimated 250,000 of them, half the industry's entire workforce, walked out. By the end of the week, that figure had swollen to more than 365,000 – making it the biggest strike in American history up to that time. Plants in all the steel towns – Lackawanna, Youngstown, Wheeling, Johnstown, Cleveland, Milwaukee and even Gary, Indiana, were forced to shut down when virtually every worker struck.

The unions claimed that the strike was about 90 per cent effective overall. In the Pittsburgh area about three-quarters of the steel plants were shut down, but this did not stop the companies putting out propaganda stories, which the local newspapers were happy to print, that American-born workers were refusing to leave their jobs. They were, the companies claimed, opposed to the radicalism of foreign workers and considered the strike 'disloyal' and 'un-American'; even the foreign workers, they said, were returning in droves. 'CONDITIONS ALMOST NORMAL IN ALL STEEL PLANTS', crowed the headlines in the Pittsburgh papers. 'STRIKE CRUMBLING', 'WORKERS FLOCK BACK TO THEIR JOBS'. The number of strikers reported as returning to work added up to 4,800,000 – almost ten times the total number of men employed in the entire industry.[22] Coincidentally, between 27 September and 7 October the same newspapers carried no fewer than thirty full-page advertisements, in nine different languages, exhorting the workers to return to their jobs and to 'Stand by America'. The advertisements implied that the 'United States' in the name of US Steel meant that the corporation was actually part of the federal government and that the strike was therefore against the United States itself. Conservative members of the US Senate encouraged such views in their attacks on the strike and on Foster. Senator Henry L. Myers, who had earlier declared that the Boston police strike could lead to a soviet government in two years, weighed in again, describing Foster as 'a notorious syndicalist, revolutionist, and enemy of organised government'.

Leading newspapers outside the steel areas played along with the companies' efforts to allay public criticism of Judge Gary's intractability by promoting the idea that the strike was purely political: it could not possibly be for higher wages, since steel workers, they wrote, were paid up to $70 a day. Some papers backed this up by reporting, quite seriously, that 'the more luxurious New York hotels expect an influx of striking steel workers who would use the occasion to take a vacation and spend their "high wages"'.[23] In fact, their only income came from a fund totalling $400,000 raised by the National Committee before the strike began, which just about managed to keep the men and their families from starving.[24]

Long before the strike began, the companies' propaganda machine was raising the spectre of violence. 'STEEL MILLS READY TO FIGHT STRIKERS – POLICE PLANS RUSHED' the *Washington Post* headline read on 21 June. The companies surrounded their mills with guards armed with rifles and riot guns: around Pittsburgh in western Pennsylvania's Allegheny County the sheriff deputised nearly 5,000 men, armed and paid for by the steel companies, and it was estimated that along the twenty-mile stretch of the Monongahela from Pittsburgh to Clairton there were 25,000 men under arms; in some places there were as many deputies as strikers.[25]

The companies were openly preparing for war – and they made sure they got it, at least in Pennsylvania and Indiana. In neighbouring Ohio, the situation was notably different, largely due to that state's more progressive labour laws. Ohio had amended its constitution four years earlier to allow open assemblies with freedom of speech, which were rigorously forbidden in Pennsylvania, and there were no 'Black Cossacks', mounted state constabulary, to break up gatherings of strikers.[26] Consequently, there were few excuses for violent clashes and the strike in Ohio remained more peaceful. It was also more complete. *Washington Post* correspondent George Rothwell Brown reported that 'the change one notices in crossing the line from smoky Pittsburgh to smokeless Mahoning is startling . . . In the Mahony valley hereabouts there are 26 solid miles of steel and iron mills, continuous ramparts of industry, one huge mill after another in unbroken rank, where are made the raw materials of the country's basic trades. All are outwardly as dead as the ruins of Babylon.'[27]

The mill operators of Ohio, Brown noted, were 'sitting tight . . . content to let the strike settle itself quietly, however long it may take'. Nevertheless, the authorities were taking no chances: in addition to augmenting the police forces, they swore in three hundred ex-soldiers of the American Legion, most of them fresh from service in France, 'for the protection of property in the business districts' – in East Youngstown, the business district had been burnt to the ground in strike disorders three years earlier – and all the mills were 'heavily guarded and protected by their own machine guns and artillery'.

In Pennsylvania, by contrast, it was Homestead 1892 all over again, but on a larger scale. In Homestead itself, 'Black Cossacks' rode through union meetings swinging long, heavy clubs at anyone within reach, women and children included, and in Lackawanna they charged groups of strikers who refused to disperse from street corners. In small mill towns they rode their horses over pedestrians on sidewalks and even into stores and company-owned houses. In Duquesne, where men were given the option of returning to work or going to jail, a local pastor provided a personal account of an unprovoked incident in a letter to William Z. Foster:

... My congregation leaving church was suddenly, without any cause what-ever, attacked on the very steps of the Temple of God, by the Constables, and dispersed by these iron-hoofed Huns. While dispersing, indignation and a flood of frenzy swayed them, being lifted by some invisible force, thrown into the flux of raging ... against the Cossacks of this State. Nevertheless, it was the most magnificent display of self-control manifested by the attacked ever shown anywhere. They moved on, with heads lowered, jaws firmly set, to submit. Oh, it was great; it was magnificent ... Oh, only for one wink from someone would there be a puddle of red horse-blood mixed with the human kind. But no, we want to win the strike. We want to win the confidence of the public ... [The next day] the little babies of No 1 were going to school. They loitered for the school bell to summon. And here come the Cossacks. They see the little innocents standing on the steps of the school house; their parents on the oppo-site side of the street. What splendid occasion to start the 'Hunkeys'' ire, let us charge the babies. That will fetch them to attack upon us. They did. But the 'Hunkey' even at the supreme test of his coolheadedness, refused to flash his knife to save his babies from the onrush of the cruel horses' hoofs ...

Needless to say, the attacks on the churchgoers and their children were not mentioned in the press.

Free speech was regarded as a crime and treated with ruthless brutality: in Farrell, police killed four strikers and seriously injured another eleven in a skirmish over the right to speak. In Clairton, state police rode down a crowd of men, women and children who had been granted a permit to hold a meeting on a vacant lot, having been refused permis-sion to hire a hall. As the crowd dispersed, a trooper intent on provoking a riot pulled down an American flag and trampled it under his horse's hooves. The union men, some of whom were ex-soldiers, took the bait and rushed at the troopers, only to be beaten down with clubs. The resulting riot made headlines throughout the state – but with no mention of the flag.[28] Press reports of such disturbances always made it appear that the strikers were at fault and the steel company men were acting entirely in self-defence, with heavy emphasis on supposed radical involvement. Neither local nor state officials, including Governor William C. Sproul, would acknowledge union complaints of brutal attacks by police or deputies, and federal officials were hardly more receptive.

Along with the belligerent police and deputy sheriffs, the companies had at least six hundred labour spies and agents provocateurs planted among the strikers, with instructions 'to stir up as much bad feeling as you possibly can'.[29] This was not unusual in America at that time: the US Attorney in Philadelphia, Francis Fisher Kane, wrote to Mitchell Palmer in July informing him that a number of the most extreme agitators in his area, who had been kept under surveillance by the Bureau of Investigation (BI), had turned out to be spies employed by private detective agencies, who had been 'actively stirring up trouble, fomenting it by their activity, and at times creating, as I believe, evils that did not exist', in order to increase business for their agencies.[30] Their job during the strike was to incite violence, undermine morale and spread rumours, which were avidly picked up by the press. One story was of a ferocious gun battle between police and an 'army of Wobblies and Bolsheviks' in Sharon, where three blocks were said to be filled with an 'arsenal' of weapons. As a result of this unfounded report, many strikers were arrested and earmarked for deportation.[31]

One of the companies' most effective methods of ensuring violence was using black strike-breakers against white pickets wherever possible, hiring more than 30,000 blacks as replacement workers. By contrast, the city authorities in Cleveland, Ohio – influenced perhaps by the fact that an election campaign for city officials was in progress – banned the importing of strike-breakers. When one mill brought in fifty men they were arrested, held in jail overnight and given the choice of getting out of town or standing trial. They got out, and the mills did not repeat the experiment. In Pennsylvania, meanwhile, the use of outside strike-breakers provoked riots between nationalities and races in towns such as Donora, where two strikers lost their lives, and Braddock, where twenty people were injured and one killed in clashes between two mobs of foreign workers. Neither of these involved the feared radical elements, but in one town there did appear to be evidence of radical complicity. Ironically, that town was Gary, Indiana.

*

Gary was seen as the most dangerous hot-spot of the dispute, with strike leaders quoted as making statements such as: 'The strike won't stop until the steel workers become the law-makers at Washington, DC.'[32] Alarmed by this, the federal government sent special agents into the area to investigate and try to control the radical elements. The companies went further, importing thousands of black strike-breakers to force a showdown – which duly came on 4 October with extensive riots. Indiana Governor James P. Goodrich immediately ordered eleven companies of the state militia into Gary, Indiana Harbor and East Chicago, to join five hundred special police and three hundred deputies in restoring order and protecting the strike-breakers, filling Gary's jails with strikers and its hospitals with wounded. Next day, 2,000 strikers, led by several hundred ex-soldiers wearing their uniforms to demonstrate their loyalty, marched through Gary taunting the four companies of militia who, numbering fewer than three hundred, were too weak to oppose them effectively without firing on the US Army uniform. At a mass meeting in a park, the strikers demanded the release of the arrested men and the withdrawal of the state troops. The gathering and the parade were entirely orderly, but they were in open violation of a ban imposed by Goodrich. Furious at the flouting of his authority, he appealed to the Commander of the Central Department of the United States Army based in Chicago, Major General Leonard Wood, for federal troops.

General Wood, a celebrated soldier who was seeking nomination as a Republican presidential candidate, was delighted to seize the opportunity of being seen as the man who saved America from the Bolsheviks. Within five hours he had led a thousand overseas veterans of the Fourth Division from Fort Sheridan into the troubled towns, and immediately imposed martial law, forbidding assembly in streets or parks and making the carrying of firearms a serious offence. Wood ordered that all men wearing army uniform should be rounded up and held in custody, though in the event only twenty or so ex-soldiers were arrested, stripped of their uniforms and released with a warning. Next day, a parade of 10,000 men, women and children, including strikers, policemen and hundreds of former soldiers in uniform, marched through south Chicago, many carrying US flags and banners with slogans such as 'We have the right to fix the price of our own labor', 'Holland is the home of the Kaiser – Judge Gary are you on your way?' and 'We got the Kaiser over there. We'll get the Kaisers over here.'[33] This was hardly the language of Red revolution, and the parade remained orderly and peaceful. Nevertheless, a further five hundred men of the Sixth Division were drafted into the area as a precaution, though they were hardly overworked – according to press reports, about eight hundred strikers gathered for an illegal mass meeting in the park near the City Hall, where the troops were quartered, but 'not a soldier was needed to scatter the mob. Five policemen did it with a few words.'[34]

With guns mounted in all the main streets, and assurances that the soldiers were not there to interfere with the strike but to protect life and property, calm was restored in Gary. Wood then brought in the army's Military Intelligence Division to investigate the alleged radical influence behind the disorders. The MID had grown from a total staff of two officers and two clerks in April 1917 to one of 282 officers, 29 non-commissioned officers and 948 civilian employees in November 1918, and it was struggling to establish itself in a permanent peace-time role in competition with the Secret Service and the Justice Department's Bureau of Investigation. During the war it had become deeply involved in domestic intelligence gathering for plant protection, and the surveillance of radical organisations that might threaten produc-tion or security. The threats of Bolshevism and industrial unrest in the post-war world offered a lifeline which it grabbed with both hands. It had already drawn up 'War Plans White', providing for the deployment of the US Army against an anticipated force of 1.5 million insurgents in the event of a general strike or even a full-scale revolution. Now its officers and agents descended on Gary, determined to discover and root out the dangerous subversives in its midst.

Steered by local police and BI reports, the MID made six raids on their first day, and seized an estimated 'ton or more' of what they described as anarchist and Bolshevik literature – local radicals, however, scoffed that there was nothing in the haul that could not be bought openly in left-wing bookstores. The MID also claimed to have found rifles and ammunition in one suspect's home. Without waiting for further verification, District Attorney Charles F. Clyne hurried off to Washington to report on progress and press for special legislation to curb Red activities.

Anticipating a flood of arrests, Wood's men began constructing a stockade to hold prisoners awaiting trial or deportation. Over the next few days the raids continued – and so did the charges, which grew ever more sensational: plots had been discovered, it was said, to blow up the homes of prominent Gary citizens and assassinate the Mayor, to destroy government property, and to 'inaugurate a general uprising of "Reds" from West Virginia to Colorado'. What was more, the reports went on, the Gary Reds were responsible for the bombs of May and June, which had been made by a chemist with the suitably alien name of Alexander Ivanhoff, who had been working as an electrician in the Indiana Steel Company's mill, and planted or posted by his brother-in-law, Anton Gorski, and a Frenchman named De Jurge. Gorski was under arrest, the other two had fled. Colonel W.S. Mapes, the army's official spokesman, gave newspapermen a demonstration of the dangers they posed by producing a jar of the guncotton allegedly used in the manufacture of the bombs, which he said had been seized by his agents. 'In this jar,' he announced dramatically, 'there is enough guncotton to blow up this building [Gary City Hall].' He proved his point by setting light to a few specks of it, producing a satisfying flash. The amount of explosives found in the suburbs of Indiana, he said, was enough 'to blow this part of Indiana off the map'.[35]

The MID raids culminated on 15 October in a massive swoop on eighty homes, netting 120 prisoners. BI agents, who had stood back from the operation until then, interrogated these 'alleged alien radicals' and cleared all but ten of them, against whom they started deportation proceedings.[36]

Meanwhile, in Washington, an MID officer told the Senate Labor Committee that followers of Lenin and Trotsky in Gary had grown so bold during the summer that they had tried to organise a 'Red Guard', with discharged soldiers as their armed force.[37] Special Agent in Charge Edward Brennan of the BI's Chicago office was not impressed by the loudly trumpeted achievements of the MID. 'It is my opinion,' he reported to Washington, 'that most all of what has been said in the press alleging to have emanated from the military authorities and the Military Intelligence is "bunkum".' J. Edgar Hoover agreed, informing the Justice Department that the dramatic disclosures 'were more fiction than truth'.[38]

True or not, the dramatic disclosures had done their work. Newspapers across the country agreed that what was happening in the steel industry was 'an attempted revolution, not a strike'. It showed, said the Boston *Evening Transcript*, 'the extraordinary hold which "Red" principles have upon the foreign born population in the steel districts'.[39] The *Washington Post* caught the popular mood perfectly when it thundered in an editorial:

Gary is shown to have been the location of a den of snakes prepared to strike their poisonous fangs into the body politic. At the beginning of the steel strike the charge was made that anti-American agitators were at the bottom of the movement; that the reds were taking advantage of the situation to spread the doctrine of discontent; that the revolutionaries and anarchists were urging the men to strike. But these statements were denied by the strike leaders and denounced as false reports circulated by the manufacturers for the purpose of discrediting the strike. Developments at Gary have demonstrated that there was entirely too much truth back of them.

The *Post* demanded that the federal authorities should deal with the situation with a nationwide operation:

Every viper's nest of anarchy in the country which can be uncovered should be stamped out. Every red should be run into jail, and all who are under suspicion of complicity in bomb outrages or other conspiracies of that sort should be put through the third degree. This is a disease which requires heroic treatment, and it is no time for mollycoddling . . . The air will be purer and sweeter and America will be a fairer land when the last red is behind the bars or on a ship eastward bound.[40]

Defeated by a combination of Gary the city and Gary the man, the steel strike was a lost cause. The events in the steel towns, and the way in which they were reported, finally destroyed public support by branding the strikers as Red revolutionaries and dangerous aliens rather than American workers seeking a fair deal and a higher standard of living in a time of rampant post-war inflation. Genuine radicals did little to help by leaping in with inflammatory statements, openly urging strikers to arm themselves and to kill police and soldiers in retaliation 'for every worker killed'. The Chicago *Communist* newspaper exhorted 'Workers, act! Out of your mass strikes will come . . . a state of the workers, proletarian dictatorship, which will crush the capitalists as the state now crushes the workers.'[41] In truth, the Reds were clinging to the coat-tails of the strike, taking advantage of the situation to further their own ambitions, but in the overheated atmosphere of the time it was difficult for most Americans to appreciate that the noise created by these few was an effect of the strike and not its cause.

Gary the man, meanwhile, was playing his part in defeating the strikers by digging in his heels and refusing to budge one inch from his position of total intransigence. On the same day that General Wood declared martial law in Gary, Indiana, Judge Gary took his seat in President Wilson's National Industrial Conference in the Pan-American Union Building in Washington DC, as one of the representatives of capital along with John D. Rockefeller Jr. Wilson had collapsed aboard his train between Pueblo, Colorado, and Witchita, Kansas, on 25 September, the third day of the steel strike, and had been forced to return to Washington, where he suffered a second and more severe stroke on the morning of 2 October. It would be foolish to blame the industrial situation and the threat of Bolshevism for the President's illness, but it would be equally foolish not to include it among the many factors that contributed to an intolerable level of stress. One of the last things he did before becoming incapacitated was to dictate a message to the conference:

At a time when the nations of the world are endeavoring to find a way of avoiding war, are we to confess that there is no method to be found for carrying on industry except in the spirit of, and with the very method of, war? Must suspicion and hatred and force rule us in civil life? Are our industrial leaders and our industrial workers to live together without faith in each other, constantly struggling for advantage over each other, doing naught but what is compelled? My friends, this would be an intolerable outlook . . . an invitation to national disaster. From such a possibility my mind turns away, for my confidence is abiding that in this land we have learned how to accept the general judgment upon matters that affect the public weal.[42]

Wilson's confidence turned out to be misplaced. With capital represented by Gary and Rockefeller, and labour by Gompers, there was never any chance that the conference would succeed in reaching any form of consensus. Gary started by having the steel strike removed from the agenda as being 'too controversial'. The conference was left to concern itself solely with seeking ways of 'resuming the natural course of industrial and economic development', though the views of the two sides on what that meant were diametrically opposed. After two weeks of frustration, Gompers brought things to a head with a carefully worded resolution for 'the right of wage earners . . . to bargain collectively . . . in respect to wages, hours of labor, and relations and conditions of employment'. It was promptly voted down, and the conference collapsed when Gompers, deprived of any function, declared: 'I have sung my swan song in this conference . . . and with a feeling of regret that I am not able with a clear conscience to remain longer, I go.'[43]

By walking out of the conference, Gompers left himself open to the charge that he was entirely to blame for its failure, a charge that the right-wing press was quick to make. The *Wall Street Journal* concluded that his action proved that the unions were under the control of 'the IWWs and Russian Bolshevists'.[44] The patriotic societies, like the employers, clamoured to condemn the strike, constantly repeating the accusation that the strike was 'an effort of anarchists . . . to destroy the government', a view that was vigorously upheld in Congress by men like Senator Miles Poindexter of Washington, who declared that if something were not done soon 'there is a real danger that the Government will fall'.[45]

The Senate Committee on Education and Labor conducted a hurried investigation of the real causes of the steel strike, which to no one's surprise roundly condemned the union leaders and concluded that 'a considerable element of IWWs, anarchists, revolutionists, and Russian Soviets' were behind the strike, which they had used 'as a means of elevating themselves to power'.[46] Another investigation at the same time, by the Interchurch World Movement, decided that it was the steel companies who were primarily to blame, attacking them for their use of 'strikebreakers, undercover men and labor spies'. The steelworkers' grievances were justified, it stated, but the companies had used their influence over the general press and the police to stifle free speech and deceive the public over the real issues involved. Naturally, Judge Gary rejected the Interchurch report out of hand. And equally naturally, it was his rejection, plus the findings of the Senate committee, that were reported to the public in the general press.

The steel strike dragged on for a further two and a half months, its support among the workers gradually dwindling, as more and more mills reopened. By 8 January steel production had recovered to about 70 per cent of normal, and though there were still 100,000 men out, the National Committee voted to end the strike. The men had gained not a single concession, but had lost some $112 million in wages. In addition, twenty people had been killed. The strike had been a complete failure, doomed from the start, like the Boston policemen's strike, by being labelled 'revolutionary' and 'Bolshevistic'.

# XIII

## THE SOVIET ARK

THROUGHOUT the whole of 1919, the British government was facing a revolutionary situation in Ireland, which added to the general atmosphere of tension not only in Britain but also in America, where there was great popular support for Ireland's independence struggle. In the British general election of December 1918, the nationalist Sinn Fein party had won seventy-three out of a total of 105 Irish seats, all but four of the remainder being in Protestant Ulster. The newly elected Sinn Fein MPs refused to take their seats at Westminster, instead setting up their own National Assembly, the Dáil Éireann, in Dublin's Mansion House. Twenty-seven members took their seats on 21 January – most of the others were in British jails, including their leader, Eamon de Valera, who escaped with two comrades from Lincoln prison in England on 3 February, using a duplicate key that had been smuggled in to him by supporters.

The twenty-nine-year-old Michael Collins, appointed Minister of Finance and Director of Intelligence, was responsible for organising and controlling guerrilla warfare against the British – which they, of course, regarded as terrorism. On the same day that the Dáil first assembled, a squad of masked Irish Volunteers, forerunners of the Irish Republican Army, ambushed and killed two policemen of the Royal Irish Constabulary who were guarding a cartload of gelignite in Solloghodbeg, County Tipperary. This was celebrated by republicans as the start of the Anglo-Irish War, and from then on, the trouble grew steadily as the rebels acquired weapons and ammunition. The resident magistrate in Westport, County Mayo, was shot in his own home by a sniper. A squad of twenty to thirty men freed a Sinn Fein hunger striker, Robert

J. Byrne, from the workhouse infirmary in Limerick, killing one constable, shooting another in the spine, tying up the warder and several other policemen and locking them in the operating theatre before making their getaway with Byrne in the unlikely transport of a donkey cart – he had been shot twice during the raid, in the back and neck, and died later that evening. A week later, the residents of Limerick declared a general strike as the city was put under martial law, with British armoured cars and soldiers in full battle order patrolling the streets, machine guns installed at strategic points and barbed-wire entanglements blocking every bridge.

By the end of April, there were 44,000 British troops in Ireland. After another jailbreak, this time by twenty Sinn Feiners from Mountjoy prison in Dublin, the British government tried to save face by declaring an amnesty for political prisoners. De Valera emerged from hiding, and was elected President of the Dáil, which sent a delegation to Paris to petition the Peace Conference for Irish independence. They were backed by an Irish-American delegation, led by Frank F. Walsh, but achieved nothing. Meanwhile, the violence continued to escalate: fifty masked men carried out an early-morning raid on Collinstown Aerodrome, four miles outside Dublin, making off with more than seventy-five rifles and 1,800 rounds of ammunition; six armed men rescued a Sinn Fein prisoner from a train at Knocklong railway station, about eighteen miles south-east of the city of Limerick, killing two constables; there were two hour-long gun battles in attacks on police barracks with minimal casualties – though the rebels made up for this two days later by ambushing and killing a sergeant and a constable.

By early September at least six policemen had been killed, but no one had been caught, though the number of troops in the country had been increased to about 200,000. On Sunday 7 September the rebels switched their target from the police to the British Army, when a party of sixteen soldiers from the Shropshire Light Infantry was ambushed while on church parade at the Methodist chapel in the garrison town of Fermoy, in County Cork. The troops carried rifles but no ammunition, and were about to stack their arms before entering the chapel when they were jumped by about a dozen rebels firing revolvers and makeshift guns. One soldier, Private William Jones, was killed instantly by a shot in the chest, and three others wounded. The rest were savagely beaten with wooden staves and spokes torn from cartwheels, before their attackers seized their rifles and drove off at speed in two cars.

The rebels had planned their escape well; they had cut telegraph and telephone wires, and blocked the roads with felled trees to hamper any pursuit. Three planes were sent up to search from the air, but could see no sign of them. Later that night, a military convoy was attacked a few miles outside the town by a large band of armed rebels, who grabbed another twenty-five rifles.[1]

The coroner's jury at the inquest on the death of Private Jones added insult to injury by refusing to declare a verdict of murder, since it decided the raiders had not intended to kill anyone, only to take the rifles. Infuriated by this tacit expression of sympathy with the killers, two hundred soldiers from Jones's regiment and the Royal Field Artillery marched into Fermoy and proceeded to smash up the town with iron bars and trenching tools, demolishing some fifty shopfronts, to the delight of many of the local poor, who followed behind, helping themselves to whatever they could grab through the shattered display windows.

The British government had tolerated the existence of the Dáil Éireann by generally ignoring it, but it now decided that enough was enough. On 12 September Lord French, the Lord Lieutenant of Ireland, declared that it was suppressed as a 'dangerous association', and banned its meetings. Troops in full battle gear made lightning searches of the Sinn Fein headquarters in Dublin and elsewhere, and the homes and clubs of known rebel sympathisers throughout Ireland. Although a great deal of nationalist literature was found, the searches turned up very few arms or explosives, though a quantity of gelignite was discovered in the Derry Sinn Fein headquarters. No doubt this was partly because at that stage the rebels had very few arms, and partly because they had clearly been warned in advance and had had time to find more secure hiding places for their precious weapons. Two members of the Dáil had been arrested when the Mansion House was surrounded by troops and police, but their prize catch, Michael Collins, escaped through a skylight and across the rooftops to plan and command a ruthless guerrilla campaign by the newly formed IRA which would bring a fatally flawed freedom to Ireland after two years of bloody warfare.

De Valera was in Providence, Rhode Island, when the Dáil was suppressed, having been smuggled out to America to make a fund-raising tour of East Coast cities. He had received a spectacular reception: in New York, he was given the presidential suite at the Waldorf; in Boston, the Massachusetts state legislature honoured him with a special joint session and his public speeches attracted audiences of 40,000 supporters. It seemed that even in the thick of the Red Scare Irish-Americans were happy to support terrorism by bomb and bullet, as long as it was perpetrated by their own people. De Valera was no Gandhi. Speaking in Providence, he declared, 'The war front is now transferred to Ireland . . .'[2]

Though the number of civil servants murdered, including police, was estimated at over a hundred, the rest of 1919 was relatively calm in Ireland with only scattered incidents – until 19 December, when Lord French was attacked by an IRA assassination squad while returning to Viceregal Lodge after a weekend at his country house in Roscommon. His motorcade was ambushed near Phoenix Park and came under a hail of bullets and grenades, but the Lord Lieutenant's driver managed to speed around and past the barricade of an overturned farm cart. The car was hit by four bullets, but none penetrated its armour. French was unharmed and reached home safely. The second car in the convoy – the position in which French normally travelled – was riddled with bullets but again no one was hurt. The guards shot and killed one of the would-be assassins, a grocer's assistant named Martin Savage. At the inquest the jury outdid their fellows in Fermoy by deciding: 'We find that Martin Savage died from a bullet fired by a military escort and we beg to tender our sympathy to the relatives of the deceased.'[3]

The troubles in Ireland were certainly revolutionary, but they had no connection with Bolshevism, despite attempts by Lenin and Trotsky to forge a link with the anti-British rebels. As far as the Red threat was concerned the British government in the autumn of 1919 was more worried about the dangers posed by a new wave of strikes. Fifty thousand iron foundry workers had begun a national strike on 22 September, the same day as the start of the great steel strike in America. The foundry workers' strike did not have the same immediate impact on the economy as the miners, but in a world before plastics, where metal components were vital to almost every mechanism and process, it was serious enough to cause substantial disruptions to industry as a whole.

Like most industrial disputes at that time, the foundry men's strike was not overtly political but a straightforward demand for higher wages. But the diehard Conservatives saw it as yet another attempt to impose workers' control, and as part of a general assault on their world by the forces of the left which were infiltrating even its most hallowed institutions. 'BOLSHEVISM AT OXFORD', a *Saturday Review* headline wailed. 'At a moment when the social structure is threatened with a more dangerous upheaval than ever before in history,' the article went on, 'the appointment of Mr R.H. Tawney to a lectureship at Balliol College is not merely an academic but a national outrage.'[4] Tawney was a leading member of the Labour Party Research Department and had been one of the three Fabian Society members supporting the miners on the Coal Commission inquiry. To the Tories it was scandalous that he should be allowed to corrupt impressionable undergraduates with his left-wing intellectual views. Their unease increased when Tawney, together with his fellow Fabian Sidney Webb, put his talents and experience at the disposal of the members of the National Union of Railwaymen (NUR) as they prepared to launch Britain's next major strike, beside which the foundry men's stoppage paled into insignificance.

The railwaymen had been pressing for a wage increase coupled with standardised rates since March. The government had controlled the railways during the war, and had granted substantial pay increases to help keep them running smoothly. But like most other workers, the railwaymen had seen their real wages eaten away by inflation so that they were now earning hardly any more in real terms than in 1914. The NUR, led by its General Secretary, the redoubtable J.H. 'Jimmy' Thomas, a Privy Councillor and Member of Parliament noted as a moderate union leader and fierce opponent of Bolshevism, demanded a minimum of sixty shillings (£3) a week for his men. For the government, Sir Eric Geddes, the Minister of Transport, a hard-nosed Scottish industrialist, was prepared to go no further than guaranteeing the existing rates until the end of the year, which in itself had an ominous ring to it, implying future cuts. The negotiations, such as they were, dragged on for six months until in September Geddes and the other principal government negotiator Bonar Law, Leader of the House of Commons and of the Conservative Party, made an offer that would have left the lower grades of railwaymen worse off than they had been before the war – when, as Lloyd George himself admitted, they had been 'disgracefully underpaid'.[5] Geddes insisted that this offer was final and non-negotiable. He was clearly seeking a showdown, and he got it: the union called a lightning strike by its 600,000 members, to begin at midnight on Friday 26 September, if negotiations were not reopened. They were not, and at that hour the railways throughout Britain came to a halt in what was, at the time, the biggest strike in British history.

Other unions, understandably seeing the government's stance as part of a general attack on wages and unionism, were quick to offer their support. First off the mark was the train drivers' union, the Associated Society of Locomotive Engineers and Firemen (ASLEF), which represented 51,000 elite rail workers and was often at loggerheads with the NUR. The members of ASLEF, its General Secretary said, had no grievance themselves since they already had a satisfactory agreement, but were striking 'entirely and absolutely in support of other grades of railwaymen getting some measure of justice'. Newspaper printers refused to set material condemning the strikers and threatened to strike unless their papers put the union's case. Lord Northcliffe, owner of *The Times* and the *Daily Mail*, made a robust response: 'Rather than be dictated to by anyone I will stop publication of my newspapers. Better a press silent by the will of its owners than a press enslaved by a class.'[6] Printing went ahead as normal. Along with all the other national newspapers which were normally distributed by rail, Northcliffe's managers lined up a massive fleet of vans and lorries to carry the papers across the country during the night.

A few trains manned by non-union staff and managers managed to pull out of the London main-line stations on the first full day of the strike, but several of those heading north were stopped by pickets who took off the engines, leaving the passengers to camp in the carriages. Freight trains carrying fish were left standing in sidings where their contents quickly rotted. Liverpool's meat supplies were held up in Birkenhead, while the manager of the rail tunnel under the Mersey worked with four assistants to operate the pumps to prevent the tunnel flooding, which would put it out of action for months. As in the Yorkshire pit strike, the navy was asked to send stokers to take over. Steelworks and coal mines were soon forced to close because of lack of transport to get men in and their products out, and power stations and businesses everywhere prepared to shut down for want of fuel.

The government treated the rail strike as a national emergency. It immediately reimposed wartime rationing of meat, bacon, sugar, butter and margarine, and issued official pleas to the public to conserve coal, gas and electricity. Field Marshal Sir Douglas Haig, Commander-in-Chief of Home Forces, and Major General Fielding, General Commanding the London District, were called to a Cabinet meeting to discuss the use of the army: demobilisation was suspended, all leave cancelled and troops were posted at railway stations to protect any railwaymen who reported for work – though since the strike was almost 100 per cent solid they had little to do. A volunteer Civilian Guard was recruited to help maintain order and keep supplies moving. Hyde Park was turned into a giant milk depot. Upper- and middle-class car owners put their vehicles at the disposal of the Ministry of Food delivering vital sustenance to the sick and elderly and to mothers with young children. As always when faced with adversity, the British rolled up their sleeves and found ways of keeping life going with the same spirit of good-natured camaraderie that they would show twenty years later during the Second World War. Indeed, in a perverse kind of way, most of them thoroughly enjoyed the experience, believing they were doing their bit in the fight against Bolshevism, their common enemy.

Lloyd George had been due to travel by train to Caernarvon in his native North Wales on 27 September to address a gathering of ex-servicemen. With typical political acumen he seized the opportunity to make his pitch to the British public in a telegram to the chairman of the Caernarvon County Council – copied to the press, of course – regretting that he would be unable to attend the soldiers' celebrations 'due to the sudden outbreak of a strike on the railways', which he promised to fight 'with all the resources at the disposal of the state'.

Having invoked the ex-servicemen as an emotive opening, Lloyd George went on to deliver a skilful political message, carefully calculated to demolish the NUR's case in the eyes of the public. Ignoring the six months of fruitless negotiations, and the government's refusal to continue them, he began: 'In a long and varied experience, I can recall no strike entered into so lightly, with so little justification, and such entire disregard of the public interest.' He insisted that the Geddes offer was a generous one. It could not be said, he claimed, that the workers were trying to wring fair wages from harsh employers who were making excessive profits: the state was running the railways at a loss, mainly due to the 'enormous increase' in the wages of the railway workers since the beginning of the war, coupled with a 'great reduction' in their hours.

The suddenness of the strike, the Prime Minster continued, gave him the impression that some individuals were determined 'to seek a quarrel at any cost'. He was convinced that it was not a strike for wages or better conditions, but had been 'engineered for some time by a small but active body of men who have sought tirelessly and insidiously to exploit the labour organisations of this country for subversive ends. I am convinced that the vast majority of the trade unionists of the land are opposed to this anarchist conspiracy. They can see the ruin and misery it has brought in other lands . . . There is no more patriotic body of men in this country than the railway men, and their conduct in the war demonstrated that fact. When they realise that they are not fighting for fair conditions for labour of their class, but are being used by extremists for sinister purposes, their common sense will resume its sway and save the country yet and their families from disaster.'[7]

Lloyd George was a master of public relations, but he had met his match in his fellow Welshman, Jimmy Thomas, aided and advised by R.H. Tawney and Sidney Webb. Thomas countered the anti-union and anti-Bolshevik scare stories in the press by taking whole-page advertisements in the newspapers stating the NUR's position calmly and unemotionally, and even making a film that was shown in cinemas across the country putting the railwaymen's case. At a mass meeting in London's Royal Albert Hall on the opening day of the strike, after the men had spent an hour singing 'The Red Flag', Thomas and the union's president, C.T. Cramp, denounced Lloyd George's statement about the purpose behind the strike as 'a deliberate lie'. 'All the powers of hell, the press, platform and perhaps the pulpit' would be invoked against the strikers, Cramp said, 'but if they remained solid, they would be victorious'.

The strike lasted nine days in all, during which there was no violence whatsoever from either side, making a nonsense of the charges of anarchy and civil strife. This was thanks largely to Thomas's highly successful PR campaign and his restraining influence: from the start, he told his members that if they kept their heads and refused to be drawn into any provocative behaviour, victory was inevitable. And so it proved to be – with a little help from their friends. On 1 October, a deputation from the Transport Workers Federation and the Labour Party, led by Ernest Bevin and Party Secretary Arthur Henderson, called on Lloyd George at 10 Downing Street and warned him that unless he reopened negotiations with the NUR the strike would spread disastrously with other unions coming out in sympathy. Bevin, leader of the dockers and a future Labour Foreign Secretary, told him that he was having great difficulty restraining his members, who were pressing him hard to call them out. Lloyd George listened, and agreed, and later that evening the delegation returned to Number 10 with the NUR leaders. The two delegations took turns to argue and plead with the Premier, until eventually, deep into the night, they began to see what Thomas called 'a ray of hope'.

Negotiations proper were resumed on 3 October, and a compromise settlement was reached two days later, on terms which Thomas described as 'honourable to both sides'. The union had obtained two-thirds of its demands: wages would be maintained at wartime levels for a year, even if prices fell, with a guaranteed minimum of fifty-one shillings a week. In return, the union pledged not to strike for any reason during that year, which in effect detached it from the Triple Alliance and removed the threat of joint action. Lloyd George could afford to congratulate himself on a successful conclusion, which he did with no false modesty in a speech at the Guildhall on 7 October, claiming that the volunteer transport organisation which had done so much to alleviate the hardships caused by the strike had been the result of his own foresight. On a less personal level, he said that the lessons learned through the strike were simple: 'The first is that you cannot hold up the community. The second is equally important. The community must make it clear to all classes . . . that it means to deal justly and fairly with their claims. A man's property, whatever form it takes, whether land or buildings or labour – if the community needs it, it must pay a fair price for it. We must make it clear that the nation means to be a just master, a fair master, a generous master – but always a master in its own house.'[8]

In America, where the steel strike was still filling the public with horror, press coverage of the British rail strike strengthened fears that the Bolshevik revolution was spreading across the world. 'Is Great Britain a nation?' the New York Times asked, 'or is it the preserve of railwaymen, miners and transport workers?' The Philadelphia Public Ledger declared that sane trade unionism could not allow 'madmen and enemies of democracy to get hold of the levers of power and run a noble ship on the shoals of disaster'. The New York World described the situation in Britain as 'gloomy almost beyond precedent' and held up as an omen the London newspaper printers' attempts to force their proprietors to publish the NUR's case: 'We all know from whom the lesson was learned. One of the first ukases of the Soviet autocrats of Russia called for the suppression of all newspapers except their own. Bela Kun adopted the same policy . . . and the Red Spartacists of Bavaria turned as naturally to the shackling of the press as to the slaughter of hostages.'⁹

In fact, for Britain, the revolutionary dangers of 1919 were already over. In the same week that the rail strike ended, Lloyd George met miners' leaders and told them he was finally rejecting their calls for nationalisation – their muted response was to thank him for seeing them. The iron founders' strike was settled the following week, a day before the last soldiers left Murmansk, ending British involvement in the Russian civil war. But in municipal elections at the beginning of November, the Labour Party scored significant successes, including winning control of fourteen out of the twenty-eight boroughs in London, a show of public support for moderate, evolutionary Socialism.

In America, meanwhile, anxiety continued to grow as the country faced further industrial and racial unrest. And with growing anxiety came growing intolerance of any deviation from total conformity of thought. Increasing numbers of teachers in schools and colleges were fired or suspended for daring even to mention Bolshevism in front of their students, never mind trying to encourage open debate or discussion. Some of the country's most distinguished professors were branded as 'parlour reds', and universities including Chicago, Yale, Vassar and Smith were denounced as 'radical institutions' because they made the writings of Marx and Engels required reading for students. Wild claims made by the patriotic associations and the press, such as that there was 'hardly a school or college in the country in which a Communist nucleus . . . has not been established' were accepted without question and used to justify an unthinking witch-hunt.¹⁰ Clergymen, especially those ministering to the poor or involved in welfare work, were attacked as closet Bolsheviks and were either muzzled or dismissed if they were bold enough to say anything sympathetic to labour and unionism, or critical of capital and employers. Government officials, even Congressmen and senators, were equally constrained, constantly aware of the dangers of speaking out. Political commentator Walter Lippmann summed it up admirably: 'So thoroughly confused are [American liberals] that the universities, the United States Congress, the government departments, every newspaper office is stoked with men who are in mortal terror . . . They tiptoe by day and quake by night, because they know that at this moment any man who in domestic policy stands about where Theodore Roosevelt stood in 1912, and in foreign affairs where Woodrow Wilson stood when he first landed in Paris . . . is absolutely certain to be called pacifist, pro-German and Bolshevist.'¹¹

In *Harper's Magazine*, a woman named Katherine Gerould had the nerve to write: 'America is no longer a free country in the old sense. Liberty is, increasingly, a merely rhetorical figure . . . No thinking citizen . . . can express in freedom more than a part of his honest convictions . . . the only way in which an American citizen who is really interested in the social and political problems of his country can preserve any freedom of expression is to choose a mob that is most sympathetic to him, and abide under the shadow of that mob.' For her audacity, she was overwhelmed with letters calling her a Bolshevik, and besieged by a mob that threatened to destroy her home.[12]

Even while the steel strike and President Wilson's conference were hogging the headlines, the next major upheaval on the industrial front was signalled. There had been increasing unrest in the coalfields all year, for the usual reason that while the industry had made huge profits from the war, wages had remained pegged at the level set by an agreement in September 1917, which was to run until the end of the war or 1 April 1920, whichever was the sooner. The miners believed that the as war was over, they were free to make a new claim. The coal operators took the view that they were not, since the Peace Treaty had not been signed and the war was therefore not officially ended.

The agitation grew month by month, and so did wildcat strikes called by small individual unions, dissatisfaction with the United Mine Workers of America union, and demands by some miners for a complete nationalisation of the industry. By September, when its annual convention was held in Cleveland, the UMW was under great pressure to take some sort of action. Finally, the acting president of the union, John L. Lewis, a tough leader and an avowed anti-Communist, persuaded the men to drop all demands for nationalisation but to terminate the wartime contract on 1 November and call a national strike if the employers did not agree to negotiate on their demands for a 60 per cent increase, a six-hour day and a five-day week.

The coal operators flatly refused to consider any negotiations until 1 April 1920. A strike seemed inevitable until Secretary of Labor William B. Wilson stepped in, calling the two sides together in Washington in the hope of reaching at least a temporary understanding. Wilson was by no means unsympathetic to the miners' case, and would certainly have understood that their excessive demands were no more than an opening bid in a fierce bargaining battle. Born in Blantyre, Scotland, but brought to Arnot, Pennsylvania, as a one-year-old immigrant, Wilson was the son of a coal miner and had himself started work in the mines at the age of nine. He had been active in the UMW, rising to the post of International Secretary-Treasurer before being elected to Congress. Appointed as the first Secretary of the newly created Department of Labor by President Wilson (no relation) in March 1913, he had won universal respect for his invaluable service to the nation during the war. However, although he was highly regarded by both sides in the current dispute, he was unable to make any real progress; the employers would go no further than to offer a modest wage increase with everything else postponed until April. Lewis's response was reported as a scornful 'In the words of Elbert H. Gary, I cannot discuss arbitration at this time'.[13] And so, the strike was called.

Lewis tried to deflect the inevitable charges of Bolshevik influence by issuing a statement to his members and the public: 'In calling this strike, the United Mine Workers have but one object in view, and that is to obtain just recognition of their right to a fair wage and proper working conditions. No other issue is involved and there must be no attempt on the part of anyone to inject into the strike any extraneous purposes.'[14] He might as well have asked for the moon. There were many members of the union, some of whom had IWW backgrounds or sympathies, who wanted more than a simple pay and hours deal, and they found it hard to keep quiet about their hopes for sweeping reforms, nationalisation and even revolutionary action. The radical press, already fired up over the steel strike, was quick to jump aboard the bandwagon and support them. And of course the Communist Party could hardly be expected to keep quiet in the face of such an opportunity. 'Workers, rally to the support of the miners,' it screamed. 'Make their strike general. Unite for a struggle against industrial slavery!'[15]

The sloganising of the left was a gift to the employers and the super patriots, who were already screaming even louder than the radicals. They deluged Congressmen with telegrams calling for action to prevent a Bolshevik revolution in the coal industry. The mine owners descended on Washington loudly demanding that something be done to crush the proposed 'insurrection'. They released totally unfounded press reports alleging that the coal strike was being undertaken on direct orders from Lenin and Trotsky and financed entirely with gold from Moscow, and delivered a continuous stream of what in later wartimes would be described as black propaganda and disinformation. The general press lapped it up enthusiastically. The New York *Tribune*, for example, attacked the miners with undiluted venom: 'Thousands of them, red-soaked in the doctrines of Bolshevism, clamor for the strike as a means of syndicalizing the coal mines . . . and even as starting a general revolution in America.'[16]

Government officials were caught up in the mounting hysteria and indeed added to it with sweeping condemnations and doom-laden predictions. Even President Wilson joined in from his sickbed in the White House, denouncing the strike as 'one of the gravest steps ever proposed in this country', and 'a grave moral and legal wrong', concluding that with winter approaching it was 'not only unjustifiable, it is unlawful'.[17] Wilson, though gravely ill, was not completely incapacitated; a very select few were permitted to see him. One of them was Attorney General Palmer, who discussed the strike situation with him on 29 October and who appears to have been given a free hand in dealing with it, free of any restrictions from other Cabinet members, who were not consulted.

Palmer's rival Cabinet members such as William Wilson could try to avert the coal strike with reasoned words and efforts at mediation. Only Palmer, as the government's chief law officer, could stop it by legal methods, and his adroit mind came up with the answer. The day after he had conferred with Woodrow Wilson, the President reactivated the wartime Fuel Administration with all its powers over coal supplies, and Palmer immediately obtained an injunction from Federal Judge Albert B. Anderson of the Indiana District Court, forbidding the UMW leaders from taking any part in the proposed strike. Faced with prison, Lewis and his fellow officials complied with the injunction, but on 1 November 394,000 miners walked out anyway. They stayed out for more than a week, during which time Palmer's rival as the nation's saviour, Calvin Coolidge, was re-elected as Governor of Massachusetts with a massively increased majority, his landslide victory giving a clear indication of the national mood. When this failed to move the miners, Palmer obtained a second injunction, ordering the UMW leaders not merely to avoid involvement but actually to call off the strike by 6 p.m. on 11 November. After agonising through a seventeen-hour session, the union's executive committee finally gave in, and Lewis announced that the strike was cancelled. 'We are Americans,' he said, 'we cannot fight our government.'[18]

Despite Lewis's capitulation, many miners refused to return to work and stayed out for almost a month, while coal stocks diminished and the Fuel Administration was forced to impose ever more drastic restrictions. Many schools and factories were closed, others reduced their working day to six hours, electric signs were allowed for only one hour a day and rail transport was cut dramatically. The miners' defiance of the law brought a fresh wave of criticism from all quarters, with renewed propaganda claims that the strike was part of a plot by Moscow to bring about the overthrow of the US government. Judge Anderson charged Lewis and eighty-three other UMW officials with violating the injunction and bound them over to a grand jury for investigation, but it was not until the President intervened personally, authorising the Fuel Administration to offer the miners a flat 14 per cent wage increase with the promise of an arbitration commission to investigate their other demands, that they returned to work. They accepted the President's plan and ended the strike on 10 December. Three months later, the promised commission recommended a 27 per cent wage increase, but no change in working hours or conditions, and the union and mine owners signed a two-year contract on those terms.

Palmer had earlier been accused of lethargy in countering the Red threat. Indeed, in early October Senator Miles Poindexter publicly denounced the Justice Department in the Senate for not rounding up and deporting radical agitators, and on 14 October, he secured a unanimous resolution demanding to know what the Attorney General was doing about the arrest and punishment or deportation of those who were trying to overthrow the government, and asking him to draft a bill that would deal with the problem. By then, however, Palmer had moved from being a leading dove to becoming the most outspoken hawk in the government, and was already making plans for a decisive attack on the radical elements that were causing so much trouble. Indeed, it is not impossible that he may have had a hand in Poindexter's resolution, which gave Congressional backing to the actions he was planning.

No doubt Palmer's conversion was partly caused by the increasing seriousness of the situation, to say nothing of the bombing of his own home in June, a fortunate escape from death which must have helped to concentrate his mind wonderfully. He must also have been heavily influenced by the reports from his protégé in the Bureau of Investigation, J. Edgar Hoover, and his General Intelligence Division, which provided ample fuel for his suspicions of increasing radical activity. There was, too, another factor that cannot be lightly dismissed: he had acquired an ambition to run for the White House, and like other potential presidential candidates saw the obvious advantages of being seen as the man who saved America.

Like many other officials, Palmer was now firmly convinced that the basic aim of the autumn strikes was revolutionary, and Hoover fed this conviction assiduously. The Attorney General put his signature to letters drafted by Hoover and distributed by his GID to all major newspapers and periodicals. 'My one desire is to acquaint people like you with the real menace of evil-thinking, which is the foundation of the Red Movement,' they began, before going on to give graphic and highly exaggerated accounts of Communist activities in America. Palmer also approved Hoover's distribution of a stream of heavily slanted press releases on Communist involvement in the strikes and race riots, often backed by 'authentic' documents specially created in the department. Such propaganda was an essential part of their preparations for action: they were determined to avoid the problems the department had had in trying to deport alien radicals after the Seattle general strike, when vociferous opposition to such arbitrary deportations had meant that only three of the fifty-four passengers on the infamous 'Red Special' train to Ellis Island had eventually been removed from the country. Next time, public opinion would be much more thoroughly prepared.

Important as the propaganda was, Hoover's main weapon was his great index. By autumn this had grown to some 200,000 cards containing cross-referenced details supplied by agents and informers of all known radical organisations and publications, with full membership rolls, names of officers and records of meetings, and including the complete case histories of more than 60,000 alleged radicals. Armed with this list, Hoover went into action – Palmer was suffering from nervous exhaustion and had been ordered to rest, so his twenty-five-year-old special assistant took charge of the operation in his name, with the support of bureau chief William J. Flynn.[19] The GID estimated that 90 per cent of those considered dangerous were aliens, and that the other, native-born 10 per cent could be safely left alone, especially since they could not be deported and would undoubtedly cause trouble if arrested. Consequently, orders were given to BI agents to concentrate on 'persons, not citizens of the United States, with a view of obtaining deportation cases'.[20]

Hoover's first target was the Union of Russian Workers. The URW had a membership of about 4,000, claimed to be composed of 'atheists,

Communists and anarchists', and preached 'the complete overthrow of all institutions of government and the confiscation of all wealth through the violence of social revolution'.[21] Its leaders, Emma Goldman and Alexander Berkman, a notorious pair of anarchists, had criminal records stretching back twenty-five years, mainly for inciting public disorder but in Berkman's case including attempted murder: he was the man who had shot Henry Frick during the Homestead Steel strike, and had served fourteen years of a twenty-one-year sentence before being paroled. Both had been born in Russia, and there had been various attempts to deport them, dating back to 1907, the year when they had founded the URW, but somehow they had managed to survive as thorns in the flesh of America's body politic.

On 7 November, the second anniversary of the Bolshevik Revolution in Russia and while emotions were running high over the coal strike, Hoover gave the order for agents to move on URW centres in twelve cities, with the help of local police forces. The main blow was struck at the New York headquarters in the Russian People's House at 133 East 15th Street, though some 250 people were also rounded up in the other cities. In New York, agents confiscated several large truckloads of radical literature and despite the fact that they had only twenty-seven arrest warrants a special police riot squad 'assisted' about two hundred men and women from the building and drove them away to Justice Department headquarters at 13 Park Row for interrogation. According to the *New York Times*, some of those arrested had been beaten up by the police, 'their heads wrapped in bandages testifying to the rough manner in which they had been handled'.[22] Other suspects were dragged from their homes and families in the middle of the night without formal charge.

Some of those questioned turned out to be American citizens and not liable to deportation, and were released at once. Others were not members of the URW or any other radical organisation, but simple workmen speaking little or no English who used the Russian People's House as a club for social contacts and useful activities such as language classes. Many of these unfortunates were held without trial or access to counsel for long periods of time – in Hartford, Connecticut, some were kept in jail for five months before even receiving a hearing.

Not to be outdone, the Lusk Committee launched a series of raids next day on seventy-three alleged radical centres in New York City. With the help of seven hundred policemen, they hauled in more than five hundred suspects and yet more 'tons' of subversive literature. Thirty-five of those arrested turned out to be US citizens, but unlike the Justice Department, Lusk's men did not release them but held them on state charges of criminal anarchy. They assessed the others, then turned over to the Justice Department all those whom they considered to be eligible for deportation. All told, the various raids brought in some 246 deportable radicals, most of them members of the URW. Hoover was delighted with the result of his operation; so, too, was Palmer, who naturally took the credit and enjoyed an overnight change of public image that placed him alongside or even ahead of Hanson and Coolidge as a national hero, dubbed by the press as 'the Fighting Quaker'.

While Palmer was basking in his new-found adulation, radicals and liberals were shocked by the blatant flouting of the American Constitution, the total disregard for civil liberties and the general brutality of the raids. But their protests were drowned by the orchestrated chorus of approval from press and public alike: at last, people cried, somebody was doing something positive about the Red menace. Any remaining misgivings were swept away four days later by events in a small town in Washington State, which appeared to bear out all their suspicions about the radical left.

Centralia was a logging town south of Seattle, with a population of a few thousand and an air of prosperity based on the huge profits generated by a rise in the price of lumber during the war from $16 to more than $120 per thousand feet. Little of this money had filtered down to the lumberjacks and loggers, and Centralia was one of the last strongholds of the IWW, whose militants were waging war on the 'slave camps' of the lumber trusts. In 1918, the companies had tried to counter IWW influence by creating a Legion of Loyal Loggers, but with little success: Centralia remained home to one of only two IWW halls that had survived closure by police or mob action in the whole of Washington. Its own hall had been shut down in March by American Legionnaires paid to sack the place, burn its literature and auction its furniture and fittings for the Red Cross, while laying into any Wobblies they could find with gas pipes and rubber hoses, all under the approving eyes of local chamber of commerce patriots. With typical cussedness, the Wobblies had hired a new hall, as a much-needed refuge for itinerant radicals, and had even increased IWW membership as a result of the persecution.

Infuriated by IWW defiance, a group of local businessmen organised the Centralia Protective Association, aimed at saving their community from the Bolshevik influence of such undesirables. During the
autumn, they began to put the word about that the IWW hall was to
be raided again, possibly during the American Legion's Armistice Day
parade on 11 November. The Wobblies met this challenge head on,
appealing for tolerance of their right to exist and charging that 'the
profiteering class of Centralia have of late been waving the flag of our
country in an endeavour to incite the lawless of our city to raid our
hall and club us out of town'.

Armistice Day dawned dank and dreary, the daylight dimmed by
a persistent sea fog rolling in off Puget Sound. At 2 p.m. the people
of the town gathered for the parade: the Elks at the front, followed
by a band, then the Boy Scouts, followed by members of the Chehalis
post of the American Legion and finally the Centralia Legion post
led by its commander, Warren O. Grimm, who was also a leading
member of the Protective Association and had organised the day's
events. The planned route passed right by the new IWW hall, and
the Wobblies prepared to defend themselves and their hall from
attack, positioning several men inside the hall itself, others directly
across the street in the Avalon Hotel and still others on high ground
about four hundred yards away, about seventy-five feet above the
street, all armed with rifles or revolvers. Among them was Wesley
Everest, an ex-army sharpshooter, wearing his uniform for the occasion. 'I fought for democracy in France,' he announced, 'and I'm
going to fight for it here. First man that comes in here, why he's
going to get it!'

At first, it seemed that there would be no violence, even though
several of the marchers were carrying lengths of rope with dangling
nooses, which they later claimed had been meant 'only as a joke'. The
parade passed by the hall without incident. Then, for no apparent
reason, the leaders turned back towards the hall, breaking through the
following ranks. From that point, there are conflicting accounts of what
happened. Some marchers claimed that they heard only shouts of 'Halt!
Close up!' Others clearly heard Legionnaires yelling 'Let's go! Up and
at 'em! Let's go get 'em!' as they headed for the hall. Immediately, a
fusillade of shots rang out from the hall, the hotel, the hilltop – and
from the Legionnaires on the street, whose bullets riddled the door of
the hall. Warren Grimm was felled by a shot in the stomach, another

Legionnaire was killed as he reached the kerb, and a third was shot through the head as he burst into the hall.

The Wobblies were quickly overcome and thrown into jail, apart from Wesley Everest, who ran for the hills. He was overtaken by a posse as he was trying to wade across the Skookomchuck River. Waist-deep in water, he still refused to surrender and emptied his revolver into his pursuers, killing one of them – the nephew of a local lumber baron – before he was seized, beaten, kicked and dragged back to town, bleeding from the mouth where his teeth had been smashed in by a rifle butt.

That night, as Everest lay bleeding on the floor of his cell, the lights suddenly went out all over Centralia. In the darkness, a mob broke into the jail, grabbed him and hauled him into the street, where he was beaten again. He was thrown into a car and driven to the Chehalis River. On the way, one of his kidnappers tore open his pants and cut off his genitals with a straight razor brought along specifically for the purpose. At the river, he was hanged by a rope from the girders of the bridge, screaming, 'Shoot me, for God's sake! Shoot me!' He was granted no such mercy. Regarding the rope as too short, his tormentors hauled him up and changed it for a longer one. This, too, did not satisfy them, and he was hanged yet again with a still longer rope. Somehow, he was still alive, and tried to cling to the edge of the bridge as he was pushed over for the third time. Someone snarled, 'Tramp on the bastard's fingers.' They did, and he fell. As he dangled, dying, they turned their car head-lights on his body and riddled it with bullets, then drove off back to town, leaving the corpse swinging.

Everest's body was finally cut down after several days and, with a foot-long neck, was taken to the jail and displayed to the other Wobblies as an example. When the local undertakers refused to handle it, four Wobblies were taken from their cells and forced to dig a grave for it in a potter's field. No inquest was held to determine the cause of death, but the Centralia coroner was reported to have ruled: 'Everest broke out of jail, went to the Chehalis River and committed suicide. He jumped off with a rope around his neck and then shot himself full of holes.' No one in Centralia disagreed.[23]

It was never established which side started the shooting, though in a trial the following year seven Wobblies were convicted of second-degree murder and given jail sentences ranging from twenty-five to forty years, while no Legionnaires were ever charged with anything. But it

hardly mattered – public outrage and sympathy at the time centred
entirely on the dead Legionnaires and the affair was immediately and
forever labelled 'the Centralia Massacre'. In truth, both sides were
victims of the Great Red Scare, forced into extreme positions by the
hysteria that swept America in 1919 and allowed only reflex, unthinking
reactions to a complex set of circumstances that were never entirely
black and white – or even Red and white.

As news of the Centralia Massacre roared across the country – initially
with no mention of the attack on the IWW hall or any reason for the
IWW shootings – virtually every newspaper ran headlines crying for
vengeance. All along the West Coast on 12 November police forces and
violent mobs went into action to clear the region of the Bolshevik
menace, declaring 'War to the Death' on all radicals. In Tacoma, thirty-
four Wobblies were seized and imprisoned, and in Spokane local
Legionnaires acting as deputy sheriffs rounded up another seventy-four.
A rampaging mob literally demolished every radical meeting place in
Oakland to show that 'law and order shall prevail'. In Seattle, another
thirty-eight Reds were locked up and publication of the *Union Record*,
the AFL's official organ in the city, was suspended and three of its staff
arrested after an editorial suggested that the IWW should be allowed
to present its side of the massacre story.

In Congress, Centralia's Representative Albert Johnson read out
dozens of telegrams from Legion posts condemning the murders of their
comrades by 'IWW draft dodgers and traitors' – conveniently ignoring
the fact that Wesley Everest had not only been an ex-soldier who had
served overseas but that he was even wearing his uniform when he was
lynched. The dead Legionnaires, Johnson said to sustained applause,
were 'victims of a long premeditated conspiracy to bring about an
armed revolution in the United States'. And in the Senate, Washington's
Senator Wesley Jones earned more applause when he cried: 'The shots
that killed those boys were really aimed at the heart of this nation by
those who oppose Law and seek the overthrow of Government.'

Also in the Senate, Miles Poindexter resumed the attack he had
started a month earlier by declaring that 'This detestable outrage is the
fearful penalty which Centralia has paid for the over-lenient policy of
the National government toward anarchists and murderous communists'. This criticism was exactly what Alexander Mitchell Palmer wanted
to hear, for it gave him carte blanche for the heroic action he and

Hoover had already started. On 14 November he delivered his answer to Poindexter's Senate resolution demanding to know what he and the Justice Department were doing about the Red menace. His long and detailed letter was accompanied by a report on the vast extent of radical activity discovered by the Bureau of Investigation through Hoover's GID, and pointed out that there were 222 radical newspapers in foreign languages and 106 in English published in America, plus 144 imported from overseas. Those figures did not include, Palmer's report said, 'the hundreds of books, pamphlets and other publications which also receive wide circulations, many of them published in foreign languages'. The IWW, it added, now circulated thirteen papers in English and nineteen in other languages, which it listed alphabetically, beginning with Armenian and concluding with Yiddish.

'These newspapers and publications,' the report charged, 'more than any other one thing, perhaps, are responsible for the spread of the Bolshevist, revolutionary and extreme radical doctrines in this country ... The reader of or subscriber to a radical newspaper uses his paper not only for his own information, but as a means of propaganda to educate his fellow workman and inoculate him with the doctrines of anarchism, Communism, and radical Socialism, and thus enlist his services in the revolution.' During the war, the radical press had been kept under control by the Espionage Act, as indeed were all radical activities by native-born Americans as well as aliens. Now that the war was over, a new Anti-Sedition Act was needed, so that American citizens could be raided, arrested and imprisoned. Palmer had drafted a stringent, catch-all bill, which he attached to his report.[24] The senators received it enthusiastically, despite the fact that many of its provisions far overstepped the limits defined in the Bill of Rights. Even the President supported the idea of such legislation in his December message to Congress.

Although Palmer could revel in the praise heaped on him by Congress and the popular press, he suddenly found himself facing an unexpected obstacle to his plans. With the President failing to provide desperately needed leadership and forbidding any meetings in his absence, the Cabinet was deeply divided over the Attorney General's methods of dealing with the radicals. Secretary of State Lansing, Postmaster General Burleson and the Presidential Secretary Joseph Tumulty were solidly behind him – and Tumulty was the only person apart from Mrs Wilson and his doctor who had regular and direct access to the President. What was more, as Palmer's closest friend in the administration and the man who had suggested him to the President for his job, Tumulty almost certainly had hopes that if Palmer did become President he would naturally want to keep him on as his secretary. Secretaries Josephus Daniels (Navy), James Houston (Agriculture) and Franklin Lane (Interior), all opposed him but could do little about it. Secretary of Labor William Wilson, however, had no hesitation in speaking out, accusing him of creating Reds through the raids rather than eliminating them. And Secretary Wilson held a trump card: deportations were the function of his Department of Labor, not Justice. Only he, or in his absence his Assistant Secretary Louis F. Post, could authorise them, and the seventy-one-year-old Post, a lawyer and former Assistant US Attorney in New York, was as hostile to Palmer's plans for mass deportations as Wilson himself. It began to look as though the radicals held on Ellis Island, their numbers now reduced after questioning to 249, would have to stay there or be released.

The stalemate was broken when a House investigation of Ellis Island discovered that between February 1917 and November 1919 more than six hundred aliens had been arrested by the federal government as anarchists, but only sixty had actually been deported by the Commissioner of Immigration, Frederic Howe, who had found the others not guilty as charged. Howe, who was suspected of harbouring radical tendencies himself, resigned to avoid being forced into ordering what he believed were unjust deportations. Amid the predictable howls of protest, his successor moved quickly to remedy the position.

Almost simultaneously, BI agents and New York police staged another raid on the Russian People's House and conveniently discovered what they said was 'a secret chamber in which was deposited enough material for 100 bombs'. This consisted of '50 or 60 small bottles' containing nondescript chemicals, which Inspector Owen Fagan of the Federal Bureau of Combustibles described as 'the most deadly and most dangerous assortment of explosives and bomb ingredients . . . seen in many a year'.[25] Coast-to-coast headlines such as 'RED BOMB LABORATORY FOUND' raised the temperature yet again.

Exaggerated reports of the supposed bombs combined with the news of Commissioner Howe's dereliction of duty to bring forth another deluge of protest at the kid-glove treatment of dangerous radicals. A number of bills were proposed to take deportation proceedings away from the soft Labor Department and give them instead to the Attorney General, that 'tower of strength', the 'lion-hearted man who has brought order out of chaos' and 'thrills of joy to every American'.[26] Nationalised citizens who espoused radical philosophies were to have their certificates revoked and be subject to deportation. Senator Kenneth D. McKellar of Tennessee suggested that even native-born Americans should be subject to deportation to a special penal colony to be set up on Guam.[27]

Overwhelmed by this tidal wave of public and Congressional fury, Secretary Wilson was forced to agree that membership of the URW was a deportable offence, and that Palmer could proceed with his plan. Hoover had found an old 5,000-ton steamer, launched in Belfast in 1890 as the British transport *Mississippi* and renamed the *Buford* when it was purchased by the US Army in 1898 to carry troops to and from Cuba in the Spanish-American War. On 21 December, he invited a host of newspaper reporters and Congressmen to Ellis Island to join him in witnessing the embarkation of the 246 men and three women on the *Buford*, which the press had christened 'the Soviet Ark'. The destination was kept secret, in sealed orders to be opened by the captain only when the ship was on the high seas. It had been provisioned with supplies for a six-week voyage and the crew had been joined by a guard of 250 American soldiers, one for every alien Red.

Most of those being deported had never taken part in any terrorist or revolutionary activity or had any criminal record. They had not been charged or tried before any court of law, or had the opportunity to contest the arbitrary decisions to expel them for their beliefs, which in many cases were purely philosophical, utopian and non-violent. A dozen of them had wives and children in America from whom they had been forcibly separated, and who had tried desperately to break through the Ellis Island ferry gates to join them, prompting the headline in the press next morning: 'REDS STORM FERRY GATES TO FREE PALS'.

There were of course a few who were genuine revolutionaries, the most notorious of whom were Emma Goldman and Alex Berkman, who were nicknamed the 'Red Queen' and 'Red King' by the press. The others were simply regarded as guilty by association. Goldman and Berkman were the only two to be interviewed by reporters – they made good copy because they were entirely unrepentant. Goldman drew on long experience to describe her quarters on Ellis Island as 'the worst dump I ever stayed in', and made a statement saying, 'I do not consider it punishment to be sent back to Soviet Russia. I consider it an honour to be chosen as the first political agitator to be deported from the United States.' As the ship pulled away from the dock, she shouted: 'This is the beginning of the end for the Unites States. I shall be back in America. We shall all be back. I am proud to be among the first deported.' Berkman, less affably, growled 'We're coming back – and we'll get you.'[28]

The sealed orders revealed that the *Buford* was headed for Finland. It docked in Hango after an uneventful twenty-eight-day voyage, and its passengers were taken across the nearby border into Russia, where they were received as heroes. None of them ever returned to the United States.

The departure of the Soviet Ark would have made a satisfying conclusion to the revolutionary year of 1919. But Palmer and Hoover, riding the crest of a wave of popular success, were plotting something bigger and better: the complete elimination of the recently formed Communist and Communist Labor parties, which were clearly at the heart of the domestic revolutionary movement. Ever since the two parties had split from the Socialists at the end of August, the Bureau of Investigation had been busily infiltrating them with undercover agents as spies and agents provocateurs. Acting as extreme Communists, many of them had quickly obtained leading positions, and were actually formulating policy, creating propaganda and organising actions. They were also providing Hoover with all the information he needed to prepare a massive move against the members of Communist parties, both native-born and alien.

Learning from the problems they had had with the Department of Labor over the November raids, Hoover and Palmer timed the new operation with care. Taking advantage of the fact that Secretary Wilson was away ill and Assistant Secretary Post was otherwise engaged, Hoover made his approach on 27 December, one week after the departure of the *Buford*, when the Labor Department's solicitor, John W. Abercrombie, was in charge as Acting Secretary. As it happened, Abercrombie was actually a member of the Department of Justice, on secondment to Labor, so he was more than willing to cooperate. So, too, was the Labor Department's top official in charge of deportation matters, Commissioner General of Immigration Antony J. Caminetti, who had bought into the Red Scare wholeheartedly. With Caminetti's support, Abercrombie signed more than 3,000 blank warrants and delivered them to the Justice Department. That same day, letters drafted by

Hoover but signed by the Assistant Director, Frank Burke, were sent to BI district chiefs in thirty-three major cities, covering twenty-three states, instructing them to carry out raids on Communist and Communist Labor Party members on 2 January. They were to get their undercover agents in the two parties to have meetings called on that night, to make it easier to arrest members en masse. Arrests were to be made between 7 p.m. on Friday 2 January and 7 a.m. next day, using local police as necessary. Any members who were not present at the meetings were to be arrested at their homes, places of business, social clubs, or wherever they could be found. Agents were ordered to 'obtain all documentary evidence possible', and to secure 'charters, meeting minutes, membership books, dues books, membership correspondence, etc'. They were not to allow any person arrested to communicate with anyone whatsoever until permission was specifically granted by Flynn, Hoover or Palmer himself.[29]

The action on 2 January was a spectacular success. More than 4,000 suspected radicals were rounded up across the nation. There were few arrests in the west and far west, where local raids after the Centralia Massacre had already put most known radicals behind bars, but mass arrests in New York, Pennsylvania, New England and the Midwest more than made up for any shortages. Every Communist cell was raided, virtually every leader arrested, often without the nicety of a warrant since there were not enough to go round.

Once again, the general press and public went wild with praise for the Attorney General, the man who had saved the nation. Those who dared to express their concerns that the raids were endangering American Constitutional freedoms, were drowned out by more strident voices. 'There is no time to waste,' the *Washington Post* proclaimed, 'on hairsplitting over infringement of liberty . . .'[30] Palmer himself had no doubts: he claimed that his raids had 'halted the advance of Red radicalism in the United States'. Equally triumphal, Flynn asserted that they 'marked the beginning of the end of organised revolutionaries in this country'. At the time, their statements sounded like a fitting epitaph for the year that had just ended – 1919, the year of revolutions and of the Great Red Scare.

# EPILOGUE:
# THE AFTERMATH, 1920

THE raids of 2 January 1920 marked the zenith, or perhaps one should say the nadir, of the Great Red Scare in the United States. The planning, execution and results of the arrests were all so far outside the bounds of legality, decency and morality that the department responsible for them could well have been renamed the Department of Injustice. The operation generated an hysteria in which law enforcement officers indulged in a frenzy of blind brutality against mostly defenceless people who had been demonised and dehumanised by the press and propaganda in much the same way as the Jews in Nazi Germany would be turned into 'sub-humans' during the thirties and forties.

Some 800 people were seized in New England towns and cities, about half of whom turned out to be American citizens who were handed over to the authorities for prosecution under state anti-syndicalism laws. Most of these were released after two or three days, when it became clear that there was no evidence against them. Thirty-nine bakers in Lynn, Massachusetts, for instance, who had been arrested for holding a revolutionary meeting, were released when it was established that they had been engaged in setting up a cooperative bakery. The other 400 or so were taken to the immigration station in Boston and then forced to march in chains to the dockside to be ferried to Deer Island in the harbour. Both in the holding stations and on Deer Island conditions were appalling, with no heat, poor sanitation and little or no food. The prisoners were all held incommunicado, with no access to legal counsel. Many were savagely beaten, usually for no apparent reason. One went insane, two died of pneumonia, another leapt to his death from a fifth-floor window.

The story was much the same in New York, Philadelphia, Pittsburgh and New Jersey – in Newark one man was arrested on the street simply because he 'looked like a radical', and another because he stopped to ask what all the commotion was about. In New Brunswick, members of a Socialist club were rounded up when agents discovered a set of 'mysterious' drawings which they thought were of 'the internal mechanism of various types of bombs' but which when sent to demolition experts for examination proved to be of a phonograph invention.

In Detroit about 800 people were imprisoned for days in a dark, windowless corridor in the city's antiquated Federal Building, where they were forced to sleep on the bare floor and had the choice of waiting in line to use the single toilet or urinating against the wall. Their only source of food was what their families brought them, once they had discovered where they were. After six days of this, and close questioning by Bureau agents, nearly half were released as completely innocent, while about 140 were marched through the streets to the Detroit Municipal Building. Since they had been unable to wash, shave or change into fresh clothes for almost a week, they presented a sorry spectacle to the public and press, who were able to print pictures of them as 'dirty, filthy Bolshevik terrorists'.

In the Municipal Building they were shoved into the 'bull pen', a bare room measuring twenty-four feet by thirty feet, designed to hold offenders for three or four hours before facing a court. The men were held there for another week, in conditions that were so bad that the citizens of Detroit eventually felt pity for them and set up a committee to investigate their situation, which found that they were not dangerous radicals but poor, ignorant foreigners who were totally bewildered by what was happening to them.

Palmer remained unmoved, asserting that the raids had produced information proving that radicals, and in particular alien radicals, posed an immediate security threat to the nation. What was more, he said, these aliens were controlled by Moscow and received their orders directly from Lenin and Trotsky. 'Each and every adherent of this movement,' he continued, 'is a potential murderer or a potential thief. . . . Out of the sly and crafty eyes of many of them leap cupidity, cruelty, insanity, and crime; from their lopsided faces, sloping brows, and misshapen features may be recognised the unmistakeable criminal type.'[1]

Through January Hoover and Flynn stepped up the propaganda campaign, flooding newspapers and magazines with free articles and cartoons. Meanwhile, Palmer continued to press Congress for a peace-time Sedition Act that would give him the powers he needed to deal with American domestic radicals. He promised that there would be more raids on aliens, producing at least another 2,720 deportations, and treating New Yorkers to the exhilarating spectacle of 'a second, third, and fourth Soviet Ark sailing down their beautiful harbor in the near future'.[2]

As it happened, however, there were to be no more Soviet Arks, and no more raids. Nor was there to be a new anti-Sedition Act. Individual states passed a rash of new criminal anarchy, syndicalist, red flag and sedition laws, in many cases at the direct urging of Palmer; the New York State Legislature went so far as to disbar five Socialist members, even though they had been elected democratically and quite properly. But there was no new federal legislation against radicalism. Some seventy bills were proposed in Congress during the winter of 1919–20, and amalgamated into the single Graham-Sterling Bill on 14 January, but this was eventually killed by a growing feeling that it was far too drastic. The tide had turned and sanity was beginning to surface again, as more bold souls found the nerve to voice their criticisms of the excesses of the Red Scare. Some newspapers even had the temerity to accuse Palmer of inventing the whole revolutionary threat in order to boost his presidential campaign.

After judges had ruled that much of the evidence against those who had been arrested had been obtained illegally and was therefore inadmissible, Assistant Secretary of Labor Louis Post began reviewing the results of the deportation hearings and the warrants issued in his absence by Abercrombie. Shocked by the flagrant disregard for civil liberties and unable in most cases to find any evidence that would justify deportation, he began cancelling warrants and ordering the release of detainees. By April almost half of them were free. Most of them, Post said, were 'wage workers, useful in industry, good natured in their dispositions, unconscious of having given offence . . . Very few, if any, were the kind of aliens that Congress could in all reasonable probability have intended to comprehend in its anti-alien legislation.'[3]

Some members of Congress naturally disagreed with Post, and began moves to have him impeached. When he appeared before the House Committee on Rules, however, he was entirely unrepentant, charging that the Justice Department, together with the general press and super-patriot associations, had manufactured a revolution that simply was not there. He blasted the Department for its high-handed procedures and illegal actions, and demolished his accusers so thoroughly and with such a wealth of firm evidence that the Rules Committee hastily backed down and left him to his work. When he had finished, he found that only 556 of the 4,000 radicals rounded up in the January raids were liable to deportation; over the following months they were quietly sent back to their native lands in small groups aboard normal American ships.

Post's vindication by the House Rules Committee came on 7 May, and was the second humiliation within days for Palmer. For weeks, the GID had been distributing dire warnings of Bolshevik plans for an uprising on May Day involving the assassination of government officials, a general strike and the blowing up of public buildings. All this, Palmer claimed, was part of a dastardly plot to overthrow the American government and force recognition of Soviet Russia. It all sounded suspiciously similar to the Independence Day scare in 1919, but nevertheless the press bought it and went to town with another set of lurid headlines. Once again, public buildings, churches and the homes of prominent individuals were placed under guard. Once again, police were put on twenty-four-hour duty, machine guns mounted at strategic points in cities, and bomb squads put on standby, while in Chicago 360 suspected radicals were locked up for the day 'just in case'. And once again, nothing happened. There was not a single disturbance in the entire country. This time, the Justice Department's claims that its warnings had worked rang very hollow indeed.

Further proof that the Great Red Scare was over came on 16 September, after a massive bomb secreted on a horse-drawn wagon exploded in New York at the corner of Wall and Broad streets, in front of the United States Assay Office and opposite the headquarters of the J.P. Morgan bank. It killed thirty-eight people and injured a further 400, and caused considerable damage. But when Palmer and Bureau chief Flynn rushed to New York City to lead the investigation, hysterically proclaiming that the bomb was part of a gigantic plot to overthrow the US government, smash capitalism and establish a soviet regime, they were ridiculed.

Most Americans accepted that the bomb was the work of a small group of dedicated but crazed Italian anarchists, and was probably a revenge attack for the arrest and indictment for murder of two of their colleagues, Nicola Sacco and Bartolomeo Vanzetti. The Cleveland *Plain Dealer* spoke for the nation when it concluded:

Capitalism is untouched. The federal government is not shaken in the slightest degree. The public is merely shocked, not terrorized, much less converted to the merits of anarchism. Business and life as usual. Society, government, industry functioning precisely as if nothing had happened.[4]

Palmer's reputation had been damaged beyond repair, and the Fighting Quaker, saviour of the nation, quickly became the Quaking Fighter, or even the Faking Fighter, with no real hope of achieving the coveted presidential nomination. It would have made little difference if he had: the Democratic candidate, Governor James Cox of Ohio and his running mate Franklin D. Roosevelt, chosen after forty-four ballots at an ill-humoured convention, were trounced by Senator Warren G. Harding, who won thirty-seven of the forty-eight states and an amazing 61 per cent of the popular vote, on a promise to return America to 'normalcy'. Harding's Vice President was Governor Calvin Coolidge, the scourge of the Boston police strikers, who succeeded him when he died of a cerebral haemorrhage in August 1923, and won the presidency in his own right the following year. The Great Red Scare was consigned to history.

In Germany, the state of siege that had existed in Berlin since the second Spartacist rising in March 1919 had finally been lifted on 6 December, but after a peaceful Christmas and New Year, 1920 soon brought reminders that the revolutionary threat was still alive and kicking. When the government introduced a bill curbing the rights of elected workers' councils in industry, the Independent Socialists called for a massive one-day strike in protest. Foreseeing trouble, General Freiherr von Lüttwitz, commander of the Berlin military district, demanded martial law for the whole of Germany, but President Ebert and his chancellor, Gustav Bauer, demurred.

Around midday on 13 January, the day the new bill was to be debated, workers from all parts of Berlin marched on the Reichstag. 'By two o'clock,' wrote the British correspondent Morgan Philips Price, 'the scene around the Reichstag resembled those of the revolution in 1918.'[5] Some of the strikers clashed with troops posted around the building by Lüttwitz and Defence Minister Noske. 'I witnessed a number of serious collisions between workers and troops between the Bismarck Monument and the Reichstag steps,' Price reported. 'A number of Noske troops were disarmed by the crowds but I did not see any of them assaulted or injured at this stage. About three o'clock the troops suddenly opened fire from the steps of the Reichstag and a terrible pandemonium followed. A large number of demonstrators fell, and isolated detachments of troops were set upon by the crowd and seriously handled. The tumult lasted some time, but the troops ultimately succeeded in driving the demonstrators away. The sitting of the Reichstag was suspended.'[6]

The newspapers next morning reported more than thirty dead – a figure later revised to forty-two – and four hundred wounded.[7] Price wrote that the pavements around the Reichstag building were covered with blood. Martial law was declared for the whole of Prussia – though not the rest of Germany, despite further demands from Lüttwitz – and Noske moved quickly to ban all public meetings and suppress Berlin Independent Socialist and Communist newspapers.

It all had a depressingly familiar ring, especially when coupled with news from the Ruhr that railwaymen had gone on strike and miners were threatening to come out on 1 February, demanding a six-hour day. But the attempted revolution, when it came, appeared to bear out British fears that the German government might be overthrown by a coup from the right, which would then open the door to a counter-coup from the left.

The Versailles Treaty had come into effect on 10 January, and three weeks later the Allies had demanded the extradition of the Kaiser from Holland and the handing over by the German government of nearly 900 former officers, starting with Hindenburg, for trial as war criminals. The army was to be reduced from its estimated strength of 400,000 to 100,000, and the Freikorps were to be disbanded, bringing to an abrupt end their involvement in the Baltic and Poland. These were bitter pills indeed for the militarists, and many refused to swallow them. Some Freikorps were incorporated into the new Reichswehr, or into state police forces, others metamorphosed into sports clubs, shooting associations, detective agencies and labour gangs on large country estates, taking their 'tools' with them.

The toughest and most ruthless of all the Freikorps, the Ehrhardt Brigade, named after its commander Naval Captain Hermann Ehrhardt, had other plans. The Brigade, now stationed at Döberitz, some fifteen miles outside Berlin, had distinguished itself in savage battles against the Poles on the eastern frontier and the Bolsheviks in the Baltic, and was one of the main units in the force that had crushed the Räterepublik in Munich. It was a formidable fighting machine, and the very thought of disbanding was anathema to its officers and men. It was also anathema to General Lüttwitz.

Lüttwitz refused the order to disband the Freikorps brigades around Berlin, and was dismissed by Noske when incriminating documents were discovered linking him with a right-wing conspiracy to overthrow the government. In the name of the Ehrhardt Brigade, Lüttwitz sent an ultimatum to President Ebert, demanding a halt to demobilisation of both army and Freikorps, plus various other measures including fresh elections, the forcible suppression of all strikes, and the restoration of the old imperial colours of red, white and black, which had been replaced under the new constitution by the black, red and gold of the revolutionaries of 1848.

When Ebert rejected the ultimatum, the Brigade marched on Berlin, led by their assault company and a field artillery battery, singing their brigade song:

> Swastika on our helmets
> Black-white-red on our band
> The Brigade of Ehrhardt
> Is known throughout the land.
>
> Worker, worker, what's to become of you
> When the Brigade is ready to fight?
> The Ehrhardt Brigade smashes all to bits
> So woe, woe, woe to you, you worker son-of-a-bitch!

As they goose-stepped through the Brandenburg Gate at 7 a.m. on 13 March, they were greeted by Lüttwitz and General Ludendorff, who happened, 'quite by chance', to be taking his early morning constitutional at that precise time and place, and Dr Wolfgang Kapp, an East Prussian civil servant and co-founder of the extreme-right wartime Fatherland Party, who was incongruously dressed in top hat and tail coat. Kapp and Lüttwitz went to the Reich Chancellery on Wilhelmstrasse, and issued a proclamation stating that the Reich government had ceased to exist. 'The full state power has devolved on Commissioner Dr Kapp of Königsberg as Reich Chancellor and Minister-President of Prussia,' it went on. 'We need two things, order and work. Agitators will be exterminated without compunction.'

Ebert and his government had wisely decamped during the night, first to Dresden and then to Stuttgart, having failed to persuade the

Chief of the General Staff, Colonel-General Hans von Seeckt, to provide military support from the regular Reichswehr units. 'Troops do not fire on troops,' Seekt had declared. '. . . When Reichswehr fires on Reichswehr, then all comradeship within the officer corps will have vanished.' Denied military protection, Ebert turned to a different weapon, one that was to prove devastatingly powerful: in conjunction with the Majority Socialists, the Independent Socialists and the trade unions, for once all acting together, the government called a general strike. Only the Communists failed to join in, refusing, they said, to support one capitalist regime against another.

It was the most complete stoppage in German history. Everything came to a halt immediately: there was no water, no power, no transport, nothing. In the midst of the ensuing chaos, there were more army and navy mutinies in various parts of the country, but the security police and troops finally declared their allegiance to the Ebert government, and after four and a half days the putsch collapsed. The Freikorps troops formed up and marched out of Berlin, watched by a hostile crowd, but the farce into which the attempted revolution had descended had a vicious edge. When a boy in the crowd jeered at the departing troopers, two of them broke ranks, clubbed him to the ground with their rifle butts and kicked him to death. As the crowd tried to intervene, other troopers opened fire on them with rifles and machine guns, before continuing on their way, leaving scores of dead and wounded behind them.

Kapp fled to Sweden, Lüttwitz to Hungary, where he was welcomed by a White government that was in complete sympathy with his views – two weeks later, Admiral Horthy dismissed the Hungarian parliament and assumed dictatorial powers, which he retained until Hitler unseated him in 1944. Ehrhardt found refuge in Bavaria, where a right-wing coup had removed Minister President Hoffmann and installed the conservative Gustav von Kahr in his place. Ehrhardt and his Brigade moved to Munich at the express invitation of its police chief, an arrogant former army lieutenant called Ernst Pöhner, a man who, when asked if he knew that there were political murder gangs operating in his city, replied 'Yes, but not enough of them!'

The reaction to the left-wing revolutionary threats of 1919 became firmly established in Munich, creating a magnet for extreme nationalists from all over Germany and a breeding ground for radicals of the right. It was no coincidence that it was at this time that the newly demobilised Lance Corporal Adolf Hitler was able to take over the small German Workers' Party and rename it the National Socialist German Workers' Party, shortened in the usual German fashion to the 'Nazi Party'. Hitler's last act before returning to civilian life had been to fly to Berlin on behalf of the Political Intelligence department to report on the situation during the putsch and to convey the Bavarian Reichswehr's greetings to Kapp and Lüttwitz. Unfortunately for him and his masters, he arrived just as they fled, but he was able to console himself with a meeting with Ludendorff, which was to prove useful four years later when he was plotting his own putsch.

Ludendorff felt secure enough in his past achievements to remain in Germany, though he had the good sense to move south into Bavaria, where he was still regarded as a hero and was presented by his supporters with a sumptuous villa in a suburb of Munich. His new home, guarded round the clock by men from the Ehrhardt Brigade, rapidly became a centre of pilgrimage for nationalist opponents of the Weimar Republic.

Having demonstrated their power so effectively in crushing the Kapp–Lüttwitz putsch, the German unions were naturally reluctant to give it up. They dictated their own terms to the government for calling off the strike, which had spread throughout most of the nation, demanding an eight-point programme of reforms which included the forcible disbanding of reactionary paramilitary organisations, the socialisation of industry and the right to be involved in selecting a new Cabinet. They insisted on the removal of Chancellor Bauer, and the hated Gustav Noske, whose remarkable career was brought to an end along with the Freikorps which he had used so effectively against the forces of the left.

Ebert bowed to their wishes over Bauer and Noske, but calling off the strike was not so simple. The flames of revolution flared up again in various places: Socialist rebels had been quick to set up workers' council governments in Leipzig, Hamburg and Chemnitz. Harry Kessler noted in his diary that there was fierce fighting between workers and Reichswehr in Berlin, Leipzig, Nuremberg, Chemnitz, Dresden and in the Ruhr. 'At various points in Berlin,' he went on, 'the mob has captured officers of the retreating Kapp forces and murdered them. The bitterness of the working classes against the military seems to be unlimited, and the successful general strike has greatly increased their consciousness of their own power. Opposed to them stand a disrupted, half-treacherous Reichswehr and a feeble, irresolute government.'[8]

In the industrial heartland of the Ruhr, the workers had organised themselves into a 50,000-strong force – which they inevitably called the Red Army – and refused to go along with the terms of the settlement. Supported by 300,000 mineworkers, they defeated the Freikorps and weak Reichswehr forces in the area, conquered Düsseldorf, Elberfeld and Essen, and seized control over the whole Ruhr valley. Under the terms of the Versailles Treaty, this had been designated as a neutral area between the zones of Allied occupation and the rest of Germany, and the size of the Reichswehr in the Ruhr was strictly limited. But Ebert and his new government, claiming that this was an emergency, sent in more troops to quell what was being called the March Revolution. This sparked a state of virtual civil war in which about a thousand rebels and 250 Reichswehr and Freikorps troops were killed, and gave the French the excuse to march in and occupy several towns and cities, including Frankfurt, Darmstadt, Hanau and Homburg.[9] Peace was finally restored and both German and French troops were withdrawn. But the brutality of the operation left a bitterness that would not easily or quickly be assuaged, encouraging yet more extremism as formerly moderate Socialist workers were driven further to the left.

When the first national elections for a new Reichstag were held on 6 June, the moderate parties of the centre suffered as the electorate swung to the right – the Majority Socialist SPD lost half its seats and the left-liberal DDP lost three-fifths. The parties of the left had been too preoccupied with squabbling among themselves to provide any worthwhile opposition in the elections. When some 350,000 Independent Socialists split from their party and joined the Communist KPD, for instance, the left wing of the KPD broke away to become the Communist Workers' Party, which wanted no truck whatever with the parliamentary system. In spite of this, however, the Communists still managed to attract some 400,000 votes in the elections, establishing themselves as a mainstream political party for the first time.

The SPD chose not to take part in the new coalition and withdrew from the government, effectively removing itself from active participation in politics for most of the next twenty-five years. Without its moderating influence, the dominating features of German politics until 1933 would be polarisation, a heritage of violence – between 1919 and 1922 there were 356 political murders in Germany – and a chronic instability.

*

France, like much of the rest of Western Europe, began the new decade with a strong swing to the right. The Socialists had been heavily defeated by an alliance of the conservative right in the general election for the Chamber of Deputies in November 1919, and again in the Senate elections on 11 January 1920, the day after the Versailles Treaty came into force, officially ending the Great War. The terms of the treaty were not universally welcomed in France: many Frenchmen thought Clemenceau had given way to pressure from Britain and America and had not been nearly tough enough on Germany, particularly over reparations and France's eastern frontier, which they believed should be extended to the Rhine.

The two houses of the legislature declined to support Clemenceau's bid for the presidency, choosing instead one of his critics, Paul Deschanel. Clemenceau resigned as premier, and retired from active politics. It may have come as some comfort to the wounded Tiger that four months later Deschanel was confined to a mental hospital suffering from a severe nervous breakdown, 'due to overwork', after he was found wandering along the railway track, uninjured but confused, having apparently falling from a sleeper train. He resigned on medical advice in the middle of September.

During the spring, France was beset by a series of strikes as the labour unions tested their strength against the government, culminating in a national rail strike at the beginning of May, supported by the General Confederation of Labour (CGT). The strike was largely political, but when the CGT called out the seamen, dockers and miners in support of the railwaymen, the response was generally half-hearted and in some places actively hostile. The government stood firm, and the strike collapsed within a week – French workers had no appetite for revolution. This came as a grave disappointment to the Socialists, who spent most of 1920 agonising over their electoral defeats, arguing over doctrinal niceties and moving steadily further to the extreme left.

In mid December the various left-wing factions held a conference in Tours, at which they voted by a majority of three to one to split from the Socialist Party and form what they called the SFIC, the French Section of the Communist International (changed shortly afterwards to the Communist Party of France), nailing their colours firmly to Moscow's mast. Among the founders of the new party was a young Indo-Chinese man by the name of Ho Chi Minh, who was later to introduce his revolutionary philosophy to his homeland of Vietnam. Although the vast majority of French people rejected the calls from the extremes of left and right, the Socialists and Communists would exert a powerful and unsettling influence on French political life for the next seventy years.

Britain, too, suffered recurring strikes during 1920, culminating in a national miners' strike in October, which lasted for two and a half weeks and brought the country to a standstill before being called off by the miners themselves. This time, the strikers were not impressed by Lloyd George's blandishments – they had heard them all too often before – but as it happened they would have been better off accepting his offer of binding arbitration on their pay claim, which was rejected by the mine owners, leaving them empty-handed. Their dissatisfaction rumbled on over the next few years, leading to the great General Strike of 1926, which involved workers from all areas of British industry and brought disruption on an unparalleled scale. The causes of the strikes, however, were mainly economic, not directly political.

In contrast to Clemenceau, in 1920 Lloyd George the Welsh wizard was still working his magic on the country as a whole, and retained his position as prime minister. His greatest challenge during the year was the Irish struggle for independence, which grew steadily more bloody and bitter as the year progressed, but which had no connection with Communism or revolutionary Socialism. In fact, although the Communist Party of Great Britain was founded that year by the amalgamation of several small groups, in direct response to a Comintern directive, it would never become a rival to the main parties, always remaining on the periphery of the political scene and never really being taken seriously by the British public.

The third of the major victorious European Allies, Italy, was the poorest and most insecure, emerging from the war exhausted and deeply in debt. At the same time, it was plagued by the instability of a political system that led to five governments between 1918 and 1922, none of which was able to get to grips with tackling the country's economic or social problems. Inflation was rampant – the lira had shrunk to one-fifth of its pre-war value, the export trade was virtually non-existent, as was tourism, and unemployment was aggravated both by the return of demobilised soldiers and by new American restrictions on immigration. There was general dissatisfaction with the territorial settlement made at the Paris Peace Conference: Italians at all levels of society felt they had been short-changed, receiving far less than they had been promised in the Treaty of London which had brought them into the war in 1915.

In the general election in November 1919, the Socialists won more than a third of all the votes and became the largest single party in the Chamber of Deputies, followed by the Catholic Popular Party, which won one-fifth of the total vote on a platform of social reform. The former ruling parties, Liberals and Democrats, lost heavily. Mussolini failed to win a seat, and immediately spurred his followers into violent protest riots, after which he and seventeen supporters were arrested and imprisoned.

Despite the election of a Socialist-led government, the unions called a general strike in December which paralysed several northern cities. There were more strikes and more riots through 1920, with Socialist agitation building steadily until it reached a climax in September with a massive sit-in, when workers occupied more than six hundred factories, and set up soviet governments in industrial towns and cities. All the conditions were in place for a Red revolution, and the world watched with apprehension. But it never came. The government promised the workers a 20 per cent wage increase, and the General Confederation of Labour accepted and called off the strike.

The strike had, after all, been economic, not political. Nevertheless, it had caused great alarm among industrialists and property holders, who saw Bolshevism lurking in the background and looked around with increasing desperation for a saviour to protect them from the Red menace. They found him in Benito Mussolini. Mussolini's only potential rival as the charismatic leader of the nationalist right, Gabriele D'Annunzio, was forced by the Italian government to quit Fiume at the end of 1920 after a fifteen-month occupation, and retired in high dudgeon to his palatial home on the shores of Lake Garda. His backers switched their support to Mussolini, and his followers swelled the ranks of the black-shirted Fascists, engaging the Socialist red shirts in increasingly vicious street battles. They attacked all forms of labour organisations, Socialist councils and newspapers, beating up and torturing their opponents, all with the connivance of the Church and liberal Italy and active help from anti-Bolshevik army officers, who provided them with arms. As the government appeared powerless to halt the violence and restore law and order, the Fascists came to be regarded by the middle classes as protectors of property, rather than the principal disturbers of the peace.

After two years of playing the anti-Bolshevik card for all he was worth, in October 1922 Mussolini was able to stage an entirely spurious 'March on Rome' (he personally travelled by train, joining his footsore followers at the end of their journey), where the King handed him dictatorial power as the 'Duce', the 'Leader', a position he was to retain for the next twenty-two years. Once again, the reaction to a perceived Bolshevik threat was to prove more lasting than the threat itself as people sought stability, at whatever the cost, instead of Trotsky's permanent state of revolution.

In Russia, 1920 brought a new and decisive phase in the civil war. After a year of fluctuating fortunes for both sides, it had seemed for a brief period in October and November 1919 that the Whites had finally got their act together and were on the verge of victory. White armies had reached the outskirts of Petrograd and were les than two hundred miles from Moscow; the Poles, invading from the west, were not much further away at Smolensk. One concerted push might have been enough to finish the Bolshevik regime. But the push never came. The Reds survived, secured the centre and drove out in all directions, smashing the White armies, carrying all before them, and eventually reconquering most of the republics in the European part of tsarist Russia.

One of the most important elements in the White generals' undoing was their determination to restore the tsarist empire to its old boundaries, encompassing all the border states which had gained their freedom in 1918. In the centre, General Denikin alienated the Poles by refusing to acknowledge Polish independence; the Poles halted their attack on Moscow and opened negotiations with Lenin, who said he was prepared to accept their historic frontiers. Denikin dithered until the Red cavalry arrived and swept his forces away. In the north-west, General Yudenich forfeited the support of the Estonians in the same way, while Lenin offered them recognition and peace in return for their neutrality. As Trotsky arrived in Petrograd to take personal command of its defences – at one stage he even mounted a horse and led his troops from the saddle – Yudenich's army, overstretched and under strength, collapsed, fled into Estonia and dissolved.

Lenin kept his word to Estonia, and extended his promises to Latvia and Lithuania. With peace talks under way, Admiral Cowan and his British naval force sailed for home on 28 December, their mission accomplished. Cowan was rewarded by the British government with a baronetcy, choosing the apt title 'Baronet of the Baltic'. The Estonians signed an armistice with Russia on New Year's Eve, and a peace treaty on 2 February. Latvia, Lithuania and Finland followed suit during the year, and freedom reigned in the Baltic until 1939, when a new Tsar, Josef Stalin, began turning the screw on the three small countries in preparation for taking them back into the Russian empire.

While Lenin was prepared to let the Baltic States go, he was less amenable to Poland, which was both more troublesome and more important to him. The war between Poland and Soviet Russia, which had broken out almost by accident in the spring of 1919, had smouldered on through that year without flaring into full-scale hostilities. Neither side had been ready for an all-out conflict: Lenin and Trotsky and the Red Army had been too heavily occupied with their civil war; the Poles, for their part, had been kept more than busy building an army from scratch and trying to re-establish their frontiers from the late eighteenth century, when their three neighbours, Russia, Austria-Hungary and Prussia, had carved up the country between them in a series of partitions. The reborn Poland became involved in fiendishly complicated struggles not only against Germany and Russia but also against most of its neighbours, including Lithuania, Belorussia, the Ukraine and Czechoslovakia, who had also been part of the three great empires. The situation was made even more complicated by the fact that Lithuania, Belorussia and the Ukraine were all fighting internal battles with their own Bolsheviks and continuing their struggles for independence from Russia.

By the start of 1920, the civil war was all but won by the Reds – there would still be fighting in the south against White forces led by Baron Wrangel until the autumn, but the outcome was already a foregone conclusion. This meant that the Red Army could concentrate its full attention on Poland, which became its principal theatre of war. Although Lenin had bought off the Poles in the previous autumn with his offer to recognise their pre-partition frontiers, he still saw Poland as his vital red bridge into Western Europe, which he was determined to take. In January, he began building up a 700,000-strong force in Belorussia, which by then had long been swallowed, in preparation for a major new offensive in late April or May. The Poles, however, demonstrating the impressive code-breaking skills that would later play such a vital role in the Second World War, intercepted and deciphered Russian radio communications. Aware of the Russians' secret plans, they launched their own offensive under Marshal

Piłsudski, invading the Ukraine with the object of establishing a pro-Polish independent Ukraine as an ally against Soviet Russia.

In May, the Poles captured the Ukrainian capital, Kiev, the birthplace centuries before of Russian civilisation. But their triumph lasted only a few weeks: the Reds counter-attacked with the Cossack 1st Cavalry Army under General Budenny, drove them out of Kiev and back across the frontier into Poland while the main body of the Red Army, commanded by a brilliant former tsarist officer, Mikhail Tukhachevsky, advanced towards Warsaw on a broad front. This was the first time the Soviets had penetrated Europe proper, and the first time they had attempted to export the revolution by force. A jubilant Lenin sent a telegram declaring: 'We must direct all our attention to preparing and strengthening the Western Front. A new slogan must be announced: "Prepare for war against Poland."' Tukhachevsky's order of the day on 2 July read: 'To the West! . . . The time of reckoning has come. Over the corpse of White Poland shines the road to worldwide conflagration. On our bayonets we shall bring happiness and peace to toiling humanity. . . . On to Vilna, Minsk, Warsaw! March!'[10]

As the Red advance continued, the Soviets set up a Polish puppet government under Felix Dzerzhinsky, to administer the territories they had already conquered and to be ready to take over when Warsaw fell, as it surely would. Delegates to the Second Congress of the Comintern, meeting in Moscow at that time, followed the triumphs of the Red Army each day on a huge map that was hung on the wall of the Congress hall. Lenin, who had insisted on the invasion of Poland against the advice of both Trotsky and Stalin, assured them that the European revolution was just around the corner.[11] And then it all went wrong . . .

Tukhachevsky was lured into a trap outside Warsaw by Piłsudski, whose codebreakers had again decrypted Russian radio messages, and his armies were encircled by a lightning Polish counter-attack. Meanwhile, Budenny's 1st Cavalry Army, which should have been protecting Tukhachevsky's flank, was occupied in a fruitless attempt to capture the industrial city of Lwow, on the orders of the South West Front's Chief Political Commissar, Josef Stalin, who was seeking to score points over Trotsky with a personal triumph. The deeply Catholic Poles hailed Piłsudski's defeat of Tukhachevsky as 'the Miracle on the Vistula', which was more than a little unfair since it was the result not of divine intervention but of a brilliantly planned and executed military operation. With sky-high morale they went on to break the Red Army in a series of crushing victories until the Russians finally sued for peace. An armistice was signed on 12 October, as the first snows of winter were falling.

The Polish–Soviet War was over, and with it the Bolsheviks' attempt to export the revolution to Europe and the rest of the world. Lenin tried to rationalise the defeat: 'Poland was not ready for a social revolution,' he told the Party Conference that autumn. 'We encountered a nationalist upsurge from the petty bourgeois elements as our advance towards Warsaw made them fear for their national survival.'[12]

However he tried to wrap it up, Lenin could not ignore the fact that the peoples of the world simply did not want his brand of international Communism. It was clear that any attempt to impose it on them from outside would provoke a violent nationalist reaction – and in any case, the Red Army was not strong enough to impose it by force. He tried to save face by claiming, somewhat unconvincingly, that his invasion of Poland had been intended as a warning to the Western powers not to interfere in Russian affairs. But what he had in fact achieved was to convince them that they no longer needed to fear a Soviet invasion, any more than they needed to fear Red revolution in their own countries. The defeat in Poland forced Lenin to abandon his grandiose international ambitions, to retreat behind his own frontiers and concentrate on developing Communism in one country, a doctrine that he and his successors would maintain for the next quarter of a century. It would take victory in another world war to change it.

# ACKNOWLEDGEMENTS

I am grateful to the following copyright holders for permission to use quotations from the books and journals listed: Pluto Press (www.plutobooks.com) for *Dispatches from the Weimar Republic* by Morgan Philips Price, edited by Tania Rose; Liverpool University Press for *Paris 1918: The War Diary of the 17th Earl of Derby*; Insel Verlag for *The Diaries of a Cosmopolitan, 1918–1937* by Count Harry Kessler; HarperCollins Publishers for *Six Weeks in Russia in 1919* by Arthur Ransome; Mrs Barbara White Walker for *A Puritan in Babylon: The Story of Calvin Coolidge*; the *New York Times* for various excerpts dated 1918 and 1919; the *Washington Post* for *A National Tonic*, © 1919.

For permission to use illustrations I thank the following: Getty Images: nos 1, 2, 4, 5, 6, 8, 10, 11, 14, 17, 18, 20, 21, 22, 25, 30, 31, 33, 34, 39, 41; AKG-images: nos 12, 19, 35, 38; Ullstein Bild: nos 7, 9, 13, 15, 16; The Library of Congress, USA: nos 3, 19, 26, 27, 28, 29, 32, 36, 40; US National Archives: no 29.

Anthony Read
August 2007

# NOTES

## Prologue

1. Webb, *Diaries*, 11 November 1918
2. Trotsky, *The Defence of Terrorism*, p. 63
3. Figes, p. 202
4. Pipes, p. 492
5. Churchill speech to the Aldwych Club, London, 11 April 1919, quoted in Gilbert, p. 278
6. Rummel, p. 39
7. Mawdsley, p. 70
8. Churchill, *The Aftermath*, p. 234
9. Memorandum, 22 June 1918: Churchill Papers
10. Trotsky, Izv V Ts I K, 22 June 1918
11. Mr John Boren, veteran of the American 339th Infantry Regiment, interviewed in BBC TV documentary *The Forgotten War*, 4 September 1971, quoted in Kettle, p. 76
12. Footman, p. 202
13. *Khronika grazhdanskoi voiny v Sibiri*, quoted in Figes, p. 577
14. *Scotsman*, 12 September 1918
15. Mawdsley, p. 100
16. Memorandum: Churchill papers
17. Graves, p. 4
18. Ibid., pp. 7–10
19. David Mitchell, p. 23
20. *Scotsman*, 12 September 1918
21. Trotsky, *The Defence of Terrorism*, p. 58
22. Rummel, p. 35
23. Ibid.
24. Figes, p. 630

25. Ibid.
26. *Izvestia*, 23 August 1918
27. Figes, p. 647, quoting R. Gul', 'Byloe'
28. David Mitchell, p. 73
29. Figes, p. 679
30. Reuter report, 8 November 1918
31. Central News report, 8 November 1918

Chapter 1

1. Dutton, pp. 274–5
2. *Kieler Zeitung*, 5 November 1918
3. *Kieler Neueste Nachrichten*, quoted in Reuter report, 6 November 1918
4. Kessler, p. 4
5. Ibid., p. 7
6. Ibid., pp. 4–5
7. David Mitchell, pp. 51–2
8. Richie, p. 300
9. Kessler, pp. 10–11
10. Allan Mitchell, pp. 66–7
11. Ibid., p. 87
12. Ibid., p. 100; Large, pp. 78–9
13. Large, p. 80
14. Dutton, p. 335
15. CAB 23/8
16. *New York Times*, 13 November 1918
17. Price, pp. 20–1, *Manchester Guardian*, 13 December 1918
18. Ibid., pp. 21–2, *Manchester Guardian*, 16 December 1918
19. Herwig, p. 410
20. *New York Times*, 28 December 1918
21. Ibid.
22. Ibid.
23. Groener, p. 467
24. *Berliner Morgen-Zeitung*, 11 December 1918
25. *New York Times*, 26 December 1918
26. Price, p. 23, dispatch of 19 December, stopped by the British censor
27. Kessler, p. 42
28. *Vorwärts*, 29 December 1918
29. David Mitchell, p. 106
30. Kessler, p. 46
31. Dallas, p. 290; Waite, p. 16; Watt, pp. 246–54

Chapter 2

1. *New York Times*, 24 November 1918
2. Macmillan, p. 14, quoting T.A. Bailey, *Woodrow Wilson and the Last Peace*, p. 87
3. Woodrow Wilson Papers, LIII, pp. 674–6; Tillman, p. 66
4. *Los Angeles Times*, 1 January 1919
5. *New York Times*, 1 January 1919
6. *Philadelphia Inquirer*, 1 January 1919
7. WO32/5248
8. WO106/329
9. *Daily Express*, 6 January 1919
10. *Evening News*, 6 January 1919
11. *The Times*, 6 January 1919
12. *Morning Post*, 6 January 1919
13. *Daily Chronicle*, 6 January 1919
14. *The Times*, 8 January 1919
15. Gilbert, p .184
16. Wilson Diary, 10 January 1919 (Wilson Papers), quoted in Gilbert, p. 181
17. David Englander, 'Troops and Trade Unions, 1919', *History Today*, March 1987
18. *Pall Mall Gazette*, 6 January 1919
19. Bennett, pp. 32–3
20. Ibid.
21. Dallas, p. 288; David Mitchell, p. 201; Watt, pp. 375–8
22. David Mitchell, p. 88
23. Ibid., pp. 88–9
24. Reuter report, *Scotsman*, 20 December 1918
25. Kessler, p. 51
26. Ibid., p. 52
27. The Avalon Project at Yale Law School: eurodocs/spartacist_001.htm
28. Kessler, p. 52
29. Central News report, *Scotsman*, 8 January 1919,
30. Kessler, p. 54
31. Reuter and Press Association reports, *Scotsman*, 13 January 1919
32. Ibid., Press Association report
33. *Vorwärts*, 13 January 1919, quoted in Dallas, p. 317
34. *Die Rote Fahne*, 13 January 1919
35. Ibid.; David Mitchell, p. 110
36. Price, p. 31
37. *Manchester Guardian*, 15 January 1919

## Chapter 3

1. *New York Times*, 6 January 1919
2. *Observer*, 5 January 1919
3. *Scotsman*, 2 September 1918
4. Ibid., 9 August 1918
5. Barbara Weinberger, 'Keeping the Peace? Policing strikes 1906–26', *History Today*, December 1987
6. Davidson Papers, 10 January 1919, quoted in Middlemas, p. 89; Rosenberg, p. 16
7. *Scotsman*, 9 August 1918
8. CAB 23/9, WC523 and 534, 31 January and 3 February 1919
9. *New York Times*, 29 January 1919
10. CAB 23/9, WC523, 31 January 1919
11. David Mitchell, pp. 125–6
12. Ibid.
13. Ibid.
14. Middlemas, p. 91; Rosenberg, p. 36
15. Gallacher, *Revolt on the Clyde* (1936), quoted in Rosenberg, p. 37
16. CAB 23/9, WC522 and 523
17. David Mitchell, p. 127
18. Riddell, *Diary*, 8 February 1919, p. 21; Churchill, *Aftermath*, pp. 51–3
19. Murray, p. 22
20. Allen, *Only Yesterday, Part II*
21. *Liberator*, quoted in David Mitchell, pp. 29–30
22. Haywood, p. 360; David Mitchell, p. 76; Murray, p. 52
23. Reuter reports, *Scotsman*, 13–15 January 1919
24. David Mitchell, p. 132
25. Heale, p. 60; Asinof, p. 134
26. Hanson, *Americanism versus Bolshevism*, p. 87, quoted in Murray, pp. 62–3
27. Report from BI Agent Walter H. Thayer, 14 February 1919, OG91928, RG65, NA, quoted in Schmidt, p. 134
28. Ibid., p. 127
29. *Baltimore Sun*, 7 February 1919
30. *Washington Post*, 5 February 1919
31. *New York Times, Boston Evening Transcript, Atlanta Constitution*, all 11 March 1919
32. *Los Angeles Times*, 1 February 1919

## Chapter 4

1. Kettle, p. 89
2. Mary Borden diary, 24 January 1919, Spears papers
3. Gilbert, pp. 243–6; Churchill, *Aftermath*, p. 173; FRUS, Vol. 3, pp. 1041–4
4. *Washington Post*, 25 February 1919
5. *Baltimore Sun*, 24 February 1919
6. Riddell, *Diary*, p. 21
7. Churchill, *Aftermath*, pp. 176–7; Churchill Papers, Char 16/20, LG to WSC, 16.2.19
8. Churchill, *Aftermath*, p. 163; Kettle, p. 141
9. Dallas, p. 371, quoting Beatrice Farnsworth, *William Bullitt and the Soviet Union* (Bloomington, 1967) p. 193, n20
10. Bullitt, p. 4
11. Lloyd George Papers, F89/2/38; FRUS, PPC, Vol. 4, pp. 121–4
12. Davies, *White Eagle*, pp. 26–7
13. *Scotsman*, 3 March 1919
14. *The Times*, 8 February 1919
15. Kessler, p. 75
16. Price, p. 35
17. *The Times*, 8 February 1919
18. Price, p. 36
19. Sterling Fishman, 'Prophets, Poets and Priests: A study of the men and ideas that made the Munich Revolution of 1918/19', PhD dissertation, University of Wisconsin, Madison, 1960, quoted in Large, p. 67
20. Oswald G. Villard, *Fighting Years: Memoirs of a Liberal Editor* (New York, 1939) p. 405, quoted in Klingaman, p. 125
21. Allan Mitchell, p. 262
22. Ibid., pp. 266–7
23. Ibid., pp. 269–70
24. 'Einheitsfront des Sozialismus', *Flugblätter*, quoted in Allan Mitchell, p. 280
25. Stenographic record of the proceedings of the Workers', Peasants' and Soldiers' Councils from 25 February until 8 March, No 1, 1, quoted in Allan Mitchell, pp. 282–3
26. Fishman, p. 115, quoted in Large, p. 104
27. GT 6978, February 1919: 'Conditions in Germany: Report by V.77'
28. Allan Mitchell, p. 168
29. Kessler, pp. 78–9
30. Ibid., pp. 81–2
31. Ibid., p. 82
32. *Baltimore Evening Sun*, 19 March 1919
33. Ibid.

34. Hecht, *A Child of the Century*, p. 291, quoted in Klingaman, p. 164
35. Service, III, p. 47
36. David Mitchell, p. 160
37. Ransome, p. 141
38. Ransome, p. 143
39. Ulam, pp. 113–14
40. Ransome, pp. 145–6
41. Ibid., pp. 147–51

Chapter 5

1. Hoover, pp. 47–51
2. Ibid., p. 154
3. Dutton, p. 291
4. Wilson Papers, LI, pp. 437–9
5. Ibid., LI, pp. 635–6
6. Hoover, p. 293
7. Ibid., p. 340
8. Keynes, XVI, pp. 391, 393–4
9. David Mitchell, p. 93
10. Hoover, p. 429
11. *Manchester Guardian*, 6 April 1919
12. N. Almond and R.H. Lutz (eds), *The Treaty of St Germain*, Stanford, California, 1933, p. 92, quoted in Macmillan, p. 256
13. Carsten, p. 13; David Mitchell, pp. 94, 96
14. *New York Times*, 30 March 1919
15. *Manchester Guardian*, 29 May 1919
16. David Mitchell, p. 94
17. *The Times*, 4 February 1919
18. *New York Times*, 22 February 1919
19. *Los Angeles Times*, 9 March 1919
20. Hoover, p. 406
21. WC 550, 24 March 1919
22. David Mitchell, p. 97
23. *Manchester Guardian*, 2 March 1919
24. *The Times*, 4 March 1919
25. Lloyd George, pp. 193–5
26. Dallas, p. 445
27. *New York Times*, 10 March 1919

## Chapter 6

1. Allan Mitchell, p. 289; Large, p. 105
2. *Münchener Neueste Nachrichten*, 19 March 1919
3. Large, p. 106
4. Ibid.
5. *Münchener Neueste Nachrichten*, 5 April 1919
6. David Mitchell, p. 165
7. Allan Mitchell, p. 310
8. Ibid., p. 311
9. Ibid., Large, p. 112
10. Wolfgang Zorn, *Geschichte Bayerns im 20. Jahrhundert*, p. 194, quoted in Large, p. 116
11. Allan Mitchell, p. 322
12. Nicolson, p. 27
13. Ibid., p. 244
14. *New York Times*, 5 January 1919
15. Ibid.
16. Molnár, pp. 2–4; *The Times*, 21 March 1919
17. Seymour, House Diary, 22 March 1919
18. Lloyd George, Vol. 1, p. 416.
19. Grayson, p. 85
20. Mayer, *The Politics and Diplomacy of Peacemaking*, pp. 725–6
21. Lloyd George, Vol. 1, p. 406; Mantoux, Vol. 1, pp. 11–15, 75–6
22. Nicolson, p. 240
23. Ibid., p. 249
24. Ibid., p. 250
25. WO32/6582
26. Churchill to Lloyd George, 8 March 1919, Churchill Papers
27. Hoover, pp. 118–19, 247–9; Macmillan, p. 89
28. Hoover, pp. 120–2; Macmillan, p. 89
29. Macmillan, p. 89
30. Gilbert, pp. 277–8
31. David Mitchell, pp. 136–7
32. Mayer, p. 212
33. Delzell, pp. 7–11

## Chapter 7

1. *The Times, Scotsman*, 4 April 1919
2. *Washington Post*, 26 January 1919

3. CAB 29/91. Vol. 6, Statement of Government of Punjab
4. Read and Fisher, pp. 1–9, 167–70; CAB 27/91, 92, 93
5. Read and Fisher, p. 184; David Mitchell, p. 187
6. David Mitchell, p. 186
7. Trotsky Papers, Vol. 1: 623, 625, quoted in Figes, p. 703
8. Press Association report, *Scotsman*, 29 May 1919
9. Klingaman, p. 348
10. Press Association report, *Scotsman*, 29 May 1919

## Chapter 8

1. *Communist International*, No. 2, June 1919, p. 271
2. Lusk Reports, Vol. 1, p. 369
3. Murray, p. 48
4. Ibid., p. 93; Schmidt, p. 33
5. *Washington Post*, 15 February 1919
6. Coben, pp. 197–8
7. Theoharis and Cox, pp. 54–5
8. *Los Angeles Times*, 22 March 1919
9. *Washington Post*, 2 April 1919
10. *Los Angeles Times*, 2 March 1919
11. Klingaman, pp. 278–9
12. *New York Times*, 12 May 1919
13. Kessler, p. 100
14. Press Association report, *Scotsman*, 25 March 1919
15. Mantoux, Vol. 2, p. 352
16. Nicolson, p. 262
17. Seymour, *Letters*, p. 220
18. *Manchester Guardian*, 5 May 1919
19. Von der Goltz, *Als politischer General im Osten, Finnland und Baltikum, 1918 und 1919*, quoted in Bennett, pp. 80–1
20. Bennett, pp. 56–9
21. Hoover, p. 461
22. Frances Lloyd George, p. 183
23. Riddell, p. 71
24. David Mitchell, pp. 213–14
25. *Washington Post*, 22 June 1919; *New York Times*, 11 and 12 May 1919
26. *Die Freiheit*, 27 May 1919; *New York Times*, 29 May 1919
27. *New York Times*, 5 June 1919

## Chapter 9

1. Conway, p. 88
2. Francis, p. 38
3. Ibid., p. 43
4. Ibid., p. 39
5. Conway, p. 91
6. David Mitchell, p. 207
7. Francis, '1919: The Winnipeg General Strike', *History Today*, April 1984
8. *New York Times*, 2 June 1919
9. Murray, p. 113; *New Statesman*, 26 July 1919
10. Conway, p. 93; Francis, op. cit.; David Mitchell, p. 209
11. *Salt Lake Tribune*; *San Francisco Examiner*; *Atlanta Constitution*; all 3 June 1919
12. *New York Times*, 3 June 1919
13. Theoharis and Cox, p. 54; Murray, pp. 78–9; Klingaman, pp. 352–4
14. *Washington Post*, 3 June 1919; *New York Times*, 3 June 1919
15. *Los Angeles Times*, 4 June 1919
16. Theoharis and Cox, pp. 56–7
17. *New York Times*, 9 June 1919
18. Ibid., 10 June 1919
19. *Caucus of the American Legion, Proceedings and Committees at St Louis, Missouri*, 1919
20. *American Legion Weekly*, June–July 1919 issues
21. Murray, p. 90
22. *New York Times*, 4 June 1919
23. New York *Call*, 13 June 1919; Cleveland *Socialist News*, 21 June 1919; *New York Times*, 13 June 1919; Murray, p. 99
24. *New York Times*, 18 June 1919
25. *New York Times*, 21 June 1919
26. Murray, p. 102; *New York Tribune*, 26 June 1919; *New York Times*, 28 June 1919
27. *New York Times*, 4 July 1919

## Chapter 10

1. *New York Times*, 2 June 1919
2. *The Times*, 17 June 1919; *New York Times*, 17 June 1919
3. *New York Times*, 19 June 1919
4. Kessler, pp. 101–2
5. K. Epstein, *Matthias Erzberger and the Dilemma of German Democracy*, New York, 1971, pp. 325–6, quoted in Macmillan, p. 483

6. *New York Times*, 14 June 1919
7. Epstein, op. cit., pp. 315–17
8. *Scotsman*, 26 June 1919
9. Mantoux, Vol. 2, p. 513
10. Kessel, p. 102
11. *New York Times*, 18 July 1919
12. Lloyd George Papers, House of Lords, F89/3/2, Memorandum from Balfour
13. David Mitchell, pp. 223–4
14. Molnár, pp. 34–5
15. Bennett, p. 106
16. Ibid., pp. 139–40; Hudson, pp. 161–2
17. Bennett, p. 119
18. Captain A.W.S. Agar, *Baltic Episode. Footprints in the Sea. Naval Operations in the Baltic. Journal of the Royal United Services Institution*, November 1928, quoted in Bennett, pp. 126–7; Kettle, pp. 473–7; Jackson, pp. 215–16; Hudson, pp. 163–4
19. Bennett, pp. 126–7
20. Ibid., pp. 130–3; Hudson, p. 164; Jackson, pp. 216–17
21. Bennett, pp. 147–56; Hudson, pp. 165–6

## Chapter 11

1. Klingaman, p. 379
2. *New York Times*, 7 July 1919
3. *Scotsman*, 2, 11, 12, 23 June, 13, 22, 23 July 1919
4. *Scotsman, The Times*, 26 June 1919; *New York Times*, 27 June 1919
5. *Scotsman, The Times*, 23 June 1919
6. Clegg, p. 287
7. Ibid.
8. *Scotsman*, 22 July 1919
9. Rosenberg, p. 25
10. *The Police and Prison Officers' Magazine*, Vol. 1, No. 16, 11 June 1919, quoted in Rosenberg, p. 27
11. Murray, pp. 114–17; David Mitchell, pp. 285–6; *New York Times, New York Call*, 4 July 1919
12. *Congressional Record*, 66 Cong., 1 Sess., 3765, 4089, quoted in Murray, p. 118
13. Quoted in Murray, p. 179
14. Theoharis and Cox, p. 57
15. *Chicago Tribune*, 28 July, 1919; *New York Times*, 28 July 1919
16. *Washington Post*, 21 July 1919

17. Cohen, p. 34
18. *Washington Post*, 30 July 1919
19. Cohen, pp. 36–7
20. Klingaman, p. 453
21. *New York Times*, 24 August 1919
22. *Washington Post*, 27 August 1919
23. Klingaman, pp. 468–71, 486–7, quoting John McCabe, *George M. Cohan: The Man Who Owned Broadway*, New York, 1973, pp. 147–8
24. *Revolutionary Age*, 5 July 1919, quoted in Murray, p. 49
25. *New York Times*, 31 August 1919; Murray, p. 50; David Mitchell, p. 287
26. Lusk Reports, I, p. 801; Murray, p. 51
27. Haywood, p. 360; Murray, p. 52
28. Private memoranda, Lansing Papers, 26 July, 1 September 1919, quoted in Schmidt, pp. 77–8
29. Link, Vol. 62, p. 281
30. Baker and Dodds, Vol. 2, p. 10; Murray, p. 202

## Chapter 12

1. Fuess, p. 206
2. Ibid, p. 207
3. White, *Puritan in Babylon*, quoted in Asinof, pp. 165–6
4. *Boston Evening Transcript*, 10 September 1919, quoted in Murray, p. 126
5. *Boston Telegraph*, 11 September 1919
6. Murray, pp. 126–9
7. *Washington Post*, 15 September 1919
8. Murray, p. 134; David Mitchell, p. 288; Klingaman, p. 502
9. Interchurch World Movement, *Report on the Steel Strike of 1919*, quoted in Murray, p. 137; Brody, p. 70
10. *Manchester Guardian*, 19 October 1919
11. Asinof, p. 179
12. Brody, p. 19
13. Ibid., p. 78
14. Interchurch World Movement, *Report on the Steel Strike of 1919*, quoted in Murray, p. 137; Brody, p. 70
15. Brody, p. 70
16. Ibid., pp. 93–4
17. Letter from J. Fitzpatrick, W.Z. Foster, et al. to President Wilson, 18 September 1919; *New York Times*, 19 September 1919

18. Senate Reports, A, No. 289, pp. 3–5; *New York Times*, 21 August 1919

19. *Los Angeles Times*, 18 September 1919

20. W.Z. Foster, *Syndicalism*, quoted in David Mitchell, p. 295; Brody, p. 138; Schmidt, p. 225

21. Murray, pp. 139–40

22. Brody, p. 129; Murray, p. 143, quoting Edward Levinson, *Labor on the March* (New York, 1938), pp. 45–6

23. David Mitchell, p. 296; Murray, 143, quoting George Soule, *Prosperity Decade; From War to Depression 1917–1929* (New York, Rinehart and Company, 1947), p. 194, and Samuel Yellen, *American Labor Struggles* (New York, Harcourt, Brace and Company, 1936)

24. David Mitchell, p. 295

25. Ibid., p. 297; Murray, p. 145; *New York Times*, 22 September 1919; *Pittsburgh Post*, 21 September 1919

26. *Washington Post*, 2 October 1919

27. Ibid., 30 September 1919

28. Asinof, pp. 191–2

29. Directive from steel officials to agents dated 2 October 1919, Interchurch World Movement, *Report on the Steel Strike*, quoted in Murray, p. 146

30. NA, DJ202600-39-2, RG60 (microfilm): Letter from Francis Fisher Kane to A. Mitchell Palmer, 16 July 1919, quoted in Schmidt, pp. 34–5

31. David Mitchell, p. 297

32. *New York Times*, 23 September 1919, quoting T.J. Vind, General Organiser of the AFL in the Chicago district; Murray, pp. 146–7

33. *New York Times*, 7, 8 October 1919

34. Ibid., 8 October 1919

35. Ibid., 15 October 1919

36. NA, OG353037, RG65: Letter from Edward Brennan to Frank Burke, 18 October 1919

37. *Washington Post*, 25 October 1919

38. NA, OG374217, RG65: Memorandum from J. Edgar Hoover to Director, 18 October 1919

39. Murray, p. 148

40. *Washington Post*, 17 October 1919

41. Murray, p. 148

42. Asinof, p. 194; David Mitchell, pp. 297–8

43. Boston *Christian Science Monitor*, 23 October 1919, quoted in Murray, p. 149

44. *Wall Street Journal*, 23 October 1919

45. *Open Shop Review*, XVI, October 1919; *Congressional Record*, 66 Cong., 1 Sess, 6869, quoted in Murray, p. 150

46. Senate Reports, A, No. 289, pp. 14–17

Chapter 13

1. *The Times*, 9 September 1919; *New York Times*, 8 September 1919
2. *New York Times*, 13 September 1919
3. *Manchester Guardian*, 20 December 1919
4. Quoted in David Mitchell, pp. 307–8
5. *New York Times*, 28 September 1919
6. David Mitchell, p. 310
7. *The Times, Manchester Guardian, New York Times*, 29 September 1919
8. David Mitchell, pp. 311–12
9. Quoted in David Mitchell, p. 310
10. *New York Times*, 20 November 1919; Murray, p. 173
11. Asinof, p. 207
12. Ibid., p. 206
13. United Mine Workers of America, *The Case of the Bituminous Coal Mine Workers* (Indianapolis, 1920), pp. 27, 33, 44–5, 47, quoted in Murray, p. 154
14. 'The Great Enterprise', *United Mine Workers' Journal*, XXX, 1 November 1919, quoted in Murray, p. 154
15. Lusk Reports, Vol. 1, p. 853
16. New York *Tribune*, 26 October 1919
17. *The Messages and Papers of Woodrow Wilson* (New York, 1924), quoted in Murray, p. 156
18. Cincinnati *Enquirer*, 12 November 1919
19. Theoharis and Cox, p. 58
20. *Investigation Activities of the Department of Justice*, Senate Doc. 153, 66 Cong., pp. 30–4
21. Murray, p. 196; Theoharis and Cox, pp. 58–9
22. *New York Times*, 8 November 1919
23. The account of the Centralia massacre combines details from Haywood, pp. 355–6; Asinof, pp. 198–202; David Mitchell, pp. 300–2; Murray, pp. 182–9, quoting *Washington Reports* 408–28
24. *New York Times*, 15 November 1919
25. Ibid., 27 November 1919
26. Boston *Evening Transcript*, 10 November 1919; Salt Lake *Tribune*, 9 November 1919; Cincinnati *Enquirer*, 10 November 1919
27. *Congressional Record*, 66 Cong., 2 Sess., 37, 990, 1334, quoted in Murray, p. 206
28. *Los Angeles Times*, 22 December 1919
29. New York *Tribune*, 25 April 1920; Theoharis and Cox, pp. 63–4
30. *Washington Post*, 4 January 1920

## Epilogue

1. 'Extent of the Bolshevik Infection Here', *Literary Digest*, LXIV, 17 January 1920; Murray, p. 219
2. *New York Times*, 29 February 1920
3. 'Justice for Alien Reds', *Literary Digest*, LXV, 22 May 1920; Murray, p. 248
4. Cleveland *Plain Dealer*, 18 September 1920, p. 6
5. Price, p. 63
6. Ibid.
7. Kessler, p. 117
8. Ibid., p. 121
9. Burleigh, p. 52
10. Davies, *White Eagle, Red Star*, p. 145
11. Figes, p. 701
12. Ibid., p. 703

# BIBLIOGRAPHY

Abella, Irving Martin, *On Strike: Six Key Labour Struggles in Canada 1919–1949*, Toronto, Lorimer, 1974

Allen, Frederick Lewis, *Only Yesterday: An Informal History of the 1920s*, New York, Harper Row, 1957

Asinof, Eliot, *1919: America's Loss of Innocence*, New York, Donald I. Fine, 1990

Baker, Ray S., and Dodds, William E. (eds), *The Public Papers of Woodrow Wilson, VI: War and Peace, 1917–1924, II*, New York, Harper Brothers, 1925–7

Bennett, Geoffrey, *Freeing the Baltic*, Edinburgh, Birlinn, 2002

Bracher, Karl Dietrich, *The German Dictatorship: The Origins, Structure and Consequences of National Socialism*, London, Penguin, 1973

Brailsford, H.N., *Across the Blockade*, London, Allen & Unwin, 1919

Brody, David, *Labor in Crisis: The Steel Strike of 1919*, Champaign, Ill., University of Illinois Press, 1987

Bullitt, William C., *The Bullitt Mission to Russia: Testimony before the Committee on Foreign Relations, United States Senate*, New York, B.W. Heubsch, 1919

Burleigh, Michael, *The Third Reich: A New History*, London, Macmillan, 2000

Caragata, Warren, *Alberta Labour: A Heritage Untold*, Toronto, Lorimer, 1979

Carsten, F.L., *The First Austrian Republic 1918–1938*, London, Gower/Maurice Temple Smith, 1986

Churchill, Winston, *The Aftermath*, New York, Charles Scribner, 1929

Churchhill, Winston S. (ed.), *Never Give In: The Best of Winston Churchill's Speeches*, London, Pimlico, 2003

Clegg, H.A., *A History of the British Trade Unions since 1889*, Vol. 2, Oxford University Press, 1985

Coben, Stanley, *A. Mitchell Palmer: Politician*, New York, Columbia University Press, 1963

Cohen, Lizabeth, *Making a New Deal: Industrial Workers in Chicago, 1919–1939*, Cambridge University Press, 1990

Conway, J.F., *The West: The History of a Region in Confederation*, Toronto, Lorimer, 1994

Dallas, Gregor, *1918, War and Peace*, London, Pimlico, 2002

Davies, Norman, *Europe: A History*, London, Pimlico, 1997
*White Eagle, Red Star: The Polish-Soviet War 1919–1920 and 'The Miracle on the Vistula'*, London, Pimlico, 2003

Delzell, Charles F., *Mediterranean Fascism, 1919–1945*, New York, Harper & Row, 1970

Doerr, Paul W., *British Foreign Policy 1919–1939*, Manchester University Press, 1998

Dutton, David (ed.), *Paris 1918: The War Diary of the 17th Earl of Derby*, Liverpool University Press, 2001

Edsforth, Ronald, and Bennett, Larry (eds), *Popular Culture and Political Change in Modern America*, New York, SUNY Press, 1991

Evans, Harold, *The American Century*, London, Jonathan Cape, 1998

Ferrell, Norman H., *Woodrow Wilson and World War I*, New York, Harper & Row, 1985

Figes, Orlando, *A People's Tragedy: The Russian Revolution 1891–1924*, London, Jonathan Cape, 1996

Fitzpatrick, Sheila (ed.), *The Russian Revolution*, Oxford University Press, 2001

Fleming, D.F., *The Origins and Legacies of World War I*, London, Allen & Unwin, 1969

Footman, David, *Civil War in Russia*, London, Faber and Faber, 1961

Francis, Daniel, *National Dreams: Myth, Memory and Canadian History*, Vancouver, BC, Arsenal Pulp Press, 1997

Fraser, Eugenie, *The House by the Dvina*, London, Corgi, 1986

Fuess, Claude M., *Calvin Coolidge: the Man from Vermont*, Westport, Conn., Greenwood Press, 1977

Gilbert, Martin, *Winston S. Churchill, Vol. IV: 1916–1922*, London, Heinemann, 1975

Graves, General W.S., *America's Siberian Adventure*, London, Jonathan Cape, 1931

Grayson, Rear Admiral Cary T., *Woodrow Wilson: An Intimate Memoir*, New York, Holt, Rinehart & Winston, 1960

Groener, Wilhelm, *Lebenserinnerungen*, Vandenhoeck & Ruprecht, 1957

Haywood, William D., *Bill Haywood's Book: the Autobiography of William D. Haywood*, New York, International Publishers, 1929

Heale, Michael, *Twentieth-Century America: Politics and Power in the United States, 1900–2000*, New York, Oxford University Press US, 2004

Herwig, H., *The First World War: Germany and Austria 1914–18*, London, Hodder Arnold, 1997

Hobsbawm, Eric, *Age of Extremes: The Short Twentieth Century 1914–1991*, London, Michael Joseph, 1994

Hoover, Herbert C., *The Memoirs of Herbert Hoover*, Vol. 1: *Years of Adventure, 1874–1920*, New York, Macmillan, 1951

Hosking, Geoffrey, *A History of the Soviet Union 1917–1991*, London, Fontana, 1992

Hudson, Miles, *Intervention in Russia 1918–1920: A Cautionary Tale*, Barnsley, Yorks, Pen and Sword Books, 2004

Jackson, Robert, *At War with the Bolsheviks: The Allied Intervention into Russia, 1917–20*, London, Tom Stacey, 1972

James, D. Clayton, and Wells, Anne Sharp, *America and the Great War, 1914–1920* Wheeling, Ill., Harlan Davidson, 1998

Kennan, George F., *Russia and the West under Lenin and Stalin: Soviet–American Relations 1917–1920*, London, Hutchinson, 1961

Kessler, Count Harry, *The Diaries of a Cosmopolitan, 1918–1937*, London, Phoenix Press, 2000

Kettle, Michael, *Churchill and the Archangel Fiasco, November 1918–July 1919*, London, Routledge, 1992

Keynes, John Maynard (ed. Elizabeth Johnson), *The Collected Writings of John Maynard Keynes*: Vol. II: *The Economic Consequences of the Peace*; Vol. XVI: *Activities 1914–1919 – The Treasury and Versailles*, London, Macmillan, 1971

Klingaman, William K., *1919: The Year Our World Began*, New York, Harper & Row, 1987

Large, David Clay, *Between Two Fires: Europe's Path in the 1930s*, New York, Norton, 1990

*Where Ghosts Walked: Munich's Road to the Third Reich*, New York, Norton, 1997

Lee, Stephen J., *European Dictatorships 1918–1945*, London, Routledge, 2000

Link, Arthur, et al. (eds), *The Papers of Woodrow Wilson*, 69 vols, Princeton University Press, 1966–93

Lloyd George, David, *The Truth About the Peace Treaties*, 2 vols, London, Gollancz, 1938

Lloyd George, Frances (ed. A.J.P. Taylor), *Lloyd George: A Diary*, New York, Harper & Row, 1971

Lusk Committee, New York, *Revolutionary Radicalism: Its History, Purpose and Tactics*, 4 vols, Albany, J.B. Lyon, 1920

McCauley, Martin (ed.), *The Russian Revolution & the Soviet State 1917–1921: Documents*, London, Macmillan, 1980

Macmillan, Margaret, *Peacemakers: The Paris Conference of 1919 and Its Attempt to End War*, London, John Murray, 2001

Mantoux, P., *The Deliberations of the Council of Four* (ed. and trans. A.S. Link), 2 vols, Princeton University Press, 1992

Mawdsley, Evan, *The Russian Civil War*, Boston, Allen & Unwin, 1987

Mayer, Arno J., *The Politics and Diplomacy of Peacemaking: Containment and Counter-Revolution at Versailles*, London, Weidenfeld & Nicolson, 1968
*The Furies: Violence and Terror in the French and Russian Revolutions*, Princeton University Press, 2001

Middlemas, Robert Keith, *The Clydesiders*, London, Hutchinson, 1965

Mitchell, Allan, *Revolution in Bavaria 1918–1919: The Eisner Regime and the Soviet Republic*, Princeton University Press, 1965

Mitchell, David, *1919: Red Mirage*, London, Jonathan Cape, 1970

Molnár, Miklós (trans. Arnold J. Pomerans), *From Béla Kun to János Kádár: Seventy Years of Hungarian Communism*, New York, Berg, 1990

Moynhahan, Brian, *Comrades: 1917 – Russia in Revolution*, London, Hutchinson, 1992

Murray, Robert K., *Red Scare: A Study in National Hysteria, 1919–1920*, New York, McGraw-Hill, 1964

Nicolson, Harold, *Peacemaking 1919*, London, Constable, 1945

Pfannestiel, Todd J., *Rethinking the Red Scare: The Lusk Committee and New York's Crusade against Radicalism*, New York, Routledge, 2003

Pipes, R., *The Russian Revolution, 1899–1919*, London, Collins Harvill, 1990

Price, Morgan Philips (ed. Tania Rose), *Dispatches from the Weimar Republic*, London, Pluto Press, 1999

Ransome, Arthur, *Six Weeks in Russia in 1919*, London, George Allen & Unwin, 1919

Read, Anthony, and Fisher, David, *The Proudest Day: India's Long Road to Independence* London, Jonathan Cape, 1997

Rees, Tim, and Thorpe, Andrew (eds), *International Communism and the Communist International 1919–43*, Manchester University Press, 1998

Richie, Alexandra, *Faust's Metropolis: A History of Berlin*, London, HarperCollins, 1998

Riddell, George, *Lord Riddell's Intimate Diary of the Peace Conference and After, 1918–1923*, London, Gollancz, 1933

Rosenberg, Chanie, *1919: Britain on the Brink of Revolution*, London, Bookmarks, 1987

Rothstein, Andrew, *When Britain Invaded Soviet Russia: The Consul Who Rebelled*, London, Journeyman Press, 1979
*The Soldiers' Strikes of 1919*, London, Macmillan, 1989

Rummel, R.J., *Lethal Politics: Soviet Genocide and Mass Murder since 1917*, Piscataway, N.J., Transaction Publishers, 1990

Sabin, Arthur J., *In Calmer Times: The Supreme Court and Red Monday*, Philadelphia, Pa. University of Pennsylvania Press, 1999

Schmidt, Regin, *Red Scare: FBI and the Origins of Anticommunism in the United States* (e-book), Copenhagen, Museum Tusculanums Press, 2004

Service, Robert, *Lenin: A Political Life*, 3 vols, London, Macmillan, 1985, 1991, 1995

Seton-Watson, Hugh, *Eastern Europe Between the Wars, 1918–1941*, Cambridge University Press, 1945

Seymour, Charles (ed.), *The Intimate Papers of Colonel House*, Boston & New York, Houghton Mifflin, 1926–8
*Letters from the Paris Peace Conference*, ed. Harold B. Whiteman Jr, New Haven, Yale University Press, 1965

Spence, Jonathan D., *The Search for Modern China*, London, Hutchinson, 1990

Suny, Ronald Grigor, *The Soviet Experiment: Russia, the USSR, and the Successor States*, New York, Oxford University Press US, 1997

Taylor, A.J.P., *The Origins of the Second World War*, London, Penguin, 1964

Theoharis, Athan G., and Cox, John Stuart, *The Boss: J. Edgar Hoover and the Great American Inquisition*, London, Harrap, 1989

Toland, John, *No Man's Land: 1918, the Last Year of the Great War*, University of Nebraska Press, 2002

Trotsky, Leon, *The Defence of Terrorism*, London, Labour Publishing Company and George Allen & Unwin, 1920
*The Military Writings of Leon Trotsky* (online: Trotsky Internet Archive)

Tuttle, William M., *Race Riot: Chicago in the Red Summer of 1919*, Champaign, Ill., University of Illinois Press, 1996

Ulam, Adam B., *Expansion and Coexistence: Soviet Foreign Policy 1917–73*, New York, Praeger/Holt, Rinehart and Winston, 1974

Viorst, Milton, *Sandcastles: The Arabs in Search of the Modern World*, London, Jonathan Cape, 1994

Waite, Robert G.L., *Vanguard of Nazism: The Free Corps Movement in Postwar Germany, 1918–1923*, Cambridge, Mass., Harvard University Press, 1952

Watt, Richard M., *The Kings Depart: The Tragedy of Germany: Versailles and the German Revolution*, New York, Simon & Schuster, 1968

Webb, Beatrice, *Beatrice Webb's Diaries, 1912–1924*, London, Longmans Green, 1952

White, William A., *Puritan in Babylon: the Story of Calvin Coolidge*, New York, Macmillan, 1938

Zsolt, Béla, *Nine Suitcases*, London, Jonathan Cape, 2004

# INDEX

www.rbooks.co.uk